THE RSS

Vijai Trivedi has travelled across the country and abroad in pursuit of news and worked in nearly every form of media—radio, print, television, digital and podcasts. His professional career started as a journalist, working for various media outlets including the Times Group, *Rajasthan Patrika*, *Akashvani*, *NDTV*, *News Nation*, *Sahara TV*, *First India TV* and *HS News* (the digital arm of *Hindustan Samachar)*. He is now associated with *Satya Hindi*. He has written for several magazines, such as *Dharmyug*, *Saptahik Hindustan*, *Ravivar*, *Dinman*, *Chauthi Duniya*, *India Today*, *Outlook* and *Lokmat Samachar*.

His books—*Haar Nahi Manunga: Ek Atal Jeevan Gatha* on Atal Bihari Vajpayee, *Yada Yada Hi Yogi* on Yogi Adityanath and *BJP: Kal, Aaj aur Kal*, tracing the journey of the national party—were bestsellers and received overwhelming support from readers.

Subha Pande is a multilingual translator fluent in Gujarati, Marathi, Tamil, Hindi, and English. Her translation portfolio includes *Krishnayan* and *Madhyabindu* by Kaajal Oza Vaidya (Gujarati to English); *Win All Your Battles* by Vishwas Nangre Patil and *An Invisible Battle* by Girish Kuber (Marathi to English); eleven novels and a short story collection by Sivasankari (Tamil to English); and *Sita's Sister*, *Fisher Queen's Dynasty* by Kavita Kane, and *Ancient Science of Mantras* by Om Swami (English to Hindi).

AF517618

Praise for the Book

'All the things documented in this book—about the public support garnered by the Sangh despite the bans on it, the contributions of the swayamsevaks, their wide-scale public service and long crusade against the caste system, about the Sangh's constant engagement with diverse sections of Indian society and its progressive attitude—present an authentic picture of the RSS.'

Nitin Gadkari, Union Minister of Road Transport and Highways

'This book could not have been more timely. Veteran journalist Vijai Trivedi, who has tracked the RSS for 30 years and is known for rigour in his writing, attempts to answer the many controversial questions about the RSS which have been in the public domain, with new information and insights. A must for all those interested in contemporary India.'

Neerja Chowdhury, columnist, political commentator and author of *How Prime Ministers Decide*

'Finally a book on the RSS that is incisive and objective. Vijai Trivedi brings his years of experience as a reporter to unravel the many mysteries surrounding the RSS. Embellished with rare anecdotes and sharp analysis, this is a must read for anyone who wants to know what makes the RSS tick.'

Rajdeep Sardesai, senior journalist, consulting editor (India Today Group) and author of *2024: The Election That Surprised India*

'The most comprehensive and complete book on the RSS till date. It introduces readers to the mysterious world of Hindutva and Vijai Trivedi is a master of facts and ruthless in his analysis.'

Ashutosh, senior journalist and author of *Reclaiming Bharat*

VIJAI TRIVEDI

THE RSS

100 YEARS OF THE INDIAN RIGHT

TRANSLATED BY
SUBHA PANDE

WESTLAND
NON·FICTION

WESTLAND
NON·FICTION

First published in Hindi as *Sangham Sharanam Gachchhaami* in 2020 by Eka, an imprint of Westland Publications Pvt. Ltd

Published in 2022 by Eka, an imprint of Westland Books, a division of Nasadiya Technologies Private Limited

Published in English by Westland Non-Fiction, an imprint of Westland Books, a division of Nasadiya Technologies Private Limited

No. 269/2B, First Floor, 'Irai Arul', Vimalraj Street, Nethaji Nagar, Alapakkam Main Road, Maduravoyal, Chennai 600095

Westland, the Westland logo, Westland Non-Fiction and the Westland Non-Fiction logo are the trademarks of Nasadiya Technologies Private Limited, or its affiliates.

Original copyright © Vijai Trivedi, 2020

Translation copyright © Subha Pande, 2025

Vijai Trivedi asserts the moral right to be identified as the author of this work.

ISBN: 9789371979221

10 9 8 7 6 5 4 3 2 1

The views and opinions expressed in this work are the author's own and the facts are as reported by him, and the publisher is in no way liable for the same.

All rights reserved

Typeset by Mukul

Printed at Nutech Print Services Pvt. Ltd.

No part of this book may be reproduced, or stored in a retrieval system, or transmitted in any form or by any means, electronic, mechanical, photocopying, recording, or otherwise, without express written permission of the publisher.

For dear Garima
Pratishtha, Shumail and Pratyaksh,
and
all those who love me unconditionally

Contents

Author's Note

The story of the completion of one hundred years of the Rashtriya Swayamsevak Sangh is not merely a diary of an organisation; it is a mirror to the changing face of the nation. At times, this mirror gathers dust—at other times, there is the fear of it cracking. To understand all of this, no single witness is enough. Expressing gratitude to all those who have been companions on this journey is a daunting responsibility, because the number of people who have contributed is far greater than my memory can hold. It is like trying to catch raindrops in one's palm. And yet, remembering some names is essential.

This book is a culmination of almost thirty years of in-depth research and reporting on the RSS and the BJP. There are anecdotes that people told me along the way, secrets people confided in me, controversies I was told of that had become buried to protect organisations and famous personalities. All these I have presented here with candour and integrity. There are those who agreed to be named in the book, and I thank them for being a part of the story. A few others were hesitant to come forth—I have respected their desire for privacy and withheld their names even as I have told their stories. I thank them for their courage in speaking to me.

This story begins at the South Delhi residence of Dr Manmohan Vaidya, the sah-sarkaryavah of the RSS. Along the way, I meet the newly appointed sah-sarkaryavah, C.R. Mukund in Nagpur; the Akhil Bharatiya Prachar Pramukh, Arun Kumar at the Udasin Ashram; the national convenor for outreach, Aniruddha Deshpande; margdarshak of the Muslim Rashtriya Manch, Indresh Kumar; the working president of the Vishva Hindu Parishad, Alok Kumar and the national convenor of Pragya Pravah, K. Nandakumar. Among the BJP leadership, Ram Madhav, along with RSS's sah-prachar pramukh, Narendra Kumar and ABVP's Sunil Ambekar, are individuals without whom it would have been difficult for me to climb these steps of understanding. It was the late Dinanath Mishra who first guided me on how to take these steps. To comprehend every room of the Sangh family, the elderly and insightful Madhav Devendra Swarup, Rajiv Tuli, Sanjeev Kelkar and Ratan Sharda were of immense help. Without the perspective of the detached yet disciplined swayamsevak, Dilip Deodhar, the Sangh could not have been fully understood.

The beauty lies in the fact that meeting all these eminent people never made me feel small—instead, it felt as though I was seeing a *mela* (fair) while perched on their shoulders, enjoying both the vantage point and the illusion of being taller than I really am.

Receiving such immense affection and support from so many people makes one feel a sense of pride. Among them are Ram Bahadur Rai, Achyutanand Mishra, B.V. Rao (Editor-in-Chief of TV9 Bharatvarsh), Ved Pratap Vaidik, writer Hemant Sharma, N.K. Singh, Nilanjan Mukhopadhyay, Rajdeep Sardesai, Narendra Sehgal, N.M. Ghatate,

Banwari Ji, Sudhanshu Mittal, Professor Badri Narayan, K.G. Suresh, and Dr Rakesh Sinha, all senior and experienced figures. Added to this is the constant contribution of hundreds of humble swayamsevaks. Also, without the knowledge preserved in the publications of the Sangh family, this book would not have been possible.

1

Unity Is Power

Nagpur—the geographical centre of India during the British Raj, the winter capital of the Central Provinces, encompassing parts of present-day Madhya Pradesh, Chhattisgarh and Maharashtra. The British government used the town as its 'Zero Mile Stone' for measuring distances across the country, and the statues of the four horses and the commemorative Zero pillar still stand there. However, Nagpur is no longer considered the 'centre' of independent India. The Zero Mile Stone is now marked 343 kilometres away, in a village called Karaundi in Katni, Madhya Pradesh, where the Ashoka Pillar has been installed.

Nagpur may no longer be the geographical centre of India, but, with the Rashtriya Swayamsevak Sangh (RSS) being headquartered there, in the current political climate, people consider it the 'remote control' city—the remote control for the Bharatiya Janata Party (BJP).

Interestingly, Nagpur has emerged as the centre of two divergent ideologies: Hindutva, the ideology propagated by the RSS, and Ambedkarism, an ideology that empowers Dalits and other marginalised classes. It is a striking coincidence that Dr Keshav Baliram Hedgewar (1889–1940) founded the RSS on Vijayadashami (the tenth day of Dussehra) in 1925, and Babasaheb Ambedkar, with 400,000 followers who were Dalits and oppressed-caste Hindus, got initiated into the Buddhist fold on Vijayadashami on 14 October 1956. Since then, the Deeksha Bhoomi has hosted a celebration for the Dhamma Chakra Parivartan Divas every year on this day.

The headquarters of the Sangh and Deeksha Bhoomi are not very far from each other. While the RSS claims to have been working significantly for the upliftment of Dalits and the oppressed classes, there has been no noteworthy coordination between the two organisations. Interestingly, both Gandhi and Ambedkar had visited a Sangh shivir (camp) once. Now, the Sangh and the BJP have embraced both leaders. The decisions to celebrate Gandhi's 150th birth anniversary and to set up a special tourist route—the Ambedkar circuit[1]—are important moves by the Narendra Modi government. The policy of reservation for Dalits and other marginalised classes has been extended for another decade. Even so, it is as if the two ideologies are like parallel railway tracks, always running together but never meeting. The third sarsanghchalak (chief) of the RSS, Madhukar Dattatreya Deoras (1915–96), popularly known as Balasaheb, gave a speech against untouchability in 1974, but the Sangh didn't start a movement against the social evil until 1981, when wide-scale religious conversion of Dalits to Islam happened at an event in Meenakshipuram in the Thirunelveli district of Tamil Nadu. The RSS did not even support the 1989 Mandal Commission report. Mohan Bhagwat, the sixth and current RSS sarsanghchalak, consistently works to bridge the gap between the Sangh and the Dalits and backward classes, concentrating on uniting all marginalised classes under the Hindutva umbrella.

The founder of the RSS, Dr Hedgewar, had two role models—Swami Samarth Ramdas and Swami Vidyanand. Both men were considered exceptional management gurus of their time. For the second sarsanghchalak, Golwalkar (1906–73), popularly known as Guruji, Vivekananda and Chattrapati Shivaji Maharaj were role models, both of whose lives and philosophies had a significant influence on the Sangh.

The Sangh has come a long way and has had its fair share of ups and downs. The Congress government at the centre banned it not once, but thrice. Following Mahatma Gandhi's assassination, the Nehru administration first banned it on 4 February 1948. Senior office bearers and swayamsevaks (volunteers), including Golwalkar, were imprisoned on 1 February 1948. RSS shakhas (branches) were disbanded, and their activities prohibited. This shook the organisation, which faced a severe financial crunch as a result. In 1969, only once the report of the J.L. Kapur Commission had clarified that the Sangh had no role in Mahatma Gandhi's assassination and that Nathuram Godse was an active member of the Hindu Mahasabha and not the RSS, was the ban lifted.[2]

During the Emergency, then Prime Minister Indira Gandhi banned the organisation for the second time on 4 July 1975. The government imprisoned lakhs of swayamsevaks and Sangh leaders, who spent nineteen months in prison. But lakhs of RSS workers continued to work underground, not only fighting the Emergency but also looking after the families of those affected by it.[3] The government lifted the ban only after the Emergency ended in March 1977.

The P.V. Narasimha Rao government imposed a third ban on the Sangh in 1992, after the demolition of the Babri Masjid. In June 1993, the Rao government lifted the ban, unable to justify its actions to a panel created for that purpose.[4]

The wheels of time have moved since Narendra Modi and the BJP came to power at the centre, and it is said that several members of the Sangh control the affairs at Raisina Hill. If you travel from India Gate to Old Rajpath (now Kartavya Path) and reach Rashtrapati Bhavan, you will find many officials and ministers associated with the RSS seated in the air-conditioned rooms of the magnificent red buildings on either side of the road and running the government. The Modi government's intention behind the new Central Vista plan, it is said, was to show Indian history in a new light by strengthening India's vibrant democracy and its cultural heritage.

Most individuals who occupy important positions in the government today have received their political and social training in the Sangh. Even parikrama darbaris—those who are not regular swayamsevaks or workers but have gained the confidence of the Sangh high command—have reached the summit of power. The Sangh has a network that spreads over forty countries. The organisation is on the verge of completing a century of its existence in 2025, and its members continue to believe that their path is rooted solely in tradition, social work and nationalism.

While people from all walks of life and religious backgrounds come to the RSS shakhas or attend its meetings, the debate on how to better align the RSS with diverse social groups is ongoing. The current RSS chief, Mohan Bhagwat, claims that he wants to reach the last man standing on the margins. Officially, the veneer of winning the confidence of the Muslim community is in place, but there is something entirely different brewing beneath the surface, which is emerging under the guise of issues such as the rewriting of history, love jihad and other contentious points.

Dr Manmohan Vaidya, the general secretary of the RSS, summarises the Sangh ideology as, 'There are four aspects to Bharat's [India's] being. First is, *Ekam Sat Vipra Bahudha Vadanti*—the Almighty or God is one and can be called by various names and can be reached by different paths. Bharat has established this through its conduct. Hence, Swami Vivekananda, in his famous Chicago address, had proclaimed that we go beyond tolerance and accept all ways to be true ... The second aspect is realising "unity in diversity". In Rabindranath Tagore's words, "To see unity in diversity and to establish unity amongst variety is the core

Dharma of Bharat." Bharat does not see diversity as "differences" and the alien as enemies. Hence, we are not scared by the advent of a new community. Bharat has an innate and incredible ability to assimilate diverse communities while preserving their uniqueness. The third feature is that Bharat believes that every soul, man or woman, is potentially divine and the goal of human life is to manifest the divinity within by controlling nature, internal and external ... The fourth aspect is that there is liberty and freedom to choose one's path to ultimate freedom.'[5]

THE JOURNEY OF A HUNDRED YEARS

In 2025, RSS will celebrate its centenary. But the organisation is already planning for the year 2047, when India will mark a century of its independence. Therefore, it is imperative to consider what the RSS would look like in 2047. Will it retain the form that it has today? Will it still be relevant? Has the purpose for which Dr Hedgewar founded the RSS been fulfilled? Pracharak Sunil Ambekar has addressed some of these questions in his book, *The RSS: Roadmaps for the 21st Century.*

As per Ambekar, the Sangh is expanding, and swayamsevaks have reached almost every sphere of Indian life. He calls this organic growth, but feels that there is still a lot more that the Sangh has to achieve. Twenty-five years from now, he predicts that India will be a 'Vishva Guru', and the RSS would be so thoroughly integrated into society that it will be indistinguishable from the social fabric. He adds that the Sangh doesn't intend to dictate terms or rule Indian society, but wants to strengthen it so that it can find solutions to its problems on its own. The Sangh wants to lose its identity and meld with Indian society the way a river melds with the sea. A new slogan was coined for this purpose—'Sangh samaj banega'—society and the Sangh will become one.[6] This, however, does not imply that the Sangh will cease to exist once that happens.

RSS ideologue and veteran journalist Dilip Deodhar believes that the aim of the Sangh is not to keep the organisation alive for a long time.

After its centenary, the RSS will merge into Indian society, and by the time India completes a century of its independence, this process will be complete. Dr Hedgewar, too, was more focused on fulfilling the Sangh's purpose and not extending its longevity. Mirroring Hindu mythology, where a deity's avatar disappears after achieving its purpose on earth, the Sangh high command advocates that once the organisation's 'avatar purpose' is accomplished and it becomes one with Indian society, there is no rationale for its continued existence.[7]

AN EMPHASIS ON ADDITION, NOT DIVISION

The Sangh talks about taking traditional and cultural values forward while adapting to the needs of present-day Indian society at the same time. As an organisation, it firmly upholds that change is the only constant. Many people hold the view that the Sangh is a Hindu outfit, but the Sangh claims it does not consider 'Hindu' to be a religious identity; rather, it recognises India as an amalgamation of cultures and calls it 'ekaatmata'. The RSS claims it may speak about the Hindu religion and of having a Hindu Rashtra, but it is not against religious freedom. Nor does it oppose Muslims or Christians practicing their faith and rituals, although it opposes conversion.

The Sangh does not entirely espouse Mahatma Gandhi's concept of 'non-violence'. For example, the national convenor of the Prajna Pravah and the writer of *Badalte Daur Mein Hindutva,* J. Nandakumar, deems the recent violence between leftist groups and the RSS legitimate. According to him, we need to look at Kerala's history to understand the violence. Although the RSS has a nationwide presence, leftist groups hold a stronger position in Kerala, enabling them, according to Nandakumar, to perpetrate violence there. In certain instances, the Sangh has had to retaliate in self-defence. Nandakumar also posits that if the Sangh was indeed against leftist groups, then there would have been violence in those places where the RSS has a stronger presence compared to leftist groups, but that is not the case.

The Sangh holds the view that social harmony in India is effective solely because of Hindus, because it believes that wherever Hindus are in the majority, there is no religious discrimination or clash between communities. It feels that if India is indeed a secular nation, it is only because of the Hindus and that, in all the places where Muslims or Christians are in the majority, Hindus and their religion are in danger, and violence and oppression are rampant. The Sangh claims to not support the conversion of Christians and Muslims to Hinduism, but it accepts that it has a mission to reconvert or bring back (ghar vapasi) those who have converted to other religions under coercion. There are several scholars associated with the Sangh who are actively working on strategies to formulate strict laws against religious conversion at the national level.

In *Pakistan or the Partition of India,* Ambedkar wrote, 'If Hindu Raj does become a fact, it will, no doubt, be the greatest calamity for this country. No matter what the Hindus say, Hinduism is a menace to liberty, equality and fraternity. On that account it is incompatible with democracy. Hindu Raj must be prevented at any cost.'[8]

So, I asked Sunil Ambekar why there is such a vast difference between V.D. Savarkar's definition of Hindutva and that of the RSS. Why has the RSS never embraced his interpretation of Hindutva? Ambekar smiled and said, 'Swami Vivekananda, Rabindranath Tagore, Savarkar, Mahatma Gandhi and several others have defined Hindutva in their own way. They have tried to incorporate their points of view into its core tenets. What is wrong with that? Hindutva itself means accepting diverse points of view. We need to churn ideas, introspect, evaluate circumstances and cultural perceptions, and reflect on patriotism from time to time. We need to understand both Gandhi and Savarkar. A nation is not built by one man.'[9]

Addressing the attacks on and the discourse around Hindutva in our country, he said, 'Hindutva doesn't seek differences; it is all about unity and harmony. The pride we take in our country is Hindutva, and it has existed for thousands of years. The Sangh is not imposing anything new on anyone. Its purpose is to rekindle the sense of national pride that is rapidly fading—to remember it and remind others of it. There is no place for conflict or strife, either in the Sangh or in Hindutva, because clashes are driven by a desire for domination. The Sangh still operates in the Hindu way, and hence it doesn't think about domination. Our focus is on not only maintaining harmony within our organisation but also in society, and it is certainly happening.'[10]

The current sarsanghchalak Mohan Bhagwat, in his speech in Aligarh on 21 April 2025, and even in his earlier speeches, effectively called for the unification of Hindu society. To weed out caste discrimination and untouchability, he proposed that every village should have a shared well, lake or common temple, and a collective cremation ground. The Sangh's volunteers have begun working towards this goal, reaching villages across the country to carry the initiative forward.[11]

The Sangh says that it supports anyone who follows Hindu culture. It is neither against Delhi's former chief minister, Arvind Kejriwal, nor does it have a problem with Bihar's Nitish Kumar. The idea is to bring veterans and old-timers back into the fold, and that is why Babulal Marandi of Jharkhand has returned to the BJP. In 2006, he had left the BJP to form his own party, the Jharkhand Vikas Morcha (JVM), but merged it with the BJP in February 2020. To that end, maintaining friendly relations with Naveen Patnaik, Odisha's former chief minister, remains a priority, as it was with Jyotiraditya Scindia, a former Congress party member now in the BJP. In its centenary year, the Sangh is actively pursuing 'addition' and not 'division'—bringing everyone together and shedding its anti-Muslim image. As Mohan Bhagwat has said, 'Hindutva is incomplete without the Muslims. The DNA of Hindus and Muslims is the same. Our ancestors are the same.'[12]

In a way, this path leads to the same path that Dr Hedgewar once took. Hedgewar's staunch belief in the Hindutva philosophy and principles characterised him as a leader with fervent Hindu sensibilities. However, his supporters say that it would be incorrect to label him as being against any other religion. They claim he was not anti-Muslim; rather, he saw that a weak Hindu society would be a major hindrance to Hindu–Muslim unity. In his view, an equal friendship could not exist between a weak and a strong community. Prime Minister Atal Bihari Vajpayee (1924–2018) had also echoed a somewhat similar sentiment, asserting that only a powerful nation could have an equal relationship with everyone else.

Perhaps many consider the RSS and the BJP to be 'upper-class' organisations, but the special thing about the RSS-BJP journey is that their leaders are of the unanimous opinion that political power can be an effective weapon for the upliftment of backward classes, especially the Extremely Backward Classes (EBCs), Scheduled Castes (SCs) and Scheduled Tribes (STs). As per the Sangh's Hindu Rashtra hypothesis, integrating marginalised sections of Hindu society into the mainstream is an important pillar of nation-building.

Deodhar says, 'The Sangh's prayer was last changed in 1940. Now, when the Sangh is looking towards the future as it completes a century, its "Hindu Rashtra" prayer will change, and it will adopt a "universal, humanitarian" form in line with the Upanishads.'[13] Deodhar says that the Sangh is the 'integrated system' of a multifaceted Hindu society, which means that the Sangh's role is to align, organise and unify Hindu society despite its internal diversity. On completing a century, Deodhar claims, the Sangh intends to be free from its attachment to Hindus and emerge in its new avatar with a new name, a new system and new programmes.

DEMOCRACY WITHIN THE SANGH

Present-day Sangh claims to be more conscious of its public image, actively using its IT cell to maintain it. Such activities began in 2012–13, well before the Narendra Modi government took charge at the centre. In the past, left-leaning political parties would invest heavily in engaging with intellectuals, who would not only create a favourable environment for their political narrative but would also allegedly distort historical facts. As per the Sangh, intellectuals aligned with left-leaning political parties have over the years also continued to advocate their ideology through the publication of extensive literature. Accordingly, to disseminate the tenets of its ideology, the Sangh too has established a new organisation called the World Association of Hindu Academicians (WAHA).

J. Nandakumar feels that the RSS's expansion over the years has adversely affected certain groups, and it is these groups that keep discrediting and defaming the Sangh. He says that the RSS is not averse to politics; in fact, there are many RSS pracharaks in the BJP and in active politics, but the RSS does not consider politics to be its be-all and end-all. He claims that the Sangh is a dynamic body working towards transforming society, eliminating social evils, uniting citizens of the country and bringing glory to India. Politics is only a minor aspect of this change.

He continues, 'This political change is not a story limited to a few days or a few years; it results from a decades-long effort. For instance, the Bharatiya Mazdoor Sangh (BMS) is the world's largest workers' union but is apolitical. The Vidyarthi Parishad is also a non-political organisation. We call them organisations associated with different sectors, while you call them the "Sangh Parivar" collectively. Usually in a parivar or a family, the elders give orders whereas the younger ones obey them. For example, the Centre of Indian Trade Unions (CITU) is a part of the Congress parivar; so are several other leftist organisations.

But the organisations affiliated with the Sangh do not take orders from the Sangh, nor does the Sangh give them any orders. They only take inspiration from the Sangh. Each one of them is an independent organisation that decides its own path and is also financially self-sufficient.'[14]

While the RSS does not operate as a political party, it believes that the advancement of a nation demands strong leadership not only within political parties but across all spheres of life. Accordingly, it endeavours to identify capable youth in every field and prepare them to contribute towards nation-building. A big change in the public image of the Sangh came when the fourth sarsanghchalak, Prof. Rajendra Singh (1922–2003)—popularly known as Rajju bhaiyya—took over leadership and began using the term 'Sangh Srishti' (Sangh Universe) instead of Sangh Parivar.

Although the Sangh claims to be a socio-cultural organisation, its programmes and activities do undeniably affect Indian politics too. The reality is that the BJP is the RSS's political arm, and it benefits from the Sangh's activities and from the enthusiastic contribution of its swayamsevaks.

Understanding the democratic structure of the RSS requires intense research. The sarsanghchalak's is the most powerful post in the organisation. His words are supreme and can neither be ignored nor disobeyed. However, can the sarsanghchalak make a point related to the RSS solely based on his own wisdom and judgement? Are such matters typically discussed and agreed upon collectively? When there are disagreements in the Sangh, they are discussed discreetly within its four walls. Members freely express individual opinions, but once a decision is made, they must adhere to it with discipline and cannot publicly express dissenting views.

Deodhar says that the RSS comprises multiple 'levels' and 'layers', but at the heart of it lies the Sangh. There is a network in place, but it's not a hierarchy. There are a total of thirty-six organisations: twelve 'mass organisations' and twenty-four 'class organisations'. Their activities sometimes overlap, but the Sangh has appointed separate 'sangathan mantris' or ministers for each outfit. The Sangh controls and regulates these organisations through its pracharaks. Discussions happen in 'pratinidhi sabhas' and 'pracharak meetings', but no organisation interferes with the activities of another organisation, nor is such intervention tolerated.

At present, the RSS has over 6,000 pracharaks who manage responsibilities of not just the Sangh but other regional organisations in the Sangh as well. With the rapid expansion in the number of organisations within the Sangh network, effective coordination has become essential to ensure smooth functioning and growth. Coordination committees were established to facilitate this. In addition, sangathan mantris oversee and control the organisations at their level.

A recent example of the consultative and collective decision-making that takes place within the RSS is the decision to change the uniform that Sangh members wear. The idea was initially proposed at a meeting of the vibhag pracharaks (divisional pracharaks) and subsequently discussed at the Akhil Bharatiya Karyakari Mandal (ABKM), which includes representatives from all provinces and zones. After this meeting, the issue was taken to the highest decision-making authority in the Sangh, the Akhil Bharatiya Pratinidhi Sabha. The change in the uniform was discussed three times, but a consensus could not be reached. Mohan Bhagwat decided to defer the decision, setting a five-year time frame for deliberation. After the stipulated period, the proposal to change the uniform was revisited and discussions began afresh, generating a variety of suggestions.

The Sangh maintains that open communication and discussion can resolve any issue, provided the decision-makers keep their egos in check and act with pure and honest intentions. The third RSS sarsanghchalak, Balasaheb Deoras, first took up the challenge of bringing about change in the organisation. In December 1973, six months after taking up the supreme post, he publicly called for reform at a winter camp held at the Hedgewar Bhavan in Nagpur: 'There is a crisis of integrity and character at this time. The responsibility has fallen on our shoulders, and it is of utmost importance. We have to accept it and fulfil it. We have been putting off a lot of our responsibilities and also trying to evade them, which is not right. We need to think about what the Sangh is, where it is today and how it should be. I cannot say for certain that our swayamsevaks do not fall prey to different enticements. There are a lot of problems, innumerable questions, and it is our responsibility to find the answers.'[15]

The Sangh claims it is intertwined with people of all social strata and religious communities in India, and does not disagree with anyone. As an example of this, Ambekar refers to the Vijayadashami RSS Sangh ceremony that was held once at the Kasturchand Park near the railway station. Balasaheb Deoras was the sarsanghchalak at the time. In his speech, he thanked the famous convent school, St Joseph High School, and its administration for providing the furniture and other things for the celebration.

The speed of expansion of the Sangh can be attributed to its effortless and efficient functioning, which attracts new members with no advertising. According to Ambekar, the RSS's greatest strength is its widespread presence, which is supported by a robust network of swayamsevaks and organisations. The number of organisations allied with the Sangh is constantly on the rise, which has led to an increase in the scope and number of programmes it organises. Moreover, the Sangh does not hesitate in distancing itself from irrelevant organisations. They prioritise the work of a particular organisation depending on current needs. For example, the Sangh prioritised the Vishva Hindu Parishad (VHP) during the 1992 Ram Janmabhoomi movement. Sometimes, the Vidyarthi Parishad is kept at the forefront. The Sangh has an effective feedback mechanism to solicit suggestions, and this system percolates to the lowest rungs of the organisation. Based on the suggestions, the Sangh not only makes changes but also ensures their implementation.

Writer Sanjeev Kelkar, a long-time associate of the RSS, highlights the Sangh's extensive use of symbolism, but adds that a deep commitment to achieving its goals is sometimes lacking in the Sangh. He gives the example of the movement against cow slaughter. The Sangh prominently took part in this movement from 1952 until 1969, incorporating protests and discussions over the issue into its programmes. And yet, despite the BJP forming the government at the centre four times, the Sangh could make precious little progress vis-à-vis the cause. Now, it is even said that the Sangh has nothing against the consumption of beef because it doesn't want to interfere with anyone's food preferences.

Even the smallest changes take time, and even against them there is a significant revolt on a larger stage. In 1973, Balasaheb Deoras had tried to introduce a few non-Indian games at the Sangh shakhas to pique the interest of children and youth taking part in games, while also bringing about a change in the image of the RSS.[16] However, senior Sangh officials had not liked the suggestion and expressed their disapproval. The result is that the games played during the RSS's initial years continue to be played to date at the shakhas, even though the world has changed a lot since then.

EFFORTS TO CHANGE THE IMAGE

Arun Kumar, a senior Sangh official, told me that there are no walls between the Sangh and society at large. The Sangh is a part of society, and they are not at all apart, be it a swayamsevak, a pracharak or a Sangh pramukh. They are all part of the blowing social winds.[17]

The Sangh claims to have made several changes to the organisation over the years to remain in step with the changing times. From the very start, Dr Hedgewar had decided that the Sangh and its members would keep changing to improve themselves based on the evolving needs of the times.

The RSS faces persistent accusations of being Brahmanical and pro-upper caste, and has failed to overcome this image, despite claiming a different reality. To support their claim, they cite the instance when Balasaheb Deoras had released a list of all the senior leaders of the Sangh and one could see that the list included people from all walks of life and from different regions of India. Throughout the seventies, the RSS says, it welcomes several individuals from socially and economically backward classes into its fold. Nonetheless, it is true that nobody from a backward class has ever held the post of the sarsanghchalak or the sarkaryavah (general secretary), and even in 2025, when the RSS completes a hundred years, the probability of there being a leader from the backward classes in either of the two posts is almost negligible.

Swami Vigyananand, who has an engineering degree from IIT Kharagpur and is the current sah-sarkaryavah (joint general secretary) of the Vishva Hindu Parishad, handles the work of the Sangh in other countries. He explains that the principles that the founders of the Sangh must have had while setting it up were remarkable because the Sangh is a 'faceless organisation'. It is an organisation of like-minded people. He adds, 'The basic unit of the Sangh is the shakha, and what do you need to run a shakha after all? A lathi and a flag.'[18]

Swami Vigyananand adds, 'It is not completely true when people say that the Sangh is an organisation that builds extraordinary character. Even its members have their human weaknesses, and there needn't be any hesitation in accepting so. To understand this, we must first consider the Sangh's founding reasons, especially since the freedom struggle was already underway. Congress was working as a nationwide organisation, but the British had understood that the most powerful institution in India was the Brahmin community. They were spread not only all across India, from Kashmir to Kanyakumari and from Assam to Gujarat, but also maintained close connections with each other. Their influence has been significant on all revolts and movements, which is why the British tried to destroy this "organisation" very strategically.'

'Look at the Brahmins not as a caste but as an institution,' says Swami Vigyananand. 'Most social movements and changes have happened under their leadership. If you look at history, even Lord Buddha's initial disciples were Brahmins. Lord Mahavir's acharya [teacher] and ganadhar [the chief disciple] were Brahmins. Ramanandacharya and Basaveshwara headed reformist campaigns, while Raja Ram Mohan Roy, Swami Dayananda Saraswati and Mahadev Govind Ranade, despite being Brahmins, led reform movements against their community. Incidentally, Brahmins have been at the forefront of other movements as well. Gopal Krishna Gokhale, Jawaharlal Nehru and Govind Ballabh Pant ran the secular movement; Vasudev Phadke, V.D. Savarkar, Hedgewar and Golwalkar spearheaded the nationalist movement; and B.L. Joshi, Namboodiripad and Rai led the communist movement. Hence, please don't call the Sangh a Brahminical organisation. There is not a single area in India in which the RSS doesn't have a presence, be it education, medicine, labour, farmers, business, religion, tribal societies. The volunteers of the RSS or its affiliate organisations have silently been rendering selfless service everywhere.'

Those in the Sangh claim that they never ask about the caste of those joining the Sangh, and they rarely discuss it either. The Sangh never even talks about the Dalits who hold prominent positions in the organisation. Moreover, it says, the rising number of leaders from the backward classes as symbols of Hindutva is neither sudden nor spontaneous. Prime Minister Modi is the most prominent Hindutva leader, a direct consequence of the RSS's efforts and strategic vision. Today, when all castes appear to be rallying together under the banner of Hindutva, along with increasing representation at the district and provincial levels, it is possible that, similar to Narendra Modi in the BJP, a Hindutva leader from a backward class may emerge from the Sangh

Parivar. The Sangh claims that if this were to happen, it would likely offer no opposition.

American scholar Jean A. Curran researched the RSS in 1951 and wrote, 'It is believed that once the Sangh comes to power, it will stand with the capitalists, zamindars and the powerful strata of society. Though a vast majority of the supporters and volunteers of the RSS come from the upper strata of society today, they believe the Sangh will protect their interests. But I don't see such a feeling among the swayamsevaks. The Sangh may not have a sound economic policy and plan today, but the pro-Hindutva socialist bent is visible in the swayamsevaks.'[19]

Curran did his research on the Sangh prior to the formation of the Bharatiya Jana Sangh—the political predecessor of the BJP—in 1951. However, his observation has come true. Although people commonly believed the Jana Sangh would favour a liberal economy, the Bharatiya Jana Sangh openly supported the abolition of the zamindari system and the privy purses. The Jana Sangh had to pay a price for its stance during the elections. Several MLAs in Rajasthan who supported the zamindari system left the party in protest. Only Bhairon Singh Shekhawat and a few other people stayed. Ironically, Shekhawat himself was a Rajput and one of the leaders who openly opposed the oppressive Sati tradition.

As far as the Sangh's policy-making agenda is concerned, Deendayal Upadhyaya's (1916–68) 'Ekatma Manavvaad ka Siddhant' or 'Integral Humanism'[20] proved to be a half-hearted effort. The second sarsanghchalak, M.S. Golwalkar, had said that the Sangh did not believe in any 'isms'. Thus, for the longest time, there was no discussion about Integral Humanism in the Sangh's shiksha vargs (summer training camps) because the Sangh believed it should not give undue importance or priority to any specific person or his ideology. The RSS claims to have been always unwilling to make itself into a purely Brahminical entity. This was the primary reason for the Sangh to not align itself with Savarkar, as it was not ready to support Savarkar's interpretation of Hindutva. Even at the time of the formation of the Jana Sangh, they say, Golwalkar had made it clear to Dr Syama Prasad Mookerjee that he shouldn't try to make this organisation along the same lines as the Hindu Mahasabha, and that the doors of the new party should be open to all regions and faiths. When Deendayal Upadhyaya delivered a speech on Hindutva at a national convention of the Jana Sangh, Golwalkar told him to follow the path of the Indian Constitution and leave Hindutva for the Sangh.[21] The Sangh Parivar chose this flexible approach to connect with all social groups and unite Hindus with differing rituals and traditions. Among these were several communities that were at loggerheads with each other. The Sangh even began organising pujas for deities, festivals and fairs at the caste and sub-caste levels.

Mukunda C.R., the sah-sarkaryavah of the Sangh, told me that changes were introduced in the working of the Sangh based on a definite vision, and along three lines: organisational, creative and awakening. Work was done to bring about social, infrastructural and other reforms. A ten-year social reform programme was formulated to address rural development, social harmony, religious awakening, cow protection, reconversion to Hinduism, preservation of family values and the mobilisation of social strength.[22]

Addressing the attacks that are made on the Sangh's image, Mukunda says, 'Dattopant Thengadi used to say that there shouldn't be too much PR, nor too little of it. The important task is to correct the image and respond to false propaganda. Karyakartas and swayamsevaks get confused by image-building efforts. Image-building is more important for political parties.' In response to a question about the Sangh's perception in the Muslim community, Mukunda explains that the Sangh was established to transform, uplift and strengthen the Hindu community, but they desire to walk with everyone, and all communities are welcome to participate in this shared effort. On the question of youth, he says, 'Apart from being the face of the Sangh, they also must be given the responsibility of social change. Today's youth is coming to us not only because they are attracted to the Sangh's ideology, but seeing how rapidly extremist and terrorist organisations are growing worldwide, such youth also want to join the Sangh in order to work against such organisations. We need to think differently about such members. Additionally, we need to think about how effectively we can utilise their experience.'

For Aniruddha Deshpande, the Sangh's former communications head, the focus is on development, and that is why, despite human tendencies, there is no sign of envy or jealousy in the Sangh. He told me: 'When an ordinary person comes to the shakha for the first time and becomes a swayamsevak, his personality is enhanced, and he learns to accept, cooperate, eat and coexist with others, play sports with them and so on. This makes him mix better in society. Then, they focus on commitment—the individual is committed to completing every task that is assigned to him. He starts to prioritise the activities associated with society and the Sangh, and his family also begins to make adjustments for him. His family too starts to realise that he needs to devote time to society and the organisation, even if it means that he would be able to devote less time to the family. The shakha also builds a sense of brotherhood, which means that a swayamsevak of the Sangh cannot be communal. The Sangh nurtures the character and values of the individual and steers him towards practicality and spirituality.'[23]

For Deshpande, communication is at the heart of the Sangh. Groups of karyakartas identify influential people from different fields in their localities and cities. They give them Sangh-centric literature, hold discussions and invite them to important occasions. However, there is no expectation that they take part in the Sangh's activities or programmes. They are free to continue contributing to society in their respective fields. The Sangh raises no objections if someone chooses not to associate with it, its programmes, or even opposes its ideology. The swayamsevaks continue to fulfil their duties despite this.

Deshpande refutes the allegation that the 'image-building exercise' targets universal acceptance: 'Why do we need image-building exercises, anyway? Everybody knows the Sangh has a powerful image in society. The Sangh is performing yeoman service in every area of society, and it is because of this that even people who didn't know about the Sangh or had preconceived notions about it want to be associated with it. When they realise the truth, they decide to become a part of the Sangh. The communication set-up is such that it not only opens windows but spreads awareness that the doors are open for everyone and we are ready to embrace them.'

THE SANGH: FROM THEN TILL NOW

It is said that the RSS's identity was strengthened around the time of Mahatma Gandhi's assassination. At that time, many believed the RSS was the second major Hindutva organisation after the Hindu Mahasabha. Nathuram Godse, a member of the latter, had shot Gandhi, causing his death. In the aftermath, the then-home minister Sardar Patel had banned the Sangh. However, a week later, Patel, in a letter to Prime Minister Nehru, mentioned that the RSS had no role to play in the assassination of Gandhi.[24] On 18 July 1948, Sardar Patel wrote another letter to Dr Syama Prasad Mookerjee, a member of the Hindu Mahasabha and a cabinet minister in Nehru's government. He mentioned that the matter of Gandhi's assassination was in court, and he would not make any comments regarding the RSS and the Hindu Mahasabha's involvement in it at this time. He added that the reports from the home ministry did, however, prove that both organisations, especially the former, helped to create the charged environment that led to the tragic event.[25] After about one and a half years, on 11 July 1949, the government lifted the ban on the RSS.[26]

Golwalkar, in the initial years of the Sangh, focused primarily on character building for its members. It was only when the third sarsanghchalak Deoras took charge that an element of activism came into the work of the Sangh. He promoted rural development, education of the Adivasis and social work. He opened the doors of the Sangh to Muslims and Christians as well.

Syama Prasad Mookerjee, an active member of the Congress, at a certain stage, became disillusioned with the party's principles and approached Sangh Pramukh Golwalkar for the establishment of a new political organisation. He asked that a group of efficient karyakartas become a part of this organisation. Golwalkar gave him young karyakartas like Nanaji Deshmukh (1916–2010), Deendayal Upadhyaya, Atal Bihari Vajpayee, Kushabhau Thakre (1922–03) and Sundar Singh Bhandari (1921–2005). Thus, was born the Jana Sangh in 1951.

The expansion of the Sangh had struck anxiety in the ranks of senior Congress leaders in the thirties itself. In a letter dated 30 October 1938, the national president of the Congress, Subhas Chandra Bose, expressed his worries to Shankar Rao Deo, president of the Maharashtra Congress, stating that compared to Congress, the Rashtriya Swayamsevak Sangh was increasingly attracting more and more of the country's students and youth. Bose sought an explanation for the same. He thought the appeal was largely because of the Sangh's discipline, its uniform and its parades, which masked its underlying ideology. Shankar Rao Deo, in a two-page reply sent on 6 November 1938, focused on the ideological reasons he thought were driving the youth towards the Sangh.[27]

From its inception, the RSS was 'ekachalakanuvartik' or supremo-led, a one-man show. This meant that at the shakha level, the sanghchalak's commands were paramount, while the sarsanghchalak's words were supreme at the Sangh level. This style of functioning was discussed at the first brainstorming meeting. A ten-day session took place in Sindi, Wardha district, Maharashtra, from 24 February to 5 March 1939. The meeting lasted for nine hours, with three segments of three hours each. The participants discussed every aspect of the Sangh—its prayer, oath, classes, officials, elections, and behaviour—in detail.[28]

At the Sangh, the sarsanghchalak's appointment is extremely important. There is no election for the head of the Sangh, and the existing head nominates his successor. However, he seeks suggestions from senior officials before making his decision. Dr Hedgewar had chosen Golwalkar as his successor very much in advance. Similarly, Golwalkar had always said that Balasaheb Deoras would be his successor even though Deoras had remained away from the Sangh for eleven years. Deoras took up no responsibilities from 1950 to 1961, though he remained involved with the activities. He joined the Sangh's work again in 1961. Seniority is not necessary to hold the reins. For example, during the tenure of H.V. Sheshadri (1926–2005), K.S. Sudarshan (1931–2012) was handed over control because Sheshadri was not keeping well. Sarsanghchalak Rajju bhaiyya had then transferred the leadership to Sudarshan. However, when Rajju bhaiyya had previously served as the sarkaryavah, he had appointed Sheshadri as the sarkaryavah in his place, while he had taken the role of sah-sarkaryavah.

The Sangh follows the practice of sending its swayamsevaks and pracharaks to different districts for its activities. In a meeting held in Sindi, the discussion veered towards finances and managing the expenses of their stay and other costs. Balasaheb Deoras had suggested sending a fixed amount monthly to all karyakartas in different districts. As the Nagpur shakha started getting increasingly burdened by these expenses, Nanasaheb Talatule suggested issuing an order requiring every shakha to remit a part of its guru dakshina (teacher's honorarium) to Nagpur. Finally, Dr Hedgewar decided to cover the expenses from the guru dakshina collected in Nagpur. But if the expenses surpassed a certain limit, other shakhas could be asked to contribute funds. However, they deferred the final decision. Dr Hedgewar also clarified that strict monitoring would be necessary to ensure that they spent every paisa collected as guru dakshina only on Sangh activities and not for personal use. The responsibility for monitoring this was assigned to the nidhi pramukh (treasury head).

One of the important links in the chain of the Sangh's functioning is the pracharak, and the primary focal point of the organisation is the Sangh Parivar. Usually, only unmarried swayamsevaks become pracharaks, i.e. lifetime swayamsevaks of the Sangh. Ambekar says, 'In fact, a pracharak is an exception in the Sangh set-up. The fundamental unit is the householder, the youth. Over ninety-nine per cent of the people in the RSS are householders or family men. There are two reasons a pracharak remains unmarried: the first is that the pracharak works to inspire society and the swayamsevaks. The second reason is that they need to work full-time; they devote a lot of their time to the work of the Sangh. However, there is also a provision for pracharaks to leave after five years or longer. Vistaraks (junior pracharaks who are householders) can leave after two years. However, the vast majority of pracharaks feel that after working full-time with the Sangh for five years, the Sangh's work becomes their life mission and they continue to be associated with it. There is neither pressure on them of any kind to do so, nor are they the most important parts of the Sangh's machinery.'[29]

The Sangh always gives its most coveted posts, which entail significant responsibility, to full-time pracharaks. Sometimes other people have also been given such positions. But the supreme authority of pracharaks in the Sangh means that other people holding these positions sometimes causes rifts within the organisation. It is also not easy to remove people from these posts. Moreover, the RSS's progress depends significantly on thousands of swayamsevaks who travel extensively, subsisting on minimal food and basic fare.

Sanjeev Kelkar says, 'There are three reasons I remained associated with the Sangh for such a long time. The first was the RSS's mission for human development. I felt this was the most important requirement for national development, and the RSS was fulfilling it. The second was that the leadership of the Sangh would not allow its organisation to become another Hindu sect. The third was that the RSS would not compromise on its ideology and principles at any cost. But when, over a long period of time, I found that the Sangh was not passing muster on these three aspects, I left the Sangh.'[30]

Kelkar now believes that the Sangh is a 'closed' organisation with very little possibility for change. He doesn't agree that the Sangh does not function like a sect or a math (a Hindu monastery). According to him, here too, there is only one supremo, and nobody dares to challenge or disobey his command. In fact, the supremo's dominance was most prominent during Golwalkar's time because of his revered spiritual personality.

A senior official and a long-time pracharak of the Sangh explains this: 'The Rashtriya Swayamsevak Sangh was born in an akhada (wrestling ring), and that is why the lathi still rules here. The swayamsevaks cannot seem to think beyond that.' But another official at the Udasin Ashram in Delhi disagrees and says, 'There is no need for the swayamsevaks to think. There are officials who can answer questions. The swayamsevak has to simply walk on the path charted by the Sangh and continue to work for nation-building. They don't need any more information than this.'

However, Sunil Ambekar and other Sangh officials have observed that the Sangh is constantly changing. For example, at the conference in Sindi, Maharashtra, a proposal to change the Sangh's prayer was brought up for discussion. The prayer was changed first. Earlier, the prayer was in Marathi and Hindi. Then, it started being recited in Sanskrit. The oath underwent changes both before and after Independence. Many organisational changes were also implemented. Golwalkar and Deoras were both present at Sindi, but Prabhakar Balwant Dani (1908–65) kept away from this brainstorming session even though he was one of the most powerful officials. It could be because when the Hindu Mahasabha had organised the Bhagyanagar Satyagraha in Hyderabad, Dani had announced his intention to participate in it despite the Sangh's stand that none of its officials would take part in such movements.

Former pracharak Ramesh Shiledar is of the view that everything has merged into one now—the Sangh alone holds power. He recalls that Dr Hedgewar used to say that if the Sangh and society became one, there would be no need to have different organisations. Golwalkar would say that any art or skill that comes with virtues, also brings its demerits with it. If a socio-cultural organisation has decided to associate itself with politics, it will have to accept the flaws that come with such an association. In earlier times, the Sangh's guiding principle was nation first, then the organisation, and finally, the individual. Today, the order seems to have been reversed. Shiledar also quotes Balasaheb Deoras, who used a telling metaphor—even the most beautiful house needs a toilet. The toilet is also the place where one is most likely to slip. So, even though it is essential to have a toilet, one must be careful of slipping while using it.

It is usually said that the Sangh keeps its distance from politics; however, it had ordered swayamsevaks to play an active role in the 2014 and 2019 general elections. During these elections, people were also greatly attracted to the Sangh ideology. And while the BJP and the Sangh are two independent organisations, the latter is the preserver of the former's ideology and ought not to be considered the 'remote control' of BJP. There is no other example like this in the history of political parties. In the case of communist parties, the ideological and political organisations are not two separate entities.

Soon after the Emergency was declared, the Bharatiya Jana Sangh, the Samajwadi Party, the Bharatiya Lok Dal and the Congress (O) came together to form the Janata Party and to fight elections against Indira Gandhi' Congress. The way the RSS allowed the Bharatiya Jana Sangh to merge with the Janata Party illustrated the leadership's confidence in its network of swayamsevaks. In his time, Balasaheb Deoras had written a letter to say that the Sangh's swayamsevaks were free to walk on the path of their chosen political ideology, but he received a lot of flak from several quarters. However, he had complete trust in his swayamsevaks and stood by his statement.[31]

Deoras had also said that he knew that a mere letter would not be enough to change the course of events—which is exactly what happened. When Samajwadi leaders started pressuring Jana Sangh leaders, who were also a part of the Janata Party, to relinquish their dual membership, most leaders had given up power rather than abandon their commitment to the Sangh ideology. Vajpayee, for instance, said that his relationship with the Janata Party was only two years old, while his relationship with the Sangh went back twenty-five years. Consequently, the Jana Sangh's relationship with the Janata Party fractured, and a new party emerged: the Bharatiya Janata Party (BJP).

The Sangh claims that they always place the organisation above the individual and are vehemently against the growth of a personality cult. However, this seems to have changed in the present day, when the spotlight seems to be on Narendra Modi and his persona. Addressing this development, Aniruddha Deshpande says, 'A lot of this depends on the leader's personality. Modi-ji's personality attracts people; the media's focus is on him, and hence it appears to be a personality cult. But the Sangh is not like this. The Sangh works in the national interest, and if this is true that a personality cult has arisen, then the Sangh will address this.'[32]

Though the Sangh may claim to be averse to politics, it has directed its efforts towards ensuring that the BJP forms the government at both the centre and in the states. This, in turn, advances their agenda of cultural nationalism. It has been widely discussed that ever since the BJP assumed power, the RSS has witnessed a significant spike in its membership and influence. Some argue that it is the RSS's organisational strength that boosts the BJP's electoral success. Regardless, the Sangh's broader mission essentially includes the BJP and its politics, and both organisations are interrelated. The Sangh believes that for nation-building, intervention in politics is essential, especially in the kind of politics which is aligned with one's ideology since it is crucial for the advancement of cultural nationalism.

Discussions about the Sangh and its relationship with politics have been ongoing since its inception. There were long and serious deliberations among Balasaheb Deoras, Dr Hedgewar, Appaji Joshi and others during the Sindi session held in 1939. At that time, the Hindu Mahasabha was an active political organisation, and most swayamsevaks from Maharashtra were fascinated by it and with Savarkar and his fiery oratory.

Dr Hedgewar's view was to allow swayamsevaks to participate in political activities during elections as long as they had the permission of the sanghchalak and returned to Sangh's work after the elections were over. But Nanasaheb Talatule expressed his concerns, noting that it would be difficult to erase the influence of politics from the swayamsevaks' minds once they had taken part in it. To prevent confusion within the organisation, Golwalkar specifically requested that the swayamsevaks be kept away from politics. However, Dr Hedgewar felt it was important to maintain cordial relationships with those who took part in political activities and those who worked for other social organisations. This approach continued under Golwalkar. Later, Balasaheb Deoras played an important role in transforming a high-caste organisation into one that was open and accessible to people from all strata. The social engineering efforts continued with Dalits and backward classes assuming important positions within the Sangh during the Ayodhya agitation. When Deoras became the sarsanghchalak in 1974, he vehemently condemned untouchability and said, 'If untouchability is not a sin, then nothing is a sin.'[33] This was a pivotal moment that led to greater inclusion of leaders from marginalised communities within both the Sangh and the BJP.

The Sangh actively and openly participated in two general elections: 1977 and 2014. Sangh officials called on their swayamsevaks and karyakartas to participate in these elections actively to make sure that the BJP succeeded. At the time of the 1977 elections, there was a feeling in the RSS that unless Indira Gandhi was defeated, the ban on the RSS would never be lifted. They feared that if she returned to power, she would take every step to dismantle the organisation. Deoras had also expressed concern that if a ban continued on the RSS during the Emergency, its state would become the same as that in 1948. But the Sangh not only worked against the Emergency under Deoras' leadership but also strengthened the organisation. Adamant on defeating Indira Gandhi, the Jana Sangh joined hands with the Janata Party and emerged hugely successful in the 1977 elections. Later, it was Deoras who decided that the BJP would play an active role in the Ram Janmabhoomi movement. He had extensive deliberations with Vajpayee and Advani, and the result was that a resolution demanding the construction of the Ram Temple in Ayodhya was passed at the 1989 national executive meeting in Palampur. This decision proved to be very valuable for the BJP.

However, during the 2004 general elections, the same Sangh leadership declared that regardless of whether the Vajpayee government won or lost, the Sangh would remain unaffected. This was also the time when the Swadeshi Jagaran Manch—an affiliate organisation of the RSS opposed to unchecked liberalisation and globalisation—launched a massive campaign against Vajpayee's administration. But the Sangh's position changed substantially by the time the 2014 general elections arrived. After a ten-year reign of the United Progressive Alliance (UPA), the RSS had realised that a third consecutive victory for the UPA would hinder its plans to advance its Hindutva agenda. Narendra Modi was projected as the BJP's prime ministerial candidate as the Sangh felt there was no better leader in the BJP capable of powerfully championing its agenda. The Sangh's high command presented the 2014 elections to its members as a matter of life or death, making clear its intention that the Sangh would make all efforts to secure victory for the BJP.

The BJP not only achieved an absolute majority in the 2014 general elections, but Narendra Modi also proved himself to be a powerful prime minister who advanced the RSS's ideology. Subsequently, the Sangh actively took part in the 2019 general elections to further its agenda and achieve its remaining objectives. And the Modi government delivered. The Ram Janmabhoomi issue that had been stuck for fifty long years was resolved. The special status granted to Jammu and Kashmir under Article 370 of the Constitution was revoked. And, ground is now being laid for the implementation of the Uniform Civil Code.

Veteran journalist K.G. Suresh says, 'Modi-ji is a lifetime swayamsevak. The Sangh flows in his veins. But those who think that he doesn't care about the RSS, or those who believe that the RSS gives orders to him, clearly understand neither the RSS nor Modi-ji. The truth likely resides in the space between the two perspectives. The Modi government has implemented many of the Sangh's suggestions. However, the relationship has evolved: previously a close, almost familial bond, it is now a more reciprocal and mutually beneficial one. Modi understands the strengths and the needs of the RSS, and the Sangh knows it needs Modi to fulfil its mission. Some people in the Sangh may dislike Modi, but it is amply clear that Modi is the need of the hour. Modi knows the role that the Sangh has played in his life. The Sangh has always believed that it is not the individual but the organisation and the ideology that are paramount. This has changed now, and Modi has become the darling of the Sangh.'[34]

Prime Minister Modi has pushed forward an agenda that combines economic progress with nationalism and Hindutva. After securing support from the Dalits and backward classes, he has sought to engage with Muslims and Christians. A key example is the Modi government's enactment of the Muslim Women (Protection of Rights on Marriage) Act in 2019, which criminalises 'triple talaq', a step that earned him support from Muslim women. Yet, a sizeable faction of the RSS and BJP continues to consider Hindutva and the Hindu identity as its foremost goal. Their hard-line efforts have posed significant challenges to the Modi government.

By introducing the Citizenship (Amendment) Act (CAA) in 2019, the Modi government took a major step that aligns with its broader

Hindutva agenda. The act provides a pathway to Indian citizenship for non-Muslim minorities—specifically Hindus, Sikhs, Buddhists, Jains and Parsis—who face religious persecution in Pakistan, Afghanistan and Bangladesh. As per the Act, members of these communities who had entered India before 31 December 2014 would be eligible for Indian citizenship; however, the same would not apply to Muslims.

Union Minister Nitin Gadkari has claimed that there was an attempt to spread misinformation regarding the CAA and that the Act aims to provide justice to the religious minorities facing persecution in the three neighbouring countries. To which other country are such religious minorities supposed to go apart from India? On the other hand, as per him, there are over a hundred Islamic nations where persecuted Muslims can seek shelter. He further clarified that Muslims living in India have nothing to do with this Act, and neither are they in any kind of danger.[35]

Additionally, the BJP government worked on making the National Register of Citizens (NRC) effective, intending to identify and remove illegal Bangladeshi immigrants from Assam. Although they made considerable progress, large-scale protests halted the process. The government also expressed an interest in creating a National Population Register of residents across the country, though it currently maintains that there are no immediate plans to move forward with it.

We need to go back in time to understand the history of the CAA and see where it all began. Soon after India gained independence and the horrifying Partition took place, Dr Syama Prasad Mookerjee, a minister in the Nehru government, raised the issue of religious persecution of Hindus. However, the discussion came to a standstill as disagreements surfaced between Mookerjee and Nehru. The former thought that the Indian government ought to intervene to protect the rights of Hindus in Pakistan. He believed it was India's responsibility to engage with the Pakistan government and put an end to the religious oppression of the Hindus in East Pakistan. But Nehru was against triggering any diplomatic disputes with Pakistan.

The Liaquat–Nehru Pact, signed on 8 April 1950, protected minorities and their property in both countries. After the finalisation of the pact, Dr Mookerjee delivered a historic speech on 19 April 1950, describing attempts to eliminate Hindus in Sindh, following similar events in the North-West Frontier Province and Baluchistan. He stated that the Pakistan government did nothing to help almost 130,000,000 Hindus driven out of East Bengal, leading to their seeking refuge in West Bengal. Mookerjee[36] had previously also demanded a separate West Bengal for Hindus.

Dr Bhimrao Ambedkar holds a unique position in the history of the Sangh. On 6 December 1993, a year after the demolition of the Babri Masjid, the head of the Vishva Hindu Parishad, Ashok Singhal, had conducted a meeting with several Hindu religious gurus. During the discussions, Dr Bhimrao Ambedkar's name was included for the first time in the list of people admired by the Sangh. The growing popularity of regional parties like the Bahujan Samaj Party (BSP) and the Samajwadi Party (SP) was posing a challenge to the Sangh's Hindutva project. The only path left for the Sangh Parivar was to welcome the backward classes and Dalits into its fold. After this meeting, several Sangh and VHP leaders even visited the residence of the 'Dom raja' of Varanasi (Doms are a community that works at cremation grounds).

When the RSS asserts that everyone living in Hindustan is a Hindu, it is important to recognise that history offers examples to support this idea. There was a time when every person who left India was referred to as Hindu. The British played a major role in ensuring that Hinduism got restricted to being only a religion. Before this, the Muslims of India were not called 'Indian Muslims' in the way they are today; there was no need to categorise them separately, as they, like everyone else, were simply a part of India.

This is the same Hindustan where the Dagar brothers, among other musicians, protected and preserved the Dhrupad style of music. I belong to Jaipur, where Dhrupad music flows like a river from Ustad Bahram

Khan Dagar's doorstep. One of the most accomplished singers of the Dagar family, Ustad Wasifuddin Dagar, now lives in Delhi, yet students from all over the world come to learn classical music under his guidance. His knowledge of Sanskrit is extensive, and he primarily performs compositions rooted in Hindu culture or praising Hindu gods and goddesses. Ustad Bade Ghulam Ali Khan, too, sang many compositions in praise of Lord Shiva. Tabla maestro Amir Hussain Khan would play the tabla during the Kali puja celebrations in Bombay's Ramakrishna ashram. Similarly, Ustad Ali Akbar Khan's father, Baba Allauddin Khan, was a devotee of the Sharada temple in Maihar. Therefore, the Islam practised in Hindustan has contributed significantly to the region's culture. There has always been an organic amalgamation of cultures in the way Hindus and Muslims in India celebrate their festivals and live their lives. Our Hindi language, for instance, is a seamless blend of Arabic, Urdu and Persian words, making it difficult to speak it without acknowledging these influences. Similarly, the cultural vibrancy of Hindu traditions has added a lot to what we understand as Islam in India today. The colours and vibrancy of Islamic festivals carry a distinct fragrance of India in them.

Nonetheless, the Sangh says there has always been a concerted effort to project the Sangh as anti-Muslim. Nitin Gadkari has said: 'During the Lok Sabha elections, some of my opponents published a photo of me at the RSS shakha in my uniform. They campaigned against me in my constituency, where there are many Muslims who support me. I said that there was nothing wrong with that and that I had nothing to hide. I have been a swayamsevak of the Sangh since my childhood and have been attending shakhas. Even now, I attend the annual Dussehra and guru dakshina programme in Nagpur every year. That doesn't make me anti-Muslim in any way. You will say that I attend shakhas, but will not reveal that I help in running 1,100 schools in my area. I work towards water conservation. I have done a lot of work in the area of renewable energy, given employment to thousands of people, and so on ... We swadeshis work towards self-sufficiency and independence. Our social and economic ideology is a nationalistic ideology. If you talk about this, your anti-Sangh agenda will not succeed. That is why you need to clean your glasses to see and understand the Sangh properly. The Sangh is an organisation that brings people together. It is not against anyone, and doesn't oppose anyone.'[37]

Still, questions remain. The Sangh's opponents often describe Golwalkar's book *Bunch of Thoughts* as the Bhagavad Gita for the Sangh's karyakartas. But is it true that the Sangh itself has distanced itself from this book written by its second supremo? Does it no longer consider this book an authorised text? Could this be because the book contains anti-Muslim sentiments?

Thinker and philosopher Devendra Swaroop says that the Sangh does not consider the book as its authorised text. The reason for this, he explains, is that the book is essentially a compilation of Golwalkar's speeches, many of which were not formally written down. The book, edited by H.V. Sheshadri, who was a senior official in the Sangh, was based on drafts of these speeches. Sheshadri himself would often joke with colleagues about working from the fourth or fifth draft of a particular speech, implying that not all the content attributed to Golwalkar necessarily reflected his thoughts. Later, in September 2018, Mohan Bhagwat clearly said that many thoughts expressed in that book were only relevant to their times. The *Shri Guruji Samagra* should be regarded as the authoritative text for understanding Golwalkar's thoughts.

Swaroop also says that the Sangh has always had a lot of reservations about Mahatma Gandhi right from the beginning, and he was for many years not accepted by the organisation. However, in a surprising move, the *Panchjanya* came out with a special edition on Gandhi in 1969 to mark his birth centenary.[38]

A. Surya Prakash, former CEO of Prasar Bharati, told me, 'The Sangh is accused of hating Muslims, but I have met and spoken to so many leaders of the Sangh and they have no such ideas. I have never heard anyone in the Sangh Parivar speak against the Muslims. They always worry about the national good and national security. Yes, of course, they do raise issues and worry about the problems faced by Hindus in areas within the country and abroad where they are in a minority.'[39]

The Sangh claims it can adapt to changing circumstances while remaining open to listening to opposing ideologies and providing a space for discussion. However, the Sangh is also steadfast in protecting its ideology and culture from external influences. Many people questioned former president Pranab Mukherjee's attendance at the Sangh's Nagpur celebration on 7 June 2018. The programme began with the hoisting of the saffron flag, and thousands of swayamsevaks and Sangh officials, dressed in white shirts, khaki pants and broad belts, stood in unison, respectfully saluting the flag. Amidst the assembly of uniformly dressed swayamsevaks, President Mukherjee in his dhoti and coat stood out like a sore thumb.

In his speech, he said, 'When I shut my eyes and dream of India, I am mesmerised that 1.3 billion people speak 122 languages, practise seven major religions and belong to three major ethnic groups. Yet, they are under one system, one flag, one Constitution and one identity, which we may call Bharatiya or Indian … A dialogue is necessary not only to balance the competing interests but also to reconcile them … Only through a dialogue can we develop the understanding to solve complex problems without an unhealthy strife within our polity.'[40]

Pranab Mukherjee's speech effectively encapsulated the fundamental principle of 'unity in diversity'. This is precisely what the Sangh says it has been doing. At the heart of the Sangh's philosophy is dialogue. The Sangh frequently asserts that discussion can resolve all issues. Dr Manmohan Vaidya asks why no swayamsevak has ever questioned the Sangh's invitation to the former president, a senior Congress leader. This highlights a key difference between the Sangh and those who claim to champion free speech. It is an intrinsic part of Indian tradition for people with diverse ideologies to come together and engage in discourse.

Opposing or condemning it is not only against 'Indianism', but it also undermines the very foundations of the world's largest democracy, its culture and living traditions.

Later, questions arose concerning a possible link between Pranab Mukherjee's attendance at the Sangh event and his receiving the Bharat Ratna, India's highest honour, six months later. Prime Minister Narendra Modi had called Pranab Mukherjee to inform him of this honour and seek his consent. However, one might ask: did the BJP remember that, during the Congress government, L.K. Avani had written to Prime Minister Manmohan Singh, urging that the Bharat Ratna be conferred upon Atal Bihari Vajpayee—only for the request to be denied? Moreover, eventually when the Modi government decided to award the Bharat Ratna to Vajpayee, prime minister Narendra Modi had suggested to the then president, Pranab Mukherjee, that another name ought to be added to the list: Madan Mohan Malaviya, founder of the Banaras Hindu University and a senior Congress leader. Given this context, what was the overriding reason behind the BJP's decision to confer the highest honour on Pranab Mukherjee, along with Bhupen Hazarika and Nanaji Deshmukh?

The RSS held its 1934 winter camp near Mahatma Gandhi's ashram in Wardha. When Gandhi had expressed a desire to witness the camp and its activities, the sanghchalak of Wardha, Appaji Joshi, had welcomed him. Gandhi observed the camp minutely and asked Appaji Joshi, 'How many Harijans are present in this camp?' 'That is difficult to say because we look at everyone as Hindus,' Appaji had answered. 'That is good enough for us.' And when Gandhi himself asked the swayamsevaks taking part in the camp about their caste, he realised that volunteers from every caste were present there, and none of them felt discriminated against based on their castes.[41]

Later, when Dr Hedgewar returned to Wardha from Nagpur, he went to meet Gandhi, who wanted to know how the Sangh was working towards eradicating untouchability. Dr Hedgewar told him, 'We don't talk about eradicating untouchability, but we inspire our swayamsevaks to think that we are Hindus and belong to one family. And because of that, the swayamsevak doesn't think about anyone's caste.'[42]

In fact, as per the RSS, the commander-in-chief of the Indian Army, General Cariappa, had attended a Sangh shakha in 1959, where he had said, 'RSS work is close to my heart. If Muslims can sing the praises of Islam, what's wrong with the RSS singing the praises of Hinduism?'[43]

THE SANGH IN THE TWENTY-FIRST CENTURY

The Sangh says that those who think of it as a conservative organisation have not delved deep into its journey to understand how it has attempted to keep up with the changing times. The Sangh has closely observed the Indian family structure and strategically leveraged its strength. It recognises the evolving dynamics within the Indian family system, including rising divorce rates and the increasing number of broken households. The organisation also supports a balanced distribution of decision-making power between men and women and acknowledges the significant role women play in the family unit.

The RSS places importance on caring for the elderly and is against female foeticide. While it supports inter-caste marriages as a progressive step towards social integration, it expresses concern over the growing trend of live-in relationships. According to the Sangh, live-in relationships may be more suited to countries and societies where the family is weak as an institution. In the Indian context, it believes that live-in relationships can undermine familial bonds and cause emotional and psychological distress. The Sangh may be against live-in relationships, but has no reservations about homosexuality. Sunil Ambekar points out that the Supreme Court had declared that homosexuality was not a criminal offense on 6 September 2018, but two years before this, Dattatreya Hosabale, the sah-sarkaryavah of the Sangh, had at the India Today Conclave on 7 March 2016 already said,

'I don't believe that homosexuality should be considered a criminal activity as long as it doesn't affect other people in society adversely.'[44] However, Ambekar adds, 'This doesn't mean that gay marriages have been given acceptance.'

On 18 September 2018, Sarsanghchalak Mohan Bhagwat had said in a lecture series in Delhi, 'Everyone is a part of this society. Society is changing, and we need to give everyone a space in society so that no one feels left out.'[45] The Sangh is strongly opposed to discrimination against the transgender community and in favour of giving them a chance to live respectfully in society. I was there when they first allowed a transgender akhada at the Kumbh Mela in Prayagraj (formerly Allahabad) in 2019. All other akhadas accepted them, including the Juna Akhada.

In the twenty-first century, the Sangh has started campaigns about the conservation of the environment and measures to address the water crisis. Efforts are being made to combat global warming and encourage healthy living. At the moment, rural development is the Sangh's primary agenda. Numerous initiatives are underway to improve conditions in approximately 8,00,000 villages across India. Nanaji Deshmukh, a prominent Sangh leader, developed a successful village development model in Chitrakoot, Madhya Pradesh, but its replication and sustainability proved limited. Even Prime Minister Modi launched the Saansad Adarsh Gram Yojana, which failed to yield the desired results because of the limited involvement of most parliamentarians. In addition, the Sangh is now working on gau seva (cow care) programmes. As per the Sangh, it is unfortunate that some individuals have misused the cause of cow protection (gau raksha) to spread fear and unrest, which has negatively impacted the credibility and effectiveness of the RSS's efforts.

According to Sangh members, the RSS is no longer an enigma. It has become more transparent and engages with the public. The Sangh not only responds to criticism but also willingly shares its programmes and ideology in the public domain. Simultaneously, it has expanded its reach into groups where its influence was previously limited, including farmers, Dalits, Adivasis, and other backward classes. As a result, both the Sangh's face and focus have undergone a visible transformation.

Not only are the affiliated organisations of the RSS growing, but the number of swayamsevaks and shakhas is also increasing rapidly. The volunteers come from across age groups, castes, professions, economic classes and from urban, semi-urban and rural areas. With the option to join online, membership has become more accessible, prompting the need for changes in the working style of shakhas and shiksha vargs (training camps), and in the overall training approach.

Traditionally, Sangh training revolved around 'character building'. However, lead trainers have now started adapting the curriculum to meet the evolving needs of the participants. The subjects taught in the shiksha vargs are being updated to include more contemporary and relevant topics. The Sangh assigns pracharaks who have completed the three-year training to its affiliate organisations; typically, those who have completed at least one shiksha varg become shakha instructors. Although the Sangh's affiliate organisations have begun conducting training programmes tailored to their specific needs, the most influential role continues to be that of the pracharaks. Those serving as sangathan mahasachivs (chief secretaries) hold particular importance. They communicate across organisational lines and share their experiences at meetings.

One more significant change that has taken place is that the key officials of the Sangh are more willing to engage with the media on important matters. Several important think tanks associated with the Sangh prepare detailed reports on critical issues and are open to contributing to the formulation of guidelines for campaigns or movements when needed.

Tensions still arise sometimes between the RSS and the BJP, as the latter must account for political, cultural and social diversity. In contrast, the Sangh focuses on advancing its ideology alone. However, the strong mutual understanding between Mohan Bhagwat and Narendra Modi has significantly eased these tensions—unlike the more strained relationship between K.S. Sudarshan and Atal Bihari Vajpayee.

The foremost responsibility of the Sangh leadership is to maintain unity within its ideological family and ensure that differences of opinion do not escalate into emotional or personal divisions. While the RSS consistently maintains that it is an apolitical organisation and the BJP is like one among several of its affiliate entities, it is undeniable that the BJP holds a special place within the Sangh—often seen as the favoured offspring.

Annual reports issued by the Sangh suggest that by 2020, the Sangh had over 1,75,000 service schemes underway, more or less, in every sphere of life. There were 5,000 service schemes underway in 1989, which grew to over 50,000 in 1998 and to 1,40,000 in 2012.[46] At one point, Balasaheb Deoras had instructed the swayamsevaks to work only during natural calamities. However, a major change occurred after the BJP–RSS conclave in 2015, where the Sangh decided it would make itself more transparent, i.e. it would make public information about its principles and programmes at the general society level.

In the eighties, the Sangh focused on increasing the number of swayamsevaks present in colleges, universities and in villages. At one time, the organisation solely focused on the Hindi heartland, using the slogan '*Hindi-Hindu-Hindustan*' to spread the Sangh's influence. However, expansionist activities in the southern and northeastern parts of India have gone hand-in-hand with the increasing usage of English in the Sangh.

Similarly, even with dietary preferences, the Sangh encourages vegetarianism, with those members who consume non-vegetarian food appearing as vegetarians in public spaces. At present, there seem to be no strict restrictions regarding food, and because of its presence in the Northeast, the Sangh claims it doesn't have any reservations about the consumption of beef. Mohan Bhagwat has even said that a person's food habits cannot determine his or her religious or national identity.[47] However, only vegetarian food continues to be served at the Sangh's public events.

The people within the Sangh itself have raised the question about the impact of their social initiatives. Keeping society aside, they ask, has there been any genuine change in the behaviour and approach of the RSS and its swayamsevaks? My friends who have held various responsibilities in the Sangh remark how it is a common practice for the officials and for the pracharaks of the Sangh to project themselves as idealists, and for the officials and swayamsevaks working under them to sing their praises and glorify them, even though Sangh members are nothing special and surely not a class apart in any manner. They have human failings like everybody else, and that is no crime. The Sangh sidelines intellectuals capable of independent work and does not accord them a special place. They say that the Sangh has become a place only for the mediocre and the average.

SANGH PARIVAR

The Sangh has started calling its affiliated organisations 'organisations of different fields'. Earlier, most people would collectively call them the 'Sangh Parivar'. Is the Sangh trying to avoid taking any responsibility for those organisations by delinking them? Sunil Ambekar clarifies that the Sangh Parivar upholds harmony. All organisations cooperate. In the past, people used the term 'parivar', implying the RSS headed the family and controlled all followers. However, Sangh members say this is not true. These organisations within the Sangh work and manage their financial matters independently, but they all work together for the cause of national glory.

During Golwalkar's time, several affiliate organisations came into being: the Akhil Bharatiya Vidyarthi Parishad (the oldest organisation affiliated with the RSS that was started with the aim to mobilise the youth), the Jana Sangh, the Bharatiya Mazdoor Sangh (BMS) and the Vanvasi Kalyan Ashram (VKA). But Golwalkar remained sceptical about their activities. He would claim that these organisations' contributions were insignificant and threaten to close them if they failed to function effectively. Therefore, the RSS did not give due importance to any significant work done by the swayamsevaks outside the Sangh, nor did it actively want to associate itself with the work of these organisations.[48]

College students carried out the RSS's activities when it was banned in 1948–49. To bring them together under one banner and consolidate their presence on university campuses, the Vidyarthi Parishad came into being in 1948. By 2003, the Vidyarthi Parishad had 11,00,000 members, which burgeoned to 35,00,000 in 2019.[49] It is generally said that, like the RSS, the Vidyarthi Parishad is also an apolitical body. Its representatives are delegates of the Akhil Bharatiya Pratinidhi Sabha, and several leaders of the BJP are believed to be products of the body. These include former vice-president Venkaiah Naidu, former minister of law and commerce Arun Jaitley, Nitin Gadkari, Ravi Shankar Prasad, Vijay Goyal and others. Sunil Ambekar, the erstwhile national secretary of the Vidyarthi Parishad, is one of the members of the Parishad who have also found a prominent place in the RSS's organisational hierarchy.

Dr Manmohan Vaidya, one of the sah-sarkaryavahs in the Sangh, speaks of a renewed focus on training the Sangh's karyakartas: 'Karyakarta Vikas Varg (karyakarta development programmes) are conducted for this purpose. Deliberations are undertaken on how to improve the training modules and bring "value addition" to them.' The Sangh holds the belief that the government alone cannot address all societal needs; rather, it is the collective responsibility of society to contribute to its own progress. Swayamsevaks have long embraced this philosophy, actively engaging in social change. Since 1998, they have dedicated themselves to rural development, and their efforts have produced visible improvements in villages.[50]

There is one name that acts as a bridge between the Sangh and Dalit politics—K.N. Govindacharya, who had wanted to teach the Sangh a thing or two about social engineering. Even today, the Sangh does not have a popular Dalit leader or a leader from the backward classes, which explains why it remained dependent on leaders like Ram Vilas Paswan and Ramdas Athawale for years, because Mayawati's growing strength intimidated them.

As much as it is difficult to understand the Sangh, it is even more difficult to consider it a nationalist organisation. Very few people would know the relief work and service that the swayamsevaks had rendered to wounded soldiers during the 1962 war. After the war in 1963, Prime Minister Jawaharlal Nehru had invited members of the Sangh for the Republic Day parade at Rajpath. Over 3,000 swayamsevaks had taken part in the event at short notice, with only two days to prepare for the march-past.

Another oft-raised question is that of the entry of women into the Sangh. Will the doors be opened to women after the completion of a century? Sunil Ambekar says, 'The question itself is flawed. The more important question is that of the empowerment of women, of their self-sufficiency and self-respect. They need to be provided opportunities in society. What are we doing about that? Are we able to give them the respect they deserve? The Sangh must empower women and give them opportunities with dignity. We have to be conscious of where the power of an organisation is being put to use.' There are serious ongoing discussions about increasing women's participation in the working committees of the Sangh Parivar. Presently, the challenge lies in finding suitable candidates for the role. Just like the Vidyarthi Parishad, the Sangh aims to enhance women's involvement in other organisations as well.

Dr Vaidya says, 'The activities of the Sangh have not been made possible because of someone's benevolence, but because of the karyakartas' hard work and sacrifices, increasing support from society and God's grace. The Sangh has faced a lot of opposition, hurdles and trouble to achieve the reach, power and influence that it has today. That is why the Sangh is being discussed everywhere. There is a lot of curiosity among people about how the Sangh will celebrate its centenary.

'The vision of the founder of the Sangh, Dr Hedgewar, was very clear. He believed that the Sangh is not just an organisation in the society but is an organisation of the entire society. Veteran ideologue Dattopant Thengadi says that conceptually, the RSS and Hindu society are co-terminus and psychologically they are one. Since the Sangh is synonymous with society, the centenary of the RSS cannot be confined to the organisational level alone. Making the efforts of the Sangh all pervasive in society should be the primary goal.'

Does that mean the Sangh will not have a momentous celebration for its centenary? Dr Vaidya answers, 'Dr Hedgewar had once said that before celebrating the silver jubilee of the organisation, we must be sure that the Sangh's vision has been fulfilled. He had entirely dedicated himself to making that happen. Accomplishing the Sangh's mission before the centenary would be the most ideal celebration. A Sangh anthem goes like, "*Karyamagnata jeevan ho aur karyapurti hi vishranti*" (To live is to be absorbed in work and only its completion is to rest).'[51]

Dr Vaidya recalls Dr Hedgewar saying in 1940, during a shiksha varg, that the Sangh's mission should not be confined to the shakhas alone and that it must be realised through active engagement with society. That it is not enough to earn a livelihood, care for one's family and attend the shakhas regularly. Sangh's true work involves dedicating time to foster social change and awareness. The integration of swayamsevaks into the broader society must be done proactively so that new sections of the population may come into contact with the Sangh and understand its ideology and nationalist vision. This engagement, Dr Hedgewar suggested, would help drive the nation's overall progress by protecting the Hindu religion, culture and communities—the pillars of Indian society.

Dr Vaidya underlines how the mission of organisational and human development is an ongoing process. Efforts towards social awakening will continue alongside it. On the front of organisational change, the swayamsevaks are active in various spheres of social life through its different affiliates. According to Dr Vaidya, the best way to celebrate hundred years of the RSS is for all swayamsevaks to commit themselves to driving social transformation—working with purpose to advance the Sangh's mission and move closer to its realisation.

Sunil Ambekar, reflecting on the Sangh's mission, describes it as a continuous journey—one that is timeless and limitless. The Sangh's stated goal is to build a healthy, cultured and disciplined society. However, the gap between this vision and reality has led to an identity crisis within the organisation. It now finds itself at a crossroads: should it remain a cultural and social body, or formally engage in politics? The Sangh has to decide which path it wants to follow. The Sangh must make a clear choice. If it wishes to pursue a political path, it should do so transparently; if not, it should fully disengage from political involvement. Remaining indecisive only harms both the Sangh and the BJP.

So, what is the RSS? A social, political organisation or a cultural organisation? The Sangh is primarily the latter, and through its many roles in society, it remains actively involved in politics. Years ago, the weekly magazine *Dharmyug* had asked various popular Indian personalities to share the mission statement that defined their lives and ideologies. Guruji Golwalkar had simply written this: '*Main nahi, tu nahi* (Not me, not you)'. He had then quoted the Sanskrit mantra: '*Rashtraya swaha, idam rashtraya idam na mama* (This is not mine, nothing is mine)'. These words reflect a spirit of complete dedication to the nation. Rooted in Indian philosophy, these words are perhaps a foundational inspiration for the Sangh itself.

2

Dedicated to the Blessed Land:

Shakha, Service, Associate

The disciplined silence in the Maharshi Vyas conference hall at the Dr Hedgewar Memorial Bhavan in Nagpur belies the presence of over 700 people there. The senior swayamsevaks taking part in the final year of the Sangh's three-year training camp have assembled. In their final year, they are preparing to take on greater responsibilities towards propagating the Sangh's message and working on social transformation. However, they must achieve their goals not by standing apart from the crowd, as political leaders might, but by remaining an intrinsic part of society. The Sangh's training allows for this seamless integration—a major reason why the Sangh has not been classified as a religious sect even after a century of its existence.

The multiplicity of languages is evident in the Sangh's shiksha vargs, where the distinctions among various identities blur. Geography becomes merely a marker, relegated to an entry in the attendance register of the Sangh office. There is no competition or race for recognition or an attempt to take credit for any accomplishment. Like the bhakti marg (path of devotion), all paths, regardless of origin, converge at a common point, uniting as one.

A generational divide exists among the various people working for the RSS. This is evident at the national, state and district levels, and between the office-bearers and the swayamsevaks. But this difference becomes irrelevant during brainstorming sessions, and while important decisions are being made. According to the Sangh, opinions supersede age or position. Great emphasis is placed on nurturing personal relationships and team spirit. This decentralisation of work and responsibilities is the secret of the Sangh's strength.

It is said that the sole goal of the RSS is *paraṁ vaibhavaṁ netumetat svarāṣṭraṁ*—we have to lead our country towards the zenith of prosperity. The Sangh has tailored its functioning to complement this goal. This way is not about self-promotion but about personal contact. Personal contact leads to closeness in relationships. Apart from taking part in Sangh camps, the Sangh also encourages communal meals as a part of its functioning. Swayamsevaks visit each other's homes for meals, and the practice of sharing home-cooked food strengthens their camaraderie.

Many consider the Sangh undemocratic because it requires all members to abide by collective decisions. Even the sarsanghchalak must adhere to the collective decisions, even if he disagrees with them in principle. The sarsanghchalak's is the highest position within the Sangh, but it is an advisory role, while the sarkaryavah is actually the de facto CEO of the RSS. Usually, the sarkaryavah is someone who finds favour with the sarsanghchalak; however, formally, an election procedure appoints the person to the post.

In the initial years, there were few voices of dissent within the RSS, probably because when the organisation was being established, Dr Hedgewar had paid great attention to the process of selecting members for the Sangh. At least two prominent people had to recommend each new member, but the organisation removed this requirement after the 1948 ban because they urgently needed many workers.

Additionally, Dr Hedgewar appointed as sanghchalaks influential champions of Hindutva, some of whom were members of other organisations such as the Hindu Mahasabha, the Arya Samaj and the Congress. Hedgewar also emphasised the need for leaders to demonstrate loyalty and eminence, so that young swayamsevaks and karyakartas coming to the shakhas would find suitable role models to emulate.

Politics is a subject that many within the Sangh feel they should not engage with. In fact, Golwalkar vehemently opposed the active involvement of the Sangh in politics. However, in Dr Hedgewar's time, many sanghchalaks fought Vidhan Sabha elections without giving up their posts, and he encouraged them in their endeavours. Over the years, there has been a lot of confusion between the Jana Sangh and the BJP over policy-related issues. During Dr Syama Prasad Mookerjee's time, patriotism and Kashmir were the main issues, but for Deendayal Upadhyaya, the principles of integral humanism were paramount. Vajpayee spoke about Gandhian socialism, while L.K. Advani stressed on the concept of cultural nationalism. For Mohan Bhagwat and Narendra Modi, nationalism and Hindutva are the central principles.

For Nitin Gadkari—a swayamsevak since his childhood, current Nagpur MP and union minister—regardless of whether he is at his private residence in Nagpur or at his official residence in Delhi, there is a constant stream of people that come to meet him throughout the day. The visitors include union ministers, MPs, MLAs from Maharashtra, farmers, industrialists and journalists. Gadkari attends to everyone with equal interest—a result of his training with the Sangh, where he learned to engage with people and to actively listen to their concerns. He says, 'Whatever I am today is because of the Sangh. I might be in politics, and in the government too, but in my mind, I am only a member of society.'[1]

He adds, 'The Hindutva of the RSS is nationalism. We have continued with Savarkar's and Ambedkar's principles of living respectfully with everyone, and providing economic and social harmony. Those who do not know the Sangh intimately have this misconception that on issues such as Hindutva, there is a lot of difference between the image that the Sangh projects and what it is in reality. Efforts to malign the Sangh have been continuing ever since Mahatma Gandhi's assassination. When the investigation found nothing, people claimed the Sangh was Brahminical and casteist. The truth is that the Sangh does not believe in casteism. It is a tradition in the Sangh to respect one and all. However, it is also true that we have failed to protest against these accusations as vehemently as we should have.'

THE FIRST WAVE

On 27 September 1925, which was the day of Vijayadashami, Dr Hedgewar decided to create an organisation in Nagpur intending to strengthen society. Just a few days later, he held another meeting, during which, for the first time, the founders decided to provide volunteer service, or swayamseva, on the occasion of Ramnavami (Lord Ram's birthday) at a large fair in Ramtek, sixty kilometres from Nagpur. At this stage, even though volunteer services had begun, the organisation did not have a name.

On 7 April 1926, a meeting took place at Dr Hedgewar's house in Nagpur, where the need for a name was discussed. Dr Hedgewar believed in having a democratic approach from the very beginning. Of the twenty-five members who voted, twenty were in favour of 'Rashtriya Swayamsevak Sangh', while the remaining five voted for 'Jaaripatka Mandal'. There were no votes for 'Bharatodhharak Mandal' and 'Hindu Swayamsevak Sangh'. At the time of the constitution of the organisation, Dr Hedgewar had given it the slogan—*Hindutva hi Rashtravad* (Hindutva is Nationalism).

Dilip Deodhar, a long-term member of the Sangh and the writer of several books on the RSS, says that Dr Hedgewar had tried to set up a body of swayamsevaks five times before he finally formed the Sangh. The first attempt was made at Wardha. In 1920, at the national session of the Congress held in Nagpur, Hedgewar created a group of 1,200 uniformed swayamsevaks. This uniform continued in the Sangh until 1942.

According to N.H. Palkar's book *Dr Hedgewar Charit*, the first shakha of the Sangh convened at Dr Hedgewar's house on 9 May 1926, with around twenty karyakartas in attendance. This meeting was called a baithak. Prominent members who attended that day included Bhauji Kavre, Anna Sohoni, Balaji Huddar, Vishwanathrao Kelkar and Bapurao—all of whom remained associated with the Sangh for a long time. The attendees discussed in detail issues including meeting every fifteen days, holding baithaks, establishing akhadas for physical fitness, and selecting uniforms for the swayamsevaks. At the baithak of 12 December 1926, it was decided that the swayamsevaks would receive military training every Sunday at 6 a.m. In those days, akhadas were seen as a part of the revolutionary tradition of the Sangh. Dr Hedgewar would visit the Nagpur vyayamshala and the Maharashtra vyayamshala[2] to select swayamsevaks. Raghunath Rao was appointed as the first interim sachiv (general secretary) of the Sangh. There was also discussion about appointing two additional secretaries.

Discussions were constantly underway regarding the structure, functioning and other aspects that were critical to the Sangh. At a baithak on 19 December 1926, participants expressed the need for a top organisational position to foster discipline and to steer the Sangh in the right direction. They unanimously chose Dr Hedgewar for this rank, although he initially resisted a formal role. Three years later, on 10 November 1929, at the strong urging of the Sangh members,

Dr Hedgewar formally took over as the sarsanghchalak. The bhagwa dhwaj, or saffron flag, started fluttering at the shakhas, and the slogan *Bharat Mata ki Jai* soon started to be heard. The saffron flag was considered a symbol of India's culture, its gallantry and sacrifice. Prior to Independence, swayamsevaks would take the oath—*Hindu Rashtra ki Azadi* (Freedom for the Hindu nation). After 1947, the oath was changed to *Hindu Rashtra ka Sampoorna Vikas* (Complete Development of the Hindu Nation).[3]

Hedgewar insisted that the word 'Hindu' should not be associated with the name of the organisation within India. Consequently, Sangh-affiliated organisations operating in India used the words 'Bharat' or 'Bharatiya' in their names and those operating outside the country used 'Hindu Swayamsevak Sangh'. Another organisation that was meant to have an international presence was called the Vishva Hindu Parishad (VHP). Dr Hedgewar was of the firm belief that none of the Sangh's affiliates' identity reflected that it was a Hindu organisation.

The first sarkaryavah was Balaji Huddar. The first sarsenapati was Martandrao Jog (later this position was dropped from the organisational structure of the Sangh). Initially, the Sangh used English as its language for communications and formal orders. However, later Sanskrit started being used. The system of pracharaks also came into place later. The Sangh's training camps traditionally included bauddhik or intellectual sessions, which were called rajkeeya bhashan, or political discourses. Discussions about the participation of women in the Sangh led to the formation of the Rashtra Sevika Samiti in 1936. This name was chosen because Hedgewar wanted the two organisations to share the same acronym. Therefore, 1936, with the founding of the women's wing, marked the beginning of the Sangh Parivar.

Dr Hedgewar believed that the organisation should be financially self-sufficient. To raise funds, he introduced the practice of guru dakshina. The first guru dakshina programme took place in 1927 on the occasion of Guru Purnima, in front of an unfurled saffron flag. Eighty-four rupees were collected that day; this symbolised the beginning of a tradition that continues to the present. The organisation keeps the amount of dakshina given confidential, therefore, a person's standing is not determined by their contribution.

Sunil Ambekar says that Anna Sohoni began imparting lathi prashikshan (lathi training) when the Sangh started the 'Itwar Dwar Prathamik Shakha'. The shakhas became a permanent feature after 2 May 1926 and began to expand. Following Nagpur, shakhas came up in Wardha. The Sangh members adopted the same khaki uniform first introduced in the 1920 Congress session for Bharat Sevak Samaj volunteers.

The Sangh began as a national organisation because Dr Hedgewar believed it would be possible to successfully establish and strengthen it over time. It was Golwalkar who took forward its work and expanded it. When Dr B.R. Ambedkar started a programme to reinstate and spread Buddhism in 1956, Golwalkar said that the Sangh too would work towards building brotherhood in Buddhist countries, after which the swayamsevaks started working in America, Europe and other Buddhist countries. The Sangh founded an organisation known as the 'Hindu Swayamsevak Sangh' to work overseas. The shakhas in these countries differed from those in India; they functioned more like family get-togethers, with entire families taking part in Sangh activities. In these shakhas, members wore trousers. A 'full-pant shakha' was started in Nagpur in 1972, which was overseen by Dilip Deodhar. This shakha had functioned during Golwalkar and Deoras's time, and had continued for nearly a year. After that, 'full-pant shakhas' reappeared only in the twenty-first century, when people felt a need for change.

In 1942, the Sangh established a system of full-time karyakartas or pracharaks. In 1950, the Sangh organised itself into provinces and regions to better manage its responsibilities. Its key decision-making body, the Akhil Bharatiya Pratinidhi Sabha, was also constituted around the same time. This body included representatives from all levels of the organisation. Before the formation of the Pratinidhi Sabha, a committee comprising senior members from all regions made major the decisions.

'*NAMASTE SADA VATSALE MATRIBHUME*' (I BOW TO YOU, EVER-LOVING MOTHERLAND)

The composition and outline of the Sangh's prayers were prepared for the first time at the Sindi session, in the presence of Dr Hedgewar, Guruji Golwalkar, Bal Apte, Balasaheb Deoras, Appaji Joshi and Nanasaheb Talatule. In the initial stages, there was a strong influence of Swami Samarth Ramdas on the organisation's prayer and its working style. At that time, the prayer started with '*Bharat Mata ki Jai*' and ended with '*Rashtraguru Swami Ramdas Maharaj ki Jai*'. The prayer was said both in Marathi and Hindi, the former a direct consequence of the RSS having been established in Maharashtra. Once the Sangh began growing though, Sanskrit was included in the prayer to give the organisation a national identity. In 1940, the prayer became entirely Sanskrit.

Narahari Narayan Bhide from Nagpur was the one who converted the prayer into Sanskrit. It was sung by Yadavrao Joshi for the first time at the Pune training camp on 23 April 1940. The prayer has thirteen lines, including three slokas and one proclamation, and it concludes with the line '*Bharat Mata ki Jai*'. The shakhas and other Sangh programmes require the recitation of this prayer.

The *Ekaatmata Stotra* (*Om Sachidananda Roopaya Namostu Paramatmane*) is another hymn that is learnt by all swayamsevaks and recited at all the Sangh offices and programmes, even at mealtimes. It has thirty shlokas and is meant to evoke national unity. This stotra pays homage to all those who have dedicated their lives to the service of the nation: kings, queens, saints, warriors, scientists, philosophers, scholars, artists, musicians, poets and writers.

The Sangh holds six primary celebrations each year—the Varsha Pratipada or Hindu New Year on Chaitra Pratipada, the Hindu Samrajya Diwas to commemorate Shivaji Maharaj's ascension to the throne, a guru dakshina ceremony on Guru Purnima, Raksha Bandhan, Sankranti and Vijayadashami.

Every shakha begins with *Namaste Sada Vatsale,* which speaks about service to the motherland and religion, without expressing reservations against any individual, religion or organisation. In the prayer, the swayamsevak declares that he has voluntarily accepted the task of bringing about social awakening, knowing fully well that it is not a simple path. During shiksha vargs and special sessions, instructors thoroughly explain the prayer so that the swayamsevaks can apply its message to their lives.

THE ROLE OF THE SHAKHA IN THE SANGH

The shakha is the basic unit of the Sangh. The identity of every swayamsevak is intertwined with the shakha he belongs to. There is often stiff competition among the shakhas within the same city. Although the shakha meets for only an hour each day, the Sangh expects swayamsevaks to be available for Sangh-related work or social duties at all times, especially during natural calamities or other emergencies. Atal Bihari Vajpayee once said, 'Once a swayamsevak, always a swayamsevak!'[4]

Discussions at shakhas typically focus on topics related to physical activities, intellectual development and social issues. Games and sports-centric conversations are tailored to local needs. The departments concerned with intellectual development and physical activities continually seek feedback and make necessary adjustments to the training they provide. Even trainers at shakhas have to undergo training. Apart from this, regional and national officials regularly visit shakhas to achieve better coordination and results.

For a time, shakhas were predominantly held in the mornings. However, with the increasing number of swayamsevaks, a need arose to accommodate people from all walks of life and professions; therefore, shakhas began being conducted in the afternoons and evenings as well. Weekly meetings were also conducted. For those members with busier routines, there would be 'sangh mandalis' or group programmes every month. Shakha timings for students are based on their academic timetables; each student is assigned a specific time.

The Sangh's website features a link titled 'Join RSS', through which approximately 50,000 new members join every month. Local swayamsevaks notify new members and organise a parichay varg (an introductory session) for them. The current system of membership differs significantly from Dr Hedgewar's approach, which required people to provide references from well-known individuals in order to be selected as swayamsevaks.

According to Sunil Ambekar, the most important lessons imparted at the shakhas are that India is a Hindu country *(*rashtra) and that it believes in unity. The Sangh is of the view that mutual respect, cooperation and peace are the central tenets of Hindutva. Ambekar says that the Sangh is a modern organisation because it is ready to change with the times, which is what keeps it connected with younger generations.

The Sangh considers the shakha as its most important unit, since it is the place where swayamsevaks take part in the Sangh's initiatives. The swayamsevaks build a connection between communities and the Sangh, and take part enthusiastically in all its activities, challenges and celebrations. Currently, nearly 50,00,000 people take part daily in over 55,000 shakhas conducted across the country. The shakhas are held at the city, district and tehsil levels and in villages. Interestingly, Kerala has the maximum number of shakhas, numbering around 5,000. In addition, there are many more people who are involved in various Sangh programmes and social initiatives, even though they might not attend the shakhas. Furthermore, many people, although not swayamsevaks themselves, are associated with the Sangh's numerous sectoral organisations, especially the Vidyarthi Parishad and the Bharatiya Mazdoor Sangh.[5]

An important aspect of the Sangh is that it becomes a part of people's homes in such an intimate and unobtrusive manner that one may not even realise when the entire family starts to follow the Sangh's path. The tradition of serving tea and snacks at a swayamsevak's home after the Sunday shakha exposes their entire family to the Sangh's values and functioning.

In the Sangh's early days, the shakhas would try to attract the attention of children by hosting games. When Dr Hedgewar founded the Sangh, the ground in Nagpur—where the Sangh head office exists today—was the site where sports for children first began. The day the present-day government abrogated Article 370 of the Indian constitution, an erstwhile pracharak of the RSS and a journalist friend told me about an incident from his childhood at the Sangh—'We would go round and round in circles and sing the song, *"Jahan hue balidan Mookerjee, veh Kashmir hamara hai. Jo Kashmir hamara hai, veh sare ka sara hamara hai"* (The place where Mookerjee sacrificed his life, that Kashmir is ours. The Kashmir that is ours is wholly ours).'[6] This demonstrates that, along with games, the ideals of the Sangh were also being instilled in children.

There is no registration fee to enrol as a swayamsevak, nor is a person asked about his caste, occupation or social status while joining. Everyone at the shakha receives equal treatment. The shakha's focus is on instilling discipline and values in the members. Besides physical training, the shakha imparts training in drill, march-past and band. The Sangh claims that in today's age, there is no better place than a shakha to receive intensive training in Indian values and culture, imparted through the medium of stories from history and the Puranas. While the shakha's training incorporates intellectual development, it avoids heavy-duty lectures or intense lessons.

People who are associated with the Sangh learn team management very early on. Youth attending the shakhas are made gatanayakas, or group leaders, either of their existing group or of a newly created group. It is among the leader's duties to ensure the attendance of his group members at the shakha every day, talk to their parents, discuss their studies and offer help when the need arises. This fosters leadership qualities in them. Some members voluntarily learn to play in the band, while others contribute through sports. Senior members also ask juniors to deliver speeches on socially relevant topics or to organise picnics for their group. Such activities naturally cultivate strong leadership skills.

THE SHIKSHA VARG

The RSS organises training camps for swayamsevaks, which were earlier called Officers Training Corps (OTC). Now, they are called shiksha vargs. In the initial years of the Sangh, Dr Hedgewar had wanted to impart military-style training to the swayamsevaks, hoping to inculcate discipline and team spirit in them. Though he lacked expertise in the field, he had invited a few of his former soldier friends, who started imparting parade training on Sundays. Like in the army, commands were issued in English, and swayamsevaks wore cross belts and RSS badges on their shoulders. In June 1927, a forty-day training was conducted for the first time. Alongside military training, the sessions included lathi-practice, four hours of physical training in the morning, and academic training in the afternoon. The Sangh's shiksha vargs evolved from this initial approach.

Now, every year, summer training camps or shiksha vargs are organised in the months of May and June. Shiksha vargs provide three years of training, and once a swayamsevak completes the final third year, he becomes a full-time pracharak. But before taking part in the shiksha varg, the swayamsevak has to participate in a week-long district-level workshop. Only someone who holds a position in the Sangh, has certain responsibilities and is involved in the other activities of the Sangh besides regularly attending the shakhas, can take part in shiksha vargs. Karyakartas in their third year of shiksha varg or those who have completed it provide physical training, while pracharaks handle academic training.

Sunil Ambekar notes that the practice of asking questions and seeking answers is an important part of the shiksha varg. First and second-year training takes place in different cities and regions, but Nagpur hosts the twenty-five-day third-year sessions. Traditionally, the sarsanghchalak stays in Nagpur during that period. Even an ordinary swayamsevak can ask the sarsanghchalak a question during this time. In one such session, a swayamsevak had asked Mohan Bhagwat about how one becomes a sarsanghchalak and the credentials needed to assume this responsibility. Mohan Bhagwat had answered that the sarsanghchalak is appointed after a lot of discussion and deliberations amongst the members of the Sangh, and the most important criterion for one to become the sarsanghchalak is his contribution to the Sangh and society.[7]

The focus of the Sangh's summer camps is 'integration'. During the twenty-five days of the final-year training, all trainees stay together. The programme divides the trainees into groups of eighteen, called 'gan' for physical training and 'gut' for academic sessions. The groups are named after national heroes, regional social reformers and prominent citizens, and often come together and practice patriotic songs in different regional languages.

The third-year training groups typically include participants from around ten states in India, exposing them to varied languages, cultures and traditions and providing them with a national perspective. In this way, the Sangh encourages swayamsevaks to imbibe the spirit of the *Ekaatmata Stotra,* both in their training and in their lives. The training emphasises strongly on personal interactions, mutual learning and understanding. Apart from the shiksha vargs, two-to three-day camps are held every winter. Attended by swayamsevaks of all age groups, these camps also include physical and academic training sessions. Though strict discipline is a must, such sessions enthuse the trainees, and they are able to work with renewed vigour after their training. Workshops are also held every month for young karyakartas and new swayamsevaks.

Academic training is an integral part of the shiksha varg, and gradually becomes more rigorous from the first to the third year. Pracharaks responsible for academic training are thoughtful and philosophical, and do not impose their views on their opponents by arguing with them. Golwalkar is known to have said that one should be open-minded while listening to people with opposing ideas and be ready to learn from them. Over time, I have met many pracharaks who begin a conversation by listening attentively and then express their views gently, gradually yet assertively. However, this attitude and maturity of thought appear to be declining among many current representatives of the Sangh. Rather than engaging with and accepting divergent views, there is now a tendency to assert one's ideas forcefully.

THE ORGANISATIONAL STRUCTURE OF THE SANGH

The most important lesson the Sangh teaches is how to create and work with consensus. As per Dilip Deodhar, the Sangh has thirty-six associate organisations, of which twelve are 'mass-based' and in direct contact with the public, while the remaining twenty-four are 'class-based'. The Sangh and its affliated organisations have close to 1,50,000 projects that are underway. In India, every Sangh organisation has a presence even at the taluka level, whereas internationally, the Sangh is present in most countries across the world. Thousands of organisations, each with its own unique purpose, are part of this wide network. However, it is crucial to remember that these bodies are autonomous and do not receive any directives from the RSS. They have a relationship centred around 'interaction' rather than 'interdependence', but their basic values remain the same.

From an organisational standpoint, the Sangh currently has forty-four provinces, each comprising several territories, with each territory having multiple districts. There are multiple departments dealing with physical training, academic training, publicity (prachaar), communications (sampark), social service and administration. In addition, there are departments dedicated to family awareness, cow-service, village development and religious awakening. The office-bearers of these departments at the national, regional and provincial levels work in close coordination. They not only collaborate with each other for implementing the Sangh's projects but also travel constantly. Travel is an important aspect of the Sangh's work—it sustains its dynamism and keeps it relevant. During their many visits, officials listen to the suggestions and perspectives of the swayamsevaks and fellow members.

In keeping with the Sangh's constitution, there is a federal structure. Although a central authority makes policy decisions, the provincial, divisional and district levels handle their implementation. As per article 19(a) of the RSS constitution, districts, cities and provincial centres send, for every fifty swayamsevaks entitled to vote, one such swayamsevak as a delegate to the Prantiya Pratinidhi Sabha. The under article 15(a) the elected members of a Prantiya Pratinidhi Sabha elect from amongst themselves one-eighth of their number as representatives of the province on the Akhil Bharatiya Pratinidhi Sabha. The elected members of the Akhil Bharatiya Pratinidhi Sabha elect the sarkaryavah. The sarkaryavah, who is akin to the general secretary in any other organisation, holds the most important position in the Sangh. He handles the day-to-day functioning of the RSS and wields significant authority over the organisation. The sarsanghchalak functions only as a philosopher and guide, and has to abide by the decisions of the sarkaryavah. Although the sarsanghchalak nominates his successor, the procedure involves extensive discussions with the sarkaryavah and the highest central working committee, the Kendriya Karyakari Mandal. Moreover, the Akhil Bharatiya Pratinidhi Sabha and the Kendriya Karyakari Mandal collectively make the major decisions in the RSS.

In the organisational hierarchy, after the sarsanghchalak and the sarkaryavah, come the sah-sarkaryavahs, the pracharaks, the head trainers, the karyavahs, the gatanayaks and the swayamsevaks. Any man, eighteen years and above, who believes in the Sangh's mission can join the shakha and become a swayamsevak. The members who are below the age of eighteen are called bal-swayamsevaks.

Pracharaks, who are full-time workers, play a very important role in the functioning of the Sangh. They do not receive any remuneration for their services, but the Sangh takes care of their expenses. The Akhil Bharatiya prachar pramukh appoints prant pracharaks with the consent of the sarkaryavaha and in consultation with the sanghachalaks concerned. The prant pracharaks, in turn, appoint pracharaks for different units in the province in consultation with the prant sanghachalak. Based on the recommendations of the Akhil Bharatiya Karyakari Mandal, the sarkaryavah has the authority to create new provincial and divisional units. Furthermore, sanghachalaks of provinces, divisions and districts form karyakari mandals (working committees), which are headed by sanghchalaks and typically include karyavahs, pracharaks, bauddhik shikshan pramukhs (chiefs of academic training), sharirik shikshan pramukhs (chiefs of physical training) and nidhi pramukh (chief financial officers).

For every fifty swayamsevaks in a shakha, the shakha selects one pratinidhi. Shakhas with fewer than fifty swayamsevaks come together to select a common pratinidhi. Typically, one member proposes a pratinidhi, and another seconds the proposal. The Akhil Bharatiya Pratinidhi Sabha then elects the regional sanghchalak. At the district, division and provincial levels, pratinidhis select their sanghchalak.

In a country where hero worship and personality cults are widespread, people consider the RSS a unique organisation because it deifies or worships no one. In the Sangh, the saffron flag takes precedence, and all activities begin with a salutation to the flag. Even the guru dakshina offerings are made to the flag. Dr Hedgewar was of the view that individuals could falter, but ideals and symbols would always endure.

An important feature of the Sangh is its inherent self-sufficiency. The RSS does not accept donations. Perhaps Dr Hedgewar knew that most organisations either shut down or compromised their principles under pressure from funding agencies or the government. To avoid such dependency, the RSS founders structured the organisation from the outset to be financially self-reliant, with members covering its expenses. The funds collected through guru dakshina are used to support daily shakha activities and to cover the living expenses of full-time pracharaks. Affiliated organisations of the Sangh are also financially independent and do not rely on the Sangh or on any other external sources for their operations.

ROLE OF PRACHARAKS

If the swayamsevak is the fundamental unit of the RSS, the pracharak is its soul. Following a three-year training course, the Sangh chooses some swayamsevaks, ready to dedicate part of their lives to social transformation and the Sangh, to become pracharaks. The Sangh requires pracharaks to remain unmarried, believing that full-time devotion to the organisation would conflict with marriage. The term of appointment for pracharaks is generally three to five years, yet many dedicate their whole lives to the Sangh. They lead simple lives, accept any responsibility given to them and are ready to work anywhere.

A former long-time pracharak, K.N. Govindacharya says, 'In fact, the organisation discourages swayamsevaks from becoming pracharaks, and fully tests them before selection. Furthermore, the organisation expects them to complete their education and to fulfil their familial duties. This is why most pracharaks have been high-performers in academics.'[8]

Pracharaks are handed responsibilities in different domains. Since they work in multiple geographical regions, most pracharaks are multilingual and blend in with the local communities to such an extent that sometimes it becomes hard to tell them apart from the locals.

Apart from pracharaks, the Sangh also has a system of vistaraks. Unlike pracharaks, vistaraks receive responsibilities for a set period of six months to a year. Once that period is over, a vistarak can become a pracharak if he continues working. The Sangh bears the living expenses of the pracharaks. Generally, they stay in the office, in a swayamsevak's home or in any other accommodation provided to them. Pracharaks are not allowed to enter active politics. If they want to do so, they have to let go of the responsibility of being a pracharak.

Govindacharya recalls how Babasaheb Bhide, a prominent Sangh official in Maharashtra, was of the view that the organisation should not overly focus on retaining people in the position of pracharaks and keep the exit gate open for them. He emphasised that it was more important to figure out what a pracharak could do after returning to civilian life. The Sangh keeps asserting that being a pracharak is not exceptionally prestigious, and leaving the role shouldn't be seen as a failure. Moreover, the duration of the pracharak's tenure should not be considered too important.

Govindacharya notes that the Sangh has been particularly active in Maharashtra, but there came a time when the state only had ninety pracharaks, compared to the 300 in Uttar Pradesh. A sense of competition existed among districts in UP over the number of pracharaks deployed. Even among the ninety pracharaks in Maharashtra, only twelve had served for about ten years, while over 150 out of the 300 in UP had served for over ten years. Despite these numerical differences, the Maharashtra pracharaks accomplished twice as much as the UP pracharaks when families affected by the MISA (Maintenance of Internal Security Act) needed support during the Emergency.[9]

Once, while answering a question from an official, Dr Hedgewar had said that he wanted householders to become pracharaks in the Sangh so that the Sangh and society would remain in harmony. Whenever people came to meet him, he would ask them to suggest a suitable bride for a certain pracharak. But Golwalkar felt that married pracharaks were not suitable and wanted full-time pracharaks. The Sangh continues this tradition to this day.

On the question of his becoming a pracharak, Govindacharya says with a laugh, 'I became a swayamsevak in 1960 and completed my third year in 1964. I had many questions in my mind before becoming a pracharak. What would I be able to do? What would I do if I didn't become a pracharak or if I left midway? Would I get a job? If I didn't find a job, would I have to beg on the streets? What if I met with an accident or something? … A slew of questions rose in my mind, but I realised such things could happen even if I did not become a pracharak, so why not lead a life in the service of the nation? Therefore, I decided that this would be my destiny, and I would blame no one else for it. There was also a talk by Guruji where he said that life is a game, so roll your dice. This thought got stuck in my mind, and I did just that. I have no regrets to this day. I feel content in having done as much work as I could.'[10]

Writer Ratan Sharda says that during Hedgewar and Golwalkar's era, a substantial number of the pracharaks came from Maharashtra. But they eventually spread to other states and remained there. As a result, some became fluent Tamil-speaking Marathis, others spoke pure Punjabi, and some adopted Gujarati. In the early days, Dadarao Parmarth was sent to the erstwhile Madras province; he was followed by Dattaji Didolkar and Shivram Joglekar. The trio laid the foundation of the RSS in the southern part of the country. Madhav Rao Mule went to Punjab, and Lakshmanrao Inamdar to Gujarat, on assignment. K.S. Sudarshan took care of Bengal and Odisha. Among the twenty-first-century politicians, former prime minister Atal Bihari Vajpayee, Lal Krishna Advani and Narendra Modi were long-time pracharaks.

During the Emergency, the Vidyarthi Parishad ran a 'Jail Bharo' campaign from 14 November 1975 to 26 January 1976. The police imprisoned thousands of people, while an equal number already were in captivity. At the time, Govindacharya remembers Atal-ji remarking that it was probably time to announce the Lok Sangharsh Samiti's dissolution. Since the movement had already produced several active karyakartas and individuals with leadership potential, the more important challenge facing them was how to channel their energy effectively. That was when H.V. Sheshadri, Dattopant Thengadi and Ravindra-ji formulated a plan of action and decided that some pracharaks should be given responsibilities in other organisations. This strategy led to Ashok Singhal, Bhanupratap Shukla, Chandrasekhar and Govindacharya receiving assignments in different regions. At the time, it was also decided that although the Sangh would send its pracharaks to different organisations, it was those organisations that would determine the respective pracharak's specific roles and responsibilities. Govindacharya was made responsible for the eastern part of the country; subsequently, from 1981 to 1986, he was assigned to the South. In 1986, because Dattatreya Hosabale started experiencing some breathing problems, Govindacharya was called to Delhi to take over North India. In 1987, the Bofors issue gained national attention, and Govindacharya, to along with his colleagues, organised several programmes to support Vishwanath Pratap Singh. L.K. Advani requested the Sangh to allow Govindacharya to join the BJP. Responding to the request, Madan Das Devi (the national organising secretary of ABVP at the time) stated that Govindacharya should not go alone and offered five or six additional names. By 1988, political activities had gained momentum in anticipation of the general elections scheduled for 1989.

According to Govindacharya, there is still not much clarity within the BJP regarding the role of the pracharaks and the regional heads, nor on how they differ from the others in the sangathan. In 1998, at a discussion in Virar, under the BJP presidency of Kushabhau Thakre, there was a discussion on the working style of the sangathans. Govindacharya told Thakre that political parties cannot always spell everything out clearly.

There are no guidelines governing the coordination between power and organisation, and the responsibilities of the sangathan increase when the party is in power. Following the Virar session, a committee was formed under Jana Krishnamurthi. The body eventually submitted its report, but by then, Venkaiah Naidu had become BJP president—and what happened to the report after that remains unclear.

The story of Govindacharya's move from the RSS to the BJP is no less interesting: 'My move to the BJP was first discussed on 25 September 1988, and on 29 September, they told me I would have to work for the BJP from then on. I said that I was a member of the Vidyarthi Parishad and did not know about the BJP. Bhaurao-ji told me what I needed to take care of while working for the BJP, but he also asked me not to change my eccentric style.'[11]

On 3 October 1988, a high-level meeting was held in Delhi, which included L.K. Advani, Rajju bhaiyya (Rajendra Singh), Bhaurao-ji, Ashok Singhal, Murli Manohar Joshi, Nanaji Deshmukh and S. Gurumurthy (representing Ramnath Goenka). They invited Govindacharya to the meeting. The Sangh had informed them that they should make Govindacharya a general secretary in the BJP. Advani replied that this was impossible because the BJP's four general secretary positions were full, and they could not remove anyone. After considerable deliberation, they decided Govindacharya would become a member of the BJP's National Working Committee, with a role equivalent to a general secretary's. Following the decision, Govindacharya told Bhaurao. 'Since I am associated with the Vidyarthi Parishad, you please talk to them first.' Bhaurao spoke to Bal Apte of the Parishad and informed him of the decision. Annoyed, Apte said, 'Are you telling me about your decision or asking me?' Bhaurao replied—'Informing you.' The response from Apte was, 'I heard you. Talk to Madan Das-ji about this.' When they took this up with Madan Das Devi, he felt it wouldn't be right to send Govindacharya alone and suggested that a few other people should be sent to the BJP as well. However, the response he received was, 'We have decided.'[12] Once Govindacharya entered the BJP, he met every senior leader. Sundar Singh Bhandari assured him that everything would fall into place within six months. Another veteran who shared invaluable advice about navigating the organisation was Kidar Nath Sahani. He cautioned Govindacharya against treating the BJP like the Vidyarthi Parishad. As opposed to the more youth-centric Vidyarthi Parishad, most members of the BJP were older and more experienced. He said that Govindacharya shouldn't feel bad if people didn't agree with his views or refused to listen to him. Govindacharya also consulted Nanaji Deshmukh and Dattopant Thengadi. His first task was to seek the resignation of the BJP's Rajasthan president, Lalit Kishore Chaturvedi. Chaturvedi was a prominent leader and did not get along with another senior member of the party, Bhairon Singh Shekhawat. With much difficulty, Govindacharya eventually convinced Chaturvedi to resign.

HARMONY WITHIN THE SANGH

The leaders of the RSS and its affiliated organisations had opposed the addition of 'secular' and 'socialist' to the Indian Constitution. Prime Minister Indira Gandhi had had these words added to the Preamble via a constitutional amendment during the Emergency. The Sangh believed that being 'secular' meant being 'impious' or 'non-religious'. It felt the word had a negative connotation. According to the Sangh, 'dharma' should not be linked to faith or religion. It could be called 'Sarvapanth Samabhav'—an identical feeling towards all religions. The Sangh believed that this was the reason the Constituent Assembly had originally not included these words in the Indian Constitution. Even though the Sangh says that it does not associate the word 'Hindu' with 'religion', Dr Hedgewar in 1925 had said, 'Yes, I, Dr Keshav Baliram Hedgewar, say that I am a Hindu and this is a Hindu nation.'[13]

According to Dr Hedgewar, the purpose of the Sangh shakhas was personality development and the building of a Hindu nation. Even though the shakha was the Sangh's primary unit, the chief work of the swayamsevaks was engaging with society outside. Every swayamsevak had to take an oath for 'the all-round development of the Hindu nation', which meant the protection of the Hindu religion, culture and society. People would refer to the collective of all the Sangh's sister organisations as the 'Sangh Parivar' even during Dr Hedgewar's time, but the RSS now calls it the Sangh Vividh Kshetra Sangathan. It is said that all the organisations under the Sangh operate in a non-political manner. They exert pressure on local governments to address issues in their areas and on the central government for favourable policy decisions, regardless of whose government it is. The BJP being in power is a significant advantage as many swayamsevaks hold positions within it, making it easy for them to understand and address their concerns. The BJP governments rarely face opposition from Sangh-affiliated organisations. Instead, they operate through what is known as 'Sangh harmony', wherein the various organisations collaborate towards the shared goal of nation-building.

The earliest affiliate organisations of the RSS—the Akhil Bharatiya Vidyarthi Parishad, Vanvasi Kalyan Ashram, Bharatiya Mazdoor Sangh, Vishva Hindu Parishad, Bharatiya Kisan Sangh, Swadeshi Jagaran Manch, Vidya Bharati and Seva Bharati—have a nationwide presence. Apart from these, there are bodies centred on certain professions, such as the Adhivakta Parishad for lawyers, the National Medicos Organisation and the Arogya Bharati for doctors, the Purva Sainik Parishad for retired defence personnel, the Seema Jagaran Manch for those living in border areas, and many more. The Shishu Shiksha Prabandh Samiti, formed in Uttar Pradesh in 1958, is active all over the country, and Vidya Bharati runs over 13,000 schools for it. A select group of officials heads these organisations, all of which operate nationally. They make autonomous decisions, launch programmes and monitor their finances by themselves. They seek suggestions from Sangh officials whenever necessary, but the final decision rests with the body.

A similar arrangement exists between the Sangh and the BJP. At the time of ticket distribution for elections, the Sangh presents the swayamsevaks' opinions to the BJP, but the party leadership takes the final decisions. A senior leader long associated with the Sangh and the BJP noted that, while this principle still holds, Sangh officials—particularly regional heads working in the BJP-ruled states—recommend names for appointments to various governmental departments, boards and committees. They also interfere with the functioning of the state governments and pressurise them. It is common for prospective candidates seeking tickets for elections to make the rounds of Sangh offices and hobnob with its officials.[14] Many Sangh officials show keen interest in the appointment of governors and chancellors of universities as well. Mohan Bhagwat says that many people take pictures with Sangh officials and use them to push their agenda, but they don't succeed because the members of the Sangh and the BJP know well that such opportunists are not real swayamsevaks.[15]

WOMEN IN THE SANGH

The truth is that there is no membership for women in the Sangh. But, in 1936, Dr Hedgewar had asked a twenty-seven-year-old widow, Lakshmibai Kelkar, to form the 'Rashtra Sevika Samiti'. The organisation's structure and culture would resemble the Sangh, and they would also have full-time pracharikas. Lakshmibai Kelkar is someone who, when faced with difficulties in arranging for her daughter's education, herself started a school for girls called Kesarimal Kanya Vidyalaya. This school is still functional in Wardha. At the time, Hedgewar had felt that it wouldn't be appropriate for women to partake in the physical training that is a part of the shakha system, but he gave his consent to start a separate body for women. Lakshmibai Kelkar was of the opinion that women were not merely the anchors of their families; they were actually the backbone of the country. Channelling their physical, intellectual and spiritual strength could build a powerful nation.

At present, women are actively involved in several departments of the Sangh such as social service, communication, village development, cow protection, religious programmes and family welfare initiatives. Another organisation for women, which is affiliated to the Sangh, is Stree Shakti. Additionally, many women are active in the Vidyarthi Parishad. It is said that the Sangh strongly supports these activities, with the sarsanghchalak and the sah-sarkaryavah taking a keen interest in the contributions of women. But a long-time member of the Rashtra Sevika Samiti says that women in the Sangh have the same status as in Hindu families: revered as goddesses, but always eating last. People do not consider women's decisions or desires pivotal or worthwhile. Until this changes in the Sangh, there is no point in boasting of the increasing number of women in the organisation. She says that even if we don't call the Sangh anti-women, the women in it certainly don't play a decisive role. If the situation improves by the time the Sangh completes its centenary, it will surely lead to a change in the Sangh's image.[16] Even Rahul Gandhi has raised this question about the absence of women from programmes of the Sangh, hinting at the Sangh's anti-women attitude.[17]

The head office of the Rashtra Sevika Samiti is in Dhantoli, Nagpur. The building, known as Ahilya Mandir, also houses the samiti's office and residential facilities for pracharikas and office-bearers. Similar arrangements are available in other parts of the country. The samiti has 4,900 shakhas, and every state is headed by a pracharika. It focuses predominantly on women-centric issues, often conducting workshops with prominent women who have achieved great heights in their fields so that the younger generation of women can draw inspiration from them.

Apart from the Rashtra Sevika Samiti, the Akhil Bharatiya Vidyarthi Parishad, too, has many women officials and members in active roles. Sunil Ambekar says that contrary to popular belief, the women associated with the Sangh have worked in diverse fields. For example, the women of the Vidyarthi Parishad have led campaigns against menstruation-related superstitions and created awareness in colleges about the use of sanitary pads. Even men have actively taken part in such campaigns.

According to Devendra Swaroop, there was scepticism about the entry of women into the Sangh. Despite the 1936 founding of the Rashtra Sevika Samiti, a majority within the Sangh remained worried about the potential problems arising from interactions between men and women. The person in charge of the Sangh in Goa, for example, had strong reservations on this matter. He had permitted the entry of women into the Vivekananda Ashram, which had led to several problems. The niece of a senior official had taken part in Sangh activities and later entered a love marriage, which became a scandal.

Aniruddha Deshpande, who has been the Sangh's national head of communications, says that no change is possible in a day. Evolution is a slow process.

AKHIL BHARATIYA VIDYARTHI PARISHAD (ABVP)

The Vidyarthi Parishad is one of the oldest student organisations in the RSS. It was established in 1948 by Prof Yashwant Rao Kelkar, a Sangh pracharak, along with Dattopant Thengadi and other pracharaks. Today, its members and workers have a pan-Indian presence in colleges and universities across the country. Although the Vidyarthi Parishad is a non-political organisation, several of its workers have been active in politics. Moreover, it has played a vital role in creating the next generation of the BJP leadership. Being a nationalist organisation, the Vidyarthi Parishad is actively involved in education and national security.

At the state level, the Parishad has contributed towards strengthening the functioning of the universities and formulating their ethics and principles. Ambekar says, 'The Parishad doesn't run its campaigns keeping in mind the impact they will have on the party in power and its government. We are an organisation that functions with a positive approach and is in harmony.' Arun Jaitley, one of the prominent leaders of the Parishad, became the minister of law and justice in India.

The Vidyarthi Parishad had started a campaign to evict illegal Bangladeshi immigrants. ABVP volunteers also actively supported the Citizenship (Amendment) Act in 2019. The initiative they created helped to move schoolchildren from the Northeast to other parts of the country, where they stayed with local families and finished their education. In the nineties, when terrorism peaked in Kashmir, forcing Pandits to flee their homes, the Vidyarthi Parishad organised nationwide college protests to raise awareness and show solidarity.

Govindacharya, who managed the Akhil Bharatiya Vidyarthi Parishad, mentions that policymakers emphasised three points: self-reliance, economy and assignment of responsibility. A relatively long review meeting takes place in the ABVP once every three years for planning and analysis. However, such structured reflection is largely lacking in the two largest organisations—the BJP and the Vishva Hindu Parishad. In these organisations, the policies and work culture are determined solely by the leadership, meaning that whatever the leadership decides effectively becomes their programmes.

Since the ABVP is a student organisation, a question arose about whether to induct girls into it. The Sangh had reservations about boys and girls working together, particularly regarding the nature of tasks and interaction. They then decided that boys and girls should not work together in closed rooms. Girls should not work beyond ten o'clock at night. They would not serve full-time before the age of twenty-four or for over four years. Girls would not stay overnight at the office, and if they had to travel, they would stay only at the homes of senior karyakartas. It was thought that, given their age, mutual affection between a boy and girl coworker would not be considered scandalous, and the Sangh would formally arrange their marriage. This was how Bal Apte married Nirmala-ji. Nirmala-ji quit working for the organisation after her wedding and didn't resume until her daughter left for medical college.

BHARATIYA JANA SANGH

The second sarsanghchalak of the RSS, Guruji Golwalkar, was against the Sangh being active in politics. However, the 1948-49 ban on the Sangh silenced the organisation, leaving it without a voice in Parliament or any public forum. The situation sparked discussions about forming a distinct political platform or party of their own. Balasaheb Deoras fiercely supported this idea. At the same time, Syama Prasad Mookerjee had resigned from the cabinet, stating his opposition to the Liaquat-Nehru Pact, and was contemplating starting a new political party. Until then, he had been a member of the Hindu Mahasabha. He held Pakistan solely responsible for the appalling state of the Hindus who had returned as refugees. He had opposed Kashmir being accorded a special status and having a separate flag and prime minister. Mookerjee had said, '*Ek desh me do vidhan, do pradhan aur do nishan nahi chalenge.*' (Ours is one country; we cannot have two constitutions, two prime ministers and two flags).

Dr Mookerjee had discussed the idea of forming a political party with Golwalkar. He stated that while the Sangh wasn't in favour of launching a political outfit, it would support Mookerjee if he started one. Following this, Golwalkar deputed several senior Sangh leaders to work in the newly formed Jana Sangh. This marked the first instance of the Sangh officially assigning its senior members to work for another organisation. Even then, Golwalkar had made it clear to Mookerjee that the Jana Sangh would not pursue the idea of a Hindu Rashtra, and its doors would be open to everyone. After the formation of the Jana Sangh, Mookerjee attempted to enter Kashmir in 1953 without a permit, and he was arrested. He later died in custody, allegedly because of a lack of proper medical treatment. At that time, Sheikh Abdullah was the chief minister of Kashmir. The Jana Sangh had taken part in the general elections in 1952, but secured only three seats. Several people hoped to assume the presidency of the Jana Sangh after Dr Mookerjee's death, but it was General Secretary Deendayal Upadhyaya who took over in 1967. In fact, the BJP still claims to follow the philosophy of integral humanism posited by Upadhyaya. A few days later, on 11 February 1968, Upadhyaya's body was found at the Mughalsarai railway station. The mystery surrounding the death of both leaders remains unsolved.

During the 1975 Emergency, the Jana Sangh and Vidyarthi Parishad leaders played an active role; subsequently, the Janata Party merged with the Jana Sangh. The then-leader of the Jana Sangh, Atal Bihari Vajpayee, had said that it was time for the lamp, the Jana Sangh's election symbol, to be extinguished. Once the Janata Party dissolved, the Bharatiya Janata Party came into existence. Atal Bihari Vajpayee, speaking at the Bombay session in 1980, said, '*Andhera chhatega, suraj nikalega, aur kamal khilega*.' (The darkness will be dispelled, the sun will rise and the lotus will bloom).

BHARATIYA MAZDOOR SANGH

The Bharatiya Mazdoor Sangh is the largest trade union in the country and marks its presence in every area of economic development. Dattopant Thengadi established the outfit in 1955. But its functioning remained very different from other labour organisations. Guruji Golwalkar had sent Thengadi to work within the Congress-affiliated organisation, the Indian National Trade Union Congress (INTUC), and understand the condition of the labour organisations and the condition of the workers. Thengadi joined the INTUC at the invitation of its president, P.Y. Deshpande. During his time, he not only engaged directly with the workers but also developed a deep understanding of industrialisation. Most labour unions were associated with political parties. The Communist Party and Congress-affiliated trade unions led to prolonged and destructive strikes. The Bharatiya Mazdoor Sangh moved away from this approach. It asserted that the workers were shareholders of the company. Therefore, they refrained from causing any damage to property or machines during strikes and protests. Back then, the trade unions wielded great power, and fluttering red flags were a common sight outside company or factory premises. Establishing the Bharatiya Mazdoor Sangh required immense effort and time. The BMS held its first session in 1967, twelve years after its establishment. By then, it had about 2.5 lakh members and over 500 associated trade unions.[18]

VANVASI KALYAN ASHRAM

Most social, cultural and political organisations restrict themselves to urban spaces so their work can receive maximum exposure and visibility. Moreover, it is not easy to extend their activities into remote areas and forested regions. In such a scenario, the Vanvasi Kalyan Ashram is India's largest organisation working for the Adivasi and tribal population in the country. It operates silently, with no noise or publicity. Ramakant Keshav Deshpande formed it in 1952. He established the first hostel for Adivasi children in Jashpur, Madhya Pradesh. Since then, the organisation has opened hundreds of schools in tribal regions and has worked extensively to promote self-reliance among Adivasi communities.

At the moment, India has 10 crore Adivasis and nobody to take care of their needs. The Vanvasi Kalyan Ashram has made concerted efforts to curb religious conversions by the Christian missionaries. In its early years, the outfit faced vehement opposition from the Church and Christian missionaries. Although the organisation has not operated with overt political interest, it is undeniable that the BJP has benefited politically from its work. Traditionally, the Congress considered Adivasis a core voter base, but many have tilted towards the BJP in recent years.

VISHVA HINDU PARISHAD

The Sangh set up the Vishva Hindu Parishad in 1964, intending to bring together, on a single platform, all the Hindu saints and ascetics, the maths (Hindu monasteries), temples, ashrams (hermitages), trusts and their heads. It is an international organisation and the only one in which the sarsanghchalak is a trustee. Guruji Golwalkar was keenly interested in this organisation, and he consistently strove to strengthen and expand it after its establishment. His involvement was so intense that he had postponed the radiation therapy for his cancer treatment for a few days so he could attend the VHP's regional meeting in Gujarat.

The VHP tried to improve the state of temples and attempted to integrate religious institutions into the waves of social change. However, they achieved nothing greater than facilitating the renovation of temples. Guruji Golwalkar was very involved in this effort and met the saints, Hindi gurus and religious leaders. Swami Shivananda, the founder of the Chinmaya Mission and Vishwesha Tirtha Swami of the Pejawar matha, played important roles in this mission. Guruji also involved another veteran pracharak, Dadasaheb Apte. In 1964, at the Sandipani Ashram in the Chinmaya Mission headquarters, the VHP formally came into being. It was Janmashtami, Lord Krishna's birthday.

Swami Chinmayananda presided over the first convenor's meeting. Religious leaders and saints of different faiths took part in the session. The VHP chose Swami Chinmayananda as its first president, and its members adopted the slogan '*Dharmo Rakshati Rakshatah*' (Those who protect the dharma are protected by the dharma).

Govindacharya recounts that Dadasaheb Apte, a key figure in the VHP, focused on spreading Hindu dharma abroad. He was succeeded by Rajabhau Devalkar, who came from Mahakaushal and concentrated on the procedures of worship. Besides the simplification of religious rites, he had a keen interest in Sanskrit, which led to the establishment of a Sanskrit organisation in Puducherry. When Swarika Prasad took charge, he started the creation of service-oriented and educational institutions like hospitals, schools, etc. He modelled them after those run by Christian missionaries, and he enlisted several wealthy individuals for this cause. However, when the Emergency was imposed, many benefactors joined the government's twenty-point programme and withdrew their support from the VHP's initiatives. Moropant Pingle launched a major fundraising effort during his tenure to protect Indian culture, thus resolving the organisation's serious financial crisis. When Ashok Singhal took over the reins, he excelled at collecting funds and mobilising people. Then, he organised the Ekaatmata Yatra (Unity March), followed by strategic planning for the Ram Janmabhoomi movement and the Kar Seva. After the Supreme Court's ruling on the temple, the VHP played a vital role in its construction.

EKAL VIDYALAYA FOUNDATION

The Ekal Vidyalaya Foundation is a unique initiative focused on Adivasi and rural areas. Its motto is 'one teacher, one school'. There are over 76,000 Ekal Vidyalayas or schools in India, teaching over 20,00,000 students. These schools are mostly located in areas that are so remote that they remain outside the reach of government schools. Local teachers teach in the local languages and use folk music, plays and stories for instruction.

Rakesh Popli, a nuclear scientist, and his wife returned from their foreign deputation and started the Ekal Vidyalaya Foundation. They began the project in consultation with experts on child education and other scholars. The VHP supported the Ekal Vidyalaya project in Gumla, Jharkhand, aiming to eradicate illiteracy in tribal zones. Later, Bhaurao Deoras and his team planned the progress and implementation of the initiative, with Rakesh Popli drafting a comprehensive framework and authoring a book, *Khele Koode, Nache Gaye* (Let's Play, Let's Dance).

The Ekal Organisation was set up to conduct research and development for the project. The responsibility for running and monitoring the Ekal Vidyalayas was entrusted to the village committees. These schools operate for three hours a day, six days a week. Apart from studies, they emphasise health and hygiene. However, critics often accuse the Ekal Vidyalaya Foundation of propagating Hindu religion and ideology.

VOICES OF DISSENT

The RSS doesn't hesitate to take action against those who don't adhere to its collective decisions. There have been several instances where the Sangh leadership had to take tough calls against rebel leaders or officials. The Sangh immediately removed them from their posts.

The first instance of a revolt in the Sangh happened in 1929, at a time when most members were Dr Hedgewar's associates or those he trusted. Upset by Dr Hedgewar's rejection of his proposal for having an akhada in every shakha, Ganesh Sohni left the Sangh and established the Hindu Nationalist Akhada in Nagpur to teach traditional martial arts.

The Sangh suspended V.V. Pendse, the Pune pracharak, immediately in 1954 after his direct criticism of the Sangh leadership. In 1955, it took stringent action against Vasantrao Oak, the Delhi provincial pracharak. According to Mukesh Sharma, a veteran leader of the Sangh associated with the Deendayal Shodh Sansthan, Oak was becoming too involved in the political activities of the Jana Sangh while serving in the key position of prant pracharak. During British Rule, Hedgewar permitted several sanghchalaks to participate in the provincial assembly elections, but in the 1952 elections, he strictly ordered all full-time pracharaks to avoid politics. After Dr Mookerjee's demise, Mauli Chandra Sharma became the president of the Jana Sangh. In 1954, he formed his working committee, which included both nationalist leaders associated with Dr Mookerjee and the Sangh pracharaks he had assigned to the Jana Sangh. Mauli Chandra Sharma had come to the Sangh from the Congress, and he was not someone who could strengthen the party, leading to an increased dependency on the pracharaks. Despite being a provincial pracharak, Vasantrao Oak believed that the Jana Sangh had to extricate itself from the Sangh circles to build its political identity. The Sangh disapproved of Oak's inclusion in the working committee, but his political ambitions were on the rise, and he raised voices of dissent against the Sangh's leadership. The Sangh removed him from the post of prant pracharak and appointed him head of physical education. However, Oak refused to take up the new designation and had to move from Delhi to Madras. Under the circumstances, Oak joined a new political party called the National Democratic Front in 1956. Those who left the Jana Sangh to join the NDF were primarily individuals unwilling to follow the Jana Sangh leadership. But this didn't continue for long, and Oak eventually returned to the Jana Sangh. Still, he could never regain his previous position or the respect he had once held within the Jana Sangh. Regarding L.K. Advani, some BJP members informed me of his diminished standing within the BJP after the NDA's formation under Vajpayee. Advani got the idea for the name National Democratic Alliance from the National Democratic Front.

In its century-long journey, the Sangh has faced many hurdles but still stands strong. However, sometimes dissent within the Sangh not only surfaced openly but also led to individuals leaving its fold. Even the highest echelons witnessed such a revolt. Balasaheb Deoras's exit from the Sangh in the fifties, reportedly in anger, stands out as an important event in the RSS's history. There is not much discussion in the Sangh about the reasons behind his departure and eventual return. Balasaheb stayed outside the RSS from 1953 to 1960. In 1973, Golwalkar appointed him sarsanghchalak—an exceptional occurrence unlikely in any other organisation. Another notable incident involved the release of many of those associated with Gandhi-ji's assassination in 1964. The Sangh expelled N.G. Abhyankar, the Pune sanghchalak, after he attended a ceremony welcoming them.

There are very few instances where someone who left the Sangh in revolt established another organisation to oppose it. Even if such a thing happened, they could not challenge the Sangh successfully, and either closed down soon or eventually merged with the Sangh. In 2017, Subhash Velingkar, the sanghchalak of Goa, started a front opposing the decision to provide financial help to English-medium primary schools. Since the RSS had supported the BJP government on this issue, he left the Sangh and started a separate organisation, but returned within a year.[19]

However, the biggest revolt in the Sangh took place in 1938–39 when the nizam of Hyderabad imposed a ban on singing *Vande Mataram* in schools and colleges. This song had become a symbol of protest against British rule and portrays the country as a sacred mother. The ban imposed on it deeply enraged the Sangh, viewing it as an insult to Hindus and India. Dissent within the Sangh erupted when the school- and college-going swayamsevaks sought permission to join the protests against the ban on the national song. However, Hedgewar denied their request, even as other Hindu organisations like the Arya Samaj and the Hindu Mahasabha were taking part in it. The swayamsevaks could join the protest individually, but the swayamsevaks associated with western Maharashtra, the Hindu Mahasabha, the Arya Samaj and other organisations formed separate contingents to participate in the protests.

Lacking strong leadership, these efforts quickly lost momentum, and either faded away or shut down entirely. In 1938, Nathuram Godse, Narayan Dattatraya Apte and J.D. Joglekar quit the RSS during this agitation. Along with a few young swayamsevaks, they started the hard-line Hindu Rashtra Dal in 1943. Godse and his associates became all the angrier with Golwalkar because, after becoming the Sangh's sarsanghchalak in 1943, Guruji focused on matters such as spirituality, human development and organisational strength instead of giving the RSS a hard-line and revolutionary character.

People voiced dissent again a year after Kannada-speaking Lingayat swayamsevaks began holding their shakhas in the Bombay Presidency because of the dominance of Maharashtrian Brahmins. The Sangh has long grappled with criticism over the perceived dominance of Maharashtrian Brahmins within the organisation—a challenge even Atal Bihari Vajpayee had to face. Vajpayee's relationship with the RSS began in 1940 when he was in high school. It was Narayanrao Tarte, a lifelong pracharak who had come to Nagpur from Gwalior, who introduced him to the Sangh. Vajpayee began attending the Lakshmiganj shakha in Gwalior. At that time, there was a rivalry between the Hindi and Marathi speakers. The Marathis were called 'kadhikhau' (kadhi eaters), while the Hindi speakers were called 'raangades' (uncouth or rustic). Vajpayee, however, learnt Marathi soon. After Gandhi's assassination, when the Sangh shifted its focus towards strengthening the organisation, a group of swayamsevaks in Nagpur rebelled. They felt the Sangh was becoming too focused on internal organisational growth at the expense of social service.

THE SANGH IN ACTIVE POLITICS

The Sangh has always been in a quandary with regard to politics. While it is a fact that the Sangh plays an important role in elections—swayamsevaks go to booths and assist voters—it continues to speak of maintaining a distance from politics. Govindacharya addresses the dichotomy: 'There had been arguments from the Jana Sangh's time itself on whether the sangh pracharak will fight elections. Will he take part in active politics? If you look at the history of the Sangh, you see that Dr Hedgewar was very agitated with the freedom struggle, but once Guruji took over the reins of the Sangh, there was an ideological momentum. It was on Guruji's insistence that the Sangh pracharaks and swayamsevaks began to play a definitive role in assisting in the political arena.'[20]

Politics was strictly avoided from 1962 to 1967. It was decided that pracharaks would avoid political rallies and shakha teachers would refrain from conducting meetings under any political organisation's banner. They would not put up posters or run campaigns, but they could take part in booth management. Sangh pracharaks could not contest elections, though there was no formal written directive to that effect. Govindacharya says, 'This important question remains unanswered, and I could not find the answer to it in the Sangh.' He had questioned Sundar Singh Bhandari and Bhaurao Deoras about this and later asked Kushabhau Thakre, but the response he received was simply, 'Mind your own business.' When Govindacharya remarked, 'I agree that pracharaks should not fight elections,' he was asked if he considered himself a greater pracharak than Deendayal Upadhyaya? After that exchange, Govindacharya decided never to fight elections. Bhaurao Deoras affirmed it was the right decision.

This rule was followed religiously, more or less, until 1972, when Deendayal Upadhyaya was granted permission to fight an election. Later, some Sangh leaders admitted it was not the right decision. In 1977, after the Emergency, the RSS relaxed this rule because it was felt that the country's politics needed serious, politically active individuals. In 1989, on the occasion of Dr Hedgewar's centenary, organisers assembled pracharaks up to the district level to discuss whether they should be allowed to enter politics or fight elections. Most people were opposed to it. At that time, a senior leader of the BJP, Pyarelal Khandelwal, disagreed and suggested there should be no restriction on entry into politics, at least within the BJP. This implied that pracharaks already associated with the BJP should not be barred from fighting elections. Khandelwal said, 'According to my personal experience, there will be conflict if there is any such prohibition.'[21] Govindacharya makes an important point when he says that the Sangh works on an esoteric tradition and a directive-based system. Everyone follows the command given to them. Loyalty is required to keep the organisation together, but it comes at the cost of initiative and courage. In the 2019 Haryana elections, the BJP was ready to accept a murder accused when it did not receive a majority. Yet nobody from the Sangh or the BJP raised questions of morality. When Uma Bharti questioned the decision, she was advised to keep away from such issues.[22]

In a democratic country like India, avoiding politics is not ideal; yet, it is often observed that the Sangh exerts its influence over politics and the government, but with no accountability. On the issue of 'power without accountability', Govindacharya says, 'No, this is called "moral authority", and its advantage is that while making any decision, the pracharak or the Sangh will not look at his personal loss or gain and will take objective and neutral decisions.'

I AM IN THE SANGH, THE SANGH IS IN ME

Most Sangh activities take place at Hedgewar Smriti Mandir Nagpur. The first shakha was held on this very ground, and one can fathom its legacy only by visiting this place.

There can be nothing better than books available here to understand the RSS's ideology and movement. Besides these, the RSS uniform, band, drum and flag are also available here. Most books are in Hindi, English and Marathi. Gangadhar Paradhikar, a pracharak since 1983, who is associated with the Bharatiya Kisan Sangh, manages the museum. Paradhikar says that swayamsevaks from all over the country aspire to visit the headquarters.

While talking about the Kisan Sangh, Paradhikar says that the Kisan Sangh has small units all over India, and these units have regular programmes at the district level. The Kisan Sangh's national convention is held once every three years. It doesn't succumb to governmental pressure from the BJP. 'We take up issues related to farmers with the government in a firm manner, but there is no political one-upmanship in all this. You have given me something; I need to reciprocate too, don't

I?' He gifted me a book, *Main Sangh Mein aur Mujh mein Sangh* (I am in the Sangh, the Sangh is in Me). Its author Madhav Govind Vaidya was ninety-five years old at the time, and his book could not have had a more apt title. Vaidya is no more now.

When I had spoken to Vaidya about swayamsevaks, he had said, 'I was never a pracharak, but I am the father of pracharaks.' That is true, as his two sons, Dr Manmohan Vaidya and Dr Ram Vaidya, have both been pracharaks. Manmohan Vaidya served as the Akhil Bharatiya Prachar Pramukh (the all-India head of media and publicity) for a long time and has now become the sah-sarkaryavah. Dr Ram Vaidya is involved in overseeing Sangh activities in America and other countries. Madhav Govind was the first spokesperson of the RSS. Though Vaidya was never formally a pracharak, he spent his entire life in the service of the Sangh. He was the editor of *Tarun Bharat* for many years and later became its chairman and managing director. He also worked with the *Panchjanya*. When someone remarked that he had ruined the careers of two of his sons by making them pracharaks, he replied, 'I keep wondering why I couldn't make my other three sons pracharaks too.'

THE SANGH AND SERVICE

The Sangh does not regard 'service' as charity, but as an attempt to return to society what it and its members have received from it. Former sarkaryavah H.V. Sheshadri shaped the service activities of the RSS. The central leadership assigns each shakha a specific social task, and a senior pracharak supports and monitors the initiative to ensure their benefits reach their intended destination. Furthermore, the Sangh doesn't hesitate to collaborate with other organisations for the cause of nation-building. It is willing to cooperate with religious and social groups. Sudhanshu Mittal, a senior leader associated with the Sangh and the BJP, notes that social service has been a part of the Sangh's vision right from the beginning. However, in 1965, after Balasaheb Deoras became the sarkaryavah, the focus on social service intensified. Before this, Golwalkar's tenure concentrated on the growth and expansion of the organisation.

The service activities of the Sangh are carried out through the Seva Bharati. In 2003, Seva Bharati was registered as a public trust under the name Rashtriya Sewa Bharati to facilitate effective collaboration with the state units and other organisations. Over 9,000 organisations involved in various aspects of life are affiliated with the Rashtriya Sewa Bharati. Currently, it runs 90,000 projects in health awareness, 39,000 projects in social service, over 25,000 projects in education and 22,000 projects for women's empowerment.[23] The All-India sah-seva pramukh oversees the activities of the Seva Bharati.

Once, someone asked Dr Hedgewar what the Sangh would do after the organisation was fully built. He replied, 'The swayamsevaks will do everything.'[24] The swayamsevak chooses a project as per his liking and then nurtures it. He doesn't get paid anything for it, and on the contrary, he spends his own money.

During a natural calamity, the swayamsevaks always step forward to help. Whether it was the 1966 Bihar famine, the storm in Andhra Pradesh in 1977, the earthquake in Maharashtra in 1993, the devastating Gujarat earthquake in 2001, the tsunami in South India in 2004, the flash floods of Uttarakhand in 2013, the Bihar floods in 2017, or the COVID-19 pandemic—the Sangh volunteers were involved in rehabilitation and rescue activities, often putting their lives in danger. The Sangh does not discriminate in terms of religion or caste during disaster management activities. Spaces for namaz were created in relief camps during the Gujarat earthquake. The Sangh believes natural calamities are a part of life, therefore, we must always be well prepared to face them. Disaster management training is now imparted in the shiksha vargs. The Deendayal Research Institute runs several projects for self-reliance, particularly in rural development. The

Seva Bharati has started a project called 'Swasthya Mitra' under which doctors run primary health projects in villages. Another crucial goal is the prevention of forced religious conversion. The accusation is that Christian missionaries and other organisations convert people through coercion and enticement. Organisations associated with the Sangh are actively working on this issue. The Sangh maintains that it is not against Christianity or Islam, but strongly opposes conversions through force or enticement.

The former director general of the Indian Institute of Mass Communication (IIMC), K.G. Suresh, is a seasoned journalist. While sharing his experience, he says, 'On 12 November 1996, a fireball from the sky spread over a village a hundred kilometres from Delhi, and the village turned into a heap of dead bodies within minutes. Charred and burnt bodies lay strewn all over. This was nothing but the world's worst aircraft accident. Two planes collided mid-air and turned 349 human beings into carcasses in a flash. 200 Indians perished in the accident. The Saudi Arabia Airlines flight had taken off from Delhi just a few minutes ago with over 200 Indian passengers flying to Saudi Arabia in search of lucrative jobs. On the other side was a Kazakhstan Airlines flight carrying thirty-seven passangers that was descending to land in Delhi. The pilot of the Kazakhstan Airlines' plane couldn't understand the instructions relayed by the Air Traffic Control and crashed into the Saudi Arabian plane. All the passengers on both the planes died in the crash. Most of the victims were Muslim.'[25]

There was nothing left to be salvaged. There were only the body parts of the deceased lying all over the fields of the Charkhi Dadri village of Haryana. The villagers were the first to reach the accident site, and with them were the volunteers of the RSS. The next morning, the *Times of India* carried a detailed article by Suresh on the front page, describing at length how the swayamsevaks had performed the arduous task of collecting the ravaged dead bodies and placing them respectfully in coffins. Although the news about the contribution of the RSS garnered a lot of attention, K.G. Suresh had to face a lot of flak. At that time, the word 'bhakt' was not much in vogue, but several mediapersons had called Suresh a 'journalist of the Sangh'.

Suresh remembers, 'I had personally gone to the accident site and witnessed the swayamsevaks working tirelessly without caring about thirst or hunger. The unbearable stench of burning bodies filled the air. Most of the deceased were Muslims, and I felt it was a story that needed to be told because it was a testament to the way the Sangh functioned.'

Suresh mentions yet another incident. On the morning of 26 January 2001, a devastating earthquake shook Bhuj and the Anjar regions in Gujarat. Thousands of houses turned into rubble within a matter of seconds, and innumerable people lay buried under the debris. The relief and rescue operations went on for days, and it was an extremely challenging task to remove the dead bodies from under the mountains of debris. The bodies had begun to decay, and their unbearable odour had spread in the air. Even the close relatives of the deceased did not dare to pull out the bodies. The Sangh's swayamsevaks were the ones who performed this task. They not only extricated the bodies but also performed the last rites because there were several families with no survivors. Suresh says, 'I must say that the BJP reaped the dividends of the commitment of the swayamsevaks towards working for the nation. (...) The BJP benefited from the credibility that it lent. You could call it a silent revolution.'

'Do the critics know that the Sangh works for the donation of bodies and organs?' K.G. Suresh continues. 'The Dadhichi Deh Dan Sanstha not only motivates others, but the members of the Sangh themselves become an inspiration. Very few people would remember that on the day the chief minister of Delhi, Mrs Sheila Dikshit, died, the regional head of the Delhi BJP, industrialist Mange Ram Garg, too, had died. His body was not cremated but donated. The working president of the

Vishva Hindu Parishad, Alok Kumar, is the current president of the Dadhichi Sansthan. Alok Kumar has been involved in this important initiative for ages. Many people would be unaware of the fact that the most noteworthy and active general secretary, Acharya Giriraj Kishore's body had also been donated as per his wishes.'

Writer Ratan Sharda says that people have now started taking note of the Sangh's social contribution, but no information is available about what the organisation did during the most difficult times for the country. Even when the fire of Partition was raging, the sarsanghchalak at the time, Golwalkar, was touring the Punjab and Sindh regions. Witnessing the volatile situation in the country, the British had moved up India's independence by ten months. Originally, they had planned it for June 1948, but they advanced it to 15 August 1947.

Sharda insinuates that the supporters of the Muslim League had made plans to assassinate central government and Hindu leaders, apart from thousands of civilians. The date for the attack was finalised: 10 December 1947. There was also a plan to hoist the Pakistani flag at the Red Fort. The volunteers of the Sangh played a vital role in thwarting their plan. During the Partition, thousands of RSS workers lost their lives and their families while saving the lives of Hindus and the refugees coming into India from Pakistan. Despite the challenges, they continued to work relentlessly.[26]

From July to October 1947, several Sangh volunteers put their lives at risk to prevent Pakistani tribal groups from entering Kashmir. Balraj Madhok was the chief coordinator of the Sangh in Kashmir then. Riots had broken out in Jammu, and the swayamsevaks of the Sangh had helped in curbing the chaos. Until then, Maharaja Hari Singh had been unable to decide whether Jammu and Kashmir should accede to India. The Sangh workers held the fort firmly until the arrival of the Indian Army. After that, the Sangh workers and supporters created a political party called the Praja Parishad, which continuously fought for the complete integration of Jammu and Kashmir with India.

Thousands of Sangh workers undertook a satyagraha (non-violent resistance) for the liberation of Dadra, Nagar and Haveli and hoisted the Indian tricolour on office buildings on 2 August 1955. The swayamsevaks had played an important role in the liberation of Goa as well. The Sangh ran free canteens for soldiers during the 1962, 1965 and 1971 wars. Following the news of such contributions of the Sangh, Prime Minister Nehru invited the RSS to the Republic Day Parade on 26 January 1963. With just three days' notice, 3,000 swayamsevaks took part in the parade, clad in their khaki uniforms. During the period of terrorism in Punjab, one of the Sangh's sister organisations, the Rashtriya Sikh Sangat, worked to promote unity between Sikhs and Hindus.

THE SANGH AND THE CONGRESS

It is generally believed that the Sangh and the Congress espouse divergent views. However, a glance at history will reveal many moments when the RSS tried to establish friendly relations with the Congress. At various times in the past, the Congress has aligned with the RSS and pursued a Hindu political path similar to the RSS's.

Dr Hedgewar was a Congress leader before he established the Sangh. While studying medicine in Calcutta, he was active in the Anusheelan Samiti, a revolutionary organisation in Bengal, and was associated with Subhas Chandra Bose. Dr Hedgewar took on the responsibility of organising the 1920 Congress session in Nagpur; he had created a band of 1,200 swayamsevaks for this purpose. Before the Sangh's formation, he not only took part in the Congress's independence struggle, but the Sangh itself maintained ties with the Congress party.

A ban was imposed on the Sangh following Mahatma Gandhi's assassination. During 1949–50, when Golwalkar was the sarsanghchalak, the Sangh lobbied with Sardar Patel to have the ban lifted, with Sarkaryavah Bhaiyaji Dani (Prabhakar Balwant Dani) and Eknath Ranade maintaining communication with him and a few Congress leaders. At that time, Sardar Patel had invited the Sangh to join the Congress, but Nehru was against the idea and refused. At the turn of the seventies, when India won the war against Pakistan and helped in the formation of Bangladesh, the Sangh had openly praised Prime Minister Indira Gandhi. The Sangh congratulated the Congress on winning the election in 1971. At the Jana Sangh convention, a leader had referred to Indira Gandhi as Goddess Durga, and it is believed that the leader was Vajpayee. However, Vajpayee himself told me that he had never used the name Durga for Indira Gandhi.[27]

Eknath Ranade remained in contact with the Congress government during the Emergency. Sarsanghchalak Balasaheb Deoras had written three letters to Prime Minister Indira Gandhi, for which he received a lot of criticism internally. Deoras's speech in 1984, the consolidation of Hindu votes, Nanaji Deshmukh's statement about nationalist votes coming together for Rajiv Gandhi—all these were directed towards the Congress. Soon after, Rajiv Gandhi became prime minister, and Balasaheb made several demands on the government: the expulsion of illegal migrants, the return of Christian missionaries to their home countries, the replacement of the Minorities Commission with a Human Rights Commission and the removal of Article 370. The Rajiv Gandhi government did not accept any of those demands. On the contrary, in 1985–86, Rajiv Gandhi gave in to the pressure from hardliner Muslim groups by overturning the Supreme Court's landmark ruling in the *Shah Bano* case and enacting a new law. This blatant appeasement of Muslim clerics greatly upset the Hindu voters, and to placate them, acting on the advice of his aides, Rajiv ordered the unlocking of the Ram Janmabhoomi in 1986.

THE LANGUAGE OF THE SANGH

According to Prof Badrinarayan of Allahabad, the biggest strength of the RSS is its language. A leader of the Congress, realising the power of its language, once said that the echoes of the five-thousand-year history of India's diverse cultures can be heard in the language of the Sangh. He also said that if the Congress wants to become stronger than the Sangh, it would have to develop a language which has the imprint of India's past, present and future.[28]

By analysing sessions conducted under the Sangh's abhyas vargs, one can understand the origin, structure and strategy of this language. The impressive speeches delivered by Sangh swayamsevaks often include the powerful element of storytelling, through which they narrate their struggles, aspirations and goals. This storytelling echoes the rich oral heritage found in the Bhagwat Purana, Mahabharata and the Satyanarayan Katha. What the Sangh karyakartas convey through such stories has a fresh perspective. Golwalkar was influenced by Madan Mohan Malaviya, who said, 'Every village should have a sabha (convention), every sabha should have a story narration, every village should have a school, every village should have a mallashala (wrestling arena).' Storytelling was a crucial aspect of Golwalkar's vision for the Sangh's interface with society. Ancient and modern poetry are frequently cited in RSS discussions, which are often built around stories.

After Golwalkar became the sarsanghchalak, a scholar once asked him why he didn't publish any literature about the Sangh or its philosophy. Golwalkar replied, 'Ours is an oral tradition, that is, we move forward and progress by listening to stories. However, when it is time to convert divine or revealed knowledge (shruti) into human remembrance (smriti), we will certainly publish it.'[29]

It is often said that the teachers and pracharaks should teach and lead the swayamsevaks by example. Exemplary behaviour is a key feature of Sangh Shiksha vargs. The training encourages swayamsevaks to connect with fellow swayamsevaks and to cultivate positive family relationships. It is a well-known fact that in the present day, the Sangh is working to unite opposing ideologies. Leaders from diverse belief systems and worldviews are invited to programmes in Nagpur. This association with divergent and opposing belief systems is one reason there has been no criticism of Ambedkar's strong views on Hinduism within the Sangh philosophy. The Sangh officials invoke Ambedkar in some way or the other on every occasion, aiming to highlight a natural connection between Hinduism and Buddhism. In the recent past, Dalit communities have tried to project certain minor figures from Hindu mythology as their leaders, portraying them as victims of past injustices.[30] The Sangh is now highlighting such characters to uphold the self-esteem of the Dalits. Initiatives like Shabari temples, stories about Lord Hanuman among tribals and education in tribal villages reflect the propagation of such a narrative. It is also true that this association is not without its challenges; it's filled with complications and contradictions.

The deliberations of the Sangh also take place in the shakhas, but the influence of the thought process and ideology of the top echelons is evident in them. The conventions and deliberations are not spontaneous; they are held with clear goals, purposes and immediate needs in mind. In 2017, Bhopal hosted the All-India convention of the Karyakari Mandal, where Mohan Bhagwat inspired the pracharaks to take up the Matrubhasha Abhiyan (a campaign for the mother tongue). Under this campaign, the pracharaks would focus on primary education being imparted in the mother tongue or native languages.

However, the Sangh should ask these questions first: how would the pracharaks implement this? Who will listen to their suggestions? Why do parents send their children to expensive English-medium schools? Even the poorest in our country aspire to educate their children and see them succeed in good jobs. What is the most essential skill required to get a government job in India? The English language! Even if you are adept at every aspect of the job, you will not get it if you don't know English. The RSS is one of the two most important organisations in the country. Even then, why does a large population of Indians view it with suspicion? No one can call the Sangh Parivar an anti-national organisation, but much still needs to be done for it to align more closely with the mainstream of the country—and it is the Sangh itself that must chart its course.

Following the era of economic globalisation, a major transformation happened in the country, especially among middle-class Indians. Instead of encouraging their children to participate in social service, parents wanted them to focus on education and securing lucrative jobs. I term this the 'placement generation'; it's focused on gaining admission to top colleges for better job placement. At one time, our generation would eagerly take part in the Scouts, Guides, NCC and the NSS programmes after college and school hours. But the number of students opting for such activities has declined considerably, especially among the middle class. Today, young men and women from the economically weaker sections work towards social transformation within their communities. This is the section that is seen in the shakhas of the Sangh, which is why you may not see Sangh shakhas in posh localities of many cities, while their numbers have been rising in villages and underprivileged neighbourhoods. To better integrate the middle-and upper classes, the Sangh has now introduced profession-based shakhas and programmes. It has launched IT shakhas for the youth, allowing them to engage with the Sangh's activities through the internet. These participants discuss issues on online forums, stay involved and meet once a month or fortnight to take part in camps. The 'One Week for the Nation' campaign, launched in Vidarbha, has received an encouraging response. Additionally, Sangh officials are continually developing and implementing new ideas to expand their outreach.

Ratan Sharda disagrees about whether participation in the Sangh is on the decline. Over 20,000 new volunteers join the shiksha vargs annually. These karyakartas undergo a week-long training, and one out of every five volunteers passes the training and progresses to the first level of the shiksha varg. This translates into 1,00,000 karyakartas taking on Sangh responsibilities every year.

While talking to Govindacharya, I asked him casually, 'An official had told Guruji Golwalkar that now that the Sangh is expanding, it should focus on fundraising and construct an office building. Guruji had responded with a smile, saying that the Sangh didn't need funds or an office but needed karyakartas. But now that a majestic new building has been built to replace the old one in Jhandewalan in Delhi, does this statement mean anything?'

Govindacharya laughs aloud and says, 'Once, S. Gurumurthy had bought a new car in New Delhi. Guruji Golwalkar was supposed to visit Delhi, and Gurumurthy wanted Guruji to ride in it. So, Guruji arrived at Surya Narayan Rao's house with Gurumurthy in his new car. There was construction work happening at the old building at that time. As the car stopped in the portico, Rao and Gurumurthy were walking a few steps behind Guruji. Guruji had told Gurumurthy not to build a magnificent structure in front of the main door and the portico; otherwise, the ordinary swayamsevak would be intimidated and hesitant to enter.' Govindacharya adds, 'I don't know about the Sangh, but Gurumurthy took that message seriously.'

While talking about political leaders who ride in cars with beacons and alienate the common man, Govindacharya narrates yet another incident. After Mahatma Gandhi's assassination, Guruji was in Nagpur. There was public anger simmering against the Sangh. An angry crowd was moving towards the head office. A few strong swayamsevaks, along with officials like Bhaiyaji Dani and Moropant Pingle, formed a protective circle around Guruji with batons in their hands. Guruji asked all of them to move away. He said that he did not need any security, and if the crowd felt so, he was not afraid of sacrificing himself. Saying so, Guruji sat calmly, and the crowd dispersed peacefully.

Soon after I heard this story, I attended a major event at the Ambedkar Bhavan in Janpath, New Delhi. Just as I was trying to get some information about the programme from a swayamsevak, another swayamsevak pushed me aside because a convoy of cars with their sirens blaring was entering the premises. Black commandos were jumping out swiftly from their cars and forming a security cordon. Ironically, the discussion inside the hall was about social equality and bringing everyone together.

3

Hedgewar

Devoted to the Motherland

The country was on the path to independence. The atmosphere was rife with revolution, and the citizens needed a strong sense of purpose. As a result, many youngsters began attending wrestling akhadas. Shivram Guru's akhada in Nagpur was very popular among the nationalists. Hedgewar would frequently visit the akhada with his friends and that is where, in 1904, Dr Balakrishna Shivaram Moonje first noticed Hedgewar. At his house, Dr Moonje taught Hedgewar how to make bombs. Dr Moonje was a prominent follower of Bal Gangadhar Tilak. That was the beginning of the Tilak era in the Central Provinces.

In the early stages, instructors taught the youth that physical exercises were a form of worship to Lord Hanuman, also known as Maruti (even Shivaji's guru, Swami Samarth Ramdas, was a devotee of Lord Hanuman and had installed his idols in the mathas he had founded). Later swayamsevaks would take their oath before the saffron flag and photographs of Lord Maruti and Swami Samarth Ramdas. Dr Hedgewar was already associated with the Anusheelan Samiti in Bengal, where the revolutionaries pledged their commitment before an idol of Goddess Kali, with the Bhagwat Gita in one hand and a revolver in the other. Along with building physical strength, the Sangh strengthened its ideological and intellectual foundations. This focus shows in the organisation's emphasis on the traditional guru-shishya parampara (teacher-student relationship) and the integration of intellectual elements into the shakhas. In 1927, Dr Hedgewar led bauddhik (intellectual) sessions for new swayamsevaks, during which they discussed questions related to the nation, its history, and its leaders. Even today, the Sangh conducts intellectual growth sessions in its training camps (prashikshan shivirs) at the district level from time to time. Initially, Dr Hedgewar did not harbour any interest in becoming a guru. Even though he had agreed to be the sarsanghchalak in 1927, he wanted swayamsevaks to pledge their true allegiance towards the saffron flag. Even today, the swayamsevaks begin their daily shakhas by bowing to the flag.

Dilip Deodhar mentions that three or four years before his death, Dr Hedgewar had said along with a few senior leaders that there was a need for establishing an organisation at the national level, and until that happened, nothing could be done. Dr Hedgewar believed that if one per cent of India's population became swayamsevaks, then anything was possible. He said that a thousand years of torture had been inflicted upon them, but Hindus should learn from some of the qualities of the British and move ahead. Hedgewar used to say: God has given us an enemy like the British, who form merely one per cent of the world population and yet rule over the world; we must learn from them.

Deodhar continues, 'I once asked a great structural engineer, Mr Masai from Nagpur, how much RCC is used to construct buildings and how much steel and cement are needed to build RCC pillars. There were four or five pracharaks seated there. Masai said that one per cent steel should be used with the RCC for constructing buildings, and the steel must be rust-proof, free from carbon impurities and flexible.'[1] Deodhar draws a parallel between Masai's ideal pillar and Hedgewar's concept for nation-building. They needed to create a dedicated pool of 'one per cent' swayamsevaks—individuals of unwavering honesty and free from any 'carbon impurities'—a metaphor suggesting that they had to be principled and resistant to corruption that would settle like rust on their intentions. The expectation was that these swayamsevaks would be both strong as steel and flexible, able to adapt to change when needed. This demonstrates Hedgewar's early vision: to shape the Sangh as an organisation rooted in values and responsive to changing times.

Between 1916 and 1926, Hedgewar managed to create a massive army of karyakartas. Lokmanya Tilak was supposed to preside over the 1920 Nagpur session of the Congress, and Hedgewar, who had created a force of 1,200 volunteers, was made responsible for managing the massive event. The success of the session would establish that Hedgewar was a skilled organiser. Sadly, Tilak died that year, and Gandhi took over the reins, marking the beginning of the Gandhian era in the Congress.

Hedgewar and his associates accepted Gandhi as their leader and began working alongside him. In 1926, Hedgewar transformed this group of volunteers into the Sangh.

A former pracharak, K.N. Govindacharya, says that Dr Hedgewar was very enthusiastic about the freedom struggle, but once Guru Golwalkar took over the command, there was an ideological intensity in the system. Following Guruji's request, the organisation limited the involvement of pracharaks and swayamsevaks in politics from 1962 to 1967. The head teachers of shakhas could not conduct their baithak under any political banner. They could not leave their shakhas for any meetings, but they could assist with booth management. This rule was more or less in effect until 1972, when Deendayal Upadhyaya was permitted to fight the election. Later, a few leaders admitted that the decision was not correct.

The RSS drew inspiration from Europe's right-wing organisations, and it gave the workers similar military-style training. It is believed that members of the Sangh admired Adolf Hitler. Golwalkar, who succeeded Dr Hedgewar as sarsanghchalak, focused on the 'racial purity' of Hitler.[2]

Lokmanya Tilak first visited Nagpur in 1891. *Kesari* and *Maratha*, two of his newspapers, enjoyed widespread readership in the Central Provinces. When he visited Nagpur for the second time in 1902, Hedgewar came to listen to his speech. The reverberations of the Bengal Partition of 1905 had started to be felt in Nagpur. In the same year, Dr Moonje had formed the Vidyarthi Samaj, delegating the responsibility of galvanising students to Dr Hedgewar. The Tilak Paisa Fund was created to gather funds, and a young Keshav Baliram Hedgewar successfully collected significant amounts for it.

As a young man, Hedgewar played an active role in popularising Swadeshi (indigenous) goods during that period. To support this cause, the Arya Bandhav Veethika was established, with the revolutionary P.S. Khankhoje among its founders. Later, Hedgewar started the Deshbandhu Samaj, a revolutionary group working towards Indian independence. He joined an established branch of the Bandhav Samaj when he began studying at Nagpur's Neel City High School. It had two units—one public, and the other secret. Hedgewar, along with Khankhoje, led the secret branch, which was known as the Samarth Shivaji Samaj. Its primary aim was to gather arms and to unite the youth who shared a revolutionary mindset. The organisation's oath was administered in Marathi.

कारित्नो सन्मित्न को निश्चये
आपल्या पपुढ़े या पणा ।
अर्पणी देहास देशकार्यी मी
जे रुचे आपणा ।

(Oh, my friend! I take you as my witness, and vow that I will offer my body and soul in the service of my loving motherland.)

Dilip Deodhar describes how the British government intensified its subjugation of the people after the Bengal Partition, further fuelling the revolutionary spirit. A ban was imposed on student participation. In 1907, the government declared via the Risley Circular that raising slogans such as 'Vande Mataram' and 'Tilak Maharaj ki Jai' was a criminal offense. Protests against this circular began in Nagpur and the Central Provinces.

In 1907, government inspectors visited Neel City High School. As soon as one of the inspectors entered Hedgewar's class, the class chanted in unison, 'Vande Mataram'. Their echoes spread to other classrooms, enraging the inspectors, who left their tour midway. They wrote a letter to the chairman of the school management committee, Bipin Krishna Bose, demanding punishment for the guilty students. A furore ensued, following which Bose advised the students to seek an apology. To defuse the tension, he told them that while he sang 'Vande Mataram' at home, it was not permitted at school. The moment he finished speaking, the students defiantly chanted again, the action led by young Keshav Hedgewar. An angry Bipin Bose suspended the class, and as a sign of protest against the decision of the management committee, the students went on an indefinite strike, which lasted for around two months; their peers from Morris College in Nagpur joined them. After a prolonged mediation, the students tendered their apologies. All tendered their apologies except Hedgewar, who declared, 'If worshipping the motherland is a crime, then I will commit this "crime" not just once but repeatedly, and accept the punishment for it with pleasure.'[3]

During his school holidays, Keshav Hedgewar would visit his paternal uncle Abaji Hedgewar in Rampayli, a small village in Balaghat district, Madhya Pradesh. There he had a band of friends, and it was there that he once hurled a bomb at the local police post. It fell into a nearby pond and exploded. This incident occurred in 1908, and the lack of concrete evidence against him prevented a case from being filed. Two months later, at a Dussehra programme in the village where people had gathered for the Ravana dahan, Hedgewar delivered a revolutionary speech, comparing the burning of the demon king's effigy with the end of British subjugation. The crowd reverberated with the sounds of 'Vande Mataram'. School officials suspended two of Hedgewar's friends, and they tried Hedgewar under Section 108 for propagating seditious matters. The police arrested him in November. Although authorities eventually dropped the case against him, they prohibited him from speaking in Rampayli for a year. Following that, Hedgewar went to the Samarth Vidyalaya in Pune and passed the exam for the Amaravati Rashtriya Vidyalaya in 1909.

According to British government data of that time, there were 230 akahdas in Nagpur division in 1921, which more than doubled to 570 at the time of 1931 census. Small akhadas had mushroomed in every nook and corner, and Hedgewar made these akhadas his laboratory. Prior to starting the RSS, Dr Hedgewar had been a member of the Anusheelan Samiti in Calcutta. But he also infused a revolutionary fervour into the training programmes held at the shakhas, incorporated elements of Anusheelan Samiti's culture into the Sangh's sessions and began drills and stick martial arts, both key components of the Samiti's regimen. The officials were divided into several categories in the Samiti: paridarshak, sampadak and dalapati. Later in the Sangh, they came to be known as mandal pramukh, mukhya shikshak and gatnayak. At that time, every member had to carry his baton or stick. In the Anusheelan Samiti, the instruction for martial arts training happened in three phases: churika (knife), chhoti lathi (small stick) and badi lathi (long stick). The chhoti lathi, about 38 inches long, was for sword training. Stick martial arts training and yoga held such significance within the Samiti that, during a raid on its Dhaka office, the police discovered over 150 books dedicated to these subjects.

Generally, children at that time would go to other cities to study, where they would find some other work or get involved in some other activity, but in Hedgewar's case it was the opposite, studying was just an excuse. The real purpose behind his move in 1910 to Calcutta, the epicentre of revolutionary activities, was to connect with revolutionaries and prepare for the freedom struggle. Dr Moonje and his colleagues arranged for his admission to the National Medical College and his accommodation in a lodge. Their underlying agenda was to have him work under the guidance of freedom fighter Pulin Bihari Das and establish a revolutionary organisation. Nationalist leaders founded the National Medical College, which only permitted students from the National Council of Education because other government medical institutions barred them. Upon arriving in Calcutta, Hedgewar immediately joined the Anusheelan Samiti, a group formed in 1901 and recognised as the most structured revolutionary outfit in the city. Firebrand leaders such as Trailokyanath Chakravarty, Aurobindo Ghosh, Bipin Chandra Pal and Jogesh Chandra Chatterjee were associated with the body. Hedgewar quickly earned a place for himself and gained the trust of the members. During his student years, Hedgewar became intrinsically tied with the robust revolutionary activities of Bengal and served as a link between Bengal and the Central Provinces. He would transport hidden weapons back to Nagpur. Furthermore, he took part in the boycott of the 1911 Delhi Darbar and, later in 1914, he led a protest against the government's refusal to acknowledge degrees from the National Medical College of Calcutta. The sustained agitation ultimately compelled the government to reverse its decision in 1916.

In 1915, during World War I, the British Army rejected Hedgewar's application to join the medical corps, giving no reason. Hedgewar had planned to use his entry into the army to stage a protest inspired by the uprising of the First War of Independence in 1857. The British Army denied Hedgewar admission for two reasons. In 1914, the government's criminal intelligence office published a book called *Political Criminals of India*, a confidential volume listing names of political criminals with bomb-making expertise and affiliations to revolutionary organisations. This list included Keshav Hedgewar's name and contained all the different details of his being associated with the happenings at Neel City High School and the activities of the Anusheelan Samiti. This was the first reason for the rejection. The second was that the British administration did not recognise the degrees of native medical colleges. When Hedgewar had staged a protest against it, the government had changed the rule and allowed graduates from native institutions to join the services, only after appearing for a separate qualifying exam. Hedgewar had fought a long battle against that as well.

This was also a time when most leaders were directing their efforts towards ensuring Britain's success in the war. Tilak, Gandhi and their supporters were part of this group. They believed the British would grant India 'dominion status' after the war. However, by 1916, Hedgewar became active in galvanising the youth and created a group of 150 revolutionaries. He called it the Kranti Dal. Nanasaheb Talatule and Bhausaheb Talatule handled the training of these recruits.[4] To fund the outfit, they came up with an indigenous idea: organise lunches with wealthy and influential citizens, and use these social settings to discreetly raise funds.

Hedgewar greatly admired Tilak. He met him in Pune and stayed with him for a few days. Although Hedgewar's attempts at armed resistance did not bear fruit, he remained unwavering in his commitment to nationalism and refused to compromise on his ideals. He realised that the strength of small organisations was limited and wasn't enough to fight a long and serious battle against the Empire. He then collaborated with selected leaders of the Congress and set up the Rashtriya Mandal. Rashtriya Mandal started a revolt for the cause of poorna swaraj (complete self-rule) and published a magazine, *Sankalp*. They organised a celebration similar to Bal Gangadhar Tilak's Ganesh Utsav and called it the Rashtriya Mandal Utsav. They celebrated community festivals like Shivaji Maharaj Jayanti (Shivaji Maharaj's birth anniversary), Shastra puja (worshipping arms and weapons), Dussehra, Ganesh Chaturthi and Sankranti. Speeches and programmes on Hindu unity were common at these celebrations.

After the Jallianwala Bagh massacre in 1919, Hedgewar went to Amritsar for a special Congress convention. Thousands of innocents had lost their lives in this brutal massacre. After returning from Amritsar, he began preparing for the 1920 Nagpur session of the Congress, responsible for its organisation. However, Hedgewar found himself at odds with Gandhi's wish—he wanted Bal Gangadhar Tilak to preside over the session. Gandhi's declaration at the All India Khilafat Congress, announcing a non-cooperation movement unless the Muslim community's demands were met, was at the core of their disagreement. Gandhi felt this stance would encourage Muslims to join the broader national struggle alongside the Congress. Tilak, opposing Gandhi's proposal, believed that the Muslims should join the freedom struggle based on a shared goal of self-rule, not because of religious demands. Hedgewar expected a rise in communalism on religious lines. Senior journalist Nilanjan Mukhopadhyay says, 'Although Gandhi's tactics, which included penance and satyagraha, influenced Hedgewar at that time, he later felt that non-violent methods alone could not remove the British from India.'[5]

In those days, several Congress members, like Pandit Madan Mohan Malaviya, Dr B.S. Moonje and Dr Hedgewar, were also part of the Hindu Mahasabha. It was possibly because at that time the Congress, the Hindu Mahasabha and other such organisations were relatively small and needed each other's cooperation from time to time. Dr Moonje and Dr Hedgewar shared a relationship similar to that of a teacher and his student, and they often supported each other. In 1934, Dr Moonje had delivered a speech at a seminar held on fascism, and Dr Hedgewar had presided over the event. Both leaders felt that Hindus could achieve Swaraj only under a strong leadership akin to that of Shivaji Maharaj, Mussolini or Hitler. Dr Moonje planned to open a 'military' style school, but he was unsuccessful. Later, he started the Bhosale Military School under the Central Hindu Education Society in Nashik, where Hedgewar served as a member of the board.

Despite agreeing with Moonje on many issues, Hedgewar chose to follow his own path. For instance, he refused to be a part of the 1938–39 Civil Disobedience movement organised by the Hindu Mahasabha against the nizam of Hyderabad. By then, Savarkar had left prison and assumed leadership of the Mahasabha. In 1937, Savarkar started the Hindu Swayamsevak Dal and the Hindu Women Protection Group, followed by the Ram Sena in 1940. When Hedgewar returned to Nagpur in 1915 after completing his studies in Calcutta, his family felt their condition would improve because there was a massive need for doctors in Nagpur. Despite the pressure from his family and friends, he refused to marry. He wrote a letter to his paternal uncle Abaji Hedgewar, stating, 'It is true that Narayanrao, Vinayakrao Savarkar, Lokmanya Tilak, Mahatma Gandhi and other patriots have worked tirelessly for the nation [while being married men]. But my own constitution is different. I am not able to gather myself for a married life. I am conscious all the while, of my social and political responsibilities and cannot divide my heart, body and soul. I do not wish to make any woman wait endlessly for me at home after getting married, nor have any desire to engage myself in social pursuits after leaving emptiness at home. There is no conflict in my mind today. I am firm in my decision, which is in keeping with my nature.'[6]

Once, Balasaheb Deoras asked Dr Hedgewar why, despite being an ascetic, he did not don saffron robes? Hedgewar replied, 'In India, the problem with our society is that when we walk the path of bhakti or devotion, we leave everything to God's will and believe that He will take care of everything. If I start the work of the Sangh wearing saffron clothes, people will think that this is "God's work" and expect Him to do it, which means that people won't do it themselves. I believe that the work of the Sangh has to be done by swayamsevaks. The Congress leaders only give orders; they do nothing themselves.'[7]

When Deoras asked why Hedgewar did not want to get married, Hedgewar smiled and answered, 'I have faith in "brahmachari sanyas" or celibate renunciation, but I am not a sanyasi. There would be nothing better than being able to work for the Sangh while having a family. This will be more effective. I am a sanyasi. I do not want to be pretentious. If I become mentally free, I will certainly get married.'[8]

Many would approach Hedgewar with marriage proposals for pracharaks and swayamsevaks. Some would even offer their names, expressing a desire to marry once they were relieved of their responsibilities. They would often ask Hedgewar to suggest good matches. Hedgewar did not insist that the pracharaks remain unmarried for life. But when Golwalkar arrived, Deoras proposed another approach: he would send men to work for the Sangh as pracharaks, and later, once married, couples could work for the Sangh together. Hedgewar believed this approach would prevent trouble, and he devised a plan for its implementation. Guru Golwalkar replied, 'I am the sarsanghchalak, and it is my responsibility to work for the benefit of the Sangh and the country. I do not want married people. A householder will work only part time and will not be able to give his full attention. This will be detrimental to the Sangh, and I do not agree with the idea of marriage.'[9] However, Bhaiyaji Dani, as an 'exception', became a pracharak despite being married.

According to Aniruddha Deshpande, 'Dr Hedgewar would say that the Hindu society had everything, but it was extremely disorganised. And that is the reason it was colonised. Dr Hedgewar said that the key was Hindu culture, and we should build an organisation based on our roots. When Hedgewar and Madan Mohan Malaviya discussed this issue, Malaviya had said that Hindus were the majority in this country, and that is why this was a Hindu nation. But Hedgewar's counter was that it was not about the numbers. Even if there is one Hindu in the country, it will be considered a Hindu nation because our civilisation is rooted in philosophy. Otherwise, there is so much diversity in terms of attire, food, language and lifestyles, but cultural nationalism is a common thread.'[10]

Dr Hedgewar often emphasised that to unite Hindu society, it was essential to cultivate not only a shared ideology but also a disciplined work culture. This led to the establishment of the daily shakha model, where individuals would assemble in one place with a unified purpose. Under Guruji Golwalkar's guidance, discussions at the shakhas became more goal-oriented. Guruji went on to start many affiliated outfits addressing various social groups: the Akhil Bharatiya Vidyarthi Parishad for students and the Jana Sangh for political participation. These came up within just two years and were all established at the national level.

At the Nagpur session of the Congress, Hedgewar had made two proposals. He asserted that while India would achieve independence; it was equally crucial to discard British culture and promote everything Swadeshi. Historically, even earlier social reform movements headed by the Arya Samaj, Brahmo Samaj or the philosophy of Sri Aurobindo, had had the revival of Hindu society at their core.

Deshpande says, 'Organisations working in different areas form the core strength of the Sangh, and some people call them the Sangh Parivar. This term is no longer prevalent in the Sangh anymore. Instead of calling these organisations supplementary or subsidiary, it would be more appropriate to call them organisations working in different areas or fields. These not only have the autonomy to complete their tasks and achieve their goals, but they also enjoy financial freedom. But the common thread that runs through all of them is coordination.'[11]

When Dr Hedgewar established the Sangh, it was not the individual but the organisation that was considered above all else. So, when he joined the Jungle satyagraha, he resigned from the sarsanghchalak's post and handed over all his responsibilities to his friend, Dr Laxman Vasudev Paranjape. He resumed the position only after the satyagraha ended.

Savarkar's book, *Hindutva*, was published in Hindi in 1923. Even before its release, Bhaiyaji Dani and Vishwanathrao Kelkar had circulated it under the title *Maratha*. Savarkar's book was published in Nagpur, and Hedgewar facilitated its publication and dissemination. However, he did not entirely accept Savarkar's definition of the ideology. Savarkar believed a Hindu is not a Muslim, a Christian, a Jew, a Parsi or a follower of any other religion. Hedgewar had a broader understanding of Hindutva. According to him, every person living in India was a Hindu, just like a person living in America was an American. His commitment lay not with the word 'Hindu', but with the ethos and values of the 10,000-year-old Hindu tradition.

After returning to Nagpur from Calcutta, Hedgewar became a member of the Congress. When Dadabhai Naoroji invited Tilak to join the Congress, Hedgewar accompanied him. The Khilafat movement, which opposed the dethroning of the caliph of Turkey, was gaining momentum in India, and so was Gandhi's support for the cause.

Dr Hedgewar did not assent to the Khilafat movement and considered it Muslim appeasement. Nonetheless, he did not quit the Congress. During that period, the Central Provinces Congress was dominated by Tilak's followers: Dr Moonje, Dr Paranjape, N.B. Khare, Vishwanathrao Kelkar. This group was merged into the Rashtriya Mandal. Dr Hedgewar did not assent to the Mandal's view of Gandhi and his political behaviour. As a result, he created a breakaway faction called the Nagpur National Union, and several Mandal members joined him. In a letter Dr Hedgewar wrote to Dr Moonje, he said, 'Congressmen are good orators who impress people in the first meeting but their impact on people's minds vanishes in two or three days. They are busy in their pursuit for money and don't have time for public work.'[12]

The year 1920 was a formative one in the relationship between Congress and Hedgewar. The twentieth Congress session was supposed to be held in Nagpur, and Hedgewar was the head of the volunteer force. Previously, the 1907 session had been called off because of the possibility of a conflict between Tilak's supporters and the liberal faction. Now, the Congress prepared to fight, and the special session in Calcutta passed the proposal for the Non-cooperation movement in September.

Bal Gangadhar Tilak's passing on 1 August 1920, a few months earlier, cast a pall of gloom on the Nagpur session held in December 1920 as they prepared to mediate on who would become the next president of the Congress. Gandhi had become well-established in the country's politics. Hedgewar, being an ardent Tilak supporter, put forth Maharshi Aurobindo's name as the new president. The Nagpur National Union passed the proposal. Hedgewar was then the joint secretary of the Nagpur City Congress. Dr Hedgewar and Dr Moonje travelled to Pondicherry with the proposal, where Shri Aurobindo had been living since 1910 as a renunciate. Both leaders tried to persuade him to return to active politics and take up the presidency, but Maharshi Aurobindo refused. After returning from Pondicherry, Hedgewar asked people to write letters and send telegrams to Sri Aurobindo, requesting him to reconsider his decision. Finally, on 20 September 1920, they received his answer in a telegram: 'reconsidering is out of question.'[13]

C. Vijayaraghavachariar's name was proposed next for the post of Congress president. Hedgewar opposed him and proposed Shyam Sundar Chakravarty's name instead, but eventually Vijayaraghavachariar became the Congress president. Being a part of several committees,

Hedgewar found himself occupied with preparations for the session. Reports indicate that approximately 30,000 people attended the session; more than 20,000 were delegates.

Hedgewar presented two proposals in the session—one asking that the object of the Congress should be to establish Indian Republic and liberate the nations of the world from the tyranny of capitalist exploitation and the other opposing cow slaughter—but the session disregarded them. He referred to the Khilafat movement as the 'Akhil Aafat' movement, loosely translating to 'All India Problems' movement. Shivaji Maharaj, who fought against the Mughals, was Hedgewar's childhood hero. Because of the Mughal rule, his family had had to leave their village Nizamabad and move to Nagpur. This may be the reason he was never entirely comfortable with the Muslim community.

Later, Hedgewar became a member of the Tilak Swarajya Fund of the Central Provinces in April 1921 and joined the Nagpur District Congress in May.

Gandhi's Non-cooperation movement had already begun, but the Swarajya Party held influence in the Central Provinces, where many people raised objections against the movement. Dr Moonje had also expressed his reservations about it, and many believed that Gandhi aimed to expand the movement through a policy of Muslim appeasement. Gandhi himself had also previously supported the Khilafat movement. Although Hedgewar opposed the Khilafat movement, he supported Gandhi's Non-cooperation movement. Hedgewar established a Non-cooperation Movement Samiti (committee) in the Marathi-speaking Central Provinces. Its purpose was to prepare workers for the movement in every way. Hundreds of youths joined the samiti and organised demonstrations and programmes that gave momentum to the movement. During this time, Hedgewar also led campaigns for prohibition. That the government filed sedition cases against twenty-five people between January 1921 and June 1922 demonstrates the success of the Non-cooperation movement in the Central Provinces and

Nagpur. Courts sentenced eleven of them to rigorous imprisonment, two to simple imprisonment, and two to special detention. They tried Hedgewar for a seditious speech he had delivered in May 1921. Indian independence was of utmost importance for Hedgewar. In 1921, when the provincial Congress Working Committee, under the presidency of Loknayak Bapuji Aney, planned to table a censure motion against the revolutionary movement for freedom, Dr Hedgewar played a vital role in stalling it. The committee ultimately withdrew the motion. Hedgewar could not tolerate criticism of the freedom fighters and revolutionaries, often stating that while one might disagree with their methods, it would be a crime to question their patriotism.

In the Nagpur court, Justice Siraj Ahmed started the hearing of the sedition case. The court set the next date for 13 June and then transferred the case to Justice Smelly's court. A prominent lawyer from Nagpur was initially representing Hedgewar, but when the judge began objecting to nearly every statement, he withdrew from the case. Hedgewar then decided to fight the case himself.

Hedgewar had never been a law student, but he began his defence by calling the judge unworthy and unsuitable. Subsequently, he appealed to District Magistrate Erwin to replace Justice Smelly. This was a unique situation where a British judge was being deemed unsuitable to hear the case of an Indian, and an appeal was being made for his replacement. Once Dr Hedgewar had concluded his arguments, the decision was supposed to be pronounced on 19 August. An enormous crowd had gathered around the court. Justice Smelly, commenting on Dr Hedgewar's arguments, said, 'His statements are far more seditious than his original speech.' Pronouncing his judgement, he said, 'Your speeches are seditious, and that is the reason you will not make any such speeches for a year. You must pay two bail amounts of ₹1000 each and ₹1000 as a legal bond with an assurance that you accept the court's conditions.'[14]

Dr Hedgewar responded to the ruling, saying, 'You may give whatever ruling you wish. I am innocent. My conscience says that I am not guilty ... I believe that there will be a time very soon when the British will have to repent for their mistake.' The judge sentenced Hedgewar to one year of rigorous imprisonment. When Hedgewar left the court, senior leaders of the Congress were there to welcome him. After Hedgewar had addressed the crowd outside the court, officials took him to Nagpur's Ajni jail. Four other revolutionaries were undergoing rigorous imprisonment along with him: Raghunath Ramachandra Pathak, Pandit Radhamohan Gokul, Veer Harkare and Inamullah Khan. On 13 April 1922, Hedgewar celebrated Jallianwala Bagh Day in prison.

On 11 July 1922, when Dr Hedgewar completed his sentence and walked out of prison, many Congress leaders and hundreds of people were present to receive him in pouring rain. The next day, organisers held a special welcome ceremony at Chitnis Park, but because of the heavy rains, they moved the programme to Venkatesh Theatre. Pandit Motilal Nehru, Rajagopalachari, Hakeem Ajmal Khan and Vitthalbhai Patel were present at the ceremony.

A lot had changed during Hedgewar's year-long imprisonment. On 5 February 1922, the revolutionaries had resorted to the path of violence in Chauri Chaura, a part of the United Provinces of Agra and Oudh. In response, Mahatma Gandhi stopped his Non-cooperation movement on 12 February 1922. The decision disappointed the revolutionaries, but Gandhi remained steadfast. On the other hand, discussions were underway regarding the Congress's participation in the State Legislative Council elections. A faction led by Chittaranjan Das, Dr Moonje, Vamanrao Joshi and Motilal Nehru viewed Gandhi's policies as impractical and were in favour of fighting the elections, while Hedgewar, reflecting a more radical nationalist view, opposed cooperating with British institutions by contesting elections.

In November 1929, all RSS sanghchalaks held a meeting in Nagpur to take decisions on the organisation's role and contribution in light of the rapidly changing political situation. This meeting went on for three days, during which the RSS decided to unconditionally support the Congress in the freedom struggle. At the time, there were thirty-seven functioning shakhas and nearly 2,000 swayamsevaks in the Sangh, including 700 youngsters. Even though a majority believed that adopting the saffron flag and the Sangh uniform would help establish the Sangh's identity, Dr Hedgewar, encouraging harmonious coexistence, said, 'Swayamsevaks are free to participate in the freedom movement with the sanghchalak's permission.'[15] Dr Hedgewar desired to unite the freedom struggle under a single platform, under one flag, one banner and one programme.

In the Lahore session of the Congress, the All-India Congress Committee was authorised to launch the freedom movement. In February 1930, at the Sabarmati meeting, Gandhi was chosen to lead the movement. Subsequently, on 30 April 1930, he started the Civil Disobedience movement in Gujarat by breaking the oppressive British Salt Laws at Dandi. This was followed by satyagrahas and protests against several other laws across the country.

A vast number of swayamsevaks were present at the special guru dakshina ceremony held in Nagpur on 12 July 1930, where Dr Paranjape announced Hedgewar's participation in the Jungle satyagraha. Those who were interested could join him, while others could continue with the organisation. At the end of the programme, Dr Hedgewar said, 'After I complete my speech, I will no longer be the sarsanghchalak. Dr Paranjape has agreed to take up the functioning of the Sangh. I thank him for this on behalf of the Sangh. We are taking part in this movement on a personal level, and there has been no change in the ideology or work culture of the Sangh. To make use of every movement that takes place in the country for one's own purpose is the duty of every organisation that is working towards making India independent.'

Thus, he ensured the Sangh's survival during the freedom struggle and prevented factionalism from taking root. After his speech, the sarsenapati of the Sangh, Martandrao Jog, felicitated Dr Hedgewar and the swayamsevaks accompanying him. On 14 July, a group of satyagrahis departed from Nagpur, and hundreds of people saw them off at the railway station.

In 1930, when the 'salt' satyagraha was going on in various parts of the nation, in Vidharbha, a 'jungle' satyagraha was launched due to the absence of a seacoast there. Dr Hedgewar, as a Congress leader, was jailed for a year after a case of sedition was filed against him. However, by then, he had already decided to start an only Hindu organisation. On 21 July, he and his group broke the Forest Laws near Yavatmal, for which he was arrested and put on trial. He received a sentence of nine months' rigorous imprisonment and three months' simple imprisonment. Additionally, the court sentenced eleven co-satyagrahis to simple detention. People brought the grass Dr Hedgewar had cut to break the oppressive Forest Laws to Nagpur and an offering of the grass was made in front of the flag..

This was Hedgewar's second stint in prison. Prison authorities kept him in solitary confinement in a 'B' category prison, while they held his colleagues in a 'C' category one. He remained in a hundred-foot-long and thirty-foot-wide room for seven days. Hedgewar was in prison when he received the news of Dr Moonje's decision to attend the Round Table Conference in London. Not only did he disapprove, but he remained sceptical of the mention of Muslim separatism in the same conference.

Dilip Deodhar says one incident particularly hurt Hedgewar. Soon after his release from prison, a senior Sangh leader, Balasaheb Huddar, took part in a political heist (dacoity) in Balaghat, leading to his rearrest in January 1931. Hedgewar suggested to Dr Paranjape that Balasaheb be relieved of his post in the Sangh. Upon his release from prison on 14 February 1931, Hedgewar arrived in Nagpur on 17 February, where a grand procession greeted him. Following this, Dr Paranjape duly handed over the tasks of the Sangh to him. Dr Hedgewar then visited Bombay, followed by Banaras, where he opened two shakhas. He met many senior leaders, including Pandit Malaviya, who offered him land on the Banaras Hindu University premises for the Sangh. However, the most important meeting of the visit was with Madhav Sadashiv Golwalkar, who was then pursuing his MSc and teaching at the university. It was Golwalkar who later took the Sangh to great heights.

The RSS's work and performance had a deep impact on V.D. Savarkar's younger brother, Ganesh Damodar Savarkar. He was popularly called Babarao. Babarao used to run the Tarun Hindu Mahasabha in 1922; his organisation merged with the RSS in 1931. Most leaders of the Mahasabha considered the Sangh as their sister organisation; the Sangh too benefited from this merger, and it was able to expand its presence in the Vidarbha and Chhattisgarh regions.

Bhai Parmanand, the leader of the Arya Samaj movement, organised the All-India Youth Congress in Karachi in 1932 and asked Babarao Savarkar to bring along Dr Hedgewar. Hedgewar's participation in the Congress helped the RSS gain recognition at a national level. Later, Babarao assisted Hedgewar in starting a Sangh shakha in Delhi and even invited him to Bombay and other areas of Maharashtra. On his tour of Maharashtra, a young man had accompanied Dr Hedgewar—Nathuram Godse.

The number of Sangh shakhas had risen to 125 between 1931 and 1933, and there were about 12,000 swayamsevaks. By the time of Hedgewar's death in 1940, this figure had reached 700, with 60,000 swayamsevaks in total. The rapid growth of the RSS attracted attention from the British, who suspected the organisation was connected with the freedom movement. But with no conclusive evidence against the Sangh, they were unable to take any further action. The British government imposed a ban on their employees joining the RSS, and when Hedgewar opposed their decision, they revoked it.

By then, Hedgewar's health was rapidly deteriorating. Despite that, he continued to expand the Sangh outside Maharashtra. During his tenure, he established Sangh shakhas in Delhi, Lucknow, Patna, Rawalpindi, Sialkot, and Lahore in the Punjab, Calcutta in the East, and Karnataka and Madras in the South. Hedgewar's refusal to transform the Sangh into a political platform or take part in elections after 1935 disappointed several swayamsevaks. The reason, however, was that the Sangh lacked a popular and charismatic leader at that time. This changed when V.D. Savarkar was released from prison.

When the swayamsevaks insisted on joining the protest against the nizam of Hyderabad, Hedgewar made it abundantly clear that the Sangh would not be a part of any political activities. Later, when Sarkaryavah Bhaiyaji Dani supported the cause, Hedgewar not only expressed his displeasure, but he also refused to include Bhaiyaji Dani in the brainstorming at the RSS's session held in Sindi in 1939.

Owing to his failing health, Dr Hedgewar decided to choose his successor. The primary agenda of the 1939 brainstorming session was to find a successor. This was probably the last session where Hedgewar, Golwalkar and Deoras sat together for several days. The decision was made to reiterate that the Sangh and its leaders must refrain from political activities and concentrate on the swayamsevaks and their daily shakhas. However, the swayamsevaks were allowed to engage in political activities in their personal capacity.

RASHTRIYA SWAYAMSEVAK SANGH

Nineteenth-century social and cultural movements, aiming to organise society, spurred the dawn of social awakening in the country. Institutions like Raja Ram Mohan Roy's Brahmo Samaj in 1828, Swami Dayanand's Arya Samaj in 1875 and Swami Vivekananda's Ramakrishna Mission worked ceaselessly towards inculcating social awareness, combating social evils and strengthening national consciousness. There was no conflict between personal religion and national duty.

Several factors contributed to the rising need for a Hindu organisation. Of particular concern were the formation of the Muslim League in 1906, the support of its interests by the British and the appeasement politics of the Congress. There had been a long history of Hindu–

Muslim riots in Nagpur—with extensive rioting happening in 1903–04 and again in 1914. By the time Dr Hedgewar was released after his first stint in jail, the Hindu–Muslim issue had gained prominence along with the freedom struggle. News about communal tension and riots came from other parts of the country, especially from the Malabar region of Kerala, where tension had increased between Hindu zamindars and Muslim farmers, with the British Army lending its support to the latter. These tensions culminated in the Moplah rebellion in 1921, the news of which Hedgewar had learnt while still in prison. After the revolt, an inquiry committee was deputed to Malabar from Nagpur under Dr Moonje's leadership. This committee brought out a report detailing the atrocities committed against the Hindus and stressed the idea of Hindu unity on religious grounds. Following the Non-cooperation movement, opposition against the Muslim League intensified, and the role of the Hindu Mahasabha came to the forefront at the Gaya Convention in 1922.

Before the findings of the Nagpur Commission were made public, Dr Moonje confided in Hedgewar that the Moplah revolt, possibly the biggest attack by Muslims on the Hindus after the Mughal rule, was not an issue related to land or farming but forced religious conversion or proselytisation.[16] In response, the Arya Samaj announced 'shuddhi aur sangathan' (purification and consolidation). Swami Shraddhanand founded the Bharatiya Hindu Shuddhi Sabha. According to Hedgewar, the solution was to bring about Hindu unity and overcome social divisions within the community. Before Swami Shraddhanand's 'ghar wapasi programme', Hedgewar reverted to Hinduism those who had been forcibly converted to Christianity while in the care of Christian missionaries. Hedgewar believed that bringing such individuals back to Hinduism was simply restoring their Hindu identity. He used to say that while modes of worship were different, the national duty of every individual was the same, and all were children of the same motherland.

However, this view led to a difference of opinion with Savarkar, who did not accept Muslims and Christians as part of the Hindu fold.

The Akhil Bharatiya Hindu Mahasabha was founded in 1915 with the former ruler of Nagpur, Raja Lakshman Rao Bhosale, as its president, Dr Moonje as vice president, and Hedgewar as the secretary. In 1924, communal riots again shook Nagpur, but this time Hedgewar led the rescue of Hindus from Muslim settlements. After the riots, Hedgewar felt the need for a stronger organisation to unite Hindus. That was when the Maharashtra Vyayamshala, the Shiksha Prasarak Mandal (Committee for the Promotion of Education) and a band of karyakartas called the Rashtriya Swayamsevak Mandal were set up. A few years prior to this, Dr Moonje had set up the Club Rifle Association to impart weapon training to Hindus—Dr Hedgewar reactivated the body. His belief that Indianism cannot progress while the Hindu nation remains weak only grew stronger with time. However, Dr Moonje did not agree with this idea.

During this time, Vinayak Damodar Savarkar, who was fast gaining popularity as a fiery national leader, entered the arena of Hinduism. Even stalwarts such as Vallabhbhai Patel had demanded his release in the Bombay Vidwan Parishad. In the meeting of the Nagpur Congress on 14 October 1923, Hedgewar had raised his voice to support Savarkar. A few days later, Hedgewar started a daily called *Swatantra* and demanded full independence.

Savarkar's 1923 book, *Hindutva: Who Is a Hindu*, presented a road map to bring this plan into fruition. Madan Mohan Malaviya, Bhai Parmanand, Dr Moonje, Savarkar, Swami Shraddhanand and Lala Lajpat Rai joined the cause, each deeply committed to its fulfilment. Right from the establishment of the Sangh, Hedgewar had emphasised creating an organisation based on Hindu nationalism and strengthening it. Moreover, the RSS had begun to take shape in his mind, but he desired a new outfit that followed neither the Hindu Mahasabha nor the

Congress. In March 1922, upon Savarkar's release on parole, Hedgewar went to Ratnagiri to seek his advice.

Dr Hedgewar had said during the establishment of the Sangh, 'There are 25 crore Hindus in our Hindustan today. Where did the total population of 35 crores come from? The 10 crores were at some time amongst us only.' Dr Hedgewar questioned, 'Why did we lose them? We were in a deep slumber, and that is why they left us?'[17]

He did not permit the Hindu nationalists' definition of being a Hindu and a Hindu nation to permeate the Sangh's foundational principles. Dr Hedgewar said, 'Please understand clearly that the Sangh is not a fitness or physical training centre, a club or a military school. The Sangh is a nationalist organisation of the Hindus, which has to be stronger than steel.'

Most Sangh leaders, including Dr Hedgewar, maintained a distance from Savarkar; he, too, never joined the Sangh, and neither did the Sangh merge with the Hindu Mahasabha. While they kept a distance from Savarkar's definition of Hindutva, it would be interesting to know what Atal Bihari Vajpayee thought about Savarkar. It was during his prime ministership that Vajpayee proposed conferring Savarkar with the Bharat Ratna, which President K.R. Narayanan did not accept. At an event of the Veer Savarkar Darshan Pratishthan in Maharashtra, Vajpayee spoke effusively about Savarkar, demonstrating how close he held the Hindutva principle to his heart. He said, 'Savarkar means speed, sacrifice, penance, ideal, logic, youth, sword, agitation ... like he says "*Sagar pran tadamala*" in Marathi, which means "a restless soul". Forbearing, spicy and sharp ... such was the multifaceted personality of Savarkar. Poetry and revolution. My first introduction to Savarkar was in the form of poetry ... I had heard about *kavita aur bhranti* (poetry and delusion), but *kavita aur kranti* (poetry and revolution) ... Poetry means imagination, creating a world of words, flying high, and even if one loses touch with the earth, breaks away from reality, there are no complaints. But Savarkar never lost touch with the ground. He possessed both height and depth.'[18]

Vajpayee added, 'I have seen that cell in the Cellular Jail in the Andaman Islands. There was security inside and outside the cell. Savarkar had to pass an important part of his life dying and being tortured every single moment, yet he said he wouldn't accept subjugation.'[19] Vajpayee, who had translated some of Savarkar's poems into Hindi, was surprised at the way Savarkar could maintain a balance between imagination and reality.

In Nagpur, on 9 and 10 November 1929, swayamsevaks held a two-day meeting, where wide-ranging discussions on the Sangh's stance on the Congress's future programmes, its policies and organisation took place. That meeting also resolved to centralise the Sangh's operations, making it function like a family where all members contribute equally and voluntarily to shared objectives under capable leadership. That's how the sarsanghchalak's post came into being. Vishwanathrao Kelkar, Tatyaji Kalikar, Appaji Joshi, Bapurao Muthal, Babasaheb Kolte, Balaji Huddar, Krishnarao Mohrir, Martandrao Jog and Devaikar attended the meeting, but Hedgewar was absent.

On the last day of the meeting, there was a huge assembly of swayamsevaks where Appaji Joshi gave a command before announcing the decision made at the meeting. He loudly commanded, '*Sarsanghchalak pranam. Ek, do, teen* (Greetings to the sarsanghchalak. One, two, three),' and the swayamsevaks greeted Dr Hedgewar as the sarsanghchalak. The situation surprised Dr Hedgewar. After the programme, he said to Appaji Joshi, 'I do not like the fact that I accept the greetings of my respected seniors who sacrificed everything for the country.'[20] Appaji replied that this was a unanimous decision of the Sangh, and you will have to accept it even if you are unhappy.

Under the sarsanghchalak, two more important positions, sarkaryavah (secretary) and sarsenapati, came into existence. Additionally, two key high-level bodies—the Akhil Bharatiya Pratinidhi Sabha and the Akhil Bharatiya Karyakari Mandal—were created by the Sangh to determine its programmes and policies. Dr Hedgewar sought the counsel of prominent members, and in 1940, appointed Golwalkar as his successor. From that point forward, the outgoing sarsanghchalak has been choosing his successor.

Dr Hedgewar had already spent time with revolutionaries in Bengal and witnessed the strategies of satyagraha and constitutional reforms during his time in the Congress. However, he thought that neither approach had succeeded in securing India's freedom or in sparking a true national awakening. From a young age, he had pondered the reason for India's repeated failures in resisting foreign invaders. He concluded that freedom and national rejuvenation would remain a far-off dream unless the nation identified and addressed the root causes of its weakness. Dr Hedgewar realised the problem was fundamentally scientific, requiring internal transformation to awaken national consciousness and foster social unity. He envisioned a body of volunteers committed to nation-building, and that establishing and sustaining a movement to revitalise the country would be possible. Guided by this vision, he launched a campaign on Vijayadashami in September 1925. One would remember that it was on the same occasion that the British administration had punished Hedgewar for singing the 'Vande Mataram' in Rampayali. Hedgewar, with the advice and counsel of twenty-five special invitees, founded a new organisation and a new work culture in Nagpur. Prominent visitors like Balaji Huddar, Bhauji Kavre, Anna Sohoni, Vishwanathrao Kelkar and Bapurao Bhedi were present at the meeting. Most were Hedgewar's childhood friends or revolutionaries.

In the initial days, the swayamsevaks came from the Brahmin localities of Nagpur. This first batch had neither a name nor a detailed plan for its activities. For five days a week, the swayamsevaks went to an akhada and attended classes on politics on Thursdays and Fridays.

The Sangh got an opportunity to prove its organisational strength and assess its readiness when the Hindu–Muslim riots broke out again in Nagpur in September 1927. This came shortly after the assassination of Swami Shraddhanand in December 1926. At that time, the swayamsevaks received training in the use of sticks, swords and knives. To test the Sangh's capabilities in a crisis, Hedgewar directed his colleagues to form sixteen groups and deploy them to neighbourhoods where the Hindus were in a minority. The 'operation' was highly successful, with the teams effectively protecting Hindu families. Following this success, the Hindu Mahasabha invited the RSS karyakartas in full uniform to their national convention in Ahmedabad in December 1927. There, Dr Moonje praised the Sangh's work.

At that time, Dr Hedgewar was a member of both the Sangh and the Congress. He even went to Calcutta in 1928 to participate in the Congress's national convention as a member of its working committee. He met Subhas Chandra Bose, who was the mayor of Calcutta then, and appealed to the leader to support the RSS. However, Bose declined because of his other pressing responsibilities.

Veteran journalist Ram Bahadur Rai observes, 'Dr Hedgewar was an excellent product of the freedom struggle, and the idea of establishing the Rashtriya Swayamsevak Sangh struck him at a vital turning point during the struggle. He had keenly observed the policies and principles of the Congress and found them frightening. The Congress that Dr Hedgewar had come from was on the path of Muslim appeasement, the result of which was the Partition of India. There are very few people who dare to wager their entire life on a new experiment, and it demands a great deal of purpose and resolve. His decision was in line with his personality.'[21]

Dr Hedgewar and industrialist Jugal Kishore Birla had a close relationship. Unfortunately, by the time Birla was prepared to purchase the campground of the Sangh and donate it to the organisation, Hedgewar had died. Sometime later, an official from the Birla company came to meet Guruji. Guruji informed him of Hedgewar's passing. When the official conveyed Mr Birla's intention to donate land, Guruji responded that such a discussion must have taken place between Hedgewar and Mr Birla. He then asked the official to tell Mr Birla that if he wished to donate the land, he should come in person and do so while standing under the saffron flag. After this, neither Mr Birla nor the official returned.

The meetings between the Congress and the Sangh took place at Hedgewar's residence. There is a swing in Hedgewar's house on which he would sit and hold discussions with his team. That swing exists even to this day.

In the beginning, only twelve people came to listen to Dr Hedgewar. Gradually, the Sangh widened its presence. Even though the lane going to Dr Hedgewar's house was narrow, it had illuminated a new path. Initially, Hedgewar conducted the shakhas himself, which were followed by a few others taking charge in Nagpur. Soon enough, the organisation spread to Pune, Yavatmal, Nashik and Central India.

A significant milestone in the RSS's growth came in 1930, when Hedgewar went to Banaras. There, Pandit Madan Mohan Malaviya offered him a space within the Banaras Hindu University campus to open a Sangh office. Rakesh Sinha highlights a key remark Malaviya made after this meeting—one that carries relevance for all organisations. Malaviya observed that while other organisations possess grand buildings and offices but lack dedicated volunteers, the RSS has an abundance of human resources but no infrastructure.

According to Ramesh Shiledar, 'Dr Hedgewar understood that the system needed to run an organisation in the long term, and that is the reason the Sangh is about to complete its centenary and is still expanding.'[22] Dr Hedgewar focused on three aspects. First, the outfit should be self-sufficient and independent, especially financially. Several people, including Malaviya, had proposed providing financial aid for the Sangh, but Hedgewar refused. He spoke of Bhishma Pitamaha from the Bhagavad Gita:

> अर्थस्य पुरुषो दासो दासस्त्वार्थो न कस्यचित् ।
> इति सत्यं महाराज बद्धोऽस्म्यर्थेन कौरवैः ॥
>
> (If we look at dharma and justice, we should not help the Kauravas, but the Kauravas have bound us with wealth, and that is why we are helpless, because man is a slave to money while money is no one's slave.)

Scholars believe the Mahabharata war was fought towards the end of the Dwapara Yuga, after the three stages of dharma (righteous living) broke down and materialism replaced spiritualism. Eminent figures like Bhishma, Vidura and Dronacharya found refuge with the Kauravas. During the episode of Draupadi's disrobing, she presented compelling arguments rooted in principle and ethics. Yet, the scholars of dharma remained silent, unable to raise their voices against Duryodhana's injustice because of their dependence on him and their financial subjugation.

Ramesh Shiledar notes that the second of Dr Hedgewar's most impactful contributions was establishing the daily shakha. The third major contribution made by Dr Hedgewar was that the pracharaks would live like regular citizens, with no distinctive attire of saffron robes typically associated with saints. This choice bridged the gap between pracharaks and the common people, making the Sangh's message more accessible and relatable—an approach that eventually benefited the organisation in the long run.

Shiledar considers Dr Hedgewar and Guru Golwalkar to be the 'epoch-makers'. He described Dr Hedgewar as a patriot by birth, just as Ramakrishna Paramahamsa or Swami Vivekananda were yogis by birth. Shiledar mentions that his father, Trimbak Rao Shiledar, was twenty-three or twenty-four years old when he met Dr Hedgewar during the time of the Second World War. Hedgewar told him that the British were in trouble, but the Sangh's functioning had not grown to such a level that they could exploit the situation and force the British to leave India.

In those days, the different groups were called pathaks, and each pathak had a different name, like Ram Pathak and Prahlad Pathak. One of the pathaks, Kush Pathak, had stalwarts like Guru Golwalkar, Balasaheb Deoras, Nanaji Deshmukh, Eknath Ranade, Bal Apte, among others. Trimbak Rao Shiledar was also a member of the same pathak.

Though Dr Hedgewar did not consider anyone as his guru or mentor, he enjoyed strong relationships with people from different ideologies. This included Dr Moonje, Savarkar and Gandhi. He would occasionally invite them to address the swayamsevaks. Dr Moonje and Savarkar were never members of the Sangh; the former was not even present at the first meeting when the organisation was established. In 1933, Dr Hedgewar assisted Savarkar's month-long tour of Vidarbha and made sure that it was a success. However, Hedgewar always ensured that influential personas did not influence the decisions of the Sangh. All decisions were made after thorough discussions with swayamsevaks.

The Sangh's image is that of a high-caste organisation dominated by Chitpavan Brahmins from Maharashtra. Hedgewar and Balasaheb Deoras were Telugu Brahmins. Guruji Golwalkar belonged to the Karade Brahmin community, and so does Mohan Bhagwat. Only Dr Paranjape was a Chitpavan Konkanastha Brahmin from Maharashtra. He was acting sarsanghchalak for ten months when Hedgewar was in prison. Lokmanya Tilak and Vinoba Bhave were Chitpavan Brahmins, while K.S. Sudarshan was a Kannada Brahmin.

Dr Hedgewar's ancestors came from a village in Telangana and worked as priests in the district of Nizamabad. At the beginning of the nineteenth century, these landless Brahmin families had to leave their village and come to Maharashtra. They settled near Nagpur city, an area that was under the Maratha Bhosale rulers. The strong tradition of Vedic education and Hindu rituals of the Brahmin society influenced Keshav Hedgewar, the youngest in his family. However, Mahadev, Keshav's eldest brother, preferred bodybuilding and weightlifting. Eventually, Keshav found himself drawn to such physical pursuits as well. Keshav was also interested in academics and enjoyed reading biographies of eminent men and books on religion and spirituality. Right from his childhood, he admired Chhatrapati Shivaji's patriotism.

Dilip Deodhar notes that when Dr Hedgewar started the shakhas, Balasaheb and Bhaurao Deoras began attending them at a young age. They lived in Nagpur's Itvari locality, about a kilometre away from the Sangh office. Dr Hedgewar was extremely fond of Balasaheb and took charge of his training. Whenever Balasaheb would come to the shakha, he would pay special attention to the modules on military training, affectionately reprimanding the young men who made mistakes during the march-past and the drills. When Guru Golwalkar became the sarsanghchalak, he would often mention in the programmes and the shakhas that those who hadn't met Hedgewar should go meet Balasaheb.

In 1940, Balasaheb had told Hedgewar that he wished to visit Calcutta as a pracharak. Dr Hedgewar had told him, 'It was your dream to be an IAS officer, why do you want to be a pracharak? If you do that, your dream will be shattered.' Balasaheb said that becoming an IAS officer had been his dream before he joined the RSS, but he had since abandoned it and now wanted to dedicate himself to the role of a pracharak. Then, Hedgewar suggested, 'You first become an IAS officer and reach a high position in the British system ... then you can do whatever the Sangh asks you to.' Balasaheb thought for a couple of minutes and then requested Hedgewar not to send him away from the Sangh, as he could not promise that he would be able to follow the RSS's commands once he joined the IAS.[23]

Most in the Sangh expected Balasaheb Deoras to be named as Dr Hedgewar's successor because of his longstanding association with the organisation. He was also Dr Hedgewar's favourite. But surprisingly, the position went to Madhav Sadashiv Golwalkar. The decision triggered a lot of discussion. Dilip Deodhar says that in 1940, Dr Hedgewar's health was in a critical state, and the doctors considered performing a 'lumbar puncture'—a procedure which could be life-altering but could also potentially fatal. Dr Hedgewar then called in Guru Golwalkar and Balasaheb Deoras; apart from this two-three other people including Nagpur Sanghchalak Balasaheb Ghatate were also present. N.S. Ghatate, Balasaheb Ghatate's son says that Akola was where they decided on the new sarsanghchalak. Dr Hedgewar said, 'Though I am very fond of Balasaheb, he lacks experience at the moment. Guruji, you have been a sarkaryavah, and that is why you will take up the responsibility of the sarsanghchalak.'

Dr Hedgewar asked Balasaheb Deoras, who had been asked to come from Calcutta, to continue to live in Nagpur. He told Golwalkar to assume complete responsibility of the Sangh and the shakhas until the organisation became a national entity. He should not engage in anything beyond his duty. He also asked Golwalkar to prepare Balasaheb Deoras to take over after him.

Then, Golwalkar stated his first condition: 'If I feel like becoming a sanyasi, I will leave everything and go away to the Himalayas, and Balasaheb will have to handle this responsibility. You need to give me a guarantee for this.' Once Dr Hedgewar agreed, Golwalkar put forward a second condition—as long as he remained the Sangh's sarsanghchalak, Balasaheb Deoras would have to adhere to his orders. The air in the room became tense for a few moments. Balasaheb paused for a while before accepting Golwalkar's condition.

Dr Hedgewar died in Nagpur on 21 June 1940, and his last rites were performed at Resham Baug. Hedgewar had bought this twenty-one-acre land for the Sangh. Twenty years later, in 1962, a memorial was constructed there for him.

After Dr Hedgewar's demise, sanghchalaks from across the country arrived in Nagpur. In their presence, Balasaheb Ghatate declared Guruji Golwalkar as Hedgewar's successor. One of the sanghchalaks, Babasaheb Padhye, opined that the Sangh's activities and work were social in nature, and revealing the new sarsanghchalak's name at such a sensitive time would resemble a military operation. Therefore, he suggested that a period of mourning be observed before going ahead with the official announcement. Balasaheb Ghatate agreed with his suggestion, and they later held Dr Hedgewar's memorial service at the Bhosale Vedashala. At the same time, news had spread outside that the RSS was not able to appoint a new chief. A misunderstanding arose between the Sangh and the Hindu Mahasabha, and the latter further helped spread the rumour.

At the memorial, there were speeches by Dr Paranjape and Dr Moonje. Dr Moonje said, 'I made Keshav start the Sangh, and he did a fantastic job and expanded the organisation very well. I have worked as an assistant to Hedgewar, and if everyone consents and everyone approves, I am ready to take up this responsibility.'[24] Dr Paranjape immediately intervened and clarified that he was aware of Dr Hedgewar's final wishes Interestingly, Dr Paranjape's daughter was married to Dr Moonje's son.

Dr Paranjape said, 'We have had a strange relationship. I was the head during the Congress session in 1920, and Hedgewar [was] my assistant. Then, later in 1925, at a meeting of the Sangh, Dr Hedgewar was the sarsanghchalak, and I was his assistant. We had no problems because there was never a power struggle between us. In 1930, when Hedgewar was arrested during the Jungle satyagraha, we did not know how long he would be in prison; that is why he appointed me as the sarsanghchalak. I even saluted the Sangh flag as the sarsanghchalak. Hedgewar was in jail for ten months, and after his release, I went back to being a karyakarta.

'Dr Hedgewar spoke to me just before his death and asked me to be the sarsanghchalak yet again, but I refused and said that he must choose a young person this time. Hedgewar liked my idea, but he died suddenly, and now I am ready to shoulder the responsibility.'

A stunned silence followed. Even Golwalkar and Deoras were surprised.

Then, Bhaiyaji Dani got up and said, 'Deoras-ji, you are Hedgewar's successor. Please tell us your thoughts.'

Deoras replied, 'I have given my entire life to the Sangh, and I was like Hedgewar's shadow. The Sangh has become a big organisation with 700 shakhas, and whoever dreams of building the Sangh has stood with it at all times. Dr Hedgewar has appointed Guruji Golwalkar as the sarsanghchalak. I have said yes; I have given my approval. Guruji is my sarsanghchalak, and that will be a real tribute to Hedgewar. We should end this discussion here.'[25]

The sarsanghchalak's seat remained vacant until Dr Hedgewar's first death anniversary. At the ceremony, in the presence of sanghchalaks from all over India, Guruji Golwalkar saluted the saffron flag as the Sangh's next sarsanghchalak.

HINDU MAHASABHA, CONGRESS AND THE SANGH

Dr Hedgewar was associated with the Hindu Mahasabha since its inception in 1923. At that time, Raja Lakshman Rao Bhosale was the president of the Mahasabha, and Dr Moonje was the secretary. The Hindu Mahasabha nominated Hedgewar to the prachaar samiti (publicity committee), and he served as secretary of its Nagpur unit from 1926 to 1927. He remained involved with the Congress's freedom struggle, and in the many instances when the Sangh detached itself from social and national movements, Hedgewar took part in them, stepping down from his responsibilities in the Sangh. Hedgewar felt that the Hindu Mahasabha had limited utility in advancing the cause of Hindutva. When the Mahasabha began to position itself as a political spokesperson of the Hindus, just like the Muslim League was for the Muslims, Hedgewar distanced himself from it. However, his connections with several Mahasabha leaders meant that some relationships continued informally. Many people conflate the Sangh and the Hindu Mahasabha, largely because, in its early years, the Sangh received some support from the Mahasabha to propel its expansion. In several regions, the Mahasabha appointed its leaders as sanghchalaks to expand the number of shakhas. However, Hedgewar's primary focus remained on the organisation's autonomy. This distinction became especially clear during the Civil Disobedience movement which began in 1930. While the Hindu Mahasabha did not take part, the RSS allowed its members to join the movement.

In 1932, the Hindu Mahasabha passed a resolution accepting the national presence of the RSS and praising Dr Hedgewar's efforts. However, it disapproved of the Sangh's participation in the Congress's programmes; it wanted the Sangh to assist the Mahasabha in its initiatives related to Hindu politics. The Mahasabha leaders were displeased with Hedgewar's different approaches to the two organisations. Savarkar, criticising the Sangh's detachment, remarked, 'The biography of the swayamsevak would say that he was born, joined the Sangh and died achieving nothing.' Following this, the Mahasabha's attacks on the Sangh intensified.[26]

In October 1938, the Hindu Mahasabha and the Arya Samaj, under the leadership of Savarkar, organised a satyagraha against the nizam of Hyderabad for his anti-Hindu policies. The leaders of the Mahasabha wanted Hedgewar to participate in it with his swayamsevaks just like he had done in the Jungle satyagraha, but Hedgewar focused his energies on the freedom struggle. He had said that the swayamsevaks were free to participate in the satyagraha against the nizam on a personal level, and close to a hundred swayamsevaks, including Bhaiyaji Dani, did join the movement. This further angered the Mahasabha leaders, who publicly criticised Dr Hedgewar, thus increasing the distance between the organisations.

On 17 March 1940, the Hindu Mahasabha established a parallel outfit called the Ram Sena and included Dr Hedgewar's name among its members. Dr Hedgewar, undergoing a naturopathy treatment in Rajgir, Bihar, instructed Golwalkar to draft a statement refuting the Mahasabha's annoucement. Furthermore, the Mahasabha established several other institutions like the Hindu Rashtra Dal, Hindu Seva Dal, Shakti Dal and Nathuram Godse's Hindu Rashtra Sena to compete with the Sangh.

Despite ideological differences, Dr Hedgewar and the Mahasabha's Dr Moonje always shared a respectful relationship. But Dr Hedgewar, who wanted no relationship with the British other than revolt, did not like Dr Moonje's attitude towards Britain.

When Dr Hedgewar went to jail in 1930, Dr Paranjape took his place as the sarsanghchalak. Dr Paranjape was a well-known surgeon in Vidarbha, and Dr Hedgewar, an allopathy practitioner. Dr Paranjape had also started a private insurance company, in which Dr Hedgewar was a registered doctor. The company paid him a thousand rupees for his services.

Prof Rajendra Singh, alias Rajju bhaiyya, worked in a college. During a visit to Kerala as the Sangh's sarsanghchalak, he required medical attention. When the local Sangh office offered to pay the bill, he refused and said, 'This is my personal expense and there is some money in my bank account.' The bill was settled from his account.

Balasaheb Deoras was a farmer and continued in agriculture. He used the income from his farming to help those in need. On the contrary, there are no bank accounts mentioned in the names of K.S. Sudarshan and Mohan Bhagwat.

Mohan Bhagwat is a veterinary doctor by training. He passed his MSc Part I in Akola before enrolling in Part II. Initially, he stayed with a relative in Nagpur, but later moved into a hostel. He was the head of his hostel, while journalist Dilip Deodhar was the provincial head of the college hostel. Deodhar used to run the full-pant shakhas at the time, and Bhagwat would attend them once in a while. Because of the Emergency, he couldn't find time to complete his dissertation. Then, he became a pracharak in the Sangh.

When Guru Golwalkar's book *We or Our Nationhood Defined* was published, the chief editor of *Tarun Bharat*, Gajanan Tryambak Madkholkar, was invited to its release. Sarsanghchalak Dr Hedgewar was also present at the occasion. During the event, Madkholkar asked Golwalkar if the book needed a review. He also posed several pointed questions. He said, 'You did your MSc, then your LLB. You started your PhD, left it and went to teach at a coaching centre. You then joined the Ramakrishna Mission, got initiated by Swami Akhandananda, and now you are a sarkaryavah in the Sangh. You are neither a sanyasi nor a professor. You are no longer a part of Ramakrishna mission and are now a part of the Sangh. Who are you actually? What do you seek? Where do you belong? You don't know what you will do in the future? You are also not of the Sangh?'

Guruji replied, 'It is good that you asked me these questions in Dr Hedgewar's presence. I want to establish an organisation based on the ideals of Swami Vivekananda. I have joined Dr Hedgewar's Sangh and want to ask Dr Hedgewar if there are any differences between Swami Vivekananda's dreams and his own dreams? Please explain.' Dr Hedgewar did not answer his question.

Dr Hedgewar used to always take some time to respond, and that would give the other person a chance to collect their thoughts. The president of the Jana Sangh, Bachhraj Vyas, was an orthodox Rajasthani Brahmin from Itwari in Nagpur. He never came to the Officers Training Corps sessions. He came to the shakhas, but not for the camps. At one point, Balasaheb asked Hedgewar if he could persuade Bachhraj to join one. Hedgewar agreed, saying that Bachhraj would come on his terms. He would cook his own food and not eat with others. However, Balasaheb was concerned that this might undermine the Sangh's discipline. In response, Hedgewar asked, 'Is discipline more important than the person?' Bachhraj eventually came, and as per his condition, cooked his food and ate alone. His solitary meal drew laughter from others, troubling him deeply. After returning to Rajasthan, Bachhraj established a unit of the Sangh there.

N.M Ghatate, a senior advocate in the Supreme Court, was one of those rare people who had seen the RSS's activities in his home since childhood, had witnessed Dr Hedgewar and Balasaheb Deoras visiting his house and watched the initial days of the Sangh up close. People fondly called him 'Appa'. People also know him as Atal Bihari Vajpayee's most trusted aide. I have known him for years. His affectionate manner and his childlike laughter never made me realise that I was in the presence of such a prominent personality. Appa's father, Balasaheb Ghatate, was one of Nagpur's landlords.

Balasaheb Ghatate and Guru Golwalkar had joined the Sangh at the same time. Ghatate became the sanghchalak of Nagpur, while Golwalkar became sarkaryavah. Balasaheb Ghatate had been with the Hindu Mahasabha for a long time.

Appa Ghatate says, 'Dr Hedgewar was seriously ill in 1939–40. We had gone to Nashik during the summer vacations. Hedgewar had come to Nashik with Guruji Golwalkar and stayed there for almost a month. During those days, there was a lot of talk about Guruji's saffron attire, his kamandal (water vessel) and his deerskin mat. Savarkar too had visited Balasaheb Ghatate's house twice. Ghatate moved to the Jana Sangh after the collapse of the Hindu Mahasabha.

'The decision to make Golwalkar the next sarsanghchalak was taken at a meeting in Akola. Dr Hedgewar had discussed this with Balasaheb Ghatate, Yadavrao Joshi and Krishnarao. Apart from Guru Golwalkar, Deoras and Appaji were also present at the meeting. Guru Golwalkar refused to accept Hedgewar's decision. A few others were also displeased with his decision because Golwalkar did not have enough experience with the Sangh at that time. In fact, Appaji was taken aback [after] listening to the decision. Everybody was under the impression that Balasaheb Deoras would be appointed as the new sarsanghchalak. Guruji was more inclined toward spirituality. But such instances have happened several times in the Sangh. Guru Golwalkar himself chose Atal Bihari Vajpayee for the Jana Sangh and furthered his presence at the national level.'[27]

4

Guruji Golwalkar

The Seer

On the evening of 6 June 1973, Guruji Golwalkar's mortal remains were cremated in Resham Baug, in front of Dr Hedgewar's statue. It marked the culmination of a significant era of the Sangh, one never likely to return. While offering his tribute to Guruji Golwalkar, Atal Bihari Vajpayee reportedly said, 'Revered Guruji's mortal body was kept in the office room for people to pay their last respects. Today, he didn't stop me from touching his feet. He did not pull his feet away. He did not bless me by caressing my head, he did not meet me with a sweet smile on his face, and nor did he ask about my well-being … He was in deep, eternal sleep. The swan has flown away, breaking open the cage of the body and disappearing forever. But Guruji will remain immortal … in our lives, our hearts, and our actions forever. The fire may burn his body to ashes, but his heart that is illuminated by the flame of patriotism and the spark of his selfless social service shall never be put off by anyone.'[1]

EXPANDING THE ORGANISATION

When Dr Hedgewar decided to expand the organisation nationally, the first name that came to his mind was Banaras, also known as Kashi. Kashi is Lord Shiva's abode and the sacred place where Gautam Buddha delivered his first discourse. Adi Shankaracharya conducted his first lecture series in this holy city, and Swami Vivekananda, too, chose the same place to share his thoughts and philosophy.

The sarsanghchalak sent a group of people under the leadership of Bhaiyaji Dani to Banaras to start a shakha there. Swayamsevaks like Tatya Talang, Babu Talang, Tatya Lokhande, Anna Pandharipande and Appa Gunde accompanied him. Dani was allowed to open the shakha while continuing his studies. Dr Hedgewar stayed in Kashi from 11 March to 1 April 1931, and with Ganesh Savarkar's help, started the first shakha in the Dhan Dhaneshwar temple at Brahma Ghat.

The shakha at the Banaras Hindu University began in July 1931, and in the same year, Madhav Sadashiv Golwalkar was appointed as a lecturer there. Bhaiyaji Dani got in touch with Golwalkar, and they became friends. Initially, the tennis and hockey-playing Golwalkar was not interested in the shakha. However, over time, he gradually began attending it actively. Later that year in December, he even took part in a Van Vihar programme in Sarnath along with forty swayamsevaks.

People addressed Golwalkar as 'Guruji' at the university, and he had a cordial relationship with Pandit Madan Mohan Malaviya. One evening, Malaviya saw a group of swayamsevaks going to the shakha carrying their lathis and a flag post. After making enquiries and gathering all the information about the shakha, Malaviya-ji called Bhaiyaji Dani and informed him he would provide space within the university to conduct the shakhas, and that they could also construct a building. Shortly, a small building was ready, and the shakhas began to be held regularly in front of it. When Golwalkar visited Nagpur in the summer of 1932, Dr Hedgewar invited him for the Vijayadashami celebrations. Along with Dr Sadgopal, he was the chief guest on the occasion.

After returning from Nagpur, Golwalkar became actively involved with the Sangh activities. He returned to Nagpur in 1933, when Dr Hedgewar appointed him as the karyavah for the Nagpur shakha. Dr Hedgewar sent Guruji to Mumbai for a few days, and in 1934, handed him the responsibility of the Officers Training Corps in Akola. At that time, Golwalkar was pursuing his law studies and would often visit the Ramakrishna Mission hostel to meet his friend, Raghuvir Dhongadi. Spiritually inclined, Golwalkar was inspired when Dhongadi told him about his intention to seek initiation at the Ramakrishna Mission Ashram in Sargachhi. Moved, he too decided to do the same and arrived in Sargachhi a few days before Diwali that year. There, he had the opportunity to be in the presence of Swami Akhandananda, a disciple of Ramakrishna Paramahamsa and Swami Vivekananda. Guruji executed every task assigned to him in the ashram with utmost sincerity.

On 13 January 1937, on the occasion of Makar Sankranti, Swami Akhandananda initiated Golwalkar into the Ramkrishna Mission. Following his initiation, Golwalkar said it was, '… the greatest day, a day to be written in golden letters, because, great fortune accrued through ages with countless births, had finally smiled on me and I was the recipient of an indescribable bliss from the kind hands of Gurudev. The experience of that day is literally most sacred. Words cannot describe that sense of sanctity. I can never forget those moments. The look in the eyes of Gurudev, his affection, his overpowering presence; the way he kindly bestowed upon me that luminous joy – I think and hope I will never forget all this. Every atom in my body was tremulous. I experienced a transformation. I was no more the person I was a few moments earlier.'[2]

Golwalkar continued to serve Swami Akhandananda, and upon his passing, decided to return to Nagpur. He picked up several invaluable items from the ashram's storeroom, which included a signed, life-size photograph of Swami Akhandananda, Gurudev's woollen blanket, the dhoti he wore while performing his rituals, two white foot towels, two ochre handkerchiefs and his pocket watch. There were a few remnants of Swami Akhandananda's ashes, a small pillar of remembrance and about twenty-five strands of Ramakrishna Paramahamsa's hair.

He first went to meet his ailing mother in Ramtek, and after he arrived in Nagpur, he began visiting Dr Hedgewar's house and the shakhas regularly. During the same time, he translated Swami Vivekananda's Chicago speech into Marathi.

In 1938, Dr Hedgewar included Guruji in his extensive efforts to expand the Sangh. Swayamsevaks from Karnataka, Bengal, Bihar, Uttar Pradesh and Punjab were scheduled to come for the shiksha varg that year. Considering the immediate need for multilingual leaders, Hedgewar appointed Guruji as the head because he could converse in Marathi, Hindi, Bengali, and English fluently. In those days, the shiksha vargs would go on for forty days. Guruji handled the duties exceptionally well and was then chosen for the shiksha varg in Lahore and North India. Aniruddha Deshpande notes, 'Guruji took up a massive challenge upon himself after the death of the founder of the Sangh, Dr Hedgewar. While Dr Hedgewar founded the Sangh, Guruji laid the foundation for its progress.'[3]

THE INCEPTION OF THE SANGH

Madhav Sadashiv Golwalkar was born on 19 February 1906 in Ramtek. His father, Sadashiv Rao Golwalkar, was an employee of the postal and telegraph department. Sadashiv quit his job in 1909 and became a teacher in Chhattisgarh. Owing to his father's frequent transfers, Madhav pursued his schooling in different cities like Raipur, Durg and Khandwa.

Sadashiv wanted Madhav to be a doctor. He entered Fergusson College in Pune in 1922, but he had to leave under certain circumstances and return to Nagpur. He then did his intermediate studies in science in Nagpur, followed by a BSc from the Banaras Hindu University and a Master of Science in zoology. After that, Golwalkar went to Madras to pursue a doctorate in marine biology. However, the climate in Madras affected his health. Around the same time, his father had retired from his job, and because of financial constraints, Madhav left Madras and returned to Banaras, where he began teaching at BHU. In 1931, he met Dr Hedgewar; however, even before that, Madhav had felt that he would not lead a householder's life and was inclined towards monkhood and retreating to Himachal Pradesh. Along with spiritual interests, Madhav was skilled at mallakhamba (the wrestler's pole). Even after joining the Sangh, Madhav abruptly stopped pursuing law, left the Sangh and his home and went to Swami Akhandananda's ashram. Madhav found out about Swami Akhandananda from Swami Amurtananda, alias Amitabh Maharaj. Amitabh Maharaj was the one who brought Madhav back to the Sangh and played a major role in his life.

At the 1939 brainstorming session at Sindi, Dr Hedgewar had asked Appaji Joshi, 'What if we make Madhav Sadashiv Golwalkar the sarsanghchalak?' Even though Appaji Joshi was the senior-most leader in the Sangh and there was a possibility of him becoming the next sarsanghchalak, Appaji Joshi's one-word reply was, 'Best!' Apart from Joshi, one of the earliest swayamsevaks, Balasaheb Deoras, too, was a contender for the post. Many continued to question the process by which Golwalkar was chosen as the sarsanghchalak, but Joshi and Deoras decided to support Hedgewar's decision and never spoke against it publicly.

Dr Hedgewar's health was steadily deteriorating, and at Nagpur, Balasaheb Ghatate requested him to rest in Deolali. Guruji Golwalkar accompanied him there, but during his stay, Hedgewar contracted a severe bout of pneumonia. His condition worsened and Guruji cared for him throughout his illness. After recovering, Hedgewar returned to Nagpur on 6 August. On 13 August, the Nagpur shakha celebrated both Raksha Bandhan and the guru dakshina ceremony, and Dr Hedgewar made two landmark announcements: Babasaheb Ghatate would be the sanghchalak of Nagpur, and Golwalkar would be the sarkaryavah of the Sangh. After the announcements, Guruji touched Sarkaryavah Appaji Joshi's feet and sought his blessings. Then, he left to travel across the country.

Even though the formal announcement hadn't been made, Dr Hedgewar's conversation with Yadavrao Joshi and Krishnarao Mohrir on 20 June had reached those closely associated with the Sangh. It was clear Golwalkar would be the next sarsanghchalak. About a decade ago in 1929, when Dr Hedgewar had been chosen as the sarsanghchalak, a meeting had been held to finalise the decision. This time around, another meeting was called at Akola on 30 June 1940, where the sanghchalak of Nagpur, Babasaheb Ghatate, the sanghchalak of Wardha, Appaji Joshi, the sanghchalak of Vidarbha, Bapusaheb Sohni and the sanghchalak of Maharashtra, Kashinath Bhaskar Limaye, were present. Everyone unanimously agreed with Yadavrao Joshi's suggestion and accepted Guruji Golwalkar as the RSS's next sarsanghchalak. It was decided that the formal announcement would be made on 3 July, on the thirteenth day of the ceremony following Dr Hedgewar's death, and on 21 July, a month after his death.

On 24 June, the fourth day after Hedgewar's death, Guruji Golwalkar sent a document to the shakhas, revealing details about Dr Hedgewar's death, the condolence messages and information about the organisation. Ranga Hari has mentioned in Golwalkar's biography, *Golwalkar Jeevancharitra*, that on 3 July, a congregation of swayamsevaks had gathered at the Resham Baug ground in Nagpur. The flag post was exactly opposite the spot where Dr Hedgewar was cremated. Over 3,000 swayamsevaks in uniform stood in formation. After the regular formalities, Babasaheb Padhye said in his address, 'Since the Rashtriya Swayamsevak Sangh is an "Ekachalakanuvartik" or "supremo-led" organisation, the wishes of the head are of utmost reverence to us. A day before his death, on 20 June, Dr Hedgewar had handed over the responsibility of the Sangh to Golwalkar-ji after him. And hence, I announce today that, according to the last wishes of our first sarsanghchalak, Madhavrao-ji Golwalkar, has become the sarsanghchalak of the Sangh. I offer my first greetings to the new sarsanghchalak.'[4]

After this, Dr Hedgewar's uncle, Abaji Hedgewar, shared his kind blessings. He said, 'Be careful, our doctor hasn't left us. We can still see him in the form of Golwalkar. We have to follow his orders, considering them as Doctor-ji's commands.'[5]

Neither speech elicited a response from the attendees. Then it was time for Guruji Golwalkar's speech.

'Revered Doctor has bestowed me with the unimaginable responsibility of being the sarsanghchalak. But this throne belongs to King Vikramaditya. Even a shepherd's son would impart justice if he were sitting on it. An ordinary human being like me has the opportunity to grace this throne. But I am sure Doctor-ji will only allow appropriate words to come from my mouth. There is no doubt that with the blessings and virtues of our great leader, I will do only deeds worthy of him. If any mistakes occur, I will be the one responsible.'[6] On 21 July, during Hedgewar's monthly funerary rites, thousands of swayamsevaks offered the first sarsanghchalak a military salute. This gesture arose from differing opinions that had emerged during the last rites. Anna Sohoni, head of the physical and military division, Martandrao Jog and a few others opined that military honours should mark the conduct of the last rites of the supreme leader of an organisation like the Sangh. On the other hand, Appaji Joshi and Babasaheb Padhye felt that the cremation should follow the traditional funerary rites acceptable to all. Guru Golwalkar made the final decision and said, 'The Sangh is a huge family and not an official military organisation. That is why the last rites of the family patriarch should be according to acceptable social norms.' However, during the monthly ceremony, it was agreed that it was necessary to highlight the Sangh's uniqueness—an approach that fosters a spirit of heroism and organisation within society. On that day, the Sangh found its second sarsanghchalak. From that moment, and for the next thirty-three years, Golwalkar dedicated himself to expanding and strengthening the organisation.

A former pracharak, Ramesh Shiledar, says, 'The longest serving sarsanghchalak of the Sangh had undergone no formal training in it. He never attended the three-year OTC camp. He completed his physical training programme within three days.' During the Quit India movement in 1942, a meeting of the Sangh officials of the Maharashtra province was held in Pune. Guru Golwalkar asked the attendees how many arms and weapons they had. At the same time, Dadarao Parmarth was discussing with Guru Golwalkar if they could fight the battle for Indian independence under the leadership of the RSS. But the Sangh was not very strong, with its presence only in Vidarbha and Central India. However, some believed that Golwalkar was adept at promoting and strengthening his "self-image", which is why he claimed he was Shivaji Maharaj and Swami Vivekananda in his previous birth.[7]

After becoming the sarsanghchalak, Guru Golwalkar focussed on fortifying his supremacy. He clarified that if anyone contested his position, they should make it clear then and there. Golwalkar also reiterated that active politics was not enough for the nation. Under his leadership, the Sangh emphasised maintaining a distance from political participation. However, the contradiction lies in the fact that, after the establishment of the Rashtra Sevika Samiti, nearly all the Sangh's associate organisations—including the Vidyarthi Parishad and the Bharat Prakashan Trust (which first published *Organise*r in English, then *Panchjanya* and *Rashtra Dharma* in Hindi)—have gravitated towards political engagement. Golwalkar maintained a certain distance from these organisations and stressed the fact that the Sangh's primary task was to unite and fortify Hindu society. Interestingly, Golwalkar remained a trustee of the Vishva Hindu Parishad while being the sarsanghchalak. However, he never supported the Hindu Mahasabha. During his tenure, he extended invitations to Congress leaders for Sangh programmes, intending to showcase the RSS as the only organisation dedicated to the welfare of Hindus.

Golwalkar's term as the Sangh's sarsanghchalak paralleled a tumultuous period for the country as it underwent massive political transitions in light of the ongoing freedom struggle. It was Golwalkar's responsibility to decide what the Sangh wanted to do. His solution was that a swayamsevak could take part in the freedom struggle as individual citizens, court arrest and go to jail, while the Sangh officials would remain solely dedicated to organisational tasks. Golwalkar believed he bore the tremendous responsibility of expanding the Sangh and focussing on the personal development of its members.

On 5 August 1940, the central government implemented an order prohibiting private organisations and institutions from wearing military uniforms and undertaking military training. This worried the Sangh because its training had been fashioned in the military style until then. In August 1940, Guruji announced that military training and the Senapati scheme for the officers would effectively cease to exist.

Even then, nothing could impede the Sangh's growth. In 1941–42, the Sangh felt an urgent need for full-time volunteers. Emphasising that there was much work to do and very little time to accomplish it, Golwalkar urged everyone to keep all personal matters aside. He called on members to dedicate themselves with the commitment of sanyasis for an entire year. He stressed on the need for pracharaks or full-time swayamsevaks. Notably, the number of shakhas had seen a rapid increase in the four years leading up to Golwalkar's appointment as sarsanghchalak.

Till then, the Sangh was predominantly visible in Nagpur and the Central Provinces; it had about 76,000 swayamsevaks at that time. Then, the Sangh spread its work to Punjab, Sindh, Delhi and other provinces, and the number of swayamsevaks rose to a lakh. According to a secret report published at that time, the number of swayamsevaks in the shakhas skyrocketed between 1938–43.[8] This was the time when

Golwalkar started the 'Indianisation' of the Sangh. After the Sindi session, the language of instruction in Sangh changed from English to Sanskrit. The RSS band was renamed 'Ghosh'. The names of different shakha units were also changed. As communal strife between the Hindus and Muslims intensified between 1945–47, and news of the Partition and the ideas of the Muslim League spread, the number of people joining the Sangh rose dramatically.

The Quit India movement was the second significant revolt during the Sangh's lifetime. Guru Golwalkar was tasked with deciding the scope of the Sangh's participation in the movement. To deliberate on the matter, he called a meeting of the provincial karyakartas in Nagpur. Following the discussions, he dispatched the revolutionary, Dr Pandurangrao Sadashiv Khankhoje, and Balasaheb Deoras to Jayaprakash Narayan with seven questions concerning the movement. After meeting Jayaprakash Narayan, Khankhoje reported that Narayan had failed to provide satisfactory answers to any of the questions. Furthermore, there was a lack of clarity about the course of action for others once the movement's leaders were arrested.

The seven questions that Guruji had asked regarding the Quit India movement were:

1. The meaning of 'die' is clear in the slogan, 'do or die', but what does 'do' mean exactly? Has the Congress Working Committee given any clear orders regarding the same?
2. What are the short-term and long-term purposes of the movement? What does it want to achieve?
3. What is the working style of the movement, and how will it be?
4. How long should the movement be continued?
5. You must have evaluated your strengths to some extent. How good is it?
6. What should be done after the success of the movement?
7. What should be done in case it fails?

Not receiving adequate answers to his questions and after consultations within the Sangh, Golwalkar decided any swayamsevak could take part in the movement as a citizen committed to achieving Indian independence. But the Sangh will not be a part of it as an organisation and will continue to work towards its social integration mission.

Golwalkar's decision disheartened many swayamsevaks, especially amid a nationwide wave of participation in the freedom struggle. They wondered why the RSS was inactive at such a crucial time. In September 1942, Dattopant Thengadi, then a pracharak in Calicut, met Guruji in Mangalore and put forward his concerns. In response, Guruji explained that even Dr Hedgewar had taken part in a revolt in 1930—but not as a representative of the Sangh—and this had been the norm. However, he added that if the Sangh's participation could hasten the achievement of freedom, there would be no objection to departing from that tradition. The Congress had not taken all organisations into confidence before starting the movement. Golwalkar had hoped that Gandhi would discuss with him before beginning the revolt, but that didn't happen, possibly disappointing and offending those who believed that the movement would not yield the desired results without bringing other organisations under the umbrella. Golwalkar believed that the Sangh was not at its full strength across the country; its influence being primarily concentrated in Central India. He felt it was not worthwhile for the Sangh to join the movement. This does not imply a desire to save ourselves, and the reality is that the people would undoubtedly suffer because of the movement.

Before this, Golwalkar had stopped military drills and military uniforms following the orders of the British government. He passed another order on 29 April 1943, which said, 'We have to function within the boundaries of law.' The British secret agencies informed the government that the RSS had kept away from anti-government activities during the Quit India movement and that there was no danger to them from the RSS.[9] The difference between Golwalkar and Deoras became publicly evident over the Sangh's stance on the issue. Golwalkar believed all political activities were immoral, while Deoras thought movements could be leveraged to become politically strong. Golwalkar used this time to empower the Sangh and increase the number of shakhas, and the impact of his effort was visible. In 1945, over 10,000 swayamsevaks took part in shakhas all over the country.

When many young men expressed their desire to be a part of the Quit India movement in 1942, Guruji stated that while swayamsevaks were free to join the movement in their personal capacity, he would not permit any Sangh official to go for it. Balasaheb Deoras recounted how Hedgewar himself took part in the 1940 Jungle satyagraha and got imprisoned, leaving all responsibilities with Paranjape in his absence. He wanted to join the Quit India movement, but when Guruji denied, he became upset. Guruji reminded him of the promise he had made to Hedgewar—to obey Golwalkar's directives—which meant he could not abandon the Sangh.

Seventy-five years later, Golwalkar continues to be criticised for this decision. Both his and the Sangh's critics allege that the organisation did not contribute meaningfully to the freedom struggle. Some question if Hedgewar's remaining the sarsanghchalak would have led the Sangh to take a different approach, considering he had been a freedom fighter and was imprisoned twice. Others speculate on how the RSS's role might have evolved if Deoras had been the sarsanghchalak during that period.

Right after taking over as the sarsanghchalak, Golwalkar became so intimately involved with his work that he thought of nothing else until the last day of his tenure. He often told Deoras he considered himself a renunciate who could exit the Sangh and retreat into the forests at any moment. For this reason, he never allowed Deoras to leave Nagpur. He also prohibited him from assuming any responsibility for the Jana Sangh. Golwalkar is said to have travelled all over India over sixty times during his time as the sarsanghchalak, often remarking that the railway compartment was his true home. Golwalkar would depend on the arrangements made by the swayamsevaks and the district offices. He would eat the food that the swayamsevak or his relatives would bring to him, and never ate the food sold at railway stations. During his journeys, Golwalkar travelled by means ranging from aeroplanes to bullock carts, but he never rode on rickshaws, as they were drawn by human beings.

Dilip Deodhar recounts a long-standing controversy involving Golwalkar. The allegation was that Golwalkar translated one of Savarkar's books, *Rashtriya Mimansa*, into English but published it under his name. However, this is untrue. When Golwalkar translated the book, he clearly stated in the foreword that this was a translation of Savarkar's original in Marathi and that none of the content was his. The confusion arose because the publisher omitted the foreword when the book was published. Deodhar later submitted the original version to the Nagpur Sangh office and made numerous photocopies for distribution. Despite this, criticism of Golwalkar continued.

Golwalkar propagated Dr Hedgewar's idea that 'Hindutva is nationalism' politically by opposing communism. Golwalkar would say, 'Not socialism, but Hindutva'. The Sangh's fundamental motto is Hindutva. Golwalkar tried to posit Hindutva against Marxism. After Independence, Marxism and socialism became synonymous with each other.

Guruji Golwalkar always stayed with swayamsevaks in their camps and the homes of the officials, swayamsevaks, karyakartas and well-wishers of the Sangh. When he wasn't travelling, he would be at the Hedgewar Bhavan, the central office in Nagpur. Sangh officials follow the same tradition even today, though some have begun staying in hotels and guest houses and even travelling by aeroplanes.

Guruji Golwalkar regularly attended camps and the shiksha vargs in the mornings and evenings. He would sit in line with the swayamsevaks for lunch, as was the norm at that time. A stickler for punctuality, he arrived at the dining hall ten minutes before everyone else, walking along the line of seated swayamsevaks, meeting and speaking to them. He would take his place at the appointed time and had no tolerance for indiscipline of any kind.

Veteran journalist Nilanjan Mukhopadhyay notes, 'The Sangh did not take up a political role after Independence, and did not take part in the negotiations with the British government and also did not become a part of the interim government. The reason for this was that Golwalkar believed that the British rule would never end, and they would not leave India. A swayamsevak at a shiksha varg in Phagwara, Punjab, had asked Guruji about the role of the Sangh after Independence. Golwalkar had asked him if he thought the British would ever leave India. The people who are being handed over the reins of government will not be able to run it for even two months, and they will ask the British to come back and take over the country again. And that is why the Sangh will continue to work as it always does.'[10]

Guruji Golwalkar was constantly travelling before the Partition and attempted to create trustworthy leaders in the provinces. He undertook two cross-country tours every year, and on these trips, he focussed on issues related to Hindutva. However, he would always evade talking about the Sangh's belief that 'an undivided India is the solution to the Muslim problem'. After Punjab, he toured Sindh, which had eighty shakhas at that time. One of the pracharaks was Lal Krishna Advani. Another massive meeting was held in Karachi, and even Pandit Nehru was in Hyderabad, Sindh, at the same time.

The situation in the country was worsening by the day. After consulting with the Sangh's officials in Punjab, Golwalkar stopped the prashikshan varg (training programmes) in Sangrur and Phagwara. The swayamsevaks were told to return to their respective locations and make plans to ensure their security during the turbulence. At the time, Home Minister Sardar Patel would stress the importance of people maintaining internal peace and security. He would that it would be impossible for the administration to provide security to one and all; each person should take care of his or her own security.[11] Guruji Golwalkar, Balasaheb Deoras, Madhav Rao Mule and Vasantrao were some of the leaders giving security orders during that time.

According to a senior official associated with the Sangh from its initial days in Jammu and Kashmir, the situation in Kashmir was challenging. Maharaja Hari Singh was anxious, and Pandit Nehru had lent his support to Sheikh Abdullah. Advocate Rai Bahadur Badridas, the sanghchalak of the Punjab province, represented the Maharaja in key legal matters and met him in September 1947, advising him to accede to India. The Jammu and Kashmir Sangh pracharak, Balraj Madhok, had cordial relations with Hari Singh and offered the same advice. After much deliberation, the king sent Harnam Singh as his emissary to Delhi with a proposal for Kashmir's accession. However, Nehru's unfavourable stance on the issue stalled the matter. A second attempt in October yielded no results. Golwalkar, who was getting all this news, decided to go to Srinagar on 17 October 1947. The province pracharak of Delhi, Vasantrao Oak, and Barrister Narendrajit Singh accompanied him. Pracharak Madhavrao Mule received them at the airport. On 18 October, Guruji went to the Karn Mahal to meet the king, where the maharaja and the queen welcomed him at the door. After their meeting, Golwalkar met Home Minister Sardar Patel in Delhi, informing him of the discussion that had happened in Srinagar. Patel took the necessary steps, paving the way for Kashmir's accession to India.

In September of the same year, Guruji was present in Delhi. The situation in the country was bad after the Partition. On the morning of 7 September at 7 a.m., Guruji met Sardar Patel to update him on the situation in Punjab and Sindh. Later, just as Guruji was about to depart for his flight to Calcutta, he received a message from Gandhi asking Guruji to meet him before he left. Golwalkar when to meet Gandhi at the Birla House on 12 September. Gandhi told Golwalkar that the hands of the RSS were steeped in blood. However, Guruji assured him that this was untrue and that the organisation did not stand for the killing of Muslims. He added that all the RSS wanted to do was to protect Hindustan to the best of its ability and that it stood for peace. He also asked Gandhi to make his views public, which Gandhi did at his prayer meeting later in the evening of the same day.[12] The next month of October, Guruji also met Nehru for about an hour, a meeting which gave him enough insights to gauge that Patel and Nehru had differing perspectives about the Sangh.

It was decided that a camp for young swayamsevaks would be held in Chinchwad near Pune in November 1947. One lakh swayamsevaks were expected to attend it. Guruji was supposed to be present, and Sardar Patel had agreed to be the chief guest. He was also the broadcasting minister and announced the news of his visit. At that time, Morarji Desai was the home minister of the Bombay province, and he revoked the permission, preventing Patel from attending the camp.[13]

On 17 January 1948, at the National Convention of the Congress in Delhi, a resolution was passed against the Sangh, and provincial governments were asked to take action against the organisation. The central government ordered that no government employee could become a member of the Sangh.

When Mahatma Gandhi was assassinated on 30 January 1948, Guruji Golwalkar was at a reception at the Ramakrishna Lunch Home in Madras. He had lunch with Rajagopalachari and a few others that afternoon. The moment Guruji heard about Gandhi's assassination, he removed himself from the group and went to a corner. His tea remained untouched. Sanghchalak Rajagopalachari's felicitation ceremony was also dispersed. Guruji planned to take the train to Vijayawada after the programme, but he cancelled it and sent condolence messages to the prime minister, deputy prime minister and Mahatma's son, Devdas Gandhi. That night, the sarsanghchalak announced a thirteen-day mourning period for every shakha and cancelled all Sangh programmes. The sanghchalak of the Delhi province, Lala Hansraj Gupta; the city sanghchalak, Harishchandra Gupta; and the province pracharak, Vasantrao Oak, headed to Birla House to express their condolences. The next morning, a condolence meeting was held at the Mohite Sanghsthan, where the swayamsevaks paid homage to Gandhi-ji and condemned his brutal assassination. Guruji took a flight to Nagpur that afternoon, but by evening, public ire and anger had intensified. An angry crowd began to gather outside Guruji's house. At one point, it appeared as though a mob might attack his residence, but the swayamsevaks responded with determined aggression. Soon after, the police arrived and controlled the situation.

A meeting was held at Chitnis Park near the Sangh office in Nagpur, attended by Sant Tukdoji Maharaj, General Avari, Samarth of the Congress and other leaders. Tukdoji Maharaj angrily said in his speech that people from the Sangh had killed Gandhi. He incited the people to attack the Sangh, and following his instigation, many reached the Sangh office in Mahaal. A large group of swayamsevaks warded off their attack, and the crowd moved towards the Hedgewar Memorial at Resham Baug. Guruji sent a message saying that if the crowd attacks the office, the swayamsevaks should not retaliate, nor fight back. If they did, there would be a civil war in the country. The swayamsevaks would walk the path of martyrdom but not retaliate with violence.

The crowd vandalised Dr Hedgewar's mausoleum. Even then, Guruji Golwalkar stuck to his promise. Later, several livid swayamsevaks criticised this decision. Why were they trained in brandishing sticks and sword fighting if they couldn't fight back? They should be ashamed of their cowardly response, simply watching their founding fathers' mausoleum being ruined. To that, Guruji said that Shivaji Maharaj was great because he understood the situation, thought about it and then decided what and when something needed to be done; he did nothing as a reaction but responded appropriately.[14]

GURU GOLWALKAR'S ARREST

The central agencies had received orders for Golwalkar's arrest on the night of 2 February 1948. The police had surrounded Nagoba Lane, where the house was situated. Guruji had learned about this through his sources and was sitting, ready to be arrested. Officer Babade arrived and read out the arrest orders, charging Guruji under Sections 302, 307 and 120 of the Indian Penal Code. Swayamsevaks stood on both sides, while most officials remained silent. As he was leaving, Guruji assured the swayamsevaks that they would face this challenge bravely and prove themselves. He was taken to the Nagpur jail in a police van. On 3 February, Sarkaryavah M.N. Kale sent a message to everyone: 'Guruji under arrest, please be calm.' On 4 February, the orders to ban the Sangh were passed, citing that the RSS does not work following the mission it claims to follow. Instead, it believes in violence, its latest victim being Gandhi-ji. The Sangh was declared illegal. When Guruji Golwalkar came to know about the ban in jail, he wrote a statement and gave it to his friend, Dattopant Deshpande, who came to visit him in jail. It was released to the press later. On 7 February, charges under Sections 302 and 120 of the Indian Penal Code were quashed, but he was put under arrest for six months under the Public Safety Act and accordingly, Golwalkar was imprisoned from 7 February to 6 August. He was eventually released, but under certain conditions, one of which was that he was prohibited from leaving Nagpur.

Over time, when it became clear that the Sangh had nothing to do with Gandhi's assassination, General Avari and Samarth came to the Sangh office and sought his forgiveness: 'We made a mistake, please forgive us. We want to contribute some funds for rebuilding the Samadhi.' Guruji told them, 'The reason for your anger is your love for Gandhi, and it is not your fault.' Guruji instructed the Sangh officials to collect funds for the Samadhi from across the entire country, gathering one rupee from each person and using the accumulated amount to reconstruct the destroyed memorial. Later, even Tukdoji Maharaj expressed his sorrow. Guruji said, 'Your anger was because of your love for Gandhi. Please continue to give us your blessings.' When Guruji established the Vishva Hindu Parishad in 1964, Tukdoji Maharaj and Swami Chinmayananda were included, and they became the organisation's founding members. Guruji believed that creativity is productive; opposition or resistance causes more strife.

On 11 August, Golwalkar wrote a letter to the Home Minister Sardar Patel seeking the removal of the ban. During this period, the trial of Gandhi's assassins was underway at the Red Fort. Barring the two absconding accused from Gwalior, authorities had nabbed everybody else. Not one of them was from the Sangh. The Sangh was not mentioned even in the charges.

Sardar Patel had set up an investigation team following Gandhi's assassination, and within seventeen days, the team, headed by Officer Sanjeevi, submitted their report. The report clarified that the RSS had nothing to do with the assassination. People considered Sanjeevi an extremely well-trained officer, and he said there could be no case against the Sangh in this terrible incident. However, the Sangh remained unaware of his findings. After the team submitted the report to Sardar Patel, he wrote a letter to Prime Minister Nehru on 27 February 1948. It is said that Nehru's lobby and the leftists considered Patel complicit in Gandhi's assassination. After allegations arose against him, Nehru banned the Sangh. Patel was told that he, too, had been involved with the RSS in the assassination. Meanwhile, RSS leader Ranga Hari criticised Patel, accusing him of being two-faced. Nehru sidelined Patel and subjugated the Sangh.

Later, on 24 September 1948, Golwalkar wrote yet another letter to Prime Minister Nehru. In October 1948, Madhav Sadashiv Golwalkar was allowed to travel to Delhi to discuss the lifting of the ban. Thousands of swayamsevaks gathered at the railway station in Delhi to welcome him. From there, Guruji headed to Sanghchalak Lala Hansraj Gupta's house. Golwalkar met the home minister the same day he reached Delhi. He met with him again on 23 October and asserted that the government should either revoke the ban on the Sangh or prove their charges in court. Even during their meeting, Patel suggested Guruji should join the Congress—it was the most practical solution. Golwalkar disagreed. He met Babasaheb Ambedkar, N.V. Gadgil, Purushottam Das Tandon and Syama Prasad Mookerjee during his visit.[15]

Fearing Golwalkar's presence in Delhi, a government emissary delivered an order on 2 November instructing him to leave the city. The order dated 28 October was that Guruji refused to accept it. The swayamsevaks were afraid that Guruji would be arrested by evening, but nothing happened. Then, on 3 November, he received a message from the magistrate of Delhi stating that he could stay in the city only if he wanted to meet the prime minister. Guruji wrote yet another letter to Nehru on 3 November, requesting the lifting of the ban and expressing his desire to meet him. In response, Nehru wrote that the Sangh's activities were anti-national—a claim that Golwalkar refuted strongly. In the meantime, Guruji wrote a letter to the swayamsevaks, outlining all the efforts taken to remove the ban and how the government responded to the situation. Furthermore, Guruji wrote, 'Hence after full consideration I hereby withdraw my directive of disbandment of the R.S.S. dated the 6th February, 1948 and request you to resume our work in the normal manner. Utmost efforts should, at the same time, be made to maintain peace and prevent discord. I have directed our General Secretary, Sri Bhayaji Dani, to communicate this decision to you and indicate to you the day and the date on which to resume our work.'[16]

LIFTING OF THE BAN

The Sangh had hastened its activities nationwide and reorganised itself from scratch. The government continued to receive reports about its initiatives and became increasingly worried. Sardar Patel made yet another attempt and sent Mauli Chandra Sharma as a mediator to Dani and Deoras, but they were no longer willing to trust the government. Mauli Chandra Sharma reiterated that the Sangh only had to provide some clarifications, following which the embargo would be lifted. Sharma then handed them a list of eight issues sent by Dwarka Prasad Mishra. It addressed subjects such as the Sangh's conviction and belief in the Indian flag and the Constitution, its view on violence and covert operations, the election process within the Sangh, the meaning of a lifetime oath, the admission of boys into the Sangh, the balanced representation of members and the accounting structure.

Most issues on the list had already been clarified, which is why Dani and Deoras raised no objections. They wrote a letter to Guruji and asked Mauli Chandra Sharma to deliver it to him. Sharma met Guruji in the Betul Jail, where Guruji signed the letter. Before handing it over to Dwarka Prasad Mishra, Sharma first showed it to Deoras and Dani. Mishra then read the letter aloud to Sardar Patel, who was recuperating from a heart attack in Dehradun at that time. Sardar Patel instructed that the letter be sent directly to the secretariat. A telephonic conversation took place between Dehradun, Nagpur and Delhi at midnight on 11 July, and on 12 July 1949, the ban on the RSS was lifted. On 13 July, his family members and a horde of swayamsevaks received Guruji when he was released from Betul. He left for Nagpur that afternoon. The next morning, Guruji's parents, Bal Apte, Bhaiyaji Dani, Balasaheb Deoras and other Sangh leaders were present at the Nagpur station to welcome him. On 17 July, the Sangh regained control of the Hedgewar Bhavan, which had been under government custody. Formal shakhas resumed the next day. In August, following the lifting of the ban, Guruji met Sardar Patel in Mumbai.

There were extended discussions between the government and the Sangh regarding the lifting of the ban. The Sangh was required not only to formulate a written constitution but to make multiple amendments under pressure from the government. However, in a programme held in Nagpur after the removal of the ban, Golwalkar said the Sangh had made no compromises and had not agreed to certain conditions put forth by the government.

When Sardar Patel died on 15 December 1950, Guruji was in Nagpur. He wanted to attend Patel's last rites, but they couldn't have reached on time by train. Instead, he went by flight to Bombay with Chief Minister

Ravishankar Shukla and attended the funeral. Ramesh Shiledar says that Guruji and Patel shared a close personal bond. A proposal suggesting that the Sangh's swayamsevaks be given primary membership of the Congress was to be tabled during the Lucknow session in 1949. Patel was in favour of the proposal, but Nehru was against it.

The Sangh's frequent run-ins with the government had left the organisation with no funds to finance its daily activities. They needed loans, and there was no one to speak in their support at the national level. Appa Ghatate said the Sangh felt a greater need for parliamentary power than ever before. Faced with the conundrum, the Sangh leadership felt an urgent need for a political wing to supplement their presence. Furthermore, the Hindu Mahasabha's Dr Syama Prasad Mookerjee also wanted to start a new political party and was in touch with Guruji. Dr Mahesh Sharma, a senior Sangh official who has written extensively on Pandit Deendayal Upadhyaya, says, 'Not Deoras but the Delhi province pracharak Vasantrao Oak was in favour of a new political party and he had aspirations of becoming the party president or taking up political responsibilities, because of which a lot of differences cropped up in the Sangh regarding him.'[17]

After Independence, Mahatma Gandhi had considered dissolving the Congress and forming a Loksevak Sangh. Meanwhile, discussions were taking place within the Sangh about launching a new political party. Sardar Patel had expressed a desire for the RSS to join the Congress.[18]

There were also conversations with leaders who were Hindu about starting a new political party. When Deoras told Guruji about this, he said, 'You are free to start a new party, but I will not allow you to leave the Sangh. You have promised that you will remain in the Sangh and you will listen to me.' Deoras was unhappy with Golwalkar's response. The Jana Sangh was born out of Deoras's constant insistence on starting a new political party, and Syama Prasad Mookerjee became the party's first president. Guruji still did not allow Deoras to join the Jana Sangh. He told him to run the Jana Sangh while being involved with the RSS.

If we were to believe Deodhar's statement, Guruji was in touch with Sardar Patel and Mookerjee at the same time.

According to a senior official of the Sangh, Sardar Patel and Guruji in 1946 desired that the Sangh and the Congress come together and form a new party. When the talks to merge the RSS and the Congress reached a standstill, Mookerjee expressed his sadness to Balraj Madhok saying, 'a lot of time is getting wasted talking to Guruji and things are not moving forward,' and then Mookerjee returned to Bengal a disappointed man. Then, Deoras told Guruji, 'Even Sardar Patel is no more; let me form a political party now. To which Guruji replied he was talking to Dr Mookerjee about it.'[19] Dr Mahesh Sharma says, 'Sant Prabhudutt Brahmachari, who was close to Guru Golwalkar and later to Rajju bhaiyya, writes in his autobiography, "Nanaji Deshmukh and Deendayal Upadhyaya came to me. They believe it is important to form a new political party to keep the Sangh alive, but Guruji is not ready to agree. You please talk to him. I spoke to Golwalkar about this."

As per Mahesh Sharma, 'Golwalkar told Prabhudutt Brahmachari that he accepted in principle that a political party was necessary to keep the Sangh alive, and he asked Brahmachari to become the president. To that, Brahmachari said that being a sanyasi, he could only give his guidance and blessings. Golwalkar replied they would form a party based on his guidance. At that time, discussions were on with Dr Mookerjee, who was in the Hindu Mahasabha. Guruji told Mookerjee that he would have to leave his Hindu Mahasabha background and give membership to Muslims in the political party. Mookerjee kept accepting Guruji's conditions, and that is how the Jana Sangh came into being.'[20]

Before the Sangh decided to foray into political representation, Guruji Golwalkar, Bal Apte and Bhaiyaji Dani had been against the creation of a party. However, Balasaheb Ghatate thought it was necessary. Appa Ghatate adds, 'When Dr Syama Prasad Mookerjee established the Jana Sangh, Guru Golwalkar had given the second in command of every state unit of the Sangh the responsibility to work for the Jana Sangh. Nanaji Deshmukh and Deendayal Upadhyaya in Uttar Pradesh, Jagendra Sharma in Punjab, Madhukar Rao Bhagwat in Gujarat, Yadavrao Joshi in Karnataka, Jana Krishnamurthy in Tamil Nadu, Kailashpati Mishra in Bihar and Kushabhau Thakre in Madhya Pradesh were given the responsibility. Atal-ji came into the Jana Sangh a little later, and he was not one of the founding members. At that time, he was handling *Panchjanya* and *Swadesh*.'

A few years after the formation of the Jana Sangh, Dr Mookerjee passed away in Kashmir in 1953. According to Dilip Deodhar, Deoras then told Guruji, 'You do not understand politics … everything is stuck in the Jana Sangh … please let me go.' But Guruji remained unmoved. He told Deodhar, 'We have an agreement, and I will not allow you to go. You control the Jana Sangh while being the head of the Sangh. I am a conditional head of the Sangh and may leave for the Himalayas at any time.' Deoras replied with displeasure, 'I respect you a lot …' and then began distancing himself from the Sangh. Meanwhile, just before the 1951 general elections, Guruji told Prabhudutt Brahmachari to stage a revolt against Nehru on the issue of cow protection and made him a candidate from Phulpur against Nehru.

Aniruddha Deshpande divides Guruji's tenure into two phases: one from 1940 to 48, and the other from 1949 to 73. The Sangh witnessed many ups and downs during this period. Guruji paid a lot more attention to the organisation after Independence, and with his efforts, pracharaks were appointed, new associate organisations were formed and organisations like the Bharatiya Jana Sangh, Akhil Bharatiya Vidyarthi Parishad, Vishva Hindu Parishad and the Bharatiya Mazdoor Sangh came into being.

Guru Golwalkar took the Sangh forward in the direction that Dr Hedgewar had desired. In a chintan baithak (brainstorming session) of the Sangh held in Pune in 1972, Guruji said, 'We have taken a lot of effort between 1925 and 1972; our activities have increased manifold. But we have to create karyakartas in every single province, from every caste, sub-caste, and place, because the representation is limited to a few sections at present. Our presence will be in villages, hills, riversides … in every possible geography. That will be the day when the Sangh will be all-India in the real sense.'

Like Gandhi, Dr Hedgewar never hesitated in raising funds from industrialists for social or organisational endeavours. But Guruji never took money because he believed that the Sangh should neither own property, nor should it boast of a bank balance. He believed that this would cause fights and quarrels in the organisation. He often said, 'I will neither indulge in corruption worth a single rupee, nor will I allow it to happen.' Until 1952, he did not permit a single rupee to be sourced from elsewhere.

According to Appa Ghatate, 'Guruji was against the accumulation of wealth and assets. He said, "Don't build a Sangh office or a building, create volunteers instead." The organisation will exist till there are karyakartas; if there is an office, there will be fights for property.' Appa's father, Sanghchalak Balasaheb Ghatate, had a house in Nagpur, where Guruji would live with his mother. But he insisted on paying a rent of seven rupees a month. Sangh meetings used to take place there, with Guruji sitting on a wooden seat and steering the discussions. After his mother's death, Guruji moved to the Sangh office and continued to live there.

Guruji Golwalkar was not only against wealth and hoarding but also focussed on the honesty and integrity of the Sangh's representatives. He believed that power begets corruption, fraud and other social ills, and perhaps that was the reason he repeatedly spoke about keeping the Sangh away from active politics. Veteran journalist and long-term associate of the Sangh, Achyutanand Mishra, mentions an incident: 'In the shiksha varg in Lucknow, representatives of all sister organisations were presenting their annual reports to Guruji Golwalkar. Ram Prakash Gupta, who was the chief minister of Uttar Pradesh for a few days, criticised the Congress, saying that everything was wrong in the government, and corruption was on the rise amongst government representatives. After Gupta presented his report, Guru Golwalkar said that corruption was a part of the government and it had nothing to do with any specific party. It will be interesting to see how you have prevented corruption only when you come to power.'[21]

There is one particular aspect related to Guruji that has been a subject of unending debate. This pertains to his belief in the varna vyavastha, the caste system, prevalent in Hindu society. It is important to narrate a particular incident in this context. In 1961, Golwalkar went to meet the president of the Akhil Bharatiya Ram Rajya Parishad, Swami Karpatri Maharaj, at his residence in Nigambodh Ghat in Delhi. Karpatri Maharaj was a staunch supporter of the varna system. During their discussion, Maharaj told Golwalkar that he should instruct all his swayamsevaks to work according to the varna to which they belonged, and they would agree with him. Guruji replied, 'I am the Sangh pramukh (head), and they are not my disciples, but my colleagues. I do not give them any orders, but I will still ask them. If they appreciate the idea, they will definitely behave accordingly. But you could create an example of framing such a society perfectly because you have thousands of disciples and you are their guru, and they should follow your command.' Angered by Golwalkar's response, Swami Karpatri retorted, 'You are placing all the burden on me.' Guruji responded, 'Please don't be angry, but tell me what is left of the varna system today? Does the caste structure exist? It is time to break away from all that and create a new social order. That is what the Sangh is doing. The Sangh believes in bringing everyone together based on the eternal concept of society and Nation and creating a well-structured society where there are no divisions left.'[22]

When the general elections took place in 1951–52, Guruji, unwilling to involve himself with political happenings, temporarily handed over the reins of the Sangh to Deoras and stayed at Lokmanya Tilak's bungalow in the Sinhgad fort for a month. The Jana Sangh fought the election but faced a massive defeat. They went into debt owing to the election expenses, and creditors came asking for their money. Deoras suggested collecting funds, to which Guruji said that spending the Sangh's money on the Jana Sangh wouldn't be right. At that time, Manohar Rao Oak (Vasantrao Oak's elder brother) and Balasaheb Ghatate were the treasurers of the Sangh, and moneylenders would often approach them, seeking repayment. They would tell the moneylenders, 'The credit papers have Deoras's signature. Why are you coming to us? The Sangh cannot pay you the money.'[23]

After Mookerjee died in 1953, Deoras sought Guruji's permission to join the Jana Sangh. Angry at Guruji's refusal, Deoras went to Balaghat. There, he began farming and kept away from the Sangh between 1953–60, not speaking with Guruji for seven years. While sending him to Uttar Pradesh, Guruji had told Bhausaheb Deoras, 'You must spend his lifetime there; we have to finish the Nehru family in UP. The Sangh must do this, and nobody else other than you is capable of this.'[24]

As per Appa Ghatate, the first year of the Sangh's Officers Training Corps was organised at Nagpur in 1954, with intellectual sessions headed by Deendayal Upadhyaya, Atal-ji and Nanaji Deshmukh. Balasaheb Deoras would attend the OTC every day but did not conduct a bauddhik session. When Appa asked Guruji why he refused to take part, he said, that what will the person who himself doesn't attend the Sangh tell the Sangh?

When Guruji received the news that Deoras was getting married, he called Bhaiyaji Dani—since their relationship was better—and with concern, asked how things would function if Deoras were married, especially as he would have to take over the responsibility if Guruji were to leave for the mountains. Bhaiyaji Dani, who held considerable clout in the Sangh, was not only a sarkaryavah despite being a married pracharak but also perhaps the only person who could openly smoke his Capstan cigarettes during the OTC. Nobody dared to stop him.

Laughing at Guruji's worries, Dani said, 'Why do you involve me when the two of you fight?' Dani clarified it was not Balasaheb, but

Bhaurao Deoras, who was getting married and was going to quit being a pracharak. He had chosen a bride, and the popular Maharashtrian dish, aloo poha (flattened rice and potato), had been eaten as per the tradition while picking a bride. Guruji heaved a sigh of relief! Dilip Deodhar had spoken to Dr Varnekar, the Sangh's first child-swayamsevak, about this, as he too had attended the ceremony. Dr Varnekar clarified that although a bride was selected, Bhaurao ultimately decided not to get married.

When Guruji turned fifty-one in 1957, Eknath Ranade and Bhaiyaji Dani came to meet him. They said, 'Deoras has gone from the Sangh, and the creditors are coming. The Jana Sangh needs money for elections, but until we return the money we owe them already, how will we get credibility? This is the main reason Deoras left. That is why we have decided to celebrate your birthday and felicitate you. We can repay the loan with the money you receive as gifts; otherwise, please allow us … some rich people are ready to donate money and help us.'

Guruji refused bluntly, saying, 'I am a sanyasi and cannot accept your felicitation.'

Then, Dani and Ranade said, 'We are not felicitating you, Guru Golwalkar. We are felicitating the sarsanghchalak.'

Even that didn't convince Guruji.

Bhaiyaji Dani, now slightly annoyed, countered, 'You are not a sanyasi; your ego is still alive, and a sanyasi cannot be egoistic. You are a man of ego.'

Guruji asked him not to talk nonsense, saying that it would create a conflict within the soul.

Dani countered him, 'But you say in your speeches that there is nothing like a soul.'

Guruji said, 'Okay, I will leave the post of sarsanghchalak; you find another sarsanghchalak and become debt-free.'

Dani replied, 'Alright, we will relieve you once we find someone better than you.'

Guruji said, 'You people neither listen to my logic, nor do you have any reverence for me. What should I do?'

Dani responded, 'You are the sarsanghchalak; you are our guide and philosopher. I am the sarkaryavah, the CEO of the Sangh. I am commanding you to accept our proposal.'[25]

Subsequently, Guruji's felicitation function was conducted and close to twenty-one lakh rupees were collected. Around this time, Guruji and Ranade's relationship turned sour. Ranade was sent away to Kanyakumari to build the Vivekananda Memorial. He returned to Nagpur only after Balasaheb Deoras became the sarsanghchalak.

Golwalkar always spoke about keeping away from politics, and yet he formed the Jana Sangh. Despite that, he chose not to participate in the election. But in the article that he wrote before the second general elections in 1957, he gave a very strong political message. Golwalkar wrote clearly, 'There is no provision in the Constitution for recalling a representative who might fail to answer to the electorate or who might go back upon the promises lavished upon the people at the time of the elections. Heavy is the responsibility of the voter, therefore. For it is in his hand now to seal the fate of the country for five long years … I belong to no political party, and no political party has any special claims upon me. I do not, therefore, advocate the cause of any particular person or party … I address myself to the great Hindu People, to strive for whom has become my Dharma, the hoary immortal Hindu People whom I worship as the veritable manifestation of the Eternal Divine. I pray to them to rouse themselves to their self-consciousness and freely and boldly exercise their right to vote without being misled, without being distracted or frightened into upholding any individual or party.'[26]

Golwalkar believed that a political party could be a vehicle for progress and that, for any political party to succeed, the individual and the organisation are equally important. He often said that a political party without committed workers was like a body with dysfunctional or helpless organs. Golwalkar always opposed the communists and the socialists, claiming that these groups took great pride in distancing themselves from Hindu identity and stood against Hindu traditions and rituals. They did not consider the cow as revered and followed the policy of Muslim appeasement. Their political conduct, he felt, was often anti-Hindu, which is why, he argued, it was time to vote like a Hindu and for the Hindu.

Despite Golwalkar's strong political appeal, it brought little electoral success to the Jana Sangh. In the first general elections, the party fielded ninety-four candidates but won only three seats, including two from West Bengal. The party had fought the elections along with the Hindu Mahasabha, and it won four seats. The Congress won 364 of the 489 seats. In the second election, the Jana Sangh won one additional seat, bringing their total to four while doubling their vote share to 6 per cent.

Achyutanand Mishra says, 'The chief minister of Uttar Pradesh, Dr Sampurnanand, was the candidate from Banaras in the 1957 election, and opposite him was the strong CPI candidate, Rustom Satin. He organised and executed an extremely impactful campaign. Dr Sampurnanand said that he was the chief minister, and every person in Varanasi was aware of his work, and that is why he would not go for any campaigning. His campaign was being managed by Kamalapati Tripathi, who was the education minister. Sarayu Prasad Dwivedi was the Jana Sangh candidate and had been the Mayor of Varanasi.'

Achyutananand Mishra and his colleagues in the Vidyarthi Parishad were handling Dwivedi's election work. As the voting day inched closer, it was clear that Sampurnanand was in trouble. Yadavrao Deshmukh was the Sangh pracharak in Banaras when the Sangh issued a message asking everyone to vote for Sampurnanand, who went on to win the election. Sarayu Prasad, who lost, created a huge ruckus. An inquiry committee was set up, and although it delivered its findings, the people had already made their choice.

After failing to achieve any success in the first elections, Golwalkar decided that movements and campaigns had to be rooted in issues related to Hindus and nationalism. After the elections, the 1952 Akhil Bharatiya Pratinidhi Sabha resolved to develop an action plan to combat cow slaughter and opposition to the Swadeshi movement, to transform these efforts into a broader movement. Golwalkar furthered Gandhi's vision for the Swadeshi movement, emphasising that love for Swadeshi should not be limited to only opposing the British, but should stem from a sense of patriotism and be reflected across all levels of national life. Golwalkar also opposed the bride and bridegroom wearing Western attire during their weddings, and he was against organising lavish wedding ceremonies. In the fifties, he protested strongly against beauty contests.

When the concept of Swadeshi was discussed in the context of nationalism, Golwalkar began a massive programme against cow slaughter to unite the Hindus. He sought a complete ban in India and ran a nationwide campaign. Fifty thousand swayamsevaks were employed all over the country. In January 1954, the Kumbh Mela was held in Prayag after the elections. A convention on cow protection was organised at the event, and under the command of Prabhudutt Brahmachari and Guruji, a letter with nearly 2,50,000 signatures opposing cow slaughter was sent to Nehru. The signed papers were sent in bullock carts to the Rashtrapati Bhavan and handed over to President Radhakrishnan. To uphold the religious sentiments of the Hindus, a demand was made for a central law on cow slaughter.

After Guruji's fifty-ninth birthday celebrations, the Sangh's Central Working Committee decided to build a memorial temple for Dr Hedgewar at Resham Baug in Nagpur. At that time, the site only had an elevated platform. A committee was formed, with Guruji appointed as its president. Although the required funds could have been collected from Nagpur and Vidarbha alone, a nationwide campaign—One Swayamsevak, One Rupee—was launched to attract participation from swayamsevaks across the country. For this, a photograph of the proposed memorial temple was prepared and sent to every swayamsevak.

Construction began in 1959 after the funds were collected. Initially, the arches in the temple's design reflected the Mughal architectural style, which Guruji modified to resemble bows. The inauguration of the temple occurred on 5 April 1962, coinciding with the Hindu New Year and Dr Hedgewar's birthday. People from across India attended the inauguration ceremony.

In his inspiring address to a gathering of swayamsevaks on the next day, Sri Guruji said that the intention of constructing this Smriti Mandir was not just to create another holy place of worship for thousands of faithful followers. He added, 'I wanted this here because this place is very sacred and pious. The RSS founder put his sweat and blood into the growth of the Sangh here in this land, and he was cremated here. This is the most sacred place for us, and it will continue to inspire us in the future. We must look at this Smriti Mandir from this point of view.'[27]

FORMATION OF THE VISHVA HINDU PARISHAD

In 1963, the atmosphere was abuzz with conversations about organising Hindus at the international level. Pracharak Lakshmanrao Bhide and Deendayal Upadhyaya, who were handling global Hindu organisations, explained the situation to Guruji. Meanwhile, Swami Chinmayananda expressed similar views in November 1963. Guruji handed over the responsibility to Dadasaheb Apte, who contacted over 200 religious heads and over forty religious organisations within nine months. On 29 August 1964, on the occasion of Janmashtami, at a meeting held at Swami Chinmayananda's Sandipani Ashram in Bombay, the Vishva Hindu Parishad came into being.

The Parishad decided in its first meeting to hold a three-day Hindu conference between 22–24 January 1966 during the Kumbh Mela in Allahabad. It would include an inter-faith conference, programmes focussed on unity in diversity and an exhibition on the continuum of the Hindu religion from the Vedic Era to modern times. During his journey to Badrinath, Guru Golwalkar offered atmapinda (offering one's being to the divine) at Brahma Kapal on 18 September 1968. After that, he was no longer the same Golwalkar as he had been before. Golwalkar inaugurated the conference for the Bharat Gau Seva Samaj organised by the RSS in Delhi in August 1964. In 1965, he permitted Sarkaryavah Balasaheb Deoras to address the Jana Sangh convention.

This movement against cow slaughter remained slow till after the India–Pakistan war in 1965 and the death of Prime Minister Lal Bahadur Shastri in 1966, but it picked up steam before the fourth general elections in 1967. The Sarvadaliya Goraksha Mahabhiyan Samiti came into being in September 1966, and Golwalkar himself served as a member of its management committee and played a key role in anchoring the entire movement. The Samiti's protest in front of Parliament on 7 November 1966 turned violent, and eight people, including one police officer, died. Prime Minister Indira Gandhi removed Home Minister Gulzarilal Nanda from the government to maintain her secular image because people perceived he had a soft corner towards Hindutva. Golwalkar, along with some members of the Samiti and a few saints, went on a hunger strike. Although one saint lost his life during the strike, it continued, and discussions about forming a new political party centred around cow slaughter gained momentum. Realising the potential political complications, Golwalkar and Deendayal Upadhyaya engaged in a dialogue with saints and ascetics. Once the government initiated talks on the issue, the protesters decided to call off the movement.

The movement greatly boosted the RSS and Jana Sangh's confidence, but it became amply clear that keeping the saints and ascetics under their control was an uphill task. During this time, Golwalkar addressed Hindu conferences in Nepal and Burma. The king of Nepal, Maharaja Bir Bikram Shah Dev, accepted an invitation to attend a Sangh's programme. However, the central government raised objections for political reasons. As a result, he could not come to the event. The

1967 general elections showed the political mileage of these activities when the Jana Sangh won thirty-five seats and formed non-Congress governments in several states with the support of other parties. After this, along with the Jana Sangh and the Sangh, other sister organisations were also strengthened.

In 1971, Jana Sangh representatives held a meeting in Nagpur, where Guruji Golwalkar emphasised the power of ideology and the importance of remaining firmly committed to it. At that time, there was intense debate within the Jana Sangh over the notion that abandoning one's ideology was necessary to attain political power. A large majority of members believed others would join them only if they distanced themselves from their ideology. Guruji Golwalkar was against this and said, '... I agree that a party that believes in a particular ideology cannot come to power. But I cannot accept that it will never come to power. The Labour Party in Britain was born in 1900, and they stuck to their ideology firmly for twenty-nine years and continued to work hard. They formed a coalition government for the first time in 1929. They were able to come to power on their own with an absolute majority for the first time ten years later in 1939.'[28]

At that time, the question likely to arise in the minds of many, including Atal Bihari Vajpayee, was whether their ideology would ever be accepted by the majority in the country? Guruji responded by saying that the time it would take for them to come to power depended on many factors. When Atal-ji specifically asked him which line they should adopt, all that Guruji said was, 'I have already said what I wanted to.'

The fruit of the seed that Golwalkar had planted decades ago was seen on 26 May 2014. The chants of 'Modi, Modi' reverberated through the Rashtrapati Bhavan premises. Energy and enthusiasm infused the environment. The lines of people waiting to participate in the event were never-ending, as if everyone wanted to witness the historic moment—the Bharatiya Janata Party's first government with an absolute majority. A long-time RSS pracharak, Narendra Modi's first swearing-in ceremony as the prime minister drew people from all over the country, along with many prominent overseas guests. The heads of government from the SAARC nations had been specially invited. It felt as though Guruji Golwalkar's words were coming true. The RSS has frequently criticised Guruji Golwalkar's book, *Bunch of Thoughts* and shown its disagreement with him. Mohan Bhagwat clearly expressed his thoughts during his lecture series in Delhi in September 2018 and said that people should see Guruji's thoughts in the context of the times.

Dr Manmohan Vaidya says, 'The clarification that sarsanghchalak Mohan Bhagwat has given regarding *Bunch of Thoughts* has led to the belief that the Sangh has rejected this book by Guruji Golwalkar, but this is not true. This book is a compilation of his thoughts on a host of issues from 1940 onwards, after Guruji became the sarsanghchalak. Its first edition was published in 1966, and the background of several of those thoughts was in the context and situation of that time. That period was a special one in India and the Sangh's history. That is why the thoughts expressed at that time should be seen in connection with the events that occurred then.

'When the responsibility of expanding the Sangh and giving it direction fell on Guruji Golwalkar's shoulder following Dr Hedgewar's death, he was only thirty-four years old. The activities of the Sangh had to be spread nationwide. The demand for Pakistan had become strong, and swayamsevaks from different parts of the country were taking part in the Quit India movement in 1942. Several swayamsevaks received a sentence of rigorous imprisonment, and some received death sentences as well. The demand for Pakistan fuelled the election of 1946. Hindus were being attacked in Muslim-dominated areas, and a gruesome genocide of the Hindus had taken place in Bengal due to "Direct Action". India had to face partition along with independence. At the same time, Hindus were being massacred en masse in Pakistan. Lakhs of Hindus had to come to their own country as refugees, and there was no one other than the swayamsevaks to care for them. The nation was in shock because of

Gandhi's assassination, and the Sangh was falsely implicated in it; a ban was imposed on it. This was the beginning of the dirty politics of hate and vengeance. The government could not prove its accusations against the Sangh. When all the doors for talks were shut, swayamsevaks went on a peaceful satyagraha, and finally the government lifted the ban. Again in 1962, there was an atmosphere of gloom in the country after India lost the war to China. The Communists openly supported the Chinese, and the conversion-related activities of the Christians were on the rise. The Justice Niyogi Commission was set up to investigate this, and once it submitted its report, the erstwhile Congress governments in Orissa and Madhya Pradesh made "anti-conversion" laws. There were protests against these laws, with support from the Church. Guruji's thoughts, which he had expressed to swayamsevaks and Indian citizens from time to time during this period, were compiled and came out as the book *Bunch of Thoughts*.'[29]

Guruji continued to guide on various subjects for eighteen years, but the book Bunch of Thoughts did not include his thoughts from this period. Therefore, a comprehensive compilation of his thoughts was published in twelve volumes in 2006 on his birth centenary, later summarised as *Shri Guruji: Drishti Aur Darshan*, which the sarsanghchalak had recommended for reading—so where does the opposition to Guruji's thoughts truly stem from?

Dr Vaidya notes that of the three dangers Guruji mentions in *Bunch of Thoughts*, the threat of Muslim fanaticism remains a global concern even today. Separatist elements within India pose a challenge to the nation's unity. Conversions driven by the church, its implicit support for anti-national activities and the threat of urban Naxalism are issues of deep concern. It is essential to remain vigilant against the extremist, jihadi and anti-national elements who, under the pretext of promoting Muslims and Christians and building a united future, are working to divide the nation. Guruji's warnings from that time continue to be relevant.

In a tribute to Guru Golwalkar published in the Sangh's mouthpiece, *Rajdharm*, in the February 1974 issue, Atal Bihari Vajpayee recalled a meeting of the Rashtriya Ekta Parishad (National Integration Council), where the views of the Sangh and Guruji on Muslims were discussed. Prime Minister Indira Gandhi chaired the meeting, while Vajpayee was a member of the council. Fakhruddin Ali Ahmed, then chancellor of the Aligarh Muslim University, was also present. During the session, Indira Gandhi referred to a marked passage from *Bunch of Thoughts* and asked Vajpayee its meaning.

Vajpayee said, 'If you want to understand its meaning, please invite respected Guruji to the meeting and ask him directly.'

'This means that there is a difference of opinion regarding this section,' replied Mrs Gandhi.

'No, there is no difference of opinion,' Vajpayee refuted, 'but I cannot give you the entire explanation. There will be some shortcomings. There are so many stalwarts present here. It won't be right if there are any shortcomings. You please call Guruji.'

Since inviting Golwalkar would be a little difficult, the prime minister suggested, 'You explain the meaning. So, it means that there is no place for the Muslims in India, doesn't it?'

'Where is this mentioned?' asked Vajpayee.

'It says here that the Muslims should merge themselves with the national mainstream,' Mrs Gandhi pointed out.

'What is written is correct,' Vajpayee agreed.

Mrs Gandhi asked, 'What is the national mainstream?' Vajpayee replied, 'If there is a difference of opinion regarding this itself, no meeting will be of any use.'[30]

In 1969, there was a suspicion that Guruji might be suffering from cancer, but he did not give it much attention. In May 1970, doctors confirmed the diagnosis during a routine health check-up. Dr Prafulla Desai, a cancer specialist from Mumbai, suggested immediate surgery, but Guruji deferred it until after the shiksha vargs are over. After Guruji concluded travels related to the vargs, he underwent tests at the Tata Cancer Hospital on 29 June. He got admitted on 30 June, and doctors performed the surgery on 1 July. Considering Guruji's fragile health, the all-India convention was held in Bombay instead of Nagpur that year. Balasaheb Deoras would go to the hospital every day and convey all the information about the meetings held between 10 and 12 July.

Around the same period, the central government in Delhi began to close in on the RSS, and the voices against the Sangh were on the rise. The administration had prohibited shakhas from being held in public parks. There were rumours that the government was going to table a bill to ban the organisation. The provincial offices of the Sangh began receiving notices levying income tax on the guru dakshina. Guruji addressed the meeting in Bombay for a short time and then returned to Nagpur on 4 August after spending three weeks in hospital. He underwent one round of tests before leaving for Nagpur amidst rumours that 'the sarsanghchalak is critically ill; there is a lot of internal strife for the post'.[31] V. Shankar, who had been Sardar Patel's secretary, presided over the Vijayadashami celebration on 8 and 9. In his speech on the occasion, Guruji stated that although the sarsanghchalak may be gravely ill, there is no conflict regarding the successor. Conflict or struggle, he said, arises only from selfishness. A tug of war is possible if the sarsanghchalak's post comes with wealth, money, a big house and luxury. But none of that existed in the Sangh. Such misinformation and slander would continue, but the Sangh must remain focussed solely on how to serve the nation. After the event, he once again left on his travels for the Sangh.

During his travels for the Sangh, Guruji Golwalkar returned to Nagpur from Calcutta by flight for the last time on 14 March 1973. He did not leave Hedgewar Bhavan after that. He would attend the shakha of the Mohite Sansthan in the courtyard of the Hedgewar Bhavan until 26 March. The Akhil Bharatiya Pratinidhi Sabha Conference took place from 22 to 25 March in Nagpur at the RSS's main office. Guruji sat through the proceedings, and on 25 March, Balasaheb Deoras requested

Guruji to say a few words. Guruji did not look too well, and he couldn't breathe properly, but still he spoke for forty minutes.

Guruji said, 'When I said on the first day of the Thane meeting that the work of the Sangh had to be done by other people, and I have little to contribute, a few senior karyakartas came and told me I shouldn't have said that. But I had spoken the truth. The Sangh won't be affected very badly, irrespective of whether this man exists or not. We have come together to create an organisation.'

He also spoke about the nation and society, and in the end, he said, 'Give importance to the programmes of the Sangh shakhas, its work-culture, the behaviour of the swayamsevaks, their character and work with deep focus. If you do this much, you will be victorious in all fields. I will only say this much today. Who knows if God will give me another chance to speak or not?'[32]

The next day, Guruji found it difficult to bathe by himself and could barely walk to the Sanghsthan. He struggled to finish his meals. In Nagpur and Vidarbha, it is tradition to announce the names of the Sangh office-bearers on Hindu New Year's Day, marking the beginning of activities for the coming year. On the last day of the year, the new moon day—2 April—Guruji penned his wish on the official letterhead, sealed it in an envelope and gave it to the administrative head of the office, Pandurang Pant Kshirsagar, saying, 'Open this once my body goes silent.' Kshirsagar's hands were trembling, and his heart was agitated when he took that envelope. That same night, the Shankaracharya of the Kanchi Math, Jayendra Saraswathi, came to meet Guruji and blessed him.

GURUJI GOLWALKAR FINAL MOMENTS

On 19 April, Guruji wrote his will and donated his family home in Ramtek to the Bharatiya Utkarsha Mandal.[33] The next day, he sent the items he would use during his puja (ritual worship) to his cousin,

Vasudev Ramachandra Golwalkar. At that point, he had only two items left: a pocket watch that had Swami Akhandananda's name etched behind it, and his kamandalu (water vessel), a symbol of his monkhood. Guruji's health was declining rapidly. On 1 June, a full moon day, he tied his holy scripture with a thread and kept it in an almirah. He cleaned his khadau (wooden footwear) and placed them on the lower shelf. On 3 June, Mausi Lashmibai Kelkar came to see him. When she enquired about his health, all Guruji said was, 'All the preparation for my departure is done.' Mausi was stunned. She left quietly after touching his feet.

Guruji woke up in the morning on 5 June, completed his daily ablutions, sat on his armchair and began chanting. He had his tea as usual at 6 a.m., his bath at 7 and started his daily sadhana. He came out at 8 a.m. when Atal Bihari Vajpayee and four or five others were waiting for him. Guruji felt tired after speaking for about half an hour and had difficulty breathing. He was served a little buttermilk and administered oxygen after his meal. He rested till 2.30 p.m. He drank a few sips of tea in the evening, but around 6 p.m., his breathing became extremely laboured. Dr Mukund Rao Shastri and Dr Bhagwat were called in, but nothing seemed to work. The evening prayers were scheduled for seven, but Guruji was finding it difficult. His aide brought him a chair for him to sit on and finish his prayers. Guruji completed his prayers but did not have his usual tea later. Abaji had left for some work, while Baburao Chauthaiwale and Vishnu Muthavali stayed. Guruji asked for water. He took two sips and stood up to go to the washroom. But he couldn't move. Baburao Chauthaiwale helped him to his room and helped him settle down in the easy chair. Vishnu called out to Guruji twice. There was no answer. However, he was still breathing. A team of doctors arrived, administered some injections and oxygen. His pulse became gradually weaker, and at 5.09 p.m., Guruji breathed his last.

The next day, on 6 June, an emergency meeting of the Central Working Committee was convened, where Pandurang Pant Kshirsagar brought the envelope that Guruji had given him. When they opened the envelope, there were not one but three letters.

Babasaheb Bhide read out the first letter: 'To all my swayamsevak friends, the activities of the Sangh will continue according to its constitution. The question is to select the next sarsanghchalak according to that very constitution. Based on my discussions with the All-India [Akhil Bharatiya] Karyakari Mandal members, I am expressing their decision in brief, which is that our own Madhukar Dattatreya Balasaheb Deoras would assume the responsibility of the sarsanghchalak's position after my death.'[34]

Balasaheb Deoras read the second letter: 'Our work is dedicated to the nation, to our purpose and is not based on personality-worship. Apart from the founder of the Sangh, who decided its purpose and ideology, there is no need to eulogise or build a memorial for anyone else.'[35]

Balasaheb read the third letter as well, a personal one. 'My dearest, respected swayamsevak friends, Dr Hedgewar's body fell silent on 21 June, and the responsibility of the sarsanghchalak post fell on my shoulders based on his will. I did not know anything, and everybody guided me. I continued to bear the responsibility. During this time, my character, shortcomings, and mistakes may have hurt several karyakartas and volunteers. I seek your forgiveness with folded hands.'[36]

5

Balasaheb Deoras

The Pioneer

In 1943, Guruji Golwalkar introduced Balasaheb Deoras at a Sangh shiksha varg in Pune. He said, 'Many of the swayamsevaks among you haven't seen Dr Hedgewar. You will see Dr Hedgewar if you see Balasaheb.'[1]

Veteran journalist and writer Ram Bahadur Rai notes, 'Balasaheb's life can be seen in two parts. In the first [part], he is Dr Hedgewar and Guruji's colleague; he complemented them. On the other hand, he is like a lotus in full bloom. A life matured and grown to its fullest through penance. He has a unique identity in this form. Having grown up under the ideology of the Sangh, he witnessed the sprouting of the seed of the Sangh. He became the instrument for the seed to grow into a sapling and to keep it safe. Babasaheb's speciality is that he grew up away from the two sarsanghchalaks, his predecessors, and he became the sarsanghchalak. But achieving this milestone meant little to him; the post just strolled towards him. Deoras aspired to bring about unity in ideological goals, and he never aspired for official posts. If this hadn't been the case, there could have been conflicts at the leadership level. Deoras will be known for creating the discipline that became a mark of the RSS.'[2]

In June 1973, the third sarsanghchalak, Balasaheb Deoras, addressed the swayamsevaks in Nagpur in his first-ever speech. He said, 'Being the sarsanghchalak, I have three things to say to the swayamsevaks. First, there will be portraits of only two sarsanghchalaks at any programme of the Sangh. Second, no memorial in my name will be constructed in Nagpur. And third, you may call me "param poojaneeya (most respected/revered) sarsanghchalak" but not "param poojaneeya Balasaheb Deoras", as you did with "param poojaneeya Guruji". The term param poojaneeya is appropriate for them, but not for me. Addressing me as maananeeya (respected) Balasaheb Deoras is enough.'

Deoras had said that the Sangh would no longer be ekachalakanuvartit (supremo-led) but would function with a spirit of teamwork. His belief in teamwork was legendary. Just about a month after becoming the sarsanghchalak, he clearly outlined his roadmap for the future at a meeting of swayamsevaks in Nagpur. Departing from Golwalkar's philosophy, Deoras placed his faith in the strength of the swayamsevaks. He believed that the commitment and energy of the organisation's workers were more valuable and powerful than ideology and philosophy.

Deoras took complete control of the Sangh's operations as soon as he took over the reins. On the very first day, he promised to transform the organisation's character and discipline without altering its ideology. But this wasn't a simple task. Before this, the words of the sarsanghchalak were considered paramount and beyond the scope of questioning. The two sarsanghchalaks preceding Deoras (Hedgewar and Golwalkar) had handed over the post while on their deathbeds, and their successors had taken over only after their passing. However, Balasaheb made Professor Rajendra Singh, alias Rajju bhaiyya, the sarsanghchalak while he was alive. During his tenure, debates often arose about whether ideology or the politics of power held greater importance for the RSS and the Bharatiya Janata Party. Politics was central to Balasaheb's personality, but he was not political in the sense of seeking power for himself.

In the real sense, the picture of the Sangh we see today is more open and inclusive than the organisation of yore that was considered walled and restrictive. Balasaheb Deoras sowed the seeds of the claim that the Sangh was *not* an organisation of 'high-class Maharashtrian Brahmins' but was something broader in its character. He envisioned a casteless organisation that, while praising the varna system, engaged with supporters of reservations. Though viewed with suspicion, it was an organisation that opened its doors to Muslims. Under his influence, the Sangh began shedding its official identity as a purely socio-cultural body, moving towards a political role and embracing a willingness to change. These shifts bear the unmistakable stamp of Balasaheb Deoras.

Balasaheb, i.e., Madhukar Dattatreya Deoras, was born on 11 December 1915 into an eleven-member Deshasta Rigvedi Brahmin family based in Nagpur. His ancestors had migrated from Andhra Pradesh and settled there. Balasaheb's father, Dattatreya Krishnarao Deoras, was a junior revenue officer. He had a small patch of farmland in Balaghat. Madhukar had nine siblings. He had three elder brothers: Diwakar was in medicine, Bhaskar was in the police force, and the third brother, Dinkar, was a lawyer. The family had hoped that Balasaheb would join the civil services and become an IAS officer, but he began attending the RSS shakhas right from his childhood and stayed with the Sangh throughout his life. In 1926, when he was eleven years old, Balasaheb attended shakhas as a bal-swayamsevak—a turning point after which he never looked back. His younger brother, Muralidhar (Bhaurao), joined him, and the two were famous in the Sangh as the Deoras brothers.

His original surname was 'Devaraju', which became Deoras over time. Vinoba Bhave once said of him, 'One who has been made with the ras (juice) of all deities is Deoras.' During his childhood, Kush Pathak became Balasaheb's army, and he was its general. In Sangh's early days, he chose a Congress bastion—an old part of Nagpur where half the city's population lived—as the base of its operations. Deoras's ancestral home was in the same area.

Balasaheb was a brilliant student and completed his high school from Nagpur's New English School in 1931. He pursued his BA from Morris College in 1935, where Sanskrit and philosophy were his favourite subjects. Although he completed his law studies in 1937, he never worked as a lawyer. He was a talented hockey and cricket player. According to Devendra Swaroop, a long-time associate of the Sangh, had Dr Hedgewar not mentored Balasaheb with great intention, he would have either been a revolutionary or an IAS officer. In 1937, Balasaheb had become the karyavah for the Itwari shakha in Nagpur, but he had been involved with the youth shakha and overseeing its activities even before that appointment.

While in the Sangh, Balasaheb became keenly interested in wars and the military, often reading books and watching films on the subjects. He often went to watch English war films at the Regent Cinema in Sitabuldi and the Liberty Cinema Hall in Sadar. He read the newspaper for almost two hours a day, an activity without which he thought he would become seriously ill. After becoming sarsanghchalak, he was once asked what path he might have taken had he not become an IAS officer or led the Sangh. He said he would have joined the army and risen to the position of chief.

Dattopant Thengadi has written that because Balasaheb's house was in the old Nagpur area, most of the neighbours were Dalits or belonged to disadvantaged social classes. Thereby, the number of Dalits in that shakha was very high. Throwing light on another aspect of Deoras's character, Thengadi notes, 'Dr Cholkar opened an orphanage for Dalit students and those from backward castes in old Nagpur. One day, Dr Cholkar asked Dr Hedgewar for a karyakarta (volunteer) to run the orphanage. Dr Hedgewar sent him to Balasaheb, who took care of the orphanage for two years apart from focussing on his studies and Sangh activities. The management of the orphanage appreciated his efforts.'[3]

Balasaheb would assist the Dalit swayamsevaks in the shakha, play with them and share his meals with them. All swayamsevaks were welcome in his home and served food. Though his mother disapproved of serving food to the Dalits alongside others, Balasaheb insisted that his swayamsevak friends eat with everyone else, use the same plates and that those utensils would not be washed and kept separately. This was unthinkable in those days, but Balasaheb's mother, despite initial resistance, eventually relented and began feeding everyone together, with the same love and care.

Golwalkar returned from Swami Akhandananda's Sargachhi ashram in 1937 and joined the Sangh. That was the year when the first shiksha varg was held in Pune. Balasaheb was its head trainer. He also attended the important 1939 Sindi meeting, and after that, he was sent to Calcutta with Golwalkar as his assistant to start the Sangh's activities in the city.

After World War II, India was in a state of great turmoil. The Muslim League had raised a demand for a separate country for the Muslim-majority areas at its Lahore session. Around the same time, there was much speculation about differences of opinion between Golwalkar and Deoras. One reason was that, by the time Golwalkar joined the organisation, people already regarded Deoras as one of its prominent leaders and saw him as a likely next sarsanghchalak. It was true that Dr Hedgewar was especially fond of Deoras.

Deoras's annoyance was obvious when he distanced himself from the first meeting that Guruji called after becoming the sarsanghchalak. When Guruji summoned him, Deoras responded that he was busy organising food for the swayamsevaks. Many had felt that Deoras would be the Sangh's chief, as he had played an important role in the organisation from its inception. However, when Hedgewar appointed Golwalkar as the sarkaryavah and sent Deoras to Calcutta, it signalled Hedgewar's inclination to pass the Sangh's reins to Golwalkar. It is said that before sending Deoras to Calcutta, Hedgewar had called both Golwalkar and Deoras and clarified that although he wished to choose Deoras as the sarsanghchalak, he felt he was not mature enough for the responsibility yet; he should be the sarsanghchalak after Golwalkar, leading him to accept the post.

There were frequent rumours about the strained relationship between Golwalkar and Deoras, but Dr Shrirang Godbole, an experienced researcher on the Sangh, notes, 'The closing ceremony of a camp for 1,300 swayamsevaks from the Vidarbha province was held in Baradwari near Nagpur in December 1946. In this ceremony, Guruji announced that Balasaheb Deoras would deliver the closing speech, who is the person because of whom people respect me as the sarsanghchalak, and [that] the camp had been a success only because of his tireless efforts and valuable guidance.'[4]

During his life, Deoras not only witnessed several major national events—such as the struggle for Independence, the Bihar revolt, the Emergency, the Janata Party's victory, the formation of the BJP, Operation Bluestar, the Ram Janmabhoomi movement and demolition of the Babri Masjid—but also played a vital role in them. Some believe that his role was controversial, and he faced criticism for the nature of his involvement. But there is no doubt that if anyone deserves credit for driving the RSS out of Mohitewadi in Nagpur and giving it a national footprint, it has to be Balasaheb Deoras.

PROPONENTS OF HARMONY

Avinash Deshpande, the former national public relations chief of the RSS, believes that Deoras had a prominent social outlook in his personality and took a strong stand against social evils and inequalities plaguing India. Emergency happened during his tenure, and the responsibility of recovering from it fell on his shoulders. He put the might of his organisation behind the Janata Party. While advocating for joining the Janata Party, Deoras would often say that if everyone didn't unite, they would end up in prison—that this was merely a parole. He had once commented in the presence of shankaracharyas and other religious leaders that no human being can be a Dalit, attracting many who were protesting against social discrimination and inequality.

Another example of his commitment to social harmony was his participation in Vasant Vyakhyanmala, a prominent event in Pune that brought together scholars, political leaders and experts of various fields from all over the country. Bal Gangadhar Tilak and M.G. Ranade started the programme in 1875, and each session featured lectures on diverse topics. Nearly a century later, on 8 May 1974, Sarsanghchalak Balasaheb Deoras delivered a lecture on the subject, 'Social Equality and Hindu Unity'.

Scholars and social researchers keenly observed Deoras's lecture. When questioned on why he chose the particular theme, he said that unity among Hindus was essential for national progress and welfare. However, the most prominent issue remains social equality, a delicate and relevant concern. Deoras stressed, 'I feel it is important to speak on this issue. I do not claim to be an expert or thinker on this subject, but I meet people and understand their feelings and thoughts.'[5]

Balasaheb asked the first question: 'Who is a Hindu?' The audience came up with several answers, but none of them felt complete. They were either short, partially developed or too descriptive. He mentioned the 1956 Hindu Code Bills, a series of legislations addressing Hindu personal laws, and said, 'This law … applies to everyone except Muslims, Christians and Jews. This bill addressed the personal problems of Hindus. There are many communities apart from the Sanatanis, Lingayats, Arya Samajis, Jains, Sikhs, and Buddhists included in the bill. We want to bring them all together and make them feel united. This does not mean creating an organisation, and this is, by no means, an easy task.'[6]

Then, Balasaheb's tone became aggressive: 'The Sangh Parivar takes pride in our religion and culture, but this alone cannot solve the problems of a society based on caste. We need to understand that whatever we believe in is not correct, and it is erroneous to think that whatever is old is good. "Old is gold" is not always true.'[7]

He emphasised the need to break the deeply ingrained habit of dividing society along caste lines, stating that Hindu society required significant reform. In his speech, Balasaheb strongly advocated for the abolition of the caste system and underscored the importance of inter-caste marriages, promoting the idea of 'roti-beti'—sharing food and familial ties across castes. Decades later, in September 2018, Mohan Bhagwat echoed the same message at a lecture session. But the conversation didn't end there. The topic was deliberated on at a shiksha varg and even at the All India Pratinidhi Sabha. The issue of reservations came up, during which someone commented that a few Dalit leaders had used insulting language against upper-caste individuals. At this point, Balasaheb interrupted and firmly stated that if upper castes had faced the same treatment that Dalits had endured for centuries, their language would have been no different. He then firmly reiterated the urgent need to abolish the caste system.

It is interesting to note that Golwalkar had supported the Hindu caste system and praised the *Manusmriti* in an interview with the Marathi newspaper *Navkaal*. However, Dilip Deodhar contests this; Golwalkar had never spoken about the varna system. During another interview in 1972, his reaction suggested that it was an ancient Indian system which has undergone a sea change. Even otherwise, this debate between Maratha versus Brahmin, that is Shivaji versus Peshwa and Bajirao-Deshpande has continued. People in North India see the Deshpandes as Kayasthas. As the Brahmin Peshwas gained strength, the Bhosales continued to weaken, and this conflict intensified during the British rule. Tilak was one of the most powerful leaders, but the Marathas became active in 1942. The four-class system continued until Gandhi and Vinoba Bhave's time.

About three years after Guruji Golwalkar's interview, senior journalist Vinayak Gokhale interviewed Balasaheb at the Dr Hedgewar Bhavan, and the interview was published in the *Kirloskar* magazine's August 1973 issue. The question was whether the Sangh had a different perspective on the caste system. Balasaheb's answer was, 'Guruji had delivered a lecture on Varna-system. But everybody has his own way of articulating things. Guruji had deep insight into our ancient literature and dharma. That's why he would refer to ancient examples. He would give you examples of Germany, Israel and Indonesia. Guruji would say things in a way that values of our ancient tradition remained intact. Still, he would call today's system a chaotic system.' Gokhale had pressed on asking what the RSS thought about the varna system. To which Balasaheb had said, 'Please write it clearly, the RSS does not believe in any kind of "varna system" … Everybody has accepted that in the RSS there is nothing like untouchability and caste discrimination … Remember this is almost a 2000-4000 years old problem. We don't need fury and stunts to resolve it … I feel that the increase of RSS "shakhas" in the so-called untouchable localities can help resolve this problem in a big way.'[8]

During the annual Vasant Vyakhyanmala programme, Deoras denounced the varna system as a 'blot on Hindu society' and said that it should be abolished. Shortly afterwards, a meeting of prominent individuals was held in Nagpur to discuss the issue of reservation. Brahmins constituted an influential majority in the Maharashtra Congress. It was deliberated that the reservation should not be permanent. Deoras listened to the discussion without offering comments. When asked him for his guidance on the matter, he finally said, 'You are all educated people; can't you understand that this is not a financial matter? You have never thought about the obstacles Ambedkar had to face. Place yourself in his position and think.' When the question arose of how long the reservation system should last and when it should end, Deoras said, 'Please understand that although reservation might bring a lot of benefits, any person would feel ashamed to call himself "backward". I feel that reservation should continue until the time that even a single person identifies himself "backwards" in our country.' During his twenty-two-year-long tenure as the sarsanghchalak, there were no discussions about this matter in the Sangh. During Deoras's stint, non-Brahmin leadership took over, especially in the RSS and the Jana Sangh in Maharashtra. However, there are very few individuals from the Dalit community occupying key leadership positions in the organisation. Mostly the upper-caste members become leaders, and all sarsanghchalaks, right from Dr Hedgewar to Dr Mohan Bhagwat, except Rajju bhaiyya, have been Brahmins.

Deoras believed that if we had to strengthen Hindu society, there was an urgent need to eliminate its weaknesses. Ram Bahadur Rai remarks, 'After Independence, Balasaheb Deoras and the then sarsanghchalak, Guruji Golwalkar, had distinct lines of thought. Their differences of opinion regarding what the Sangh should do after independence were clear within a year itself. But in 1948, when the Sangh was banned for the first time after Mahatma Gandhi's assassination and Golwalkar was arrested, Bhaiyaji Dani and Balasaheb Deoras handled the leadership of the Sangh.'

Golwalkar was the sarsanghchalak, but Deoras was out of his post between 1953–60 and was no longer in the Sangh. It is said that Deoras did not follow Golwalkar during that time. He later joined the Sangh and eventually became its chief. According to Deodhar, this proves that the Sangh does not oppose individuality; otherwise, Golwalkar would never have taken him back. The Sangh focuses solely on what is beneficial for the organisation.

Vasantrao Oak was considered the head of the Sangh in Delhi and northern India, and he was Sardar Patel's friend. Patel was the minister for Home Affairs, who was also in charge of refugee welfare. The Sangh used to run camps for refugees. Vasantrao Oak, Balasaheb Deoras and Sardar Patel wanted to form a political party together. However, Dr Mahesh Sharma, a BJP Rajya Sabha member, believes that it was only Oak who wanted to start a political party, and Patel and Deoras were not a part of this.

In the 1967 general elections, the Jana Sangh had won a maximum of thirty-seven seats, and over 250 legislators of the Jana Sangh were elected in different states. Balasaheb Deoras's decision proved to be correct when he appointed Deendayal Upadhyaya as the president of the Jana Sangh. Apart from this, the party joined coalition governments in Uttar Pradesh, Rajasthan and Madhya Pradesh. Balasaheb and Deendayal Upadhyaya saw this as a temporary arrangement, but a leader like Vajpayee was very pleased with this political success.

However, the coalition governments did not last long. Balasaheb, who had been observing the political developments keenly, could visualise the future. Consequently, he directed the general secretary of the Jana Sangh, Nanaji Deshmukh, to accompany Jayaprakash Narayan. JP agreed, subject to certain conditions, after which Sangh members were included on several committees. Balasaheb was reaching out to many individuals who were considered critics of the RSS, one of whom was Vinoba Bhave. Balasaheb went to his Paunar ashram to meet Bhave. After the meeting, Bhave said, 'I am an unofficial member of the RSS.'[9]

BALASAHEB BECOMES THE SARSANGHCHALAK

Despite all the discussions and misunderstandings, Golwalkar had decided to appoint Balasaheb as the Sangh's sarsanghchalak much earlier. After his death on 5 June 1973, one of the three letters he had left behind confirmed his decision. Balasaheb had no inkling about this and found out only on 6 June when the letters were read out. However, Guruji had already discussed this with the provincial coordinators. By the time Deoras ascended to the post of sarsanghchalak at the age of fifty-eight, he had spent decades in the RSS.

Guruji's discussion to select Deoras mildly upset Dattopant Thengadi, a senior leader who had felt that Guruji would make him the sarsanghchalak. Guruji then sent Deoras's younger brother, Bhaurao Deoras, to Uttar Pradesh with the responsibility of ousting the Nehru dynasty from the state and setting up the Sangh. After the Pakistan war in 1971 that led to the formation of Bangladesh, Prime Minister Indira Gandhi's popularity was at its peak. She had won the general election in March of the same year with an overwhelming majority. But there was also increasing anger in the country over the allegations of corruption against the central government.

Deoras understood the political climate and instructed the Jana Sangh's leadership to channel public anger against the government into political demonstrations, organising them nationwide with citizen support. At the party's convention in Kanpur in February 1973, the president had already outlined a blueprint for this. This was likely the first time that the RSS had come forward to collaborate with its political ally, the Jana Sangh. Deoras tried to present the anger against Indira Gandhi as public angst, and soon enough, voices began to rise against her.

Balasaheb was keen to join the Quit India movement in 1942, but Guruji did not permit him to do so. Simultaneously, Balasaheb and JP developed a strong friendship. But after Gandhi's assassination in 1948, JP believed the Sangh had a role to play in the killing and protested in front of its offices. He also staged a protest in front of the *Organiser*'s office in Delhi. The work the swayamsevaks had done during the 1966–67 Bihar famine had impressed JP. When Balasaheb became the sarsanghchalak in 1973 and JP was leading a movement against Indira Gandhi, Deoras called Nanaji Deshmukh and asked him to meet JP with a message: 'Tell him I cannot take part in the movement being a swayamsevak, but you are our leader and the Sangh will back you on the condition that you have to acknowledge publicly that there are no differences between you and the Sangh.' Deoras conveyed a message through Nanaji, 'I will stand by you like how Lakshman stood with Ram and will obey all your orders.'[10] After this, JP and the RSS came together.

Describing an incident from the same period, Govindacharya said it was only thanks to Balasaheb that he survived, as many within the Sangh were targeting him. In 1974, during JP's political agitation in Bihar, Govindacharya was the vibhag (division) pracharak in Bihar. That a Sangh vibhag pracharak would enthusiastically take part in a political movement was unexpected. However, Govindacharya was deeply involved in that agitation, and many irate Sangh members were prepared to take action against him. Meanwhile, Balasaheb visited Patna and said that it was not right to treat the Bihar movement as just a law and order issue, but acknowledged that there was an aspect of truth and injustice in it. Govindacharya was advised to present his justification directly to Balasaheb. Though eager to meet Balasaheb, he could not do so initially because of the fear of arrest. Eventually, he was summoned to Nagpur for a meeting attended by several Sangh leaders. Govindacharya says, 'I felt like I was standing in the accused box in court at that meeting. There were a lot of opinions expressed, but most were against me. However, Balasaheb encouraged me to give out all the details right from the beginning.' Govindacharya spoke for two hours about the role of the Sangh in the Bihar movement. Once he finished, Balasaheb said, 'You have entered the arena with no preparation. This will create trouble, but there is no cause for worry. We will find a way.' Govindacharya added that this movement was aimed at change, and that the Sangh, as an organisation, was not involved.

Balasaheb requested Govindacharya to stay back after the meeting, and asked him in private, 'What do you want to achieve from this agitation?'

With a sparkle in his eyes, Govindacharya said, 'I was a young man brimming with enthusiasm, and I said that we want systemic change and this movement offers a lot of possibilities.'

'Look,' Balasaheb answered, 'so much will not happen ... but it would be enough if the movement can stop corruption and pressurise the people sitting in government to change themselves.'

Balasaheb was considering the Bihar agitation as an opportunity for social change and encouraged the swayamsevaks who wished to participate in it. JP and Balasaheb met in Delhi, and after that, Balasaheb stated in Delhi on 1 December 1974, 'Jayaprakash Narayan is a saint and has come forward to pull our society out of bad and tough times.'

After returning from Delhi, JP said, 'I am extremely impressed with Balasaheb Deoras.'[11]

A while later, Deoras had sent Manohar Andhare and Mama Bhomre, editors of *Yugdharma* and *Tarun Bharat,* respectively, to Bihar. He asked them for a ground report on the Sangh, its offices and karyakartas in Bihar. Both travelled the length and breadth of the state and concluded that the Sangh is in terrible shape in Bihar. The shakha offices were invisible, and the organisation's karyakartas had joined JP's movement, working as his soldiers and devotees. Deoras laughed, listening to their account. Shocked at his reaction, the editors asked him, 'We are worried about the terrible state of the Sangh, and you seem to be happy?' Deoras said that they had seen Hedgewar's Sangh alive and kicking, and JP's movement is a part of the Sangh. However, many members of the cadre said that this was against the Sangh's principles. To prevent further misunderstandings, Balasaheb praised JP in his capacity as the sarsanghchalak and criticised Indira Gandhi. Deoras addressed a rally at the Ram Leela Maidan in Delhi, speaking openly about the policies of the government and the situation in the country. Traditionally, sarsanghchalaks refrained from delivering such overtly political speeches.

The coming together of JP and the RSS, along with the growing Bihar movement, deeply worried Prime Minister Indira Gandhi. A section believed that if she hadn't lost the case in the Allahabad High Court, Mrs Gandhi would have considered imposing another ban on the Sangh. Balasaheb expected something like this to happen, which is why he said at a shiksha varg in Rohtak on 16 June 1975, 'Talks about banning the Sangh again started soon after they lifted the ban in July 1949 and continue even now. We didn't take this seriously initially, but I did make a statement in January–February where I said that the Sangh cannot be finished just by locking up 1,000 or 2,000 swayamsevaks. We don't do our work thinking about whether the Sangh will be banned or not. We are running the Sangh with steely determination and commitment. If there is a ban, we will convert even that into an opportunity.'[12]

Balasaheb's apprehensions came true, and the government declared Emergency at midnight on 25 June 1975. JP, Vajpayee, Advani and other Opposition leaders were arrested. When Balasaheb reached Nagpur on 30 June, he was imprisoned too in Pune's Yerwada Jail. On 4 July, the government banned twenty-seven organisations, including the Sangh. Balasaheb saw this ban as an opportunity and sent a message from prison, declaring that the time had come to achieve what had previously remained out of reach. Deoras kept repeating that victory would be theirs; one simply needed to be patient and face the challenges with courage—that was the only way. While Balasaheb was in prison, the underground leadership had called a meeting in the last week of July to discuss future strategy. Madhavrao Mule had been nominated as the sarsanghchalak for this meeting. Zonal supervisors were appointed at the meeting: Yadavrao Joshi (South), Moropant Pingle (West), Bhaurao Deoras (East) and Rajju bhaiyya (North). Rambhau Godbole was placed in charge of Bihar and Bengal and made the organisational secretary; he was additionally tasked with coordinating with opposition parties. Moropant Pingle headed the Lok Sangharsh Samiti, while Eknath Ranade managed lines of communication with the government. Eknath Ranade had to speak directly with Indira Gandhi, and his role was kept under wraps. Even when the Sangh was banned soon after Mahatma Gandhi's assassination, Eknath Ranade and Bhaiyaji Dani had played a crucial role in negotiating with the government and getting the ban revoked.

Balasaheb would write to Mrs. Gandhi whenever the opportunity arose, suggesting she should lift the ban on the Sangh. While a few in the organisation believed that he shouldn't have written the letters, the majority believed Balasaheb had acted in the spirit of democracy, so communication remained intact. Balasaheb wrote the first letter in August, in which he praised her Independence Day speech. In the second letter, written in November, he congratulated Indira Gandhi after the Supreme Court upheld her election from Rae Bareli. Nilanjan Mukhopadhyay says, 'There are no discussions regarding these letters in the Sangh. In his third letter, written in July 1976, Balasaheb had sought information about the improvement in relationships with Islamabad and Peking. Ranade used to act as a bridge for these letters. Balasaheb involved the Sangh so deeply in this conflict, forcing Indira Gandhi to say that even ten per cent of Sangh karyakartas had not been caught and that they had gone underground. Even with the ban, the Sangh stayed functional and whole, increasing its presence in Kerala. The difference between the ban in 1948 and 1975 was that, in 1948, the ban had weakened the Sangh, leaving it with hardly any funds to run the families of the swayamsevaks and leaders. The pressure from the government was more severe ... but after the emergency, the Sangh had converted the ban into an opportunity and had grown stronger. It gave strength to the movement while being underground, and the swayamsevaks helped the families of the leaders of other parties who had been imprisoned.[13]'

Balasaheb was the first person to actively involve students in politics during the Gujarat Navnirman agitation in 1974. After that, it became almost a norm in Indian politics to mobilise students onto the streets to force the corrupt and ineffective governments to resign. This tactic was tested once again in Bihar. Ram Bahadur Rai mentions, 'I was a member of the Chhaatra Sangharsh Sanchalan Samiti (Student Struggle Committee) in 1974. There used to be common meetings between

Jayaprakash Narayan, the Jan Sangharsh Samiti and the Chhaatra Sangharsh Samiti. Once, when JP came to Delhi in February 1974, there was a small piece of news in the newspapers that there had been a long meeting between JP and Balasaheb Deoras. We asked JP about what he had spoken to Deoras about. JP had asked Deoras what Hindutva meant. His answer was, "Hindutva is not a religion; it is nationalism." I was very impressed with that.'[14]

Ram Bahadur Rai, who edited a book on Deoras, *Hamare Balasahab Devras: The Life and Legacy of a Towering Political Pioneer*, notes that in March 1975, Balasaheb accomplished something politically significant: he succeeded in convincing Jayaprakash Narayan to attend the national convention of the Jana Sangh. Earlier, JP had invited the Jana Sangh to be a part of the Opposition parties' protests in Delhi. It was during this convention that Jayaprakash Narayan gave the Sangh a clean chit when he said, 'If you are fascists, even I am a fascist.'[15] Following his comment, Deoras compared JP to Mahatma Gandhi, Vinoba Bhave and Golwalkar. By placing Golwalkar and Gandhi next to each other, Deoras had distanced the Sangh from Nathuram Godse and freed it from the accusation of Gandhi's assassination.

Samajwadi leader Madhu Limaye writes in the book *Janata Party Experiment*, 'Deoras had congratulated Indira Gandhi for winning the appeal in the Supreme Court on her election. Distancing himself from the JP movement, he had asked Indira Gandhi to remove the ban on the RSS. Even Vinoba Bhave had been requested to intervene in this matter.'[16]

A few believed this step was part of Balasaheb's strategy, which the common karyakartas of the party did not appreciate. At the time this letter was written, those operating underground attempted to convince Indira Gandhi to agree to contest elections. They had even decided that, if necessary, they would not hesitate to seek a pardon to make that happen. Within the RSS, Balasaheb's letter drew two contrasting reactions. Some felt it was the right move, given the strategic thinking behind it. Others, who viewed the struggle as one rooted in ideology, were disheartened by his decision to write the letter.

After he took over as the sarsanghchalak, Deoras faced an important question: how would Muslims be brought under the Sangh's umbrella? Although the Sangh's foundation lay in Hindutva and creating a Hindu nation, its definition of a 'Hindu' differed vastly from the Hindu Mahasabha's and Savarkar's. Though the Sangh had accepted the Muslims living in India, Muslims did not come to the Sangh shakhas, and there was a distance between the organisation and the community. The Emergency offered a chance to bridge the gap, because the government imprisoned RSS and Muslim leaders together. There, they interacted with each other, built mutual understanding and found answers to many unanswered questions. When the Janata Party came to power, the Shahi Imams would visit the RSS office, and if it was time for their prayers, they would perform their namaz there itself with no hesitation. Morarji Desai's advice was for the RSS to not restrict the Sangh to the Hindus alone, but to open it to everyone. Balasaheb was in favour of this.

There were in-depth deliberations regarding the question of Muslims and the Sangh at the RSS's Pratinidhi Sabha in 1977. In that meeting, Balasaheb's view was that the RSS should be opened for the Muslims, but when he saw that most opposed his idea, he put an end to the chapter in his closing speech. Had the decision been left to Balasaheb, he would have allowed everyone to come for the shakhas, and maybe the face of the Sangh would have changed, and as a result, taken away a key cause for criticism from its detractors.

THE RSS'S FIRST ELECTION

Before the elections were announced in 1977, the Indira Gandhi government had received enough indications that the Sangh was preparing to put its full strength into the elections and make the Emergency a central issue.

Hence, Indira Gandhi sent her emissaries underground. During that meeting, attempts were made to both entice and threaten RSS leaders. Madhavrao Mule and Bapurao Moghe represented the RSS, but by then it was too late. The Sangh clarified that since the government did not heed Balasaheb's letter, there was no point in further dialogue. The Sangh leadership had resolved to confront the situation head-on and decided to participate directly in the general elections for the first time. However, Opposition leaders George Fernandes and Madhu Limaye were against contesting, believing that the elections wouldn't be fair and were leaning towards a boycott. Even Raj Narain was reluctant to fight the elections from Raebareli. At that critical moment, Balasaheb sent a message urging them to fight the election, warning that if they didn't, Indira Gandhi would claim that the people were with her. Everyone knew Balasaheb was right.

After the election results were out, Indira Gandhi decided to lift the Emergency at a cabinet meeting. Eventually, the government lifted the ban on the RSS, and released Balasaheb from prison after twenty months and twenty days. He travelled from Pune to Mumbai and then to Nagpur. At the Sangh's working committee meeting in Nagpur, there was a detailed discussion on the Emergency, after which Deoras decided to tour the entire country. In 1948, even Guruji Golwalkar travelled across the country after the ban on the RSS got lifted, but the circumstances now were very different. This time, it was a Sangh-backed government, and the swayamsevaks were in positions of power.

Deoras reached Delhi from Nagpur on 9 April 1977, and decided to start his all-India tour from the capital. He met Prime Minister Morarji Desai, and the next day, was felicitated publicly. At a press conference the following day, answering a question on including Muslims into the RSS, Deoras replied, 'As a principle we have agreed that despite differences in our modes of worship, Muslims too can blend harmoniously with national life; and they should.'[17] He said the Sangh would ponder over this issue in the Pratinidhi Sabha.

Opening the doors of the Sangh for the Muslims was top priority for Deoras. He took up the issue at the Pratinidhi Sabha of the Sangh, but the Sabha rejected it. He then admitted that he had failed to change the Sangh's traditionalist attitude.

The egos of the leaders began to create obstacles from the very beginning of the Janata Party government, and soon they targeted the RSS. Amidst this, Balasaheb tried to find a way forward. Chandra Shekhar once called Balasaheb to meet him at the Nagpur airport and at the meeting that took place in the VVIP room, he asked Balasaheb to set aside the word 'Hindu' for a few days, explaining that many were trying to break the Janata Party on this very pretext—and if that happened, the blame would fall on Balasaheb.

Around this time, some leaders raised the issue of dual membership and the mastermind behind it, possibly because they had not made him a minister in the Janata Party's government. Limaye told his colleagues, 'Raise the issue of dual membership in the Janata Party. The Sangh will not approve of it.' This debate had started in August 1977, soon after the Janata Party government was formed. In the same month, Limaye raised the topic of 'Hindu Rashtra' in the Janata Party's working committee, along with the roles of the Vidyarthi Parishad and Bharatiya Mazdoor Sangh. According to him, the RSS should amend its constitution and remove the concept of 'Hindu Rashtra' from it. He wanted the Vidyarthi Parishad and Bharatiya Mazdoor Sangh to become the social arms of the Janata Party. Limaye even made this a point of contention regarding the presence of central ministers at Balasaheb's reception in Delhi. Morarji Desai remarked he did not want his ministers to attend such programmes, though one of the cabinet ministers present at the reception questioned what was wrong with it. Subsequently, the Samajwadi leaders said that all the organisations affiliated with the Sangh should merge with the Janata Party. However, those organisations opposed the move, as they were not part of the Jana Sangh. It was then insisted that Jana Sangh leaders and members of Parliament sever their ties with the Sangh, arguing that since the Sangh believed in the concept of a Hindu Rashtra and could not be secular, they should either quit the Sangh or leave the Janata Party. When the issue sparked widespread discussions within the Sangh, the swayamsevaks expressed their displeasure. Balasaheb, Rajju Bhaiya and Bhaurao Deoras resolved the issue. The Sangh told the Janata Party leaders it was up to the Jana Sangh leaders to decide on the matter. As far as the Sangh was concerned, the organisation would not ruin its relationship with the swayamsevaks, come what may.

By 1979, the issue of dual membership had intensified. Balasaheb decided it was time to convey a powerful message. A rally was organised in Delhi on 4 March 1979, attended by Vajpayee, Advani, Kedarnath Sahni, Vijay Kumar Malhotra and other parliamentarians. Many leaders present wore the Sangh's uniform. Balasaheb said in the rally, 'Politics is important and it has a significant role in public life, but we must understand clearly that the Sangh does not need any political protection. Despite a lot of political blows, the Sangh has continued on its journey based on its strength, and it is only gaining more momentum.'

A week after Balasaheb made the Sangh's standpoint clear, Biju Patnaik and Mohan Dharia met him on 11 March 1979. They wanted the Sangh to announce that it had nothing to do with the Jana Sangh faction of the Janata Party. They suggested that the Vidyarthi Parishad and Mazdoor Sangh should merge with the Janata Party. Balasaheb reminded the leaders that they were independent organisations, and the Sangh had no control over them.

The sarsanghchalak did his best to resolve the issue of dual membership, and he said during his annual speech on Vijayadashami, 'Some people suggest the Sangh should change. Change is a natural process, and the Sangh too has been changing and will do so in the future as well. This is an indication of its progress. What is incapable of change can never remain alive. However, this change cannot be adopted by cutting the veins of the stream of life.'

Ram Bahadur Rai wonders, 'What would have happened had the Sangh bowed down to one faction of the Janata Party? At least five things would have happened. First, the Janata Party would have become a political battleground, and the Sangh would have continuously crushed under it. Second, the BJP would not have been born. Third, the creative abilities of the Sangh would have been stunted. Fourth, the Sangh would have been deprived of stepping into new areas, or it would have become directionless and distracted. Balasaheb did not allow the RSS to fall prey to any of these possibilities.'[18]

During the Janata Party government, the Sangh made several forward-looking decisions. It focussed on expanding where there was no existing competition and creating new organisations accordingly. For this purpose, Balasaheb reactivated many individuals who had become inactive within the Sangh. He also made efforts to bring the Dalits and Muslims with the Sangh—something that today's political leaders pursue merely as a matter of political fashion or electoral compulsion.

Balasaheb Deoras used to say, 'I have to accept that the youth of today do not find the activities of the Sangh as attractive as they used to be. We are thinking of bringing changes to our programmes so that more and more youths can join the Sangh. Not only today, but such deliberations had taken place even when Guruji Golwalkar was alive. But change is not as easy as it appears to be. The organisation cannot make decisions as fast as an individual can. But what is more important is that we strongly believe that the youth will be attracted when the appropriate changes are made. When the Sangh can decide to change its prayer, what can be difficult in changing its activities and programmes? Furthermore, it is not our purpose to gather a crowd; we do need large numbers, but we must not forget that our primary goal is to inculcate values and culture in our youth. We have to build confidence in our swayamsevaks so that they can speak their minds openly with the Sangh officials. I make a lot of effort in this direction. Instead of taking intellectual sessions, I interact with the swayamsevaks, and my sessions are such that they ask questions and I answer them. Despite that, if any swayamsevak is not convinced, he can take up the issue with me later.' [19]

When Deoras joined the Sangh at an early age, he did not perform any religious rituals, leading some Sangh members to label him as a communist. He started prayers and worship only after becoming the sarsanghchalak. Until the Government of India Act came into being and the elections were held in the various provinces, Savarkar's Hindu Mahasabha was ready to contest. The Sangh, however, remained on the fence. Hedgewar himself was not ready to fight elections or allow the Sangh to play an active role in politics. Golwalkar followed the same path. Deoras, however, recognised the importance of political participation. Right from the beginning, he worked with the Bharatiya Mazdoor Sangh and the Vidyarthi Parishad, believing that he could harness the strength of these organisations for political participation in the future. In the fifties, the Sangh, bruised after its 1948 ban, began to expand its interests into the labour movement. Golwalkar asked Dattopant Thengadi to work with the Indian National Trade Union Congress (INTUC), the labour organisation associated with the Congress, so the Sangh could establish a large labour organisation aligned with their organisation's ideology. As a result, the Bharatiya Mazdoor Sangh was born in July 1955. Despite all such efforts, work did not progress rapidly. Apart from the Vidyarthi Parishad, Deoras started taking an interest in the activities of the Mazdoor Sangh. In 1964, Thengadi was sent to the Rajya Sabha, and in 1967, the Bharatiya Mazdoor Sangh held its first national convention in Delhi. By 1984, the Bharatiya Mazdoor Sangh had become the second largest organisation in the country, and by 1996, the union had become the workers' biggest strength.

Balasaheb started the Bharatiya Shikshan Mandal in Mumbai in 1979 to propagate Indian and Sangh ideology and was associated with it even after he became the sarsanghchalak. Before Balasaheb took over as sarsanghchalak, 1940–49 was a crucial period from the Sangh's point of view. The Mahal office of the Sangh was constructed between 1941–45. One cannot overlook Balasaheb's role in communicating with the Nehru government after the 1948 ban, drafting the Sangh's constitution and the acquisition of *Tarun Bharat*.

It is often said that the Sangh functions under one command, but Balasaheb proved this wrong. He stressed initiative, experimentation and collective decision-making in the Sangh. In 1947, the Sangh leadership debated whether the structure of training and education sessions should be uniform at the national level or tailored by each state according to its needs. Discussions continued late into the night, and it felt they wouldn't be able to decide until Balasaheb asked everyone to vote on the issue, thereby arriving at a resolution.

In his book, *Teen Sarsanghchalak*, Dr V.R. Karandikar has written about Balasaheb's role in the last stages of the ban on the Sangh. During the ban, Balasaheb had taken up the responsibility of all the external tasks along with Bhaiyaji Dani. Dwarka Prasad Mishra had come to Nagpur to speak on behalf of Sardar Patel, and he met Balasaheb. Mishra wanted Golwalkar to write a letter to Jawaharlal Nehru, but Balasaheb did not allow it. Even Golwalkar accepted Balasaheb's decision.[20]

BAN ON THE SANGH

The Sangh celebrated when they lifted the ban on it following Gandhi's assassination, but Balasaheb did not get carried away by his emotions. In an article titled 'The Next Step of the Sangh', published in *Yugdharma*, Balasaheb mentioned the Sangh would start working in every area of society. When Guruji got to know about the article, he said jokingly, 'I don't even know what the next step of the Sangh would be, and the decision has already been taken!'[21]

Rambahadur Rai believes that two of Dr Hedgewar's successors had differences of opinion on the Sangh's next steps. But they did not lose mutual respect because and stood firmly by their views. If it had been someone else, conflict would have arisen. Preserving the dignity of the sarsanghchalak's position and considering the respect he had for Guruji, Balasaheb chartered a different path. He did not withdraw from the Sangh activities; instead, he became even more active and chose a new area for his work. He did these experiments for the sake of his relevance. Balasaheb became involved with farming and also faced much ridicule, with people commenting that instead of working for 'culture', he had got busy with 'agriculture'. Apart from this, he also gave a new direction to journalism through *Nar Kesari*.

While Deoras considered politics as a path for change, Golwalkar kept away from it. Deoras's style of functioning revolved around the pillars of organisation, revolution and promotion. This approach didn't garner support within the Sangh. Deoras had his definition and style of work, believing in goal-driven action. He always saw politics not only as a powerful medium for service, but also for social change. Before and after the formation of the Jana Sangh, he frequently spoke about starting a separate political organisation and leading it.

The Jana Sangh fought its first general elections under Deoras's guidance. A post-election review meeting was held in Gadarwara, where Deoras not only presented his analysis in his two and a half hour-long speech, but he also highlighted the need for the Sangh to work in other areas. On Golwalkar's instructions, he spoke at length about the priorities of the Sangh. But after this meeting, Deoras became inactive in the Sangh activities. Deoras might have distanced himself from the Sangh, but he never made any comments about Guruji Golwalkar and simply immersed himself in his work. When Sangh karyakartas and leaders came to meet him, Balasaheb would say, 'This is between Guruji and me. You please don't worry about me.' When the pressure mounted, he said firmly and clearly, 'Whatever happens, I will not create a situation where there will be two different Sanghs, one of Guruji and one of Deoras. Dr

Hedgewar taught me this.' On the other hand, Guruji would say that Balasaheb was the organisation's anchor.[22]

Though Balasaheb remained detached from the Sangh from 1953 to 1960, he was never distant from the organisation. He kept telling people that the power of the Sangh is far more than what it appears to be. Devendra Swaroop says that around the same time, the Jana Sangh held a working committee meeting in Nagpur. Deoras attended the meeting with no prior intimation, sat through and listened to the proceedings, but left without saying a word.[23]

After being away for seven years, Deoras returned to the Sangh in 1960. Reportedly, Guruji Golwalkar sent Balasaheb a message through M.N. Kale, asking him to return. Guruji opined that if karyakartas like Balasaheb kept themselves away, what impact would it have on the swayamsevaks? Balasaheb responded positively to his message and said that he would return after two to three months.

BALASAHEB'S DETACHMENT FROM THE SANGH

After distancing himself from Golwalkar, Deoras left Nagpur and moved to Balaghat and started farming there. But whenever he visited Nagpur, he would stay at the Sangh office. He took part in the annual Vijayadashami celebrations several times. However, Golwalkar and Deoras never spoke to each other in the interim. Deoras would send the questions he had regarding the Sangh to Guruji Golwalkar through his friend Talatule, a seasoned karyakarta. Golwalkar would, in turn, send his responses to Deoras by the same messenger. Nonetheless, Golwalkar continued his efforts to bring Deoras back into the Sangh. Two veteran leaders, Bhaiyaji Dani and Ranade, made relentless attempts to convince Balasaheb. Finally, they succeeded, and Deoras returned as the karyavah of Nagpur. In April 1962, a day before the inauguration of the Hedgewar Memorial in Resham Baug, he was made the joint prant pracharak.

Balasaheb was appointed as the sah-sarkaryavah and then became the sarkaryavah following Bhaiyaji Dani's death in 1965. Those seven years could not create a wedge between Golwalkar and Balasaheb. Golwalkar welcomed Balasaheb with respect, and Balasaheb honoured him. This was no straightforward task. After his return, Balasaheb focussed on increasing the Sangh's participation in the areas of social work and opened several new organisations to achieve his goals.

BALASAHEB'S LEGACY

Deoras played a vital role in the third general elections held in February 1962. Although it was believed that the Sangh does not interfere in ticket distribution and candidate selection, Deoras influenced the final list of candidates in this election. In the by-election of 1963, it was Balasaheb who had decided to field Deendayal Upadhyaya as a candidate. Though Deendayal was initially reluctant to contest, he fought the elections from Jaunpur on Balasaheb's insistence but unfortunately faced defeat. Writing in his diary about the reasons for his loss, he noted that the Congress had campaigned against him as an outsider. It is said that Deoras had chosen Deendayal in place of Atal Bihari Vajpayee for the elections, sparking much debate within the Sangh since Vajpayee was a more popular leader and would have won. Moreover, it was believed that Deendayal Upadhyaya was more suited for strengthening the organisation. Golwalkar felt that instead of politics, pracharaks should focus only on the organisation, and even in 1967, he expressed opposition to making Upadhyaya the president of the Jana Sangh.

Balasaheb, despite being an idealist, was a very practical person. But he was not averse to taking risks. More than success, he believed in experimentation and possessed a scientific bent of mind. He considered democracy as a 'guiding principle', believed in changing the world, but had no desire to create one of his own. He supported change while remaining within the national mainstream. Deoras was always mindful of proportion and used the glorification of the past only as long as it served as a source of inspiration.

An example of this can be seen in the journey of the Jana Sangh to the BJP. Indira Gandhi had returned to power after the Janata Party government fell because of internal conflicts. Later that same year, on 6 April 1980, the BJP was formed. The president of the BJP, Atal Bihari Vajpayee, advocated Gandhian socialism, leading to many arguments in the Sangh. Despite that, Balasaheb allowed Atal Bihari Vajpayee to walk in his direction. He felt the BJP was digressing from its path, but it would return only once it suffered a rude shock. By 1980, the interference of religion in politics had increased, and in January of that year, Indira Gandhi made a sensational comeback to power. Three years before this, Balasaheb had taken full control of the Vishva Hindu Parishad. Since Guru Golwalkar's time, the sarsanghchalak has served as a trustee in the Parishad. Over 150 full-time pracharaks were managing the Parishad, which had over 300 district units. Before this, Balasaheb Deoras's younger brother, Bhaurao Deoras, was overseeing the activities of the Vishva Hindu Parishad, which was involved predominantly in non-political efforts such as running orphanages, hospitals and medical centres.

When Balasaheb's health began to decline, he appointed Moropant Pingle as a trustee of the Parishad in his place. Despite the Parishad's expanding activities, there were no large-scale programmes related to Hindu unity and harmony—something Balasaheb had been contemplating for some time. Then, on 9 February 1981, a serious incident of religious conversion was reported from the Meenakshipuram village of Tirunelveli district in Tamil Nadu. Over 8,000 Dalits, angered by the oppression by high-caste Hindus, had converted and accepted Islam. This news created a big furore in the nation. Prime Minister Indira Gandhi, too, acknowledged its seriousness.

She sent a committee of representatives to Meenakshipuram, and its report was tabled in Parliament, followed by a long discussion on the issue. Balasaheb felt that this was the right moment to organise the Hindus and that there should be no delay in the issue. He believed the VHP should take up the matter vociferously. Balasaheb had understood that the primary cause for such religious conversion was the oppression of the Dalits by the higher castes, and he elaborated on the issue at the Vasant Vyakhyanmala.

Balasaheb called for a five-day conference of the zila pracharaks at a venue near Bengaluru. After this conference, the Sangh decided on its approach towards the Dalits. A new organisation called the Virat Hindu Samaj came into being, with Dr Karan Singh as its president. Close to a lakh attended the conference held in Delhi, which was managed by Ashok Singhal. Furthermore, Balasaheb started to strengthen the Vishva Hindu Parishad, and Singhal was given a new leadership role. Until then, the Parishad had been like a hermitage of renunciates. The organisation embarked on a campaign for Hindu awakening. Later, the Sangh moved away from the Virat Hindu Samaj, and it eventually wound down. The Sangh organised conferences all over the country. Hermits and ascetics joined the Vishva Hindu Parishad in large numbers. The Sangh desired their support but did not want them to be part of the decision-making body. Therefore, a kendriya margadarshak mandal (central advisory board) was set up in March 1981, and the Dharma Sansad (a gathering of religious leaders and scholars) took place a few months later. Its purpose was to contemplate Hindu interests and come up with programmes to fulfil them, giving hermits and ascetics a sense of importance and inclusion.

In 1981, the Hindu Samajotsav was held in Karnataka, the Hindu Samagam in Bengaluru and the Virat Hindu Sammelan in Kerala. The Hindu Munnani Sangathan was formed in Tamil Nadu. On Dr Ambedkar's birthday in 1983, the Samajik Samarasta Manch was started in Maharashtra, and the Manch organised an Ambedkar and Mahatma

Gandhi March, which went on for 7,000 kilometres. At the time, Balasaheb was focussed on the safety of Hindus. During that period, the Vishva Hindu Parishad had collected funds close to five crore rupees for Hindu unity. In the early 1980s, they conducted an Ekaatmata Yatra (Unity March), and the 85,000-kilometre-long yatra received widespread public support. In this journey, huge cans of Ganga river water were carried between villages; the impact of the march was such that the prime minister decided to participate in it when the procession reached Delhi on 17 November, but for some reason, she didn't do so. The yatra boosted the Parishad's social standing. This was the first time that the Vishva Hindu Parishad had registered its presence all over the country. In April 1984, the Parishad announced it would initiate the Ram Janmanbhoomi movement from Ayodhya.

In 1984, the RSS created a youth wing of the Vishva Hindu Parishad called the Bajrang Dal. In the same year, the Parishad took out a Ram–Janaki Yatra under its leadership. This march started from Sitamarhi in Bihar and reached Delhi on 30 October, via Lucknow and Ayodhya. This movement too received wholehearted support from the Hindu community, but before any political mileage could be garnered from the yatra, Indira Gandhi was assassinated in Delhi on 31 October 1984. Terrifying anti-Sikh riots broke out all over the country. The mood in the country had changed drastically.

After about a week, on the occasion of Vijayadashami, the annual celebration was held at the Sangh headquarters in Nagpur, where Deoras delivered a speech. Although it was an annual ritual, the sarsanghchalak's address that year created a storm in political circles. It was as if Balasaheb had crossed all limits and broken all rules, and his anger was palpable. There was hardly any matter that he didn't address. Deoras spoke at length about the perils of terrorism, the relationship between the centre and the state, the contribution of Sikhs and Indira Gandhi. He accused her of selfishness and of being a prime minister without values and ideologies. While speaking about the Congress, the BJP and other political parties, he said that because there was no alternative to the Congress, no one could remove it. At the same time, the BJP and the other parties were grappling with internal conflicts. They were headed for worse times, as these parties could neither unite nor form a strong platform against Congress. The possibility doesn't look like it will happen shortly.

People reacted differently to Deoras's speech. Several politicians saw it as supportive of Indira Gandhi, and some also believed that Deoras had helped her during the 1980 elections. After his Vijayadashami speech, Balasaheb set out on a national tour to unite the Hindus, urging them to collectively vote only for those who addressed their needs. Deoras's speech served as a mirror to the political scenario, mocking all the political parties. It was indeed true that there was no alternative to the Congress then, and none of the other political parties were willing to take meaningful steps to improve the situation.

The most important aspect was Deoras's efforts to convince the Hindus to vote for the benefit of their community, aiming to transform that unity into political strength. Some interpreted this as an invitation for the Congress to support the Sangh. A few days later, the government announced the next general election, and all the political parties began their preparations. Indira Gandhi's assassination became the central election issue for the Congress, leading to a largely negative campaign. Meanwhile, other parties, including the BJP, appeared clueless and confused. That was when Nanaji Deshmukh, who had retired from active politics, observed that Rajiv Gandhi needed the backing of nationalist forces. Balasaheb remained silent throughout the campaign, and when the results came in, the BJP suffered a devastating defeat, winning only two seats—even stalwarts like Vajpayee failed to secure a victory. This led many to believe that the RSS had voted for the Congress.

By then, a lot of water had flowed under the bridge. Vajpayee was the Sangh's target; the organisation was ready to marginalise him. Every decision—especially Vajpayee choosing Gandhian socialism instead of integral humanism and secularism over Hindutva—was under scrutiny. He was going to be made a scapegoat. Even his leadership in the Sangh came under questioning.

Generally, sarsanghchalaks answer letters personally, and the letters have their signatures. Deoras used to take a lot of interest in reading letters and newspapers, but did not enjoy writing letters or answering them very much. He would discuss the annual Vijayadashami speech with the editor of the *Tarun Bharat*, Madhav Govind Vaidya, and then Vaidya would write it. Before the Dussehra festival in 1985, M.G. Vaidya had gone to his native village, and Deoras did not call him back. The reason was that Deoras had extolled Prime Minister Rajiv Gandhi's work that year. Deoras had said in his speech, 'The Rajiv Gandhi government is toeing the Sangh line.'

Dattopant Thengadi approached M.G. Bokare, a retired Marxist scholar who had been the chancellor of the Nagpur University, and convinced him to join the Swadeshi Jagran Manch and the All-India Intellect Project. Bokare wrote a book called *Hindu Economics*, citing Hindu ideology and the Vedic times. When Bokare gifted the book to Deoras, he said, 'You have done the right thing.'

Bokare replied, 'I am keen to know your reaction to my book as the RSS's sarsanghchalak.'

Deoras wanted to avoid the question, but when Bokare insisted, Deoras said, 'In the Sangh, we do not directly criticise anyone, but the thing is that Dr Hedgewar always emphasised on the fact that the Sangh does not consider any idea as lasting and doesn't keep itself in that frame because according to the Sangh, ideas are contextual and current. It is not a given that everything old need be gold, and everything new be something bad. Ideas and thoughts change with time, and that is why there is a thing as Hindu Economics. "Hindu" means "eternally fresh". I appreciate you for writing the book, but I do not accept its concept.'[24]

The Sangh was set to complete sixty years in 1985, a time of political turmoil. Rajiv Gandhi was prime minister with a brute majority, and though the Sangh had done good work, the impact and outcomes were unsatisfactory. Balasaheb had told the swayamsevaks, 'We have to look inwards. Renounce laziness and carve a new path.' His speech had the intended effect, and a renewed churning of ideas began.

The BJP was in a quandary. The party was abuzz with discussions regarding ideology and organisation. Balasaheb met Vajpayee and Advani in Kochi. He suggested the Congress was trying to adopt the principle of Hindutva, but it could not do so under Rajiv Gandhi's leadership. If the BJP takes this path, it will gain immense support from the people. Following this meeting, the BJP passed a resolution in Palampur in June 1989 and changed both its line of functioning and the party's leader. Now, it was Advani's face instead of Vajpayee's, and he was on his way to becoming the Hindu Hriday Samrat (emperor of Hindu hearts).

A senior leader of the Sangh, Bapurao Varadpande, had compiled a report on the Sangh's processes, internal discord and affiliated organisations. Varadpande said that Sarsanghchalak Balasaheb Deoras was trying to find ways to eliminate the organisation's lack of harmony and mutual coordination at a time when the Sangh Parivar was on the verge of disintegration. Deoras had suggested that the only way to set this right was to entice them with the possibility of political power—but for that, they all needed to be aligned and at least in tune with each other. The path to achieving this goal was found in 1989, when Dr Hedgewar's centenary was organised.

DR HEDGEWAR AND DR AMBEDKAR'S BIRTH CENTENARY

The BJP celebrated Dr Hedgewar and Dr Ambedkar's birth centenary in 1989. Balasaheb Deoras toured the country despite his ill health.

He identified three tasks for swayamsevaks: first, to spread awareness about Dr Hedgewar's life before his time with the Sangh; second, to promote the ideology of 'Hindu Rashtra'; and third, to expand the Sangh's social service initiatives in society at large. On the occasion of Dr Hedgewar's birth centenary, the Sangh requested the release of a commemorative stamp in his memory, but the Rajiv Gandhi government disagreed. The Sangh then found an alternative path. They printed 1 crore postcards, which had Dr Hedgewar's image on one side and the image of 'undivided India' with the saffron flag on the other. The Sangh distributed these postcards all over the country and also set a target of reaching 2,00,000 villages. Fifty thousand small and large committees were set up, and between November 1988 and April 1989, eighty public meetings were held. They also aimed to reach one and a half crore families through these efforts.

The Vishva Hindu Parishad celebrated its twenty-fifth anniversary the same year on 24 March. The Sangh and its other organisations held a meeting in Ahmedabad, which Balasaheb Deoras, H.V. Sheshadri, Rajju bhaiyya, Ashok Singhal, Bhaurao Deoras, Yadavrao Joshi, Dattopant Thengadi, Lal Krishna Advani, Sundar Singh Bhandari and other prominent leaders attended. After this meeting, Balasaheb handed over the charge of the Ram temple movement to Moropant Pingle. This movement, which Balasaheb believed the Sangh should conduct under its aegis and supervision, brought the Hindutva ideology to the forefront. By then, the Bharatiya Mazdoor Sangh had also grown to be the second-largest workers' union in the country. The Vanvasi Kalyan Ashram was expanding rapidly. The Sangh Parivar was prospering, but every organisation was treading a distinct path, with little coordination among them.

Two months before the demolition of the Babri Masjid in 1992, the Sangh headquarters in Nagpur hosted the annual Vijayadashami programme. The chief guest was writer and journalist Arun Shourie, who then became the minister of Disinvestment, Communication and Information Technology under Vajpayee's prime ministership. Sarkaryavah Rajju Bhaiyya believed the sarsanghchalak should adopt a hard line regarding the Ayodhya movement in his address. That year, it was decided to hold a karseva (voluntary service) programme in Ayodhya on 6 December, and the RSS's Uttar Pradesh unit also supported this, as the sarsanghchalak's backing would have empowered them. Rajju bhaiyya decided to visit Nagpur to ensure Balasaheb addressed the issue in the speech. He met Balasaheb's close associate, Shrikant Shankar Joshi, in Nagpur and asked him for the sarsanghchalak's speech, which M.G. Vaidya had written as usual. Rajju bhaiyya's concerns were confirmed—the speech did not reflect the firm stance the RSS desired. When M.G. Vaidya learned Rajju objected to that portion, he rewrote it.

The next morning, Balasaheb Deoras called M.G. Vaidya and asked him if he thought it would be right for the RSS chief to express his views so strongly. Vaidya explained the reason for revising the speech without mentioning Rajju bhaiyya's involvement. Nonetheless, Balasaheb disagreed and read the original draft. This incident demonstrates how seriously Balasaheb regarded the dignity of the sarsanghchalak's position. Regarding the Ram Janmabhoomi issue, Deoras always maintained that the Sangh's view on the matter had always been crystal clear, having passed several resolutions between 1980 and 1991. The resolutions stated that the Hindus have to be ready to make any kind of sacrifice for the construction of the Ram temple. Victory was certain. The BJP won a majority in the Uttar Pradesh Legislative Assembly elections in 1991. On 6 December, Babri Masjid was demolished while Deoras was the sarsanghchalak.

Balasaheb was the sarsanghchalak for twenty-one years. His tenure, from 1973 to 1994, is remembered for three reasons: first, he mobilised people to take to the streets against Indira Gandhi; second, he played a crucial role in bringing a non-Congress government into power at the centre after the Emergency and mainstreaming of the Sangh; third, and most importantly, he brought the Ram Janmabhoomi movement to the national stage. Balasaheb Deoras also witnessed Atal Bihari Vajpayee take over as the BJP's first prime minister. He may have well said that there would be no memorial for him in Nagpur after his death, but he continues to live in the hearts of countless swayamsevaks even today. In the truest sense, Balasaheb was the embodiment of a true swayamsevak.

6

Deendayal Upadhyaya

Integral Humanism

The year 1963 marked an important milestone in Indian politics. In the Lok Sabha by-elections for four seats, the landscape saw a clear polarisation between the Congress party, and the left-wing and right-wing opposition parties. In Uttar Pradesh, the opposition parties had united and fielded three prominent leaders: Acharya J.B. Kripalani from Amroha, Dr Ram Manohar Lohia from Farrukhabad and Deendayal Upadhyaya from Jaunpur. Minocher 'Minoo' Masani, the co-founder of the Swatantra Party, was the joint opposition candidate from Rajkot in Gujarat. The Jaunpur seat had fallen vacant following the death of Thakur Brahmajit Singh, a Jana Sangh MP. Other than Deendayal Upadhyaya, both remaining candidates won the by-elections.

Dr Mahesh Sharma, who has deeply researched Upadhyaya's life and written his biography, *Deendayal Upadhyaya: Kritatva Evam Vichar*, says, 'The biggest reason for Upadhyaya's loss was that he was not fighting to win the election. Upadhyaya himself was not in favour of fighting the elections, and Golwalkar was also not keen on making him fight the election. Golwalkar would say, "Whether we win or lose, it will harm us ... though we will be harmed more if we win than if we lose".'[1]

Upadhyaya was of the view that pracharaks should not enter politics and should solely work for the organisation's growth. Under pressure from prant pracharak, Bhaurao Deoras and other Jana Sangh workers, Upadhyaya had agreed to enter the fray. Additionally, Balasaheb Deoras had convinced non-Congress parties to fight the elections as a united front. The fight was between the Rajputs and Brahmins in Jaunpur. The Congress sought to mobilise support through Rajputvad, and in response, the Jana Sangh had attempted to invoke Brahminism. This approach had displeased Upadhyaya, who firmly stated that if such tactics were used to win elections, he would withdraw from the electoral process.

Upadhyaya would speak only about the principles of the Jana Sangh and various economic issues during his campaign. While filing his nomination, he had told his party, 'I will be the first person to congratulate the winning candidate. I will write it, and you can send it to the candidate.'[2] People were surprised when later, after losing the elections, Upadhyaya addressed a rally where he congratulated the winner publicly, and announced that he would render all his support to him for all measures of public interest.

Veteran journalist Achyutanand Mishra notes that during the Jaunpur elections, Murli Manohar Joshi was serving as the karyalaya pramukh in Jana Sangh. Post the by-elections some newspapers had incorrectly reported that Kripalani and Lohia had lost, while Upadhyaya had won. When Achyutanand Mishra had asked Murli Manohar Joshi, the latter had said that if Upadhyaya loses, it will be because of his own reasons. Upadhyaya had come to cleanse politics, but politics had degenerated by then.

Hedgewar Memorial Bhavan in Nagpur. People are sitting alert and with discipline in the Maharshi Vyas Memorial Hall. The training's third year would focus more on bauddhik (intellectual) sessions, where national-level Sangh officials delivered lectures. That day, the topic was the philosophy of integral humanism. The sah-sarkaryavah began by saying that when Pandit Deendayal Upadhyaya had introduced this philosophy in the 1970s, it had not been something new. It had been a part of Hindu thought for thousands of years, but people had forgotten about it. That's why there was a historical need to re-emphasise it.

When Upadhyaya first presented this thought in a bauddhik session at a shiksha varg in 1964, the discussions continued for two days. In the same year, he presented a document on the principles and policies of ekatma manavvaad or human integralism, and the Jana Sangh's all-India convention of the pratinidhi sabha in Vijayawada accepted the proposal in January 1965. A four-day discussion followed in April 1965. Upadhyaya delivered four speeches in Bombay to explain the concept of ekatma manavvaad. In those days, conversations about individualism, religious systems and socialism were centred around the West. By religious systems, people specifically meant the rule of the church, while socialism referred to the rule of humans. In his speech, Upadhyaya spoke at length on topics like the state, democracy, extremism and integralism. He also addressed the question: Is India a nation?

Integral humanism was Upadhyaya's identity and social philosophy—an extraordinary effort from an ordinary-looking man! Not only the Jana Sangh, but even the BJP and its governments later invoked this principle. There remains a vast difference between Deendayal, who placed emphasis on political integrity and ideological purity, and the BJP of today, which places electoral victory above all else. On one side stood Upadhyaya, who practised financial frugality and discipline, travelled third class in trains and dressed in a simple dhoti and kurta; on the other are BJP leaders criss-crossing the country by chartered flights![3]

Later Senior BJP leader Lal Krishna Advani made it clear that after the death of Dr Syama Prasad Mookerjee, although there was a succession of Presidents between 1953 and 1967, everyone knew that the general secretary Deendayal Upadhyaya was the mind, heart and soul of the Jana Sangh. He was not just the organisational head of the party, but also its philosopher, guide, and motivator all rolled into one.[4] Deendayal ran the Jana Sangh as 'a party with a difference', which Advani used as a slogan in the nineties with the idea being the same. Perhaps for this reason, when they chose Advani as the president of the Jana Sangh at the Kanpur session in 1973, the Sangh mouthpiece, *Organiser Weekly*, had run the headline—'Another Deendayal at the helm of the Jana Sangh'.

Senior journalist Nilanjan Mukhopadhyay told me of an incident—'25 January 2013 was a special day for Narendra Modi. The BJP announced him as the prime ministerial candidate, and that too in the presence of Lal Krishna Advani. In the meeting conducted in Bhopal, Advani, Rajnath Singh, and Shivraj Singh Chauhan were present. After the announcement, Modi said, "The founder of the Jana Sangh, Dr Syama Prasad Mookerjee, had once said that 'Give me two Deendayals and I will completely change the face of the nation.' And when the country celebrates Pandit Deendayal Upadhyaya's birth centenary in 2015–16, BJP will be in power in most states in the country." In November–December 2014, the BJP won the Vidhan Sabha elections in Maharashtra, Haryana, Jharkhand and Jammu and Kashmir, but by 2019, before the Vidhan Sabha election in the same five states, BJP already held power in two-thirds of Indian states. However, by 2020, even though the BJP held majority power at the centre, the number of its state governments had fallen to less than fifty per cent. When Narendra Modi became prime minister for the first time on 26 May 2014, he put forth Deendayal Upadhyaya's idea of "antyodaya" (upliftment of the poorest), and said that our government will work for the underprivileged and marginalised.'[5]

Upadhyaya would say that as long as the country was under British rule, the goal of all movements and protests was to attain freedom and self-rule, but there was little thought given to what the country would look like or what direction it would take after Independence. Gandhi-ji had outlined his vision for post-Independence India in *Hind Swaraj*, but no serious action was ever taken on it.

Upadhyaya would also say, 'We had taken pride in resisting things – British while they (Britishers) ruled us, but strangely enough, now that the Britishers have left, Westernisation has become synonymous with progress … Western science and the Western ways of life are two different things. Whereas Western science is universal and must be absorbed by us if we wish to go forward, the same is not true about the Western ways of life and values … Independence can be meaningful only if it becomes an instrument for the expression of our Culture … Both from the national and human stand point, it has become essential that we think of the principles of Bharatiya Culture … The fundamental characteristic of Bharatiya Culture is that it looks upon life as an integrated whole … There is diversity and plurality in life but we have always attempted to discover the unity behind them … Hegel put forward the principles of thesis, anti-thesis and synthesis; Karl Marx used this principle as a basis and presented his analysis of history and economics; Darwin considered the principle of survival of the fittest as the sole basis of life; but we in this country saw the basic unity of all life.'[6] He would also say that it was necessary for every nation to think about its own self and that self-rule had no meaning without independence.

THE PRINCIPLE OF INTEGRAL HUMANISM

Ekatma manavvaad darshan refers to the integral relationship between human life and the whole of nature. The cumulative thoughts of a human being are the sum of the thoughts of the body, mind, intellect and soul. To fulfil needs, demands, desires and expectations, and to ensure holistic development, Hindu culture has established the ideal of the four purusharthas (aims of life).

For Upadhyaya, the four purusharthas are: dharma (righteousness), artha (wealth or material success), kama (desire or pleasure) and moksha (liberation or spiritual freedom). Humans are attracted to these goals, and their devotion to the purusharthas gives them peace. But it is a mistake to consider any of these purusharthas as the sole yardstick, the inspiration for effort or the benchmark for the success of human life. The integral human being, inherent in the balance of the four purusharthas, was meant to be the focal point for our thought process and systems. An integral human—one who has contemplated the four purusharthas holistically, worked diligently towards them, has an all-encompassing view of human life, rises above narrow group identities like nations and realises oneness with the 'Supreme'—was considered the ideal in this philosophy.

When Sarsanghchalak Golwalkar lived in Nagpur, he would read all the newspapers but paid special attention to *Tarun Bharat*. In those days, news arrived at the newspaper office via teleprinters, and Golwalkar would be on the lookout for any news related to the Sangh. Mama Thombre was the editor-in-chief of the *Tarun Bharat* at that time. A Jana Sangh convention was taking place in Nagpur, and a piece of news was published that Deendayal Upadhyaya had introduced a proposal about a Hindu Rashtra, and that a discussion supporting it was scheduled. Golwalkar told Upadhyaya that he should leave the matter of Hindu Rashtra to the Sangh. He had taken an oath on the Constitution and should work towards secularism. Later, when the proposal for integral humanism was made at the Kerala convention of the Jana Sangh, Golwalkar said, 'We don't believe in any "vad" (isms), and there need not be any discussion on it.'

Subsequently, Prof. Rajendra Singh and H.V. Sheshadri removed the concept of integral humanism from the Sangh bauddhik sessions, citing that Hedgewar's rationale was to keep the Sangh away from personality cults or any individual's opinions.

THE AXIS OF THE SANGH

Deendayal Upadhyaya's political life became associated with the Jana Sangh ever since its establishment when the then sarsanghchalak, Guruji Golwalkar, had made him join the Dr Syama Prasad Mookerjee-led organisation. Craig Baxter, the writer of *The Jana Sangh: A Biography of an Indian Political Party*, says, '… the Jana Sangh is the result of a party-less leader, Syama Prasad Mookerjee [and] the leaderless party RSS coming together.'[7] Dr Mahesh Sharma believes this is incorrect; the situation is more complex. Sharma asserts that no one can cast aspersions on the leadership abilities of Golwalkar.

In light of the Sangh's growing predicament after Gandhi's assassination in 1948, Bhaiyaji Dani had written a letter to Eknath Ranade on 25 March 1949 saying, 'The government will not invite us; we have to start our party. We will get its constitution and other documents formulated by someone like Puntambekar and make all the necessary preparations. Let's not waste any time …'[8]

Dr Mahesh Sharma says that when the ban on the organisation was lifted in July 1949, calls for a new political party did not subside but grew stronger. Dadarao Parmarth, Balraj Madhok and K.R. Malkani wrote articles on this issue in various magazines, including the *Panchjanya* and *Organiser*. At that time, many Sangh leaders, including Golwalkar, opposed the idea of forming a political party. In a speech delivered in Lucknow in December 1949, Golwalkar had expressed similar views. He believed that no political party can fulfil the goals of the entire Hindu society, and that doing so would lead to division and factionalism. Golwalkar did not agree with the statement that '… people say that it is possible that after the party is formed, it may not have any culture … that it is impossible to rise beyond party lines once it is formed. That is why we have not given ourselves the structure of a political faction, party or sect … The members of the Congress may have fallen, but we will not … this belief is nothing but false pride.'[9]

At a meeting of karyakartas held in Nagpur from 18 to 22 October 1949, Golwalkar gave a speech in which he stressed that the organisation's fundamentals should not be changed to pursue political goals, and that instead the focus must be on organisational development and social initiatives. During this time Balasaheb Deoras's essay on Sangh's next step was published in the magazine *Yugdharm*. In this Deoras said that the Sangh will take the society along and present solutions to social problems as per the Sangh's own policies.

At that time, the chronology of political events was rapidly evolving amidst the problems posed by the Partition. On 8 April 1950, the Nehru–Liaquat Pact was signed. Before this, Dr Syama Prasad Mookerjee had resigned from the Nehru cabinet, calling the pact a 'betrayal of the Hindus of East Bengal'. Following his exit, efforts to form a new political party gathered steam. Between May and October 1951, provincial teams were organised, and on 21 October 1951, the all-India Jana Sangh came into being under the presidency of Syama Prasad Mookerjee in Delhi. Key figures active at that time included the prant sanghchalak of Delhi, Lala Hansraj Gupta; the prant pracharak of Delhi, Vasantrao Oak; the prant karyavah of Punjab, Dharmvir; Balraj Madhok and Bhai Mahavir. Guruji Golwalkar facilitated the appointment of several leaders from the Sangh to different states. These included Deendayal Upadhyaya and Nanaji Deshmukh in Uttar Pradesh, Manohar Rao Moghe in Central India, Sundar Singh Bhandari in Rajasthan and Thakur Prasad in Bihar. Dr Bhai Mahavir was appointed the first general secretary of the Jana Sangh. All these leaders were second-ranking Sangh leaders in their respective states. Earlier, in May 1951, Syama Prasad Mookerjee had also founded the People's Party in Bengal.

Dr Mahesh Sharma explains that the Jana Sangh's provincial unit in Uttar Pradesh was set up in Lucknow in September 1951, and

Upadhyaya was chosen as its pradesh mahamantri (general secretary). Until then, he had been the sah-prant pracharak in the RSS. Before the Jana Sangh was officially formed, a meeting was held in Delhi on 8 September to prepare the party's manifesto, which was attended by Upadhyaya. The Jana Sangh's first national convention was held in Kanpur from 29 to 31 December 1952. Nanaji Deshmukh served as the convenor of the convention, and that was when Upadhyaya replaced Bhai Mahavir as the party's national general secretary. The second general secretary was Mauli Chandra Sharma.

The ideological impact of Upadhyaya's leadership can be measured by the fact that seven out of the fifteen proposals that were passed at the first convention of the party. These included protesting against apartheid in South Africa, foreign colonies in India, tax policy and multi-point sales tax, amendment in election rules, rehabilitation, five-year plan and revival of culture. Out of the seven, cultural revival was of prime importance. It was suggested that the foundation of education should be Indian culture, that Sanskrit should be promoted, and that all languages in the country must be written in the Devanagari script. Indian history had to be accurately revised and was to be based on Indian culture rather than on the perspectives of foriegn invaders. Public awareness campaigns were required to promote Indianisation among the people.

If we examine the history of the relationship between the Sangh Parivar and Jana Sangh-BJP, it is clear that the Sangh sought to maintain dominance over its affiliated political organisations, though publicly, it described the relationship as that of an 'advisor'. After the sudden death of Syama Prasad Mookerjee, there was no other leader of comparable stature. Following the Sangh's directive, Vice President Mauli Chandra Sharma was given the responsibility of heading the organisation. Mauli Chandra Sharma looked after the functioning organisation when the government banned the Sangh after Mahatma Gandhi's assassination. He maintained a cordial relationship with the central government, and by creating a Jan Adhikar Samiti, he assisted members of the Sangh

Parivar. He also played an active role in having the ban on the Sangh revoked. For this, Sharma had sought the help of the former home minister of the Central Provinces, D.P. Mishra. The government had demanded a written assurance from the Sangh that it would refrain from future political activities, however an imprisoned Golwalkar was not willing to give this assurance at the time.

Sharma then found a middle path—Golwalkar wrote a letter to Sharma in this regard, who presented it to the authorities and got the ban lifted. Sharma had fought in the first general election from the Outer Delhi constituency, but had lost. Perhaps the Sangh considered Sharma a weak leader, so they handed him the reins of the Jana Sangh so the Sangh could run it the way it wanted. But the moment he became party president, Sharma's attitude changed, and he would not allow any Sangh interference. He refused to accept the Sangh's recommendations for party posts and appointed officials according to his wishes. This angered the RSS, and they used Upadhyaya as a tool to remove Sharma.

When Upadhyaya constituted a working committee to improve the Jana Sangh's functioning, Sharma opposed the move. A power struggle continued between the leaders for almost a year, and eventually, Sharma had to resign. However, Sharma was not one to accept defeat easily, and after his resignation on 3 November 1954, he publicly denounced the increasing interference of the Sangh Parivar in Jana Sangh matters in the past year. Upadhyaya had realised by then that leaders with strong political inclinations could not run the Jana Sangh, and hence he appointed the sanghchalak of Bihar, S.A. Sohoni, as the president. However, voices of dissent against this appointment began to arise in the Jana Sangh, and several leaders made up their minds to resign. But Upadhyaya remained unmoved. He had decided that only a leader associated with the Sangh could head the Jana Sangh. Nonetheless, after Dr Mookerjee, the position of the Jana Sangh's president became largely ceremonial. In practice, the most powerful figure in the organisation was the general secretary, Deendayal Upadhyaya himself.

The presidency of the Jana Sangh was then handed over to Pandit Prem Nath Dogra of Jammu for a year, followed by Debaprasad Ghosh, a relatively weak leader from Calcutta. Ghosh operated under the instructions of the RSS, and Upadhyaya too continued to carry out Jana Sangh's duties according to the Sangh's directives. Pitambar Das, a former long-time Congress leader from Uttar Pradesh and a member of the RSS, became the president in 1960. A. Rama Rao from Andhra Pradesh succeeded him. During this period, the Jana Sangh's participation kept increasing in the general elections, but its public support remained stagnant. In the 1962 elections, the Jana Sangh won fourteen seats, but leaders like Vajpayee and Balraj Madhok experienced defeat.

Following this, Upadhyaya took complete control of the organisation and assigned the responsibility of the Jana Sangh to select pracharaks. At the 1965 Vijayawada convention, Bachhraj Vyas was made the president. He became the first karyakarta–president of the Jana Sangh. The decision was not well-received by senior leaders such as Vajpayee and Balraj Madhok, who boycotted the convention. However, Upadhyaya remained unfazed, believing that the issue was one of principles rather than personalities. Devendra Swaroop says that Upadhyaya and Vajpayee had a good relationship. When Upadhyaya returned to Delhi from Vijayawada after the convention, he stayed at Vajpayee's house, but to Vajpayee's surprise, Upadhyaya refrained from discussing any organisational matters with him.

Upadhyaya was the general secretary of the Jana Sangh from 1952 to 1967, even though the Jana Sangh went through a succession of presidents in that period. According to Dr Mahesh Sharma, 'The political discussions in the Sangh at that time were not merely ideological, and the reason was that some people had political ambitions. One such person was Vasantrao Oak. Oak was the Delhi prant pracharak and harboured ambitions to head the Jana Sangh. He was in direct contact with Mookerjee. Golwalkar, who was aware of this, made him the all-India sharirik pramukh (physical education chief) in the Sangh and sent him away from Delhi to Nagpur. Oak, annoyed with this move, became a rebel.'

The official convenor of the Jana Sangh, Balraj Madhok, was an ambitious man too, which is probably why he was never made the president; instead, the responsibility was given to Dr Mahavir. Remarking on the goal of attaining political power, Upadhyaya said, '[The] Bharatiya Jana Sangh is an organisation with a difference. This is not a group of people who want to come to power by any means. Jana Sangh is not a party; it is a movement.'[10] Contrary to this sentiment, many individuals actively vied for the position of president after Dr Mookerjee's sudden passing. His death had created a leadership crisis, as the party's constitution lacked any provisions for choosing a new president in the event of the incumbent's death or departure, even though the constitution states that the president could only serve a one-year tenure in the Jana Sangh.

Leaders like N.C. Chatterjee, who were associated with the Hindu Mahasabha, also tried hard to become the president of the Jana Sangh. Many believed at the time a merger between the Hindu Mahasabha's charismatic leaders and the Jana Sangh's strong organisational foundation would benefit both organisations. However, Upadhyaya firmly refused. The prospect of leveraging the Sangh's power attracted the Mahasabha and the Ram Rajya Parishad, but at the same time, they were afraid of the devotion that the young leaders had towards Guruji Golwalkar. Dr Sharma says, 'Savarkar and the leader of the Parishad, Swami Karpatri, considered themselves to be equally influential leaders.'

Apart from this, there were three key reasons, from Upadhyaya's perspective, which made the coming together of the two organisations with the Jana Sangh an impossible feat. The first was a fundamental difference in the definition and understanding of Hindu nationalism between the Jana Sangh and the Hindu Mahasabha. The second reason was that leaders like Golwalkar believed Savarkar was not entirely committed to organisation building. Finally, although Savarkar had been acquitted of involvement in Gandhi's assassination, the matter was still fresh in public memory and might have adversely affected the Sangh's image. If Dr Sharma is to be believed, Upadhyaya may have been young and lacking in political experience, but he had a clear vision about the Jana Sangh's goals, and though he looked innocent, he certainly wasn't naïve.

FROM DEENA TO DEENDAYAL

In a typical North Indian lower-middle class Hindu family, in the village of Nagla Chandrabhan in Mathura district of Brajbhoomi, a son was born to Bhagwati Prasad and Rampyari on 25 September 1916. They named him Deendayal, but affectionately called him 'Deena'. Owing to familial problems, Bhagwati Prasad was forced to send Rampyari and his sons, Deena and Shibu, to his father-in-law Chunnilal Shukla's home in the Dhankya village near Jaipur in Rajasthan.

From an early age, Deendayal was forced to face extraordinary circumstances. When he was just two and a half years old and living in his maternal grandfather's home, news came of his father's death. A few years later, his mother Rampyari developed tuberculosis, and by the time Deena turned seven years old, she too had passed away. Two years later, his grandfather Chunnilal died too, forcing Deena to move to his maternal uncle's home, where he took on the responsibility of taking care of his younger brother, Shibu. At the time, he had been studying in Kota, but upon hearing of his aunt's demise, he had to leave Kota and move to his uncle's home in Rajgadh, Alwar. At eighteen, Deena was in the ninth standard when Shibu fell seriously ill. Despite every possible treatment, nothing could save his life. Now, only Deena and his maternal grandmother remained in the family. He passed his tenth-standard exams in 1935, and later that winter, his grandmother also passed away. He then shifted to his cousin Ramadevi's house. While he was pursuing his MA in English, tragedy struck again—Ramadevi fell seriously ill and died in 1940.

Despite his trials and tribulations, Deendayal was always an excellent student. When he ranked first in his tenth-standard exams, Maharaja

Kalyan Singh presented him with a gold medal, a cash prize of two hundred rupees and a monthly scholarship of ten rupees. He earned first-class marks in his BA and first-year MA examinations, but he could not complete the second year of his MA because of his cousin's illness. Pressured by his uncle, he appeared for the administrative exams and passed them too, but he didn't take the job and went to Allahabad (now called Prayagraj) to do his B.T., marking the beginning of his public life.

In 1939, while he was pursuing his BA in Kanpur, Deendayal came into contact with the RSS through Sundar Singh Bhandari, who was his fellow student. The first all-India pracharak, Bal Apte and Pracharak Dadarao Parmarth would also often stay in his hostel. He also met Dr Hedgewar there. Once, when Savarkar visited Kanpur, Deendayal organised a bauddhik session in the Sangh shakha. While pursuing his education, Deendayal completed the first year of the Sangh's shiksha varg in 1939 and the second year in 1942. He stood first in the bauddhik session of the shiksha varg, became a Sangh pracharak and never married. His first posting as zila pracharak was in Lakhimpur, Uttar Pradesh.

Balasaheb Deoras's younger brother, Bhaurao Deoras, then prant pramukh of the Central Provinces, on meeting Upadhyaya had been very pleased with his work and had written a commendation letter praising his efforts. When Upadhyaya became the sah-prant pracharak, he worked with the education department and took charge of spreading the Sangh's ideology through educational initiatives. Seeing the impact of his work, Balasaheb Deoras founded 'Vidya Bharati', the educational wing of the RSS.

Upadhyaya then started the monthly publication *Rashtra Dharma* from Lucknow to propagate the organisation's belief system. Upadhyaya started the Sangh's mouthpiece *Panchjanya* in 1945. On 14 January 1948, *Panchjanya* was relaunched on a large scale, with Vajpayee taking over as its first editor. Upadhyaya played an important role in the formulation of the constitution of the Sangh in 1949 too.

Bhaurao Deoras, recognising Upadhyaya's talent, asked him to write historical stories for children to provide them with authentic knowledge about Indian history. The Sangh held the belief that left-wing parties and the Congress had misrepresented history. Upadhyaya wrote a book about Emperor Chandragupta, and after its success, started writing about Adi Shankaracharya.

In 1962, the question of maintaining the Jana Sangh's identity and character arose when discussions about the Swatantra Party and Ram Rajya Parishad merging with the Jana Sangh emerged. Upadhyaya viewed the Swatantra Party as a party of kings and landlords, and the Ram Rajya Parishad as espousing a Hindutva ideology different from the principles of the Jana Sangh. Upadhyaya firmly rejected the merger. Even during the elections, he refused to align with any party that might have adversely affected Jana Sangh's image, and despite all the resistance he faced, he remained steadfast in his stance. Even when Jana Sangh was in the opposition, Upadhyaya was not in favour of the party's constant criticism of the government. He called it 'negative democracy' in contrast to a 'controlled democracy', which he supported.

He advocated that better governance called for efficient administration, capable candidates, strong political parties and responsible voters. He was in favour of erstwhile kings and rulers fighting elections and felt that they should be active in politics. However, he was also of the view that political parties ought not to field them as candidates based solely on their wealth and stature. According to Upadhyaya, 'The candidate, the party, and its ideology—all have to be considered. A bad candidate cannot claim a premium just because the party he belongs to is good. An evil is an evil and, like the proverbial ill wind, cannot blow good to any one any where. The party High Command in giving a ticket to such a man might have acted on a partisan basis or, with the best of intention; it might have committed an error of judgment. It is the duty of a responsible electorate to rectify such a mistake.'[11]

Like Golwalkar, Upadhyaya too did not consider democracy the best form of governance, but rather its least evil form. According to him, the greatest cause of political instability was a lack of political morality. In 1960, during Jana Sangh's national convention, he passed a proposal that formulated a code of conduct for MPs and MLAs, which incuded strict guidelines against creating an uproar in the Parliament or the legislative assembly or storming the well of the house. Achyutanand Mishra believes that until 1973, that is, during Golwalkar's tenure, politics did not actively influence the Sangh. The Sangh leaders did not work for the elections, but after Balasaheb Deoras became the sarsanghchalak, the Sangh's proximity to politics increased, and its political dependence kept increasing gradually.[12]

Political character was one among Upadhyaya's worries. He expressed concern over 'party defection' and 'cross-voting', particularly in light of the 1967 elections. No single party had won a majority in Kerala, West Bengal, Punjab, Bihar, Uttar Pradesh, Madhya Pradesh and Rajasthan. In these states, the governors had dismissed the elected governments, citing the breakup of parties and defections as justification for it. However, at the time the Constitution lacked clear guidelines regarding the governor's role in such dismissals of governments. During the president's address in 1967, Upadhyaya warned against the arbitrary behaviour of governors and called for transparency in appointments. He stated that although India had adopted the Westminster system of government, it needed to be adapted to suit the country's specific needs. Upadhyaya believed that any government should be made to resign only after a no-confidence motion on the floor of the assembly had passed successfully. If the majority of the members demanded a meeting, the speaker of the assembly should convene the same.[13] Since the Supreme Court's verdict in the *S.R. Bommai* case[14], there has been little change in the role of governors in political events.

In 1967, Upadhyaya had to face other hurdles within the Jana Sangh. Many new members had joined from other parties but struggled to adapt to the Jana Sangh's mode of functioning and its ideology, causing challenges for Upadhyaya. Upadhyaya came up with two ways to overcome the problem. First, he included many pracharaks in the party and assigned them various responsibilities. Second, he linked legislators directly to the party organisation. In 1960, he appointed a pracharak in every district to work for the party. Moreover, he instructed the cadre that they should take the party and the government's programmes directly to the people.

The appointment of Sangh pracharaks strengthened the Jana Sangh, but the party faced setbacks when the Janata Party formed the government at the centre in 1977. Several Janata Party members raked up the issue of dual membership, demanding that Jana Sangh members relinquish their RSS membership while being part of the Janata Party. Eventually, the Jana Sangh withdrew from the Janata Party over this issue.

Even after the bitter experience of the Janata Party's breakup and the formation of the BJP, the underlying conundrum remained unresolved. Between 1998 and 2004, when the NDA government was in power at the centre, tensions arose between the BJP and the Sangh. BJP leaders repeatedly clarified that the Sangh did not hold the party's 'remote control' nor did it interfere in the functioning of the government. Notably, one major reason for the Vajpayee government's defeat in 2004 was the disapproval of the Swadeshi Jagran Manch and Sangh's K.S. Sudarshan's displeasure with the BJP. Before the elections in 2004, the Sangh had stated that it was largely unaffected by the Vajpayee government's victory or loss. As a result, despite its 'Shining India' campaign, the Vajpayee government failed to retain power.

Upadhyaya was always against viewing India as a union of states, and he opposed the federal structure of governance enshrined in the Constitution. In a historic speech in Mumbai, he said, 'We have accepted a system of single citizenship. Despite having different states, we don't have different citizenships for the states and the nation, like it is America. We are all Indian citizens, and we have not given the states the right to secede from the country. It is only the Parliament and not the legislative council that can decide the borders and names of the states. All of these are the correct provisions. Despite all this, we have made the Constitution federal, and whatever is in practice has been essentially unaccepted. In a federal structure, the individual units do not have any power or sovereignty. They entrust their rights to the central government and the federation according to a mutual agreement. As per this idea, the Constitution considers the power of the state to be fundamental and the centre as a group of states. This is against the idea of the unity and integrity of India.'[15]

Upadhyaya was in favour of an ekatma rajya (a unitary state) and clarified that this did not mean a 'free-willed' or an 'autonomous' state, nor did it mean the abolition of states. Instead, he supported strengthening local government systems like janapadas and panchayats. He would say, 'We must recognise and accept the independent power of the panchayats. This will lead to decentralisation of power, and it will reach right down to the grassroots. Multiple centres of power will exist, but there will be a united state at the centre.'[16] Upadhyaya opposed the division of states based on language and demanded the constitution of a state reorganisation commission. The Nehru government constituted such a commission in 1954.

The first five years, 1952 to 1957, since the formation of the Jana Sangh were tough, and Upadhyaya toured extensively across the country and created the foundation for the organisation. In 1957, the Jana Sangh had 243 Mandal Samitis (committees) and 889 local Samitis with a total of 74,863 members. But the results of the first general election were unsatisfactory, with Jana Sangh getting only 3 per cent of the votes and three seats. The result of the local body election in Uttar Pradesh were better. In the second general election in 1957, the Jana Sangh fielded 127 candidates for the Lok Sabha and 650 candidates for the legislative assemblies. They won four seats in the Lok Sabha and fifty-one seats in the Legislative Assembly elections with a 6 per cent vote share, which was double than that of the previous elections. It was decided to hold the Jana Sangh convention in Bangalore in 1958, as Upadhyaya wanted to expand the party's presence in the South. This decision reaped rich dividends.

By the third general elections, factionalism within the Congress was on the rise, and other political parties sought to capitalise on this development by forming alliances with non-Congress parties to contest the elections together. However, Upadhyaya rejected any sort of coalition, citing the example of the pratinidhi sabha in Banaras. The Jana Sangh contested the elections independently, fielding candidates in 198 Lok Sabha seats and 1,162 Vidhan Sabha seats. Upadhyaya viewed shortcuts or opportunistic alliances as weaknesses, but at the same time, he considered political untouchability as wrong.

Pandit Nehru's passing in 1964 was a massive jolt for the Congress, while for the Jana Sangh, it became a significant year in terms of organisation and ideology. From 11 to 15 August 1964, the Jana Sangh's pratinidhi sabha held a prashikshan shivir (training camp) in Gwalior, where they finalised the party's principles and policies, formulated by Upadhyaya. On 23–24 January 1965, at the convention held in Vijayawada, Bachhraj Vyas was elected president.

In 1965, violent anti-Hindi protests erupted in the southern states of India, leading to widespread unrest. The provision for English to remain the official language at the Centre was expiring on 26 January 1965. Upadhyaya supported the use of Indian languages and emphasised that North Indians too should learn at least one regional language. However, he considered Urdu to be a language associated with separatism and communalism. According to him, Hindustani or Urdu-mixed Hindi was an impractical and artificial language. Simultaneously treating Sanskrit-based Hindi as tough and Urdu-based Hindi as easy was a myth. Upadhyaya said, 'No language is indeed specific to any particular religion ... but to consolidate themselves as a separate nation, the Muslims, under the protection of the Muslim League, created a movement to make Urdu the language solely of the Muslims. This was the reason the official language of Hyderabad was Urdu and also the medium of instruction in the Osmania University; however, nobody spoke the language there ... till the time Urdu exists in this country, the communal and separatist mindset will never end.'[17]

Meanwhile, the rapidly evolving political scene heightened the importance of the general elections in 1967, in which for the first time, the Jana Sangh won thirty-five seats and secured the second place in seventy-five seats. In fifteen seats, they lost by a margin of less than 5,000 votes. Overall, the Jana Sangh won 257 seats in the legislative assemblies.

After Bachhraj Vyas, Balraj Madhok became the president in 1966, but Upadhyaya was elected president at the Calicut convention in the same year. Madhok opposed Upadhyaya's election, as he wished to continue in the post. However, the Sangh supported Upadhyaya, and Sundar Singh Bhandari of Rajasthan became the vice president. The general election results influenced Upadhyaya's selection, after which discussions started on forming coalition governments in some states. Like Vajpayee, Upadhyaya supported joining the government, but a large faction of the Sangh was against it.

Upadhyaya's presidential address at the Calicut convention reflected the effort he had invested in playing an active role in politics, expanding the organisation and safeguarding his ideology. Dilip Deodhar says that when Upadhyaya went to meet Golwalkar after becoming president at the Calicut convention, Golwalkar had been annoyed and had said, 'I told you while giving you the responsibility of the Jana Sangh that you will always remain the general secretary, and not be a leader. You will never become the pinnacle of a temple.' When Upadhyaya responded, citing Deoras's orders, Guruji said, 'Let's leave everything to God.'[18]

After Upadhyaya's untimely and mysterious death, Deoras said, 'I have understood Guruji's importance today. Guruji did not allow me to become the president of the Jana Sangh for eight years. He did not permit me to be the face of the organisation. Guruji did not change even after eight years. I returned and now understood why Guruji had said that. What had happened to Syama Prasad Mookerjee and to Deendayal Upadhyaya could have happened to me as well. He gave me life; if I am alive today, it is all because of Guruji.'

THE MUSLIM 'ISSUE'

Upadhyaya considered Muslims to be anti-nationalists, separatists and politically ambitious. His complaint with Muslims was not because of their religion, but because of their beliefs about nationalism. In a way, he was totally against the principles of Hindu-Muslim unity. He considered this subject itself to be incompatible and the policy of appeasement of Muslims to be disastrous.

In a booklet titled *Akhand Bharat Kyon?* (Why Undivided India?), Upadhyaya addressed the concept of 'Akhand Bharat' (undivided India). Analysing the freedom struggle and its outcomes, he wrote, 'While announcing Independence, we are hoisting the national flag at the Red Fort, but today the bank of the Ravi river where we had taken the oath for Poorna Swaraj (complete self-rule) has been snatched away from us.' Criticising the two-nation theory, he said, 'It is a mistake to consider the Khilafat movement a national movement. It is not only a blot on nationalism, but it also creates a feeling among Muslims that they can remain nationalist Indians despite following people from outside India.'

Upadhyaya, who had led a frugal and simple life, could not adjust to the luxury he received towards the end of his life. After he became the party president in 1967, he was even advised to travel first class instead of third class on the train.

On 10 February 1968, while in Lucknow, Upadhyaya received an urgent message asking him to attend a working committee meeting in Patna. That same night, party workers saw him off at the Lucknow railway station as he boarded the Sealdah–Pathankot Express to Patna. But the train's route was changed at the last minute; it would no longer go to Patna, and his first-class coach was attached to the Delhi–Howrah Express at the Mughalsarai station. The next morning, when the train arrived at Patna, Upadhyaya was missing.

The workers who had come to the station to receive him grew worried. Soon after, they received news that an unidentified body had been found lying on the railway track just beyond the Mughalsarai railway station. Upadhyaya had been murdered. His last rites were conducted at the Nigambodh Ghat in Delhi on 12 February 1968, where thousands of workers bade him a tearful farewell.

When Balasaheb Deoras received the news of Upadhyaya's death, he broke down and cried like a child, blaming himself for Deendayal's murder. In a memorial meeting of swayamsevaks held in Delhi, Deoras expressed his sadness, saying, 'Deendayal-ji's death has rendered all of us lifeless. It is extremely difficult for us to imagine a life in his absence. Everyone loved him, and had he fallen ill, thousands of swayamsevaks would have eagerly come forward to serve him. If he had needed blood, there would have been a long line of swayamsevaks ready to donate blood for him. If any of us had had an inkling that his life was in danger, any swayamsevak would have endangered his own life to save Deendayal-ji. However, he has left us without giving us a chance to serve him. This is the reason for our unbearable sorrow ... Dr Hedgewar would say that a good swayamsevak creates several swayamsevaks like himself. Deendayal Upadhyaya was like that. He made innumerable karyakarta-leaders all over the country. That is why thousands of Deendayals will rise from Deendayal Upadhyaya's ashes.'

In his condolence message, Golwalkar compared Deendayal to Yudhishthir, who never behaved harshly in thought, action or word.

On 12 February 1968, Atal Bihari Vajpayee paid a tribute to Deendayal Upadhyaya at the Lok Sabha. In his speech, he said, 'Simple in appearance but a great thinker, a skilled organiser, a visionary leader, the quality of taking everyone along which he displayed in his life will serve as a guide for the new generation. He acquired the highest of degrees but never held a job. He never bound himself to family ties and dedicated every cell of his body and every moment of his life in the nation's service to ensure that his motherland prospered.'

The BJP headquarters in Delhi is on the Deendayal Marg. Most leaders sitting in this swanky facility remember Deendayal Upadhyaya in their speeches. I am reminded of an incident in this context. A senior party official, after offering a flower garland to Deendayal Upadhyaya's statue at the headquarters, scolded a junior worker for not arranging a new and larger vehicle for him. He wanted to know how many karyakartas would receive him at the Mumbai airport and insisted that they hold his press conference not at the party office, but at a five-star hotel. Ironically, he planned to speak on integral humanism at another event; after that, he was going to hold a grand press conference where a few legislators from another party would join the BJP in his presence. Deendayal Upadhyaya now, however, remains confined to photographs and books—his ideals, it appears, have become inconvenient to the party in its pursuit of growth.

7

Mohan Bhagwat

The Outspoken Chief

For a long time, the phrase 'remote control' was often used to describe the relationship between the RSS and the BJP. But this term has faded recently, largely because of the current and sixth RSS sarsanghchalak, Dr Mohan Bhagwat.

A significant transformation has occurred in the relationship between to the party in its the Sangh and the BJP. During Deoras's tenure, the RSS played the role of 'big brother' to the BJP. But now, under Narendra Modi and Mohan Bhagwat, the relationship has evolved into one of 'twin brothers'. The work ethic and harmony between the leaders of the two organisations are so seamless that even close aides and observers struggle to detect any differences. There is a distinct harmony in the relationship between the Sangh and the central government—neither side seeks dominance, nor does either appear subordinate. Bhagwat and Modi have become a cohesive team, walking the path of Hindutva and committed to advancing its agenda.

There appear to be no strain or fissures in the relationship between Prime Minister Modi and Bhagwat. Modi understands that Bhagwat's primary interests lie in India's history and culture, and he aligns with him on these fronts. This ensures that the Sangh does not interfere in the government's economic and foreign policies. Furthermore, the two leaders engage on these subjects exclusively—no other politician or affiliated organisation is allowed to take part. One of the most notable changes from the past is that during the Vajpayee era, the RSS leadership, comprising figures such as Deoras and Golwalkar, was significantly more experienced and older, commanding greater deference. In contrast, Modi and Bhagwat are contemporaries. Both were born in September 1950 and have risen to the highest positions within their organisations, which has resulted in a deeper mutual understanding and a more equal partnership.

Bhagwat and Modi have completed, with considerable effort, the tasks that Prime Minister Vajpayee and Sarsanghchalak K.S. Sudarshan could not accomplish during their tenure. Individuals who strongly advocate for the Sangh's ideology, including committed karyakartas, have been appointed to various governmental organisations. Even journalists sympathetic to the RSS worldview have received leadership roles in government-affiliated bodies. Reportedly, ministers in BJP governments at both the centre and the states have received instructions to appoint only people associated with the Sangh as their private staff, instead of hiring relatives. The Sangh's ideological preferences have influenced the appointments of most governors. In the academic sphere, the RSS's endorsement has become increasingly important in the selection of vice-chancellors in universities. However, Bhagwat says that nowadays some people click photographs with RSS officials and include them in their resumes to bolster their credentials but such tactics are not tolerated in the Sangh and that everyone knows that a true swayamsevak of the Sangh will never do such things. Bhagwat has also placed a strong emphasis on rewriting history and reviving the ancient gurukul system of education, believing that an in-depth understanding of Indian culture, ideology and history can come only from traditional models of learning.

The Sangh's increasingly political character shows another vital change. Earlier, the Sangh believed that politics was just one part of life, and it focussed its energies on social transformation. But over time, the Sangh has realised that political power is the most important aspect of the game and, rather than merely playing a critical role, it has transitioned into an active political partner.

After the ten-year reign of the UPA government at the centre, Mohan Bhagwat mobilised the RSS apparatus, both on the ground and at the strategic level, with an aim to achieve a BJP victory at the centre in 2014. It marked the first time since 1977 that the Sangh had taken part so openly in electoral politics. Many within the Sangh believe that the BJP's resounding victory in 2014 was not solely because of people's anger over UPA's corruption or Modi's popularity, but also the result of the Sangh's strategic planning and spirited involvement in the campaign. While it was the most significant political triumph of Modi's career, for Bhagwat, it represented a crucial step towards the goal of realising a Hindu Rashtra. Bhagwat has consistently spoken about this vision, which encompasses a broad dream of positioning India as a 'vishva guru' (world leader). This includes key objectives such as overhauling the education system, constructing the Ram temple at Ayodhya, implementing a Uniform Civil Code and addressing significant national issues. Bhagwat is of the view that Indian history has become distorted and must be rewritten to reflect what he sees as a more authentic narrative.

Tensions were high at the Sangh headquarters in Resham Baug, Nagpur, on 21 March 2009. At the Akhil Bharatiya Pratinidhi Sabha meeting, key agenda items included the election of the sarkaryavah and sah-sarkaryavah, along with a crucial discussion on the Sangh's role in the upcoming general elections. As the election manager, Madhav Govind Vaidya—also the Sangh's first spokesperson—prepared to announce the result of the sarkaryavah election, an unexpected moment unfolded. Then Sarsanghchalak K.S. Sudarshan, seated nearby, abruptly took the mic from Vaidya's hand and declared that he was stepping down from his role. In a surprise move, he announced that Mohan Bhagwat would succeed him as the new sarsanghchalak.

At that time, Mohan Bhagwat's third term as the Sangh's sarkaryavah was ending. He had held the position from 11 March 2000 to 20 March 2009. While it had been long expected that he would one day assume the responsibility, even Bhagwat may not have expected that the moment would come so soon. At fifty-eight, he would be the youngest sarsanghchalak after Hedgewar and Golwalkar (Sudarshan had been selected for the post when he was sixty-eight). By stepping aside, Sudarshan had paved the path for the young generation of leaders. In doing so, he lived up to the slogan, 'Catch Them Young', even before Bhagwat could act on it. This was an important step in the RSS's journey, exemplifying the principle of applying the organisation's discipline and ethos to oneself. In earlier years, it was Sudarshan who had asked stalwarts like Vajpayee and Advani to step down to make way for younger blood.

Today Bhagwat is considered the most powerful non-political personality in Indian politics. In June 2018, when former President Pranab Mukherjee visited Dr Hedgewar's residence to pay his respects, he wrote in his tribute: 'Today I come here to pay my respect and homage to a noble son of Mother India.'[1] By doing so, he made it clear that the Sangh is not 'untouchable' for anyone. The credit for bringing the former president, who had been a Congress leader all his life, to the RSS's founding father's residence must go to Bhagwat. It is said that Bhagwat had been working towards this moment for a long time, consistently striving to change the Sangh's image and broaden its outreach.

~

June, 2005. The political temperature within the BJP was hotter than the peak of Delhi's summer. As Advani, then deputy prime minister of India and BJP president, landed at the Indira Gandhi International Airport following his six-day trip to Pakistan, Venkaiah Naidu and other leaders pulled him aside in the airport lounge. Advani's remarks at Jinnah's tomb during his Pakistan trip had created a furore in India. His statement had visibly annoyed the RSS, VHP, and BJP leadership, causing widespread discontent. They urged him to retract the comment or at least claim that it had been misrepresented. Advani was not ready for either. There was an enormous crowd of media personnel waiting outside the airport. I had been on the six-day trip to Pakistan with Advani and was present when he wrote in the visitors' book at Jinnah's tomb. Advani's description of Jinnah as a secular leader—relying on Jinnah's speech given at Pakistan's constituent assembly on 11 August 1947—had not been well-received in India. As soon as the news of what he had written in the visitors' register reached Delhi, protests erupted outside his residence. The RSS spokesperson was the first one to express his displeasure. At that time, Bhagwat was the sarkaryavah, and Sudarshan, the sarsanghchalak. Within forty-eight hours, Advani—who had played a significant role in shaping the Sangh, the Jana Sangh and the BJP over a period of fifty years—was compelled to resign. Strikingly, even BJP leaders considered close to Advani did not step forward to defend him. At that time, I recalled Pramod Mahajan's response, once when he had been asked which of the two men he considered a greater leader—Advani or Vajpayee. Mahajan had remarked that in the BJP, leadership isn't about being a big figure; only a person backed by the

Sangh could lead. Without the Sangh's support, you couldn't remain a leader in the BJP even for a day.

Despite all his efforts, Advani could never stage a political comeback. In 2005, following the BJP's national working committee meeting in Chennai, he publicly criticised the nature of the RSS–BJP relationship at a conference. Advani remarked that an image is being created that the BJP could not function without the Sangh's instructions, and this perception was detrimental to both organisations. It was the BJP's silver jubilee year. For Sarkaryavah Mohan Bhagwat, no leader stood above the Sangh's ideology, not even Advani—a man who had been with the Sangh since even before Bhagwat was born, whom his father, Madhukar Rao Bhagwat, had trained, and who had dedicated his life to the growth of Jana Sangh and BJP. The primacy of Hindutva was non-negotiable for Mohan Bhagwat. Soon after, Rajnath Singh was handed the BJP presidency.

In 2013, Mohan Bhagwat did not heed Advani's objections to Narendra Modi's candidature for the post of prime minister for the 2014 elections. Expressing his displeasure, Advani resigned from the BJP's parliamentary board, its national executive and its election committee. At that critical moment, his confidant and advisor, S. Gurumurthy, came forward to defuse the problem. When Gurumurthy spoke to Bhagwat, the man who had by then become the sarsanghchalak made it unequivocally clear that unity—both real and perceived—was of utmost importance, and Advani's resignation would only harm the party. Accordingly, Advani took back his resignation.

During K.S. Sudarshan's tenure as the sarsanghchalak, there had been considerable instability in the relationship between the Sangh and the Vajpayee administration, and they would often air these differences publicly. The Swadeshi Jagran Manch would frequently criticise the Vajpayee government openly. Possibly, the intention behind making Bhagwat the sarsanghchalak was to improve the coordination between the BJP and the Sangh.

Following the BJP's defeat in the 2009 elections under Advani's leadership, Bhagwat became doubly focussed and strategic in his preparations for the 2014 elections. He understood that a third term for the UPA would severely undermine his ultimate goal of creating a Hindu Rashtra. During that time, the number of RSS shakhas was noticeably on the decline. When the UPA came to power in 2004, the RSS had 48,329 shakhas, which fell to 44,417 in 2007 and further reduced to 43,905 by 2009, and this was naturally a genuine concern for Bhagwat.[2]

To strengthen the BJP's machinery and improve its electoral prospects, Bhagwat deployed over 500 well-trained pracharaks to assist the party. There was a growing sentiment that the BJP had failed to adequately safeguard Hindus and their interests. After becoming the sarkaryavah in 2000, Mohan Bhagwat had begun closely monitoring leaders in Delhi who, according to him, were failing in their roles as the torchbearers of the Sangh's ideology. At one point, Pramod Mahajan had been his favourite, but Mahajan's untimely death in 2006 altered that equation. Bhagwat then began to seriously consider Narendra Modi after he won the Gujarat state elections for the second time in 2007. Around the same period, Rajnath Singh paved the path for pracharaks to enter the party, changing the organisation's constitution to facilitate this move. Bhagwat turned his gaze towards the BJP leaders outside of Delhi, and zeroed in on Nitin Gadkari in Maharashtra, Manohar Parrikar in Goa and Narendra Modi in Gujarat.

In December 2009, Bhagwat chose Nitin Gadkari—then a relatively young leader from Nagpur—as the BJP president. Gadkari was only fifty-two years old at the time, becoming the youngest BJP president and a new face in Delhi's political circles. Narendra Modi had also been considered for the post of party president, but he did not want to move to Delhi until after the 2012 Gujarat elections. Bhagwat reportedly was so pleased with Gadkari's performance, that in May 2012, BJP's constitution was amended to allow Gadkari a second term as the party president. The amendment was ratified in October 2012, however internal politics within the BJP ultimately blocked Gadkari's reappointment. If he had secured a second term, Gadkari would have led the 2014 election campaign. It was Mohan Bhagwat who played a critical role in making Narendra Modi the prime ministerial candidate for the 2014 election. Surprisingly, Bhagwat remained silent as the party increasingly sidelined Gadkari. Even after the BJP lost the election in Himachal Pradesh, Bhagwat agreed to extend J.P. Nadda's tenure as BJP president.

The RSS's interference in BJP's operations has been a popular and long-standing subject of debate. In recent years, the conversation has reversed, with growing speculation that it is Narendra Modi who is exerting influence over the Sangh. In 2015, Sarkaryavah Suresh 'Bhaiyyaji' Joshi had completed two terms, and a new sarkaryavah was supposed to be chosen at the Akhil Bharatiya Pratinidhi Sabha held in Coimbatore. At that time, Narendra Modi allegedly lobbied for his favourite, Sah-sarkaryavah Dattatreya Hosabale, to be chosen as the next sarkaryavah.

The sarkaryavah, often considered the 'CEO' of the RSS, is the most important functional post in the organisation; however, Suresh Joshi was re-elected and given a third term. The matter didn't end there. Reports about Joshi's ill health began circulating as his third term neared its end in 2018, leading people to assume Hosabale would finally take over the position. However, yet again, Bhagwat reappointed Suresh Bhaiyyaji for a fourth term as the sarkaryavah. After H.V. Sheshadri, he was the only person to be chosen for the post four times, though, like Sheshadri, he was never elevated to the post of sarsanghchalak. Ironically, Mohan Bhagwat had been made the sarkaryavah without ever having served as the sah-sarkaryavah. After this, the number of sah-sarkaryavah posts were increased from four to six. Akhil Bharatiya prachar pramukh Manmohan Vaidya received the responsibility of managing the posts. Vaidya, Bhagwat's trusted aide, was the former prant pracharak of Gujarat. The Sangh appointed C.R. Mukund of Karnataka as the new sah-sarkaryavah.

In fact, in 2000, a senior RSS functionary, K. Suryanarayan Rao, had written a letter to the then sarkaryavah, H.V. Sheshadri. In it, he stressed the need to avoid lifelong tenures in leadership and argued that younger members should be inducted and given opportunities to lead. At that time, Rajju bhaiyya was the sarsanghchalak. Rajju bhaiyya, Sheshadri, Moropant Pingle and M.G. Vaidya had all voluntarily stepped down from their respective positions, and before them, even Balasaheb Deoras had set a precedent by relinquishing his role willingly.

As the sarsanghchalak, Mohan Bhagwat moved away from several existing ways of functioning and made far-reaching changes. Several officials were handed responsibilities to boost the organisation's hold on the BJP. Attention was refocussed on coordinating meetings between the BJP and the Sangh. Reportedly, Bhagwat had instructed that, regardless of what BJP leaders decided for the party, the RSS representatives had to ensure that the Sangh's influence over BJP continued to remain strong.

In political terms, the most important developments unfolded in the Northeast, where, before this, the BJP's presence was conspicuous by its absence. The impact of Bhagwat's strategic vision and the Sangh's groundwork was first evident in Assam, where the NRC issue was effectively leveraged to destabilise the Tarun Gogoi-led Congress government. This was followed by another breakthrough in Tripura, ending twenty-five years of uninterrupted left-wing rule. Soon after, the BJP expanded its footprint across other states of the Northeast, and the Congress was completely wiped out from that landscape. Bhagwat's influence was also significant in Jammu and Kashmir, where, for the first time in 2014, BJP formed part of the state government. The Sangh's sustained pressure made the BJP-led government at the centre decide to revoke Articles 370 and 35A of the Constitution. The Sangh entrusted Arun Kumar with overseeing its work in Jammu and Kashmir, a role he had held before he moved to Delhi. His current focus remains on facilitating the return of Kashmiri Pandits to the valley, though he remains wary of complications.

In June 2015, during the first term of the Modi government, Sarsanghchalak Mohan Bhagwat was given Z-plus category security. The sangh pramukh notes how people mistakenly perceive the RSS to be an institution providing simple physical training or musical instruction, but such a view is akin to the story from the *Panchatantra* called 'The Blind Men and the Elephant' (a story in which four blind men imagine and describe an elephant differently based on the different parts of the elephant's body they touch). As per Bhagwat, one needs to go to a shakha to understand the Sangh. The doors of the shakha are open for everyone, and it requires no fees or registration to attend.[3]

Bhagwat is of the view that once someone joins the Sangh, he never goes back, but it is difficult to understand the Sangh from a distance.[4] The Sangh shakha is seen as a space for discipline and penance, and the Sangh's work itself is regarded as an act of lifelong dedication. While the focus on youth has been central since Dr Hedgewar's time, Bhagwat gave this a renewed push, by coming up with the slogan—'Catch them young!' He calls for the injection of ideology in a playful manner. He says that by involving the youth in the Sangh, ideology can be easily explained to them. At the same time, this increases the strength of the Sangh and the student council at the college level. With the BJP government in power at the centre and in several states, the ABVP has witnessed a rapid rise in membership across college campuses nationwide.

During Bhagwat's tenure as the sarsanghchalak, one of the most visible and symbolic changes was the transformation in RSS's uniform, an issue that had been discussed for years. On 11 October 2016, during the annual Vijayadashami celebration, RSS swayamsevaks formally bid farewell to their iconic khaki shorts, which they had worn since the organisation's inception in 1925. Although he had been in favour of change since he became the sarsanghchalak in 2009, there was strong resistance in the organisation at the time, and the proposal was shelved. In 2015, as the RSS intensified its efforts to connect with the country's youth, it became clear that a newer generation wouldn't like to wear baggy khaki shorts as their uniform. At the Akhil Bharatiya Karyakari Mandal meeting held in Ranchi in October 2015, Bhagwat formally raised the subject. Some swayamsevaks even attended the meeting wearing full-length trousers, giving others a sense of how the proposed change in uniforms would look and feel. Bhagwat and Bhaiyyaji Joshi supported the change, yet they faced resistance from veteran pratinidhis in Maharashtra.

After this meeting, some prant pracharaks and a team of twelve members of the central executive toured across the country, attempting to understand what the swayamsevaks thought of the change. In March 2016, a report on the subject was tabled at the Akhil Bharatiya Pratinidhi Sabha held in Nagaur, Rajasthan. There the Sangh adopted coffee-brown trousers, matching socks, a white shirt and a black cap as its new uniform. In colder regions, a dark brown sweater could be worn over the white shirt. Before settling on this combination, several alternatives had been considered: navy blue and grey trousers or black trousers with white T-shirts. To ensure that the change came into force in unison, 6,00,00 trousers, 2,00,000 sweaters and bales of fabric were sent to the various shakhas. The swayamsevaks could buy the new uniforms at extremely subsidised rates.

It took almost ninety years to bring about a change in the Sangh's uniform. When Sarsanghchalak Hedgewar had founded the organisation, he had chosen the swayamsevak's attire, drawing inspiration from the uniform of the Seva Dal of the Congress. Initially, the cap's colour was khaki, but in 1930, it was changed to black. In 1940, the British government imposed a ban on the Sangh's marches and the wearing of its uniform. Sarsanghchalak Golwalkar complied with the government's orders. In those days, military boots were also part of the uniform. Interestingly, in 1971, the Sangh explored the idea of including trousers or pants at a Nagpur shakha, of which Bhagwat was also a part. In 1973, military boots replaced the black leather shoes. After that, even black rexine shoes were allowed. On the suggestion of Jain monk Muni Tarun

Sagar, who saw the use of leather as being against the concept of non-violence, the Sangh switched from leather to canvas belts.

At fifty-eight, Dr Mohan Bhagwat was the youngest person to have been chosen as the sarsanghchalak. He is seen as a straightforward, gentle and practical person, frequently quoting Swami Vivekananda and his ideas, anecdotes from the Ramayana and Mahabharata and shlokas from the Bhagavad Gita and the Vedas in his speeches.

Shrirang Godbole, a close observer of Savarkar and Mohan Bhagwat, notes that the Bhagwat family has been associated with the Sangh for three generations. Mohan Bhagwat's relationship with the Sangh began early; he was brought to a shakha as a toddler, sitting on his father's shoulders. He voluntarily joined the organisation at fourteen, and his brothers, Chittaranjan and Ravindra, also became involved with the Sangh. He completed his schooling at the Lokmanya Vidyalaya and pursued his college studies in Chandrapur, later graduating in veterinary science from Akola. During the Emergency in 1975, he quit his postgraduate studies and became a Sangh pracharak. In 2017, the Maharashtra Animal and Fishery Sciences University accorded him an honorary doctorate. He was the first person to receive such a distinction from the institution, despite not having completed his postgraduate studies.

After the Emergency, Bhagwat continued as a pracharak in Akola, and from 1980 to 1987, he was the prant pracharak in Nagpur. From 1987 to 1994, he served as Vidarbha's prant pracharak and joined the central executive in 1987. Between 1991 and 1994, he held dual responsibility as the all-India physical training co-chief. In October 1994, he was assigned to Bihar as the regional pracharak. In 1995, he became the all-India head of physical training. His ascent continued when he was appointed as the all-India pracharak pramukh in 1999–2000.

Ramesh Shiledar and Mohan Bhagwat became pracharaks roughly around the same time. Shiledar says Mohan-ji possessed sound knowledge of music and a good command over Marathi. Over the years, he has contributed significantly to physical education in the Sangh, scientifically remoulding its instruction in physical training. He has helped in composing the tunes for many of the Sangh's songs.

In September 2025, when RSS will celebrate its centenary, Mohan Bhagat will also turn seventy-five years old. In 2000, Sarsanghchalak Rajju bhaiyya had to retire for health reasons. The senior-most sarkaryavah at that time, H.V. Sheshadri, refused to take up the responsibility, also owing to poor health. Finally, the third Sangh leader in terms of seniority, K.S. Sudarshan, became the sarsanghchalak. At that time, Madan Das Devi's name was also doing the rounds. He was supposed to become the sarkaryavah, but Mohan Bhagwat was appointed in his place. One reason for this decision was the Sangh's internal principle that individuals who have worked primarily outside the core organisation, particularly in affiliate bodies, should not be given the top posts of sarkaryavah and sarsanghchalak. Madan Das Devi had been handling the ABVP for a long time and had been working on improving coordination between the Sangh and the BJP. But it was suggested to Sudharshan that Mohan Bhagwat would be a better sarkaryavah, being from Maharashtra. At that time, Madan Das Devi was asked to consult with Bhagwat on BJP-related issues. When President Venkaiah Naidu was forming his team as the BJP president, he had discussed the selection with Bhagwat and Devi. Another name considered for the sarkaryavah's position was K.N. Govindacharya. However, his candidacy was dropped because of Vajpayee's displeasure with him. Reportedly, Advani, who was managing the coordination between the Sangh and the BJP, said that he wouldn't object if the Sangh took Govindacharya back. But the Sangh stood its ground—they would not reinduct someone who had left the organisation. The same reasoning had earlier led Bhaurao Deoras to remove Dattopant

Thengadi—a powerful leader of the Bharatiya Mazdoor Sangh—whose things had been removed from the Sangh's Delhi office. Thengadi never returned to the Sangh.

Fifty-year-old Bhagwat had not even become the sah-sarkaryavah by then. Before that Sheshadri had been the sarkaryavah from 1987 to 2000. At that time, senior RSS leader Moropant Pingle had suggested that there was a need to bring young and experienced people to higher positions in the RSS. This is the reason Bhagwat was first made the all-India pracharak pramukh and then the sarkaryavah.

After almost fifteen years of non-Maharashtrian leadership, finally in 2009, the responsibility of the Sangh fell on a Maharashtrian Brahmin. After Deoras left his post of sarsanghchalak in 1994, Rajju Bhaiyya from western Uttar Pradesh became the sarsanghchalak and after him, it was Sudarshan from Karnataka.

While Bhagwat was Vidarbha's prant pracharak, he had become very close to Balasaheb Deoras. Like Deoras, he was focussed on advancing the Sangh's sphere of influence to the present generation. Though Bhagwat's moustache was similar to Hedgewar's, his outlook resembled Deoras's. Dilip Deodhar and Mohan Bhagwat were at one point of time together at the Sangh in Nagpur. According to Deodhar, Bhagwat was widely believed to be an amalgamation of the personalities of Hedgewar, Paranjape, Golwalkar and Deoras. Dr Hedgewar had both a social and spiritual temperament. Dr Paranjape from Vidarbha, who was the sarsanghchalak for ten months, was a surgeon, but Lokmanya Tilak's ideologies had influenced him. During his tenure, the Sangh had grown most rapidly. Guruji Golwalkar was an ascetic, while Deoras was the opposite—he did not believe in God but was a Hindu reformer working towards social harmony.

Deoras had studied Islam and Christianity in depth. He not only removed the chapters titled 'Internal Enemies' from *Bunch of Thoughts*, but he also made significant changes to it. Mohan Bhagwat adopted this task seamlessly from Deoras. He also clarified his stand on the questions being raised about the Sangh and Guruji.

K.S. Sudarshan had once said that the Indian constitution should either be changed or discarded. Following his statement, the Congress, the socialists and the Dalits had banded together to strongly oppose him. Some time later, on one occasion, Sudarshan had garlanded the Ambedkar statue at the Deeksha Bhoomi in Nagpur. Ambedkarites had claimed that his act had desecrated the statue. Thereafter, the statue was bathed in milk to purify it—another action that recieved a lot of criticism.[5] Eventually, Sudarshan declared that he accepted the Constitution. Rajju bhaiyya had directed the Sangh's energies towards gaining political power, projecting Vajpayee as a key leader. During Sudarshan's tenure, personal arrogance increased. Sudarshan would say that the sarsanghchalak was supreme, while the prime minister was irrelevant. Bhagwat did not repeat Sudarshan's mistake and instead, worked towards upholding the dignity of both posts.

During Balasaheb Deoras' tenure, the number of shakhas had reached 70,000, and even after fifty years, the number remains, more or less, the same. Many in the RSS think that Vajpayee's re-election in 2004 would have proven detrimental to the organisation. However it was also said that the Sangh would have remained unaffected whether Vajpayee won or lost, as it had not taken part actively in those elections. After the 2004 elections, Bhagwat positioned the Sangh on an equal footing with the BJP. In 2014, Modi improved his infrastructure with the Sangh's help. During the time of the Modi government, money from the Corporate Social Responsibility (CSR) fund of companies was utilised to build social infrastructure and bolster the initiatives of the Sangh's sister organisations.[6]

While Dr Hedgewar had empowered the Sangh alone, Balasaheb had strengthened both the Sangh and its Parivar. Guruji Golwalkar had promoted the latter, creating new organisations in multiple spheres and training members for them. Bhagwat, on his part, has appealed that every swayamsevak should induct at least one new swayamsevak into the Sangh each year, which would translate into an annual increase of over 60,00,000 swayamsevaks. In 2014, when BJP became more powerful, there had been a possibility of the party overpowering the Sangh. But Bhagwat did not allow that to happen. At present, there is stability between the Sangh and the BJP; the latter cannot ignore the Sangh's socio-political stronghold. Both Modi and Bhagwat have emerged as powerful players.

Dilip Deodhar says that Guruji had empowered the Sangh. The other organisations of the Sangh Parivar were like its children. Deoras brought those children—the sister organisations of the Parivar—at par with the Sangh. Bhagwat went on to strengthen the entire ecosystem. Earlier, only full-time pracharaks would emerge from the Sangh. But now there is a provision for paid pracharaks: married or retired people, capable of working for the Sangh, who are assigned specific projects and provided financial support.

A few years ago, researchers conducted a study to ascertain the psychological and behavioural changes among unmarried pracharaks. A number of pracharaks serve for many years, eventually stepping away to get married and settling into their family lives. Within the Sangh, it is often noted that the number of unmarried pracharaks is significantly smaller as compared to the broader base of swayamsevaks. The Sangh supports the family system and has a structured plan to involve entire families. But I must mention a notable incident at this point. When the BJP government came to power in 2014, a senior Sangh official was asked to step down at the same time. He was, at that time, the sah-sarkaryavah. The mistake this gentleman in his fifties had made was that he had fallen in love with a woman, and they had started living together. The Sangh dismissed him. A while later, the erstwhile official got married to that woman, and he now lives in Kerala.

Guruji Golwalkar was opposed to the Sangh owning any property or buildings. Today, the Sangh has numerous buildings across India, with over fifty big buildings in Nagpur alone. Every organisation and the projects it undertakes have designated venues. Earlier, whenever the need arose to acquire land or a building for building a head office, Guruji had refused. He believed that the desire for property could lead to future disputes. As a result, he did not buy a single building in the name of the Sangh, and instead, formed a separate trust for this purpose. The Sangh itself is not a registered organisation. It was only during Deoras's tenure that buildings began being constructed for service-related activities. The Sangh now has schools, colleges, hospitals, cooperatives and housing societies. Other organisations in the Parivar too have their buildings. During Dattopant Thengadi's time, the Bharatiya Mazdoor Sangh built thousands of housing societies. Farmland was acquired, plots sold and colonies built—even shakhas started being conducted there. The community halls were used for the shakhas' programmes.

During the COVID-19 lockdown, the Sangh conducted all its activities online. Bauddhik sessions conducted by Sarsanghchalak Bhagwat, shakhas, interactions with foreign journalists—everything happened through video conferencing. Ram Madhav was the first one to adopt IT for Sangh-centric tasks and also taught the senior leaders how to utilise it. Even the Sangh prayer began to be held nationally through online video streaming.

Bhagwat remains in touch with other intellectuals through the Pragya Pravah, the Sangh's intellectual arm, and he takes a keen interest in public relations. In 2017, Bhagwat met political leaders of over fifty countries in New Delhi. He was the first RSS chief to address the Bombay Stock Exchange. Bhagwat regularly meets administrative officers, former judges, senior ex-officers of the army and scholars. Ram Lal, the BJP's longest-serving national general secretary, has been called back. He is now taking care of Bhagwat's meetings with powerful and prominent people from every field.

With Bhagwat at the helm, the Sangh does not want to repeat its old mistakes and wants to shed its previous image. The sole purpose of

Bhagwat's nationwide tours is not merely to make his presence felt or to deliver speeches. Generally, he spends significant time at the camps with swayamsevaks and Sangh officials. According to Dilip Deodhar, the preamble of the Sangh's constitution now makes a mention of 'corporate life', effectively meaning collective life. It is said that Hindus lack a spirit of collectivism which causes them to lag in certain spheres. Dr Hedgewar stressed the organisation's constant superiority over the individual and would often say that individual egos harm the organisation when they take precedence.

Aniruddha Deshpande views Bhagwat as an 'organisation man', a natural communicator who interacts freely and informally with karyakartas. Such interactions are a highly valuable source of guidance for the swayamsevaks in shiksha vargs. Bhagwat was the sarkaryavah before he became the sarsanghchalak, and although he has a decisive personality, he believes in consensus. He gathers in-depth information on an issue and makes no decision until he has satisfied himself about the minutest detail. Such a process is time-consuming, but it reflects his belief in teamwork. According to Deshpande, 'Mohan is assertive, but not obstinate.' Bhagwat welcomes change, but never distances himself from the Sangh's fundamental principles and ideology. He remains committed to the vision of a Hindu nation and social harmony, encouraging peaceful coexistence among faiths.

Talking about Hindutva, Bhagwat says, 'We consider Hindutva as only one … It is the set of values which we believe in. It is the same one about which Vivekananda, Subhas Chandra Bose, Gurudev Rabindranath Thakur, Babasaheb Ambedkar have spoken.' He clarifies that while RSS believes in truth and non-violence being the core values of Hindutva, however if somebody attacks those values, then to protect them one will have to fight. To fight and practise truth and non-violence is Hindutva as per Bhagwat.[7] After Balasaheb Deoras, Bhagwat is the one sarsanghchalak who really emphasises on social harmony. He says, 'Hinduism is incomplete without Muslims. Our DNA is the same and our ancestors are also the same.' Bhagwat also emphasises on bringing Dalits into the mainstream of Hindu society. For this reason, he has talked about having one well, one temple and one crematorium for the entire society in every village so that there is no discrimination of any kind.

A long time ago, *Panchjanya* and *Organiser* had published an article on vegetarianism saying that any person who consumed meat or was non-vegetarian was not a Hindu, not a nationalist and someone who did not belong in the Sangh.[8] A national newspaper had at the time published a column questioning whether members of the Sangh themselves consume non-vegetarian food. Deodhar says that ever since Mohan Bhagwat has become the sarsanghchalak, he has not eaten any non-vegetarian food. The last time he had such food was when he was the sarkaryavah. While a large majority of the swayamsevaks consume non-vegetarian food, the Sangh likes to project a connection between 'vegetarianism' and 'nationalism'.

Another pracharak who has been with the Sangh for a long time and is heavily involved in social work says critically, 'Mohan Bhagwat was the sarkaryavah for nine years before he became sarsanghchalak, but played no decisive role. The three sarkaryavahs before him—Madhavrao Mule, Rajju bhaiyya, and H.V. Sheshadri—were all giant personalities, but Mohan Bhagwat did nothing effective in those nine years. A lot of pracharaks within the Sangh consider him a weak leader, and he likes only people similar to him on the team.'

Another ex-pracharak supported this argument, but also added that if one observed the Sangh's associate organisations, it would become clear that there wasn't a single powerful figure capable of becoming a prominent leader and challenging the status quo. There was a time when the Sangh had people such as Madhavrao Mule, H.V. Sheshadri, Moropant Pingle, Dattopant Thengadi, Madan Das Devi, Ashok Singhal and Praveen Togadia. They not only built organisations but spearheaded massive movements. At the moment, there is only the Sangh and Mohan Bhagwat—'Only one Brahm.'

The UPA government raised the issue of Hindu terrorism and saffron terror during Bhagwat's tenure as the sarkaryavah. Even though it was claimed to be a part of an international conspiracy, but instead of opposing it, Bhagwat chose to keep quiet, fearing that this might lead to the Sangh getting banned. A powerful pracharak remarked that the RSS had endured three bans in the past, and never had a sarkaryavah or sarsanghchalak shown such fear.

Deshpande believes that Bhagwat's tenure has seen clarity about the role of women for the first time in the history of the RSS. Their role in Sangh programmes has been outlined, and and it has been made clear that the organisation does not differentiate between the contributions of men and women. Under Bhagwat's leadership, the number of programmes centred on women's empowerment has increased. The sarsanghchalak has stressed that interested women shouldn't be simply redirected to the Rashtra Sevika Samiti. Instead, there should be a focus on identifying the roles women can play within shakhas and other Sangh programmes.

Bhagwat believes that society trusts swayamsevaks, therefore, swayamsevaks must embody integrity to improve society. If their actions align with their words, this trust will only grow. The society will align with the Sangh only if the organisation genuinely cares for its welfare. Bhagwat recalls that Dr Hedgewar had once said that society defines a gentleman as someone who leaves for work with his head down and returns home by five in the evening without indulging in frivolous activities. However, a true gentleman thinks about society, recognises what is happening outside the four walls of his home and takes responsibility to rectify all that is wrong. Dr Hedgewar himself was an example of this ideal.

One critical voice was that of Vijay Chauthaiwale, who was the head of the bauddhik department of the Sangh in the US for a long time as well as the head of the pragya pravah. He later returned to India and settled down in Surat. His father, Baburao Chauthaiwale, had been a prominent RSS leader. Vijay Chauthaiwale wrote a letter to Mohan Bhagwat when the latter had been the sarkaryavah stating that while the Sangh claimed to be a flexible and progressive organisation, that was not true. Sangh had become rigid and inert, and Bhagwat had done nothing to change that. He also sent a hundred copies of this letter to prominent people, something which greatly angered Bhagwat. Vijay, along with his friend Ajay Dhakras, was called to the Nagpur head office. Dhakras was Mohan Bhagwat's friend too. Ajay Dhakras, Mohan Bhagwat and Guruji Golwalkar were all Karadi Brahmins. Bhagwat made Dhakras sit in the meeting and addressed Chauthaiwale, saying that it was not true that inertia had gripped the Sangh and that change in the Sangh would often take place according to need and time. Bhagwat then questioned him, 'When you had already addressed the letter to me, why did you send it to others? Why did you publish a private letter? If you hold a post in the Sangh, you cannot do such things. You can leave your post and then do whatever you want, but criticising the Sangh publicly while being its member is unacceptable.'

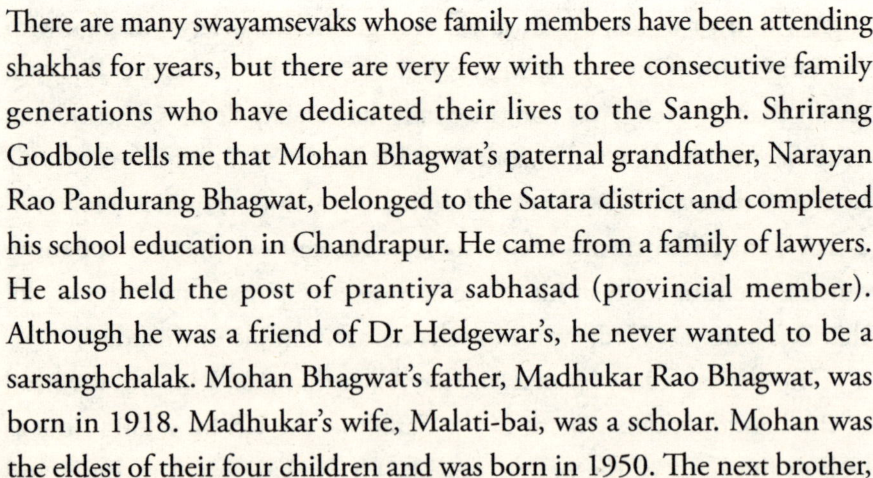

There are many swayamsevaks whose family members have been attending shakhas for years, but there are very few with three consecutive family generations who have dedicated their lives to the Sangh. Shrirang Godbole tells me that Mohan Bhagwat's paternal grandfather, Narayan Rao Pandurang Bhagwat, belonged to the Satara district and completed his school education in Chandrapur. He came from a family of lawyers. He also held the post of prantiya sabhasad (provincial member). Although he was a friend of Dr Hedgewar's, he never wanted to be a sarsanghchalak. Mohan Bhagwat's father, Madhukar Rao Bhagwat, was born in 1918. Madhukar's wife, Malati-bai, was a scholar. Mohan was the eldest of their four children and was born in 1950. The next brother,

Chittaranjan, was born in 1954, then came Ravindra in 1957 and the youngest sister, Nivedita, was born in 1962.[9]

Godbole says that during Madhukar's Sangh-related travels in 1934–35 under Dr Hedgewar's guidance, he was asked where he would like to go for higher studies. Dr Hedgewar had wanted to send him to Pune. However, Madhukar Rao joined the Fergusson College in Pune without Hedgewar's knowledge. But since Madhukar joined the college without the support of the Sangh, he was denied the post of vistarak. Later, Madhukar started Ghosh, the Sangh's band in Pune. At that time, the band played only military tunes. Madhukar would often travel overnight from Pune, in trucks loaded with vegetables, to watch English war movies being screened in Mumbai and to learn their tunes. He would then return to Pune and compose tunes for the band.

According to Godbole, Madhukar became a pracharak in 1938–39 when the Sangh's centre was in Baroda, and all the work was done in Marathi. He shifted the Sangh's centre from Baroda to Karnavati (in present-day Ahmedabad), prohibited the use of Marathi in the shakhas and insisted that Gujarati should be spoken instead. When he married in 1942, he was the prant pracharak. Post-Independence, when the government banned the Sangh, he went underground and then returned to Baroda, since there was no ban in Baroda because it was a separate state. In 1949, he went to Nagpur and completed his studies in law, while simultaneously taking on the role of the prant karyavah of the Nagpur province. In 1952, Madhukar became the district karyavah of Chandrapur and later became the zila coordinator. From 1972, he was the shareerik shiksha pramukh and was a forceful advocate for having physical training for the swayamsevaks. During the Emergency, Madhukar was imprisoned for nineteen months. He emphasised English education, and he would show his children English films so that they could learn the language. He would also read Savarkar's poems to his children. While he was in the Nagpur jail, he delivered speeches on the Mahabharata and Saptashati.

After he turned seventy, Madhukar curtailed his movement, travelling again in 2004 from Chandrapur to Nashik to participate in a prantik shivir in Karnavati. Sadly, he couldn't make it there because of his ill health. At the time of his father's death, Mohan Bhagwat's bauddhik was in progress at the Vishwa Sangh Shivir in Bengaluru and he was not able to attend his father's last rites.

There is a possibility that by the time the Sangh completes its centenary, Mohan Bhagwat will still be at its helm as the sarsanghchalak. In the RSS, it is often said that the swayamsevak is as important as the sarkaryavah, and the sarkaryavah is as important as the sarsanghchalak. The Sangh belongs to one and all, and everybody is a swayamsevak. At one time, there were discussions about 'Who after Nehru?' In a similar context, somebody had asked Guruji Golwalkar. 'Who after you?' Guruji had answered, 'Why not you? All this is not happening because of me. There are so many people involved.'

8

'There Is No Rest for Me, Until I Do Ram's Work'

Lord Ram, in his child form as Ram Lalla, has now been gloriously enthroned in a magnificent temple in Ayodhya, on the banks of the Sarayu River. In a historic event, the prime minister himself played the yajaman (host) for the prana pratishtha (consecration) ceremony held on 22 January 2024. Sarsanghchalak Mohan Bhagwat, Governor of Uttar Pradesh Anandiben Patel, Uttar Pradesh Chief Minister Yogi Adityanath and thousands of prominent personalities graced the occasion. The newly sculpted Ram Lalla idol, breathtaking in its divine beauty, is said to have left thousands of people physically present at the temple and the crores watching the ceremony being streamed live on television, emotionally overwhelmed and spiritually uplifted. Adorned with a dazzling crown encrusted with diamonds and precious gems, radiant earrings, the divine Vaijayanti garland and with a gentle, adolescent form, the idol of Ram Lalla can truly be called a vision of celestial grace. His deep, limpid eyes, serene smile, and divine presence evoke profound devotion and reverence in all who behold him.

On the day of the consecration, saffron flags adorned almost every street in the country, and chants of 'Jai Shri Ram' reverberated all around. Amidst this surge of devotion and veneration, the prime minister spoke about 'Vijay nahi vinay' (Not victory but humility), while Sarsanghchalak Bhagwat stressed upon 'Josh mein hosh' (Wisdom in enthusiasm).

While addressing the religious saints and other invitees at the ceremony, Bhagwat said, 'But why did he (Ram) leave? He left because there were disputes in Ayodhya. Ram Rajya is coming, and we have to shun all disputes and stop fighting among ourselves over petty issues. We will have to shun ego and stay united ...'[1] In preparation for the occasion, Prime Minister Modi observed a special fast for eleven days and undertook a vow of purity before the consecration ceremony. Sarsanghchalak Bhagwat commended him for his spiritual discipline. When the prime minister rose to speak, his speech reflected the same restraint that marked the Sarsanghchalak's address. Modi said, 'Today's occasion is not just a celebration but also a moment of realisation of the maturity of Indian society. This occasion is not only about victory but also about humility for us ... The generations after a thousand years will remember our nation-building efforts today.'[2] Undoubtedly, given the many controversial statements that had been made in the past regarding the Ram temple, such carefully measured remarks carried great significance. Yet, beyond the speeches, the consecration ceremony has sent the country into a state of rapture. The moment marked the culmination of a long and arduous journey, won through years of struggle and sacrifice. The joy was so profound that the country celebrated not one but two Diwalis! From the smallest villages to bustling towns in every corner of the country, homes and streets were bathed in lights, and the skies resounded with the sound of crackers in the evening. Ayodhya has turned a new leaf, with newly built roads, modern buildings, a gleaming railway station and even a brand-new airport. The city has been transformed beyond recognition. However, amid this wave of development, some voices have expressed concern that in embracing this 'newness', the essence of Lord Ram's Ayodhya might be lost. What of the akhadas (religious sects), ashrams, ochre-clad saints and sadhus? The pilgrims balancing bundles on their heads, feeding bananas to monkeys, distributing and receiving free food? What of the sacred dips in the Sarayu and the tapping of the khadaus (wooden footwear) on the rough and bumpy roads through the town? What will become of the vibrant markets selling Ram Lalla attire, brass bells, and oil lamps—of the eager guides shepherding pilgrims towards Hanuman Garhi, the ongoing Bhagwat discourses and the many stages set up for the dramatic retelling of the *Ram Lila*? Will this be the same Ayodhya that was beloved to Kevat, Shabari, Janmbavant, Sugriv and Hanuman? Or are we witnessing the rise of a new city, one that dazzles with the promise of Ram Rajya, yet risks leaving behind the values and people that defined it? Will this Ayodhya become a city where commerce eclipses faith, grandeur overshadows simplicity and the poor and underprivileged are pushed to the margins?

Apprehensions and fears can also be unfounded. Alok Kumar, the president of Vishva Hindu Parishad's international working committee, assures us they have consistently urged the government to not reduce Ayodhya to a mere tourist destination, rather to maintain its spiritual character. For them, faith is paramount. Attempts were made to shape the pran-pratishtha of the Ram temple into a true people's movement. Water from sacred rivers from 110 countries was brought to Ayodhya, along with water from the small ponds, wells and rivers from every village, gathered through religious processions and pilgrimages. This water was then used for the consecration ceremony, symbolising the collective devotion and participation from around the world. Even before this, the stones and bricks used in constructing the Ram temple had been sourced from every corner of the country. Alok Kumar says, 'The purpose of the Ram Janmabhoomi movement is not restricted to the construction of the temple at the Ram Janmabhoomi site; this is just a milestone. After the construction, Hindu awakening is the most important task, and this is an ongoing process. This has nothing to do with politics, and it never did. This aspect needs to be understood and underlined.'[3]

However, the construction of the Ram temple and its premises is being carried out by the Shri Ram Janmabhoomi Teerth Kshetra, while the broad development of Ayodhya city is under the Uttar Pradesh Government, led by Chief Minister Yogi Adityanath. For decades, the Ram temple movement has been at the heart of Indian politics; governments rose and fell, and more than one chief minister lost their position over it.

It is noteworthy that in 2023, the central government awarded the then chief minister of Uttar Pradesh, Mulayam Singh Yadav, with a Padma Vibhushan, despite his controversial decision in 1990 to order police firing on Ram devotees. In contrast, in 2022, the central government honoured the former chief minister of Uttar Pradesh, Kalyan Singh, who had once declared that no force would be used against karsevaks (volunteers), with the Padma Vibhushan.

On 5 August 2020, at the bhoomi pujan (groundbreaking) ceremony of the Ram temple, Prime Minister Narendra Modi declared, 'The construction of Shree Ram Temple is a task to unite the entire nation. This celebration is an occasion to unite belief with the reality, man with the Supreme God, mankind with conviction, the present with the past, and self with ethos. People across the globe will recount today's historical moment for ages, and it will bring laurels to our country. This day is proof of the honesty of the millions of determined devotees of

Shree Ram. This day is a unique gift from the law abiding India to truth, non-violence, faith and sacrifice.'[4]

On the occasion, Dr Mohan Bhagwat had said, 'So there would be a glorious temple here, the process of construction has begun, responsibilities have been allocated. Those who have been entrusted with various duties would carry out their work. While this is happening, what do we have to do? We have to get ready with Ayodhya in our hearts. The "dharma" to which Prabhu Ram belongs, unites people, helps them progress and move up. This "dharma" is all-inclusive. We have to be the flag bearers of this "dharma" and ensure that we build a Bharat that brings peace and happiness to the world. Even as the construction of the temple progresses here, the Ayodhya in our hearts should also get ready. Before this temple is ready, the temple in our heart should be ready.'[5]

While Prime Minister Pandit Nehru chose not to participate in the inauguration of the Somnath temple after its reconstruction, Narendra Modi sought to write a new chapter in history by personally taking part in the bhoomi pujan (groundbreaking) ceremony of. Modi said, 'Not only is a new history being created with this temple, but history is repeating itself.' Someone remarked that Modi hasn't only performed the ceremony of the Ram temple—he simultaneously laid the foundation for victory in the 2024 general elections. The shilanyas (foundation) ceremony was held on 9 November 1989, and the construction work of the temple began thirty years, eight months and twenty-seven days later. The construction of a Ram Mandir in Ayodhya started after 492 years. 'History will remember Kalyan Singh's tenure for the demolition of the Babri Masjid, while people will know Yogi Adityanath's term for the construction of the Ram Mandir,' a BJP leader said to me.

Historians believe Mir Baqi, a Mughal commander under Babur, built the Babri Masjid in Ayodhya in 1528. Over the past 492 years, the site has witnessed many turbulent phases. The first instance of violence erupted about 167 years ago. Disputes formally began in 1858—nearly 330 years after the mosque's construction—when an FIR was filed over prayers and a havans (fire ritual) being performed at the site. The matter eventually reached the courts 135 years ago. Kishore Kunal, the author of *Ayodhya Revisited*, tells us, 'On 1 December 1858, the Police Inspector of the Awadh, Sheetal Dubey, wrote in his report that a platform had been constructed. This is the first legal document that shows evidence of Ram's symbols inside the premises. Twenty-seven years after this incident, the matter reached the court. At that time, Mahant Raghubar Das filed a petition in the Faizabad court seeking the construction of a temple at the Ram Janmabhoomi site. The court dismissed his petition. In 1886, an appeal was filed against the ruling, but it was dismissed yet again.'[6]

Between the night of 22–23 December 1949, someone placed an idol of Lord Ram at the disputed site. An FIR was filed the next day. In response, the gates of the premises were locked, but the mayor of the municipal corporation, Priya Dutt Ram, was appointed the receiver of the disputed site on 5 January 1950. The matter reached the court that same year, and the legal battle continued for nearly seven decades, concluding on 9 November 2019.

Alok Kumar says, 'The premises of the Shri Ram Janmabhoomi Teerth Kshetra are spread over an area of over 70 acres, while the main temple is being built on 2.7 acres. The total built area is 57 thousand 400 square feet. The temple is 360 feet long, 23 feet wide and 161 feet tall, including the height of the spire. Now, the temple will have three floors instead of two. Each floor's height is intended to be 20 feet. The basement of the temple will have 160 pillars, the first floor will have 132 pillars, and the second floor will have 74 pillars. The temple will have five spires and mandaps (pavilions). Twelve doorways will be constructed. The existing idol of Ram Lalla will be installed in the sanctum sanctorum as the utsava murti (processional deity), while a magnificent Ram Darbar is being constructed for devotees to worship. Two special Shaligram (sacred black fossil stone) rocks are being brought in from Nepal for this. Sixteen images will be carved on each pillar. Along with, in the vast 70 acre premises of the temple, a Shri Ram Kund Yagyashala (altar for fire worship), Anusthan Mandap (ceremonial hall for religious rituals), a large idol of Lord Hanuman in Hanuman Garhi, Guru Vashisht Peethika, Bhakti Teela, Tulsi Ram Leela Kendra open-air theatre and a Ram Darbar Projection theatre are being planned to be constructed. With the construction of the Ram Mandir, the city of Ayodhya, which has been in a state of neglect, will also see a turnaround. The government is building an international airport and a high-tech railway station here. We hope that the number of tourists and pilgrims visiting Ayodhya will reach a lakh a day, which, at the moment, stands at five thousand a day. There will be arrangements to accommodate two lakh devotees a day on special occasions.'

Dr Manmohan Vaidya notes, 'The struggle for reinstating Ram Mandir on Ram Janmabhoomi was a movement to reinstate the dharma of Bharat, which was being systematically distorted in the name of secularism.'[7]

प्रबिसि नगर कीजे सब काजा । हृदयँ राखि कोसलपुर राजा ॥

(Enter the city and accomplish all tasks, keeping the King of Kosala, Lord Ram, in your heart.)

On 25 March 2020, the first day of the Chaitra Navratri (the nine-day Hindu festival dedicated to Goddess Durga), Ram Lalla, along with his brothers and Lord Hanuman, was ceremoniously installed in a temporary temple made of pinewood and glass at 3 a.m.. Since 6 December 1992, Ram Lalla had been housed in a temporary tent temple. For the first time after 1528, the idol was placed on a silver throne. Following the Supreme Court's ruling, the central government announced the formation of the fifteen-member Shri Ram Janmabhoomi Teerth Trust on 6 February 2020. Mahant Nritya Gopal Das, a long-time figure in the Ram Janmabhoomi movement, was appointed its president.

Funds for the construction of the Ram Temple in Ayodhya have been collected from the public, and the government has clarified that it will not contribute financially to the project. Instead, the government will focus on the development of Ayodhya. The VHP clarified that its role is now complete, and the responsibility for temple construction lies entirely with the trust. However, the Parishad led the fund collection drive. The working styles of the Sangh and the Parishad reflect their aim to ensure maximum participation from across the country and even from abroad in the temple's construction. A similar approach was seen earlier, when bricks and stones engraved with 'Shri Ram' were brought in from all corners of India. In the 1960s, when the memorial for Dr Hedgewar was to be built in Resham Baug, Vidarbha, Nagpur offered to fund the project. However, Sarsanghchalak Guruji Golwalkar insisted every swayamsevak contribute one rupee, emphasising shared responsibility and participation. The Ram Janmabhoomi Trust was constituted along the lines of the historic Somnath temple. After the Partition, when the princely state of Junagadh acceded to India, the question of reconstructing Somnath arose. Sardar Patel and K.M. Munshi approached Mahatma Gandhi with the idea. Mahatma Gandhi advised against spending government funds on the reconstruction and suggested that the citizens of India could voluntarily raise the money and rebuild the temple if they so desired.

Despite the Nehru government's efforts to promote a secular image and distance itself from the initiative, Patel moved ahead with the plan, navigating support and opposition. On 23 January 1949, a conference was held in Jamnagar where it was decided to set up a trust with two donors, two Union ministers, two prominent citizens and two representatives of the Saurashtra government as its members. After the death of both Gandhi and Patel, K.M. Munshi took up the responsibility for the temple reconstruction. In 1950, he formed an additional trust under the Bombay Public Trusts Act to supervise the temple's functioning and ensure that the government remained formally distanced from the process. Once the temple was finally ready in May 1951, despite Nehru's displeasure, President Dr Rajendra Prasad attended the inauguration ceremony of the temple.

राम कृपा नाशहिं सब रोगा। जौं एहि भाँति बने संजोगा॥

(If the grace of Lord Ram is present, all diseases will be destroyed.
If such a fortunate union takes place, all the ailments will disappear.)

On the morning of 10 November 2019, a sense of relief washed over Ayodhya. The resolution of a centuries-old conflict brought a sense of calm to the holy city. However, just a day earlier, there had been an air of apprehension from the banks of the Sarayu River to the areas surrounding the temple's site. Meticulous security arrangements were in place in anticipation of the court's ruling. A five-judge Supreme Court bench comprising Ashok Bhushan, S.A. Bobde, D.Y. Chandrachud and S.A. Nazeer, led by the then Chief Justice of India Ranjan Gogoi, had even held a meeting with the senior officials of the Uttar Pradesh Government to review the law and order situation and ensure that preparations were in place.

In its decision, the Supreme Court addressed the appeals concerning the 2010 Allahabad High Court ruling, which had divided the disputed land into three equal portions, allocated among Ram Lalla Virajman, the Nirmohi Akhara, and the Sunni Waqf Board. Over a forty-one-day stretch, the Supreme Court had heard arguments from all parties. The Ayodhya title dispute involves 120 issues, which were framed for trial, and the case records span the depositions of eighty-eight witnesses running into 13,886 pages and 257 documents. The judgement sought to legally resolve a dispute spanning the 'Mughal era, the colonial period and the present-day Constitutional era'. In its landmark ruling, the Court awarded the entire disputed site to the Ram Janmabhoomi Trust for the construction of the temple. It directed the government to allow a piece of five-acre land anywhere in Ayodhya for the construction of a mosque. The Supreme Court overturned the ruling of the Allahabad High Court, stating clearly that a verdict could not be based solely on matters of faith. Throughout the daily hearings, the bench ensured all parties had ample time to present their arguments, so that no side could later claim denial of a fair opportunity to be heard. Following the exhaustive proceedings, Chief Justice Gogoi delivered the final judgement of his career, acknowledging the significance and sensitivity of the case. A few months after the verdict, the president of India nominated former chief justice Gogoi as a member of the Rajya Sabha—a move that drew widespread criticism from across the political spectrum.

It is important to closely examine key aspects of the Supreme Court's decision. Notably, the court had held that the act of placing the idol of Ram Lalla in the central dome of the mosque in the night between 22 and 23 December 1949, and subsequently, preventing Muslims from performing their namaz in the mosque there, was illegal. The Supreme Court had pronounced the demolition of the Babri Masjid on 6 December 1992 to be an unlawful act. These findings serve as a significant rebuke to those who celebrated or justified the demolition, marking a legal condemnation of both events.

Apart from the Ram Janmabhoomi dispute, the Supreme Court reaffirmed the importance of maintaining the sanctity of the Places of Worship (Special Provisions) Act of 1991, which mandates the preservation of the religious character of places of worship as it stood on 15 August 1947. To ensure that the decision was just and balanced, the Supreme Court, invoking its extraordinary powers under Article 142 of the Constitution, directed that five acres of land should be granted for the construction of a mosque in Ayodhya. The court noted that in 1986, erstwhile prime minister Rajiv Gandhi had exerted pressure to have the locks of the disputed site opened to allow worship. Later, in 1989, the permission granted to Hindu organisations to perform the shilanyas was procedurally flawed. Most people have been considering the Ram Janmabhoomi a matter of Hindu faith, but most religious texts have no mention of it. However, the tenth chapter, 'Ayodhya Mahatmya', of the Vaishnava Khanda, a part of the eighth-century *Skanda Purana,* mentions Ram's geographical birthplace.

तस्मात् स्थानत ऐशाने रामजन्म प्रवर्तते।
जन्मस्थानमिदं प्रोक्तं मोक्षादि फल साधनम् ।।

(Therefore, from this northeastern place, the birth of Ram occurred. This birthplace is declared as a means to attain liberation and other spiritual fruits.)

विघ्नेश्वरात् पूर्वभागे वासिष्ठा दुत्तरे तथा।
लौमशात् पश्चिमे भागे जन्मस्थानं ततः स्मृतम् ||[8]

(To the east of Vighneshwara, to the north of Vasistha [hermitage], and to the west of Lomasha—The place situated there is remembered as the birthplace [of Lord Ram])

The trouble is that the Vighneshwara temple and the hermitages of Rishi Vashishtha and Loumesha no longer exist.

राम पियारे राम का नगर बस्या भरपूरि

(Beloved Ram founded his city in the land of abundance.)

In the 1980s, the Congress-led government in Uttar Pradesh, under Chief Minister Sripati Mishra, had acquired 42 acres of land surrounding the Ram Janmabhoomi–Babri Masjid premises for developing a public space, Radha Park. The banks of the Sarayu River were dug up, and the 'Ram ki Paidi' was created. During this period, President Giani Zail Singh also visited Ayodhya. This event spurred the Sangh into action. Sarsanghchalak Balasaheb Deoras had intensive discussions with Vajpayee and Advani. On 6 March 1983, Maharaj Vijay Kaushal and others associated with the Sangh organised the Virat Hindu Sammelan in Muzaffarnagar, under the banner of the Hindu Jagran Manch. The gathering saw participation from notable figures, including former deputy prime minister Gulzarilal Nanda, senior leaders of the Congress and Dau Dayal Khanna. It was at this conference that the proposal for freeing the Ram Janmabhoomi was first passed. It was at this time that the Sangh and the Vishva Hindu Parishad decided to protest against the incidents of religious conversions in Meenakshipuram. Moreover, in 1983, Swami Swaroopanand Saraswati publicly voiced his support for the construction of the Ram Mandir. On the other hand, the VHP had moved a step further and organised a Dharma Sansad (religious conclave) at the Vigyan Bhavan in Delhi on 7 and 8 April 1984. The aim was to formulate a strategy for mobilising protests against the mosques in Kashi, Mathura and Ayodhya, which were allegedly built over ancient temples. During the conclave, resolutions were passed for the liberation of these three religious sites. However, since the mosques in Kashi and Mathura were near other temples, the movement squarely placed the emphasis on Ayodhya. As a follow-up, on 27 July 1984, the Ram Janmabhoomi Mukti Yagya Samiti was set up. Mahant Avaidyanath, the head of the Gorakhnath Math, was appointed its president, and Dau Dayal Khanna was named its general secretary. On 25 December, the Samiti decided to launch a Ram–Janaki Yatra all over the country. In this procession, a chariot displaying the idols of Ram and Janaki behind bars was created, and it started from Sitamarhi in Bihar. The

Samiti demanded the opening of the Babri Masjid's locks and the land's handover to Acharya Shiv Ramacharya of the Ramanandi Sampradaya for the temple's construction. Before the yatra reached Ayodhya in October, the outrage in the Hindu community was palpable. VHP leader Ashok Singhal came into the limelight owing to his involvement with this yatra. Beginning on 11 June 1989 with the BJP's national convention in Palampur, the politics surrounding the Ram temple began to take shape, as the party decided to support the Ram Janmabhoomi movement. Lal Krishna Advani drafted the resolution, but Atal Bihari Vajpayee was against it. The resolution stated, 'This conflict cannot be resolved legally through the courts. With the same respect that Prime Minister Jawaharlal Nehru decided on the Somnath temple reconstruction, the Congress government should take decisions. The government should respect the emotions of the Hindus and hand over this site to them. If possible, they should resolve the matter through mutual discussions, or the parliament should pass a law. However, this can under no circumstances be resolved by the courts.'[9]

On 22 September 1989, a Maha Hindu Sammelan was organised at the Boat Club in Delhi under the presidency of Mahant Avaidyanath. At the event, a proposal was adopted, and the date for the foundation ceremony was announced. On 9 November 1989 at 1.33 p.m., a havan and prayers were held at a predetermined spot roughly 192 metres away from the sanctum sanctorum. Kameshwar Prasad Chaupal from south Bihar placed the first brick for the temple. He was a Dalit, an active member of the VHP and continues to be a member of the Shri Ram Janmabhoomi Teerth Trust. During the Hindu month of Magh (January–February) in 1989, the third Dharma Sansad convened at Allahabad and resolved to ask every Hindu to contribute a symbolic donation of one and a quarter rupee along with a brick for the construction of the Ram temple.

Meanwhile, the groundwork for the temple's construction had already begun under Prime Minister Rajiv Gandhi. In a clever move to counter the pro-Muslim image he had acquired after the *Shah Bano* case, Gandhi took a strategic step by ordering the unlocking of the Babri Masjid premises—an act interpreted as an appeal to Hindu sentiments. As the 1989 Lok Sabha elections approached and the accusations of corruption mounted, he once again attempted to rally Hindu support. Rajiv Gandhi began his election campaign in 1989 from Faizabad, promising to establish Ram Rajya. Simultaneously, the Congress attempted to attract Muslim voters by proposing a bill to grant Urdu the status of an official language. However, this strategy did not yield results for the Congress. On the contrary, the BJP gained traction. From a mere two seats in 1983, the party won eighty-five seats this time around. Within the party, it marked the era of Advani's rise and Vajpayee's marginalisation. The BJP and the left parties supported the National Front government's formation in 1989 after the elections. After the National Front government took over, Prime Minister V.P. Singh, amid a power struggle with Deputy Prime Minister Devi Lal, decided to implement the Mandal Commission's report. This move awarded a 27 per cent reservation to OBCs in government jobs and educational institutions. In response, the BJP, under Advani's leadership, sought to consolidate its Hindu vote base by launching a Ram Rath Yatra, a grand chariot procession from Somnath to Ayodhya. The Janata Dal government led by Lalu Prasad Yadav halted this procession in Samastipur. In retaliation, the BJP withdrew its support for the National Front government, leading to the collapse of the coalition.

In 1990, the VHP announced that it would do karseva in Ayodhya, but the Allahabad High Court ordered that the status quo at the disputed site had to be maintained. Despite this, the karseva proceeded, resulting in violent clashes. Police action led to several deaths and hundreds of injuries. Right before the karseva, the then chief minister of Uttar Pradesh had challenged that he would make sure that not even a bird flew up to the mosque, leave alone any karsevak. BJP capitalised on this incident in the state assembly elections, eventually forming a government under Kalyan Singh's leadership. During his short forty-day stint as prime minister, Chandra Shekhar attempted to resolve this deadlock, but the BJP and the VHP's obstinate attitude thwarted his efforts. During this phase, the Parishad popularised provocative sayings such as, 'Ram Lalla hum aayenge, mandir vahin banaenge, Teen nahi teen hazaar, nahi bachegi koi mazaar (Lord Ram, we will come and build your temple there; Not just three, but three thousand will come, no mausoleum will be spared).'

In December 1991, the BJP and the VHP announced yet another round of karseva at Ayodhya. Although the court issued an order for maintaining the status quo, and the Kalyan Singh government filed an affidavit promising that it would grant no permission for tampering with the mosque, it did not uphold the assurance. Central security forces were stationed outside the disputed area, and yet, on 6 December 1992, the mosque was demolished. In the aftermath, the central government under Narasimha Rao suspended the BJP governments in six states and constituted the Babri Masjid Action Committee. Despite the communal tension, it appeared that the BJP would benefit from the 'Ram wave'. But in the subsequent Uttar Pradesh Legislative Assembly elections, a counter-narrative came to the forefront. The slogan, '*Mile Mulayam Kanshiram, Hava Ho Gaye Jai Shri Ram* (When Mulayam and Kanshiram come together, Jai Shri Ram vanishes) gained popularity, and the BJP lost. Samajwadi Party leader Mulayam Singh Yadav and the Bahujan Samaj Party formed a coalition government. In the 1996 general elections, the BJP remained politically isolated. Consequently, the first BJP government under Vajpayee's leadership lasted only thirteen days. The BJP leadership under L.K. Advani and Vajpayee, with guidance from Sarsanghchalak Rajju Bhaiya, decided to set aside contentious issues like the Ram Mandir, Common Civil Code and Article 370. Therefore, the National Democratic Alliance (NDA), which came to power in 1998 with the BJP at the helm, was formed with core ideological issues remaining on the back burner.

The political history of the Ram Mandir is as long as its legal past, and Rajiv Gandhi, Vishwanath Pratap Singh, Chandra Shekhar and Narasimha Rao have been key figures in this complex trajectory. At one time, Arif Mohammad Khan, who was a minister in the Rajiv Gandhi government says, 'Ali Miyan Sahib of the Muslim Personal Law Board did not make any statements till Rajiv Gandhi was alive … Rajiv Gandhi had told me he had informed Ali Miyan and a few other selected Muslim leaders about the lock of the mosque being opened which meant that a deal had been struck to give these people Shah Bano and open the locks for the other side. What does it mean to open the locks? A letter was sent to Pandit Nehru in 1947 stating that the idols should be removed. At that time, the district magistrate of Faizabad had warned that doing so could cause a blood bath, and please think if the status would change by opening the locks?'

Khan says that he represented the government in the Ram Mandir case. The Supreme Court had said that some solution could be found if both parties agreed. When the chief justice looked at both parties, he realised that nobody was ready.[10]

सबहि नचावै राम गुसाईं

(Lord Ram makes everyone dance to His will.)

When Vishwanath Pratap Singh quit the Rajiv Gandhi government in protest against the Bofors scandal, it was almost certain that the Congress rule would collapse. In 1989, the BJP decided to go for the polls with the Jan Morcha, and Atal Bihari Vajpayee was given the responsibility to come to a consensus about the distribution of seats. His colleague Govindacharya, the party's chief organisational secretary, looked after the finer points of the negotiations. The government was formed. The VHP had, by then, decided the date for the karseva programme for the Ram temple construction: 30 October 1990. A meeting of all the associate organisations of the Sangh was organised for the allocation of responsibilities.

Senior journalist Ram Bahadur Rai says, 'Prime Minister Vishwanath Pratap Singh could understand the politics of the Sangh Parivar and the BJP on the Ayodhya issue, and that is why he pulled out a trump card. Devi Lal was applying pressure from the other side. In such a scenario, on 7 August 1990, Singh announced the implementation of the Mandal Commission report, and he did not find it necessary to consult the coalition partners, the BJP and the Left parties.'[11]

Govindacharya, who had been the chief secretary of the BJP, says, 'The temple issue had almost reached the resolution stage during the V.P. Singh government. The prime minister had proposed that political parties should keep themselves away from this issue and that attempts should be made to find a solution to this matter through non-political people from both communities. The proposal suggested handing the disputed site and place to a new Hindu Trust, requiring it to build a temple without touching the disputed site, and to build a wall between the temple and the disputed site. Singh had given this responsibility to the then-governor of Andhra Pradesh, Krishan Kant, and he was told to garner support for the matter. Krishan Kant proposed they make Jayendra Saraswati, the Shankaracharya of the Kanchi Kamakoti Peetham, the head of the new Trust. Krishan Kant also had arranged for a meeting between the main petitioner, Ali Miyan, and Jayendra Saraswati. Moreover, he also had deliberations with Vishwesha Tirtha Swami.'[12]

On the other hand, the prime minister appointed S. Gurumurthy as the mediator for this discussion, and Gurumurthy put forward a three-point programme. Three days later, acting as the prime minister's emissary, he met George Fernandes and P. Upendra and informed them that the central government was ready to issue an ordinance on the Ram temple issue. That same evening, the prime minister called Govindacharya and Additional Solicitor General Arun Jaitley and discussed the consequences of accepting the three-point formula. They worked through the night and prepared the ordinance. Singh also discussed the matter with Advani, but by the evening, the situation had shifted. A meeting was held at the prime minister's residence, attended by Gurumurthy, Jaitley, George Fernandes, Arun Nehru, Ajit Singh and Dinesh Goswami. Along with the proposed ordinance, the central government imposed a condition: the VHP must drop its demands concerning the religious sites in Mathura and Kashi. The Muslim faction had agreed to the construction of the temple, but the VHP pulled back as its leaders were unwilling to abandon the Kashi and Mathura issues. In light of the stalemate, the decision to issue the ordinance was ultimately shelved. Bilateral talks resumed during Prime Minister Chandra Shekhar's tenure (10 November 1990–21 June 1991). On 1 December 1990, members of the Babri Masjid Action Committee and the VHP representatives held a meeting. The VHP's delegation comprised Vishnu Hari Dalmia, Badriprasad Toshniwal, Shrish Chandra Dikshit, Moropant Pingle, Kaushal Kishore, Bhanupratap Shukla, Giriraj Kishore and Suryakrishna. A second round of discussions happened on 4 December 1990, attended by Minister of State for Home Affairs Subodh Kant Sahay, along with three leaders believed to be close to Chandra Shekhar: Uttar Pradesh Chief Minister Mulayam Singh Yadav, Maharashtra Chief Minister Sharad Pawar and Rajasthan Chief Minister Bhairon Singh Shekhawat. The most significant achievement of Chandra Shekhar's tenure was the attempt to resolve the conflict through rational dialogue. For the first time, the Archaeological Survey of India was brought into the discussion, allowing the matter to be approached through evidence-based inquiry. When the central government under Narasimha Rao assumed power, Subodh Kant Sahay, who was not a member of the Congress at the time, received an unexpected phone call from the prime minister. Rao asked whether he would help initiate the mediation process yet again. Sahay accepted his request. Under his guidance, a significant meeting was convened, attended by Sharad Pawar and Chimanbhai Patel from the Congress, Bhairon Singh Shekhawat and Rajmata Vijaya Raje Scindia from the BJP, the Shahi Imam of the Jama Masjid, and leaders from Hindu organisations and other parties. The primary objective of these meetings was to assuage the communal hysteria that was gripping the country. According to Sahay, the core issue during mediation was not whether the Ram temple should be built. Rather, the parties debated how they should build it—through consensus and mutual respect or through confrontation—and what process they should follow. On the evening of 2 October 1992, a crucial meeting was underway at Vigyan Bhavan in Lutyens' Delhi, attended by the key stakeholders in the Ram temple issue: the chief minister, senior officers and political leaders. Subodh Kant Sahay had hoped for a concrete resolution. However, everything changed with a piece of news. Hindu organisations had announced a karseva at Ayodhya on 6 December during a meeting held at the nearby Ramlila Maidan.

Attendees questioned the utility of their efforts given the unilateral announcements. Consequently, an official meeting held on 9th December decided that all related parties should submit their opinions in writing to the home ministry. After the demolition of the Babri Masjid, the Congress government introduced an ordinance in January 1993, which the BJP had opposed. President Dr Shankar Dayal Sharma assented to the ordinance that same month. Home Minister S.B. Chavan then presented the ordinance in the Lok Sabha, and the 'Ayodhya Act' was passed. This legislation allowed the central government to acquire the 67.7 acres of land surrounding the disputed site. The Rao government, under Article 143 of the Constitution, sought the Supreme Court's counsel on whether a pre-existing Hindu temple or structure stood at the Ram Janmabhoomi–Babri Masjid disputed site. A five-judge bench of the Supreme Court, comprising Justices M.N. Venkatachaliah, J.S. Verma, A.M. Ahmadi, and S.P. Bharucha, deliberated on it but declined to offer an opinion. On 7 January 1993, the erstwhile president specifically asked the Supreme Court: was there a Hindu religious structure or a temple that was demolished before Babur constructed the mosque in 1528 in Ayodhya? The Supreme Court sought clarification from the central government regarding the president's question. In September 1994, Solicitor General stated in his affidavit: 'If the answer to the president's question comes out to be positive, that the disputed structure was built after destroying a Hindu temple or a Hindu structure, then the Government of India will act according to the feelings of the Hindu community. If the answer is negative—that is, there was no Hindu temple or structure before 1528—the Government of India's actions would be in line with the emotions of the Muslim community.'[13]

A senior Sangh leader affirmed, 'The President's question is the central point of the entire controversy. This is the only way the ownership of the disputed site can be decided.' To find an answer to the president's question, the Allahabad High Court in 2003 commissioned radar photography of the land near the Ram Janmabhoomi site in Ayodhya. A Canadian expert executed the assignment, reporting that the remains of a building were visible deep under the ground.

The matter resurfaced during the NDA government in 2001. VHP leader Ashok Singhal and Mahant Ramchandra Das Paramhans of the Ram Janmabhoomi Nyas renewed pressure again on the Vajpayee government. Prime Minister Vajpayee responded by creating a dedicated cell within the PMO for the assignment, with Ashok Saikia appointed to lead it. Shatrughna Singh, a retired IAS officer of the UP cadre, headed the unit, which had a space in the PMO and Vigyan Bhavan. This cell prepared a proposal for the prime minister, outlining three potential avenues of resolving this conflict:

1. Hindus should be allowed to build the temple, and the mosque should be built at a designated spot a few kilometres away where the commander of Babur's army had camped. However, this was contingent on giving up the demands for the temples in Kashi and Mathura.
2. The land of the disputed site should be divided into two equal parts.
3. A mosque should be built at Ara Ghar, at a short distance from the disputed site on land that had already been acquired by the government.

Vajpayee received all the information about this in February 2002, but offered no reaction during the meeting. The organisations associated with the Babri Masjid did not pursue the matter further, and no progress was made on the issue.

In further investigating the photography report, the Allahabad High Court, in 2003, ordered the Archaeological Survey of India to excavate the site. The excavation report confirmed the presence of a Hindu temple in the Uttar Pradesh style. Based on these scientific reports, the Allahabad High Court delivered its judgement on 30 September 2010. The three-judge bench comprising Justice D.V. Sharma, Justice S.U. Khan and Justice S. Agarwal was split, with two in favour and one against. The bench determined that in the Ram Janmabhoomi title suit, Triloki Nath Pandey, who represented Ram Lalla, Nirmohi Akhara, and the Sunni Waqf Board, should each be granted one-third of the disputed land and that all three should hold the title jointly. Justice Sharma was against awarding one-third of the land for the construction of the mosque.

The court dismissed the Waqf Board's petition seeking permission to build the mosque on the disputed site, stating that the Ram Lalla Virajman should receive the land in the central part of the Babri

Masjid, but ensuring that it would not inconvenience the other two sides. Furthermore, the land of the Ram Chabutra, Sita Rasoi and the Bhandara was to be given to Nirmohi Akhara, implying that the outer parts of the land should go to the Hindus, as they had historically used that land for worship. The Waqf board should receive the remaining, but the portion must be no less than one-third the total area. To facilitate this, a portion of the land acquired by the government could also be utilised if necessary. The key aspect of this judgement is the court's acceptance of the Hindus' claim that Lord Ram was born there. Justice Agarwal and Justice Sharma accepted that the original temple at the site had been demolished to build the Babri Masjid. Justice Khan, however, argued that the mosque was built on the site of a dilapidated temple that was in ruins, and some stones of that temple were used in its construction of the mosque. Justices Agarwal and Khan affirmed the existence of a mosque at the site until 1992, but Sharma disagreed that the disputed structure qualified as a mosque, because he posited the construction violated Islamic traditions and beliefs, thus one could not consider it a mosque. The Supreme Court dismissed this judgement in its ruling on 9 November 2019.

एक राम का सकल पसारा

(The entire creation is the manifestation of one Ram.)

When Bhaurao served as the VHP's coordinator, he also acted as an intermediary between the Sangh and the Jana Sangh. He maintained very close relationships with Sanjay Gandhi and Indira Gandhi. During that period, Indira Gandhi was actively supporting the VHP. Bhaurao's strategy was to form a trust, similar to the one for the Somnath temple, to clear the way for the construction of the Ram temple. At that time, the Ram Janmabhoomi movement was aligned with the Congress. Bhaurao successfully convinced the Sangh high command that even if the Congress took credit for the temple's construction, their ultimate mission is to create 'Ram Rajya'. To hasten the movement, the VHP created an affiliated organisation called the Bajrang Dal on 1 October 1984. The fiery Vinay Katiyar, a young pracharak and the founder of the Hindu Jagran Manch, was made its president. The Bajrang Dal workers made the Janmabhoomi movement even more aggressive.

Later, Bhaurao became the in-charge of the Ram Mandir movement, while Moropant Pingle, as the head of the VHP, was the key strategist. Senior journalist Dilip Deodhar observes Pingle had cordial relations with both S.B. Chavan (the home minister) and Sharad Pawar (the defence minister). Deodhar claims that Moropant Pingle had carefully planned the entire karseva of 6 December 1992, drawing inspiration from Shivaji Maharaj's guerrilla tactics. Each participant received a different task assignment and information solely pertinent to their role. Chief Minister Kalyan Singh, it is said, was instructed to first issue an order prohibiting firing upon the karsevaks, and that he would be informed later when to tender his resignation. The karsevaks were not only divided into groups and assigned different responsibilities, but they also underwent secret training. On 6 December, when the entire structure was demolished, and the ground flattened, Kalyan Singh's resignation was accepted. This ensured that even if another mosque were to be built there, it would not be the Babri Masjid. The makeshift temple was installed, and the idols were placed only after President's Rule had been imposed. Throughout the entire operation, Narasimha Rao had conspicuously vanished from the scene.

Hemant Sharma, veteran journalist and author of *Yuddha Mein Ayodhya*, believes that the shilanyas ceremony was an important milestone in the Ayodhya movement. He says, 'The shilanyas gave momentum to the dream of the temple construction. But neither the BJP, the VHP, nor the Sangh was behind the shilanyas. A saint ordered this task, and a prime minister accomplished it. The prime minister was from the Congress.'[14]

This was around the time when Ramchandra Das Paramhans declared that the VHP's chosen spot for the ceremony would not be altered. He strongly believed that disputing this piece of land was impossible since he had already registered it in the Trust's name. Even if the government considers it to be Nazul land (government-acquired land), the burden of proof would lie with the government. On the other hand, the state government wanted the shilanyas to proceed, but insisted on a change of location. The government proposed an alternative—an empty piece of land next to the designated spot—but the VHP rejected this offer outright. They then contacted Devraha Baba, requesting his intervention. Devraha Baba was already functioning as a mediator between Rajiv Gandhi and the VHP. Baba had close ties with the Gandhi family because Indira Gandhi would visit him, seeking his counsel during difficult times. Baba unequivocally told Rajiv Gandhi when they met at Vrindavan that the temple must be built. He instructed Rajiv Gandhi to ensure the shilanyas was performed at the designated spot. Rajiv Gandhi immediately began efforts to facilitate the process. The next day, Baba called Shrish Chandra Dikshit and said, 'You [be] rest assured, I have asked the prime minister to do the Shilanyas at the spot where you people have planted your flag. This meant that the decision for the Shilanyas was not made in Delhi or Lucknow, but in Vrindavan; that too with Devraha Baba's blessings.' Hemant Sharma says, 'It is clear from the later events that Rajiv Gandhi did what Baba asked him to do. A day before the Shilanyas, Baba had rejected the government's suggestion of changing the spot for the Shilanyas. According to Vinay Katiyar, some leaders of the VHP had agreed to change the designated spot.'[15]

The government, at the last moment, intended to shift the site of the Shilanyas to Plot 576. That piece of land was undisputed and located just seven yards away from the original location. On 5 November, a few senior officials visited the area to facilitate the change. The plot in question was leased by Ramkripal Das, who readily agreed. The bathing room and wall at the site were broken down to prepare for the ceremony. However, on 6 November, the state government filed a petition in thc High Court, questioning whether 586 was part of the disputed site. In response, a special division bench of the Allahabad High Court clarified its interim order, explicitly designating the site where the VHP should perform the shilanyas as disputed. The bench's judgement stated that the land, where the VHP had planted flags and erected scaffolding, was disputed and that the status quo had to be maintained. The court clarified that this specific plot was indeed part of the disputed land. Had the VHP been prepared for this, there would have been no issues, and it could have performed the ceremonies at the non-disputed site with the assent of the Babri Masjid Action Committee. The government would have been able to placate both the Hindus and the Muslims. The VHP leaders found themselves in a quandary with the government, and internal divisions plagued them on the issue. At this juncture, Devraha Baba called Ashok Singhal and the former police inspector general to Vrindavan. Singhal said, 'Devraha Baba clcarly said that we must do the Shilanyas at the designated spot only.' The government found itself in a spin, caught between the High Court ruling and Devraha Baba's instructions. Rajiv Gandhi promptly dispatched Home Minister Buta Singh to Lucknow the next morning, 8 November. An agreement on the shilanyas could not be reached between Rajiv Gandhi and Uttar Pradesh Chief Minister Narayan Dutt Tiwari because the latter was not in favour of the ceremony. Rajiv Gandhi wanted the state government to clearly inform the High Court that the proposed site was not disputed after the High Court issued a stay on 6 November, but Tiwari refused to comply.

According to Hemant Sharma, 'After a lot of quibbling, it was decided that the District Magistrate of Faizabad would conduct a land measurement and make a statement that the site for the shilanyas is not disputed. This annoyed Tiwari. Although people used to call him "New Delhi Tiwari" because they knew he made all decisions with permission from Delhi, he unusually stuck to his guns on this matter. History proved him right later on.'[16]

After the demolition of the structure, the High Court delivered its highly anticipated judgement on 11 December 1992. Had this ruling been issued just five days earlier, the course of history might have been altered, and the karseva on 6 December would have been deemed legal. The High Court, in its judgement, scrapped the state government's acquisition of 2.77 acres of land surrounding the disputed structure. The court had reserved this judgement since 3 November.

Before the karseva on 6 December, the Uttar Pradesh Government, VHP, and BJP leaders had completed all necessary procedures, aiming for the court to pass its judgement on the 2.77 acres of land before that critical date. Had the court pronounced this acquisition legal, the land would have remained with the Ram Janmabhoomi Nyas. Furthermore, had the state government handed over this land to the Nyas immediately after its acquisition, the karseva itself would have been legal. Even if the court had dismissed the order, the ownership of 2.07 acres out of the 2.77 acres would have returned to the Ram Janmabhoomi Nyas. This is because various individuals had originally purchased the land and held possession of it before the acquisition process. Notably, the 2.77 acres of land were separate from the disputed site, and the planned karseva would have happened away from the contentious area. In both situations, the karseva would have been legally permissible. Kalyan Singh had told Hemant Sharma, 'I had created a "safety valve" of the 2.77 acres by separating it from the structure. Kar Seva had been performed on this land before as well. The *shilanyas* too had been performed on the same land. In July 1992, karseva was conducted on the same 2.77 acres of land. The platform had not been built at that time.'[17]

Both the state government and the VHP were seeking a rapid legal resolution. The key issue in the discussions among the central government, the Sangh and the BJP was that the Centre should request the court to fast-track its proceedings and deliver a verdict before 6 December. When the court finally gave its decision, the structure had already been demolished.

The moot question was how so many karsevaks had managed to gather in Ayodhya. It was perplexing because the Congress government was in power in more than half the states and at the centre, with Lalu Prasad in Bihar, Biju Patnaik in Orissa, Jyoti Basu in West Bengal. Why, then, did no one attempt to stop the karsevaks? The Supreme Court's order for the central government to publicise that there was no prohibition on any kind of symbolic karseva also contributed significantly to the burgeoning crowd.

On 10 December, Narasimha Rao went against his usual self and imposed a swift ban on the Sangh, VHP, Bajrang Dal, Jamaat-E-Islami, and the Islamic Sevak Sangh. He dismissed the state governments of Rajasthan, Madhya Pradesh and Himachal Pradesh based on their relationship with the banned organisations.

According to *Yuddha Mein Ayodhya*, a day before Operation Flush Out, a message arrived for Vinay Katiyar from the prime minister. It conveyed the government's desire not to use force against the karsevaks and requested that the karsevaks be made to leave. That night, an announcement was made that the karseva would be postponed.

Hemant Sharma writes about Operation Flush Out: 'At 3.30 in the morning on 8 December, we heard some chaos outside our hotel and we saw convoys of paramilitary forces racing towards Ayodhya, piercing through the deafening silence of the night. A battalion of the 108 Rapid Action Force and a company of the CRPF reached Ayodhya. Exactly at

3.30 a.m., RAF commandos entered the Janmabhoomi premises from behind the disputed structure, along the Manas Bhavan and Sita Rasoi. Around 5,000 karsevaks sat wrapped in blankets, singing bhajans. In the pandals (tents) on the side, karsevikas (female volunteers) were fast asleep. Soon after, a stampede ensued, and the premises were evacuated with very minimal force. In the entire operation, only five shells of tear gas were used along with a minor lathi (baton) charge. The loudspeakers of the Ram Katha Kunj stopped playing devotional hymns and started announcing, "The CRPF has come, you people leave the premises".'

In Ayodhya, the image of the 'central forces' had become 'anti-temple'. The state government fuelled this perception, blaming central forces and creating an impression among the people that the CRPF was obstructing the temple's construction. This was inaccurate. Ironically, these same security forces provided protection while prayers and worship were conducted at the makeshift temple.

Any discussion about the Ram temple movement would be incomplete without acknowledging the VHP. Once the VHP took over the reins, the movement significantly sped up. However, the VHP's involvement extends far beyond the Ram Janmabhoomi movement.

Following independence from the British, the Hindu community has faced many hurdles both within India and in other countries. Hindus in Bangladesh and Pakistan have been victims of religious conversions and mass killings, often forced to abandon their belongings and flee their homes. Even within India, Hindus have been forced to compromise on their welfare. Apart from these, Hindus have endured discrimination in Africa, Mauritius, Sri Lanka, Malaysia, Indonesia, Fiji and the Caribbean nations because of their religious identity. Crucially, there was no established organisation to champion Hindu welfare and rights during that period.

In those times, several prominent Hindu leaders, including Swami Chinmayananda, Guruji Golwalkar and Shivram Shankar (Dadasaheb) Apte, stepped forward. They garnered support from

Master Tara Singh, Jain saint Sushil Kumar and Rimpoche Kushok Bakula. Subsequently, a meeting was convened, gathering over forty social, spiritual, religious, and Hindu political leaders, and representatives from different faiths. After extensive deliberations, they decided to formally constitute the Vishva Hindu Parishad. The announcement was made on 29 August 1964, on the occasion of Krishna Janmashtami. The VHP's primary aim was to unify the Hindu community, strengthen it and propagate the spiritual philosophy of the religion worldwide. This campaign received a major fillip through the Ram Mandir movement, which witnessed the Hindus rise above caste differences and unite. Because of the VHP's campaign, not only central and state governments but even political parties seemed to grapple with its growing influence.

Driven by a vision to instil in the global Hindu youth an understanding of their religion, its importance and spiritual philosophy, the VHP has developed special programmes, weekly meetings and classes. To firmly establish and propagate Hinduism abroad, the VHP has either built grand temples or has contributed towards their construction, leading to a point where Hindu temples are now present in almost every nation. This initiative is further bolstered by the growing political participation of the Hindus.

Remembering the vision of the Ram Rajya at the bhoomi pujan ceremony, Prime Minister Narendra Modi had said, 'Lord Ram has taught us to be dutiful, and how to fulfil our duties! He has shown us the path of awareness and search and moved us away from the path of resistance! We have to join the bricks of the Ram temple with the glue of mutual love and brotherhood. We have to remember that whenever humanity has believed and devoted itself to Lord Ram, development and progress have happened; whenever we have wandered from the path, paths to destruction have opened.'[18]

He was perhaps referring to this verse from Tulsidas's *Ramcharitmanas*:

नहिं दरिद्र कोउ दुखी न दीना।
नहिं कोउ अबुध न लच्छन हीना॥
सब गुनज्ञ पंडित सब ज्ञानी ।
सब कृतज्ञ नहीं कपट सयानी।।

(No one was poor, miserable, or downtrodden,
No one was ignorant or devoid of noble qualities,
All appreciated virtue, learned, and wise,
All were grateful, and none were deceitful or cunning.)

9

The Dharma of Being Hindu

When Swami Vivekananda was returning to India in 1897, after spreading the glory of the country and Hindutva across America and Europe, an English friend asked him, 'After having experienced the life of developing, rich and powerful Western countries for four years, how will you feel in your motherland?'

Vivekananda answered, 'Before I left my motherland, I used only to love India, but now for me the air, and every grain of [her] dust is purer than heaven. India is a sacred land. She is my mother. India is my pilgrimage.' Just as the shores of India came into sight, Swami Vivekananda's eyes began streaming with tears. He stood with his gaze transfixed on the shore, his hands folded, as if beholding Mother India herself. The moment the ship anchored, he ran down the deck like a madman, and as soon as he set foot on the soil, he prostrated himself on the land and rolled in the mud like a child who had reached his mother's lap. Swami-ji said, 'All my stains have been washed away in my mother's lap.' He continued bowing to the sacred land, singing its glory. Swami Vivekananda had earlier said in his famous Chicago address, 'I feel extremely proud to say that I am a follower of such a religion (dharma) whose divine language is Sanskrit, and it has no synonym for "exclusion".'[1]

There is another story related to Guru Nanak. It was a night, perhaps one of a new moon night in August. Lightning shone amidst the deafening thunder of the clouds. Fear gripped the village. Nanak-ji sat alone, singing through the night with the lamp in his room aglow. Nanak's mother knocked on his door and said, 'Son! Go to sleep now. It's going to be daybreak very soon.' Nanak stopped singing, and just then a cuckoo cooed.

Nanak said, 'Listen, mother, even the cuckoo hasn't fallen silent. [If] he calls out to his love, [then] how can I become silent? While his love is somewhere close by, mine is very far away. I will be able to reach Him only if I keep singing for the lives to come.'

Nanak resumed his singing, and some say that he attained God through his song. His penance in seeking the Divine could not have been ordinary—for the pursuit of God is never ordinary.

In Hinduism, there is a deep and constant striving to attain God. Each individual seeks the Divine through their path, in their way, using their means, and every path is valid, because the goal is the same. Mira reached her Lord through dance, while Kabir, a simple weaver, found his Supreme God through daily work at the loom. Adi Shankaracharya changed the course of Hinduism, elevating philosophical and metaphysical enquiry to such heights that it remains unparalleled to this day. Shabari attained Lord Ram by offering him berries she had first tasted herself, and Bhakta Prahalad became one with God by stepping into fire with unwavering faith. This is perhaps the unique essence of Hinduism: every individual has the freedom to choose his or her path.

Nearby, a bhajan (devotional song) echoed from a temple: '*Kaun kahta hai bhagwan aate nahi, ham Mira ke jaise bulate nahi* (Who says God doesn't come? We don't call out to Him like Mira).' The fundamental mantra or core of Hindutva is ekaatmata (unity or oneness). This means that while one can express truth in many ways, its essence and ultimate goal are the same. Hinduism inculcates a sense of oneness into our conduct, which is why people often describe it not only as a religion, but as a way of life. Even the Supreme Court of India has acknowledged it as such.[2] This timeless, eternal spirit is Sanatan.

The word 'Hindutva' was first used by Bengali litterateur Chandranath Basu in 1892. Basu served as the president of the Bangiya Sahitya Parishad and had deeply studied the spiritual and political aspects of the Hindu Dharma. His book, *Hindutva: Hindur Prakrita Itihas,* was published in 1892. During the Independence struggle, patriot and thinker Nabagopal Mitra started the Hindu Mela to awaken national consciousness through the medium of Hindu culture. Additionally, the publication of the newspaper *National Paper* began in Calcutta in 1867. It featured articles on enhancing self-pride and promoting reverence for Hindu culture, intending to revive the glory of India's ancient heritage and inspire the people. Sunil Ambekar asserts that 'Hindu Rashtra' has been derived from the concept of 'Hindutva'. The concept of a Hindu rashtra represents a nation that believes in non-violence, where peace and prosperity prevail, where there is complete freedom of worship and where women enjoy equal rights. The relationship between Hindutva and Hindu rashtra is that of thought and action—they are inseparable and must be understood together. Hindu rashtra does not imply opposing Muslims, nor has it ever done so. Hindutva has three core principles: cooperation, agreement and equality. Hindutva upholds equanimity towards all forms of worship and harmony across diverse spiritual paths.

Ambekar stresses that Hindutva is not a tool to acquire political power or authority. If that had been the intention, Dr Hedgewar would have founded a political party and not a socio-cultural organisation like the RSS. The understanding of Hindutva is not limited to spirituality alone. For the Sangh, Hindutva represents a more refined and meaningful way of living.

Vinayak Damodar Savarkar wrote a book on Hindutva using the pseudonym 'Ek Maratha', which was published by Nagpur-based lawyer V.V. Kelkar. Although the British banned the book, Vikram Savarkar later reprinted it. In this book, Savarkar doesn't present Hindutva as a religion; instead, he seeks to decode it through a rational and scientific lens. Before this, Savarkar had written a book in Marathi, *The Indian War of Independence 1857*. Its English translation was published in the Netherlands in 1909, but it could be published in India only after Independence. This book offers valuable insight into Savarkar's attitude towards Hindutva and its historical context. Notably, Savarkar viewed Hindu–Muslim harmony as essential for national unity and praised the last Mughal emperor, Bahadur Shah Zafar, as an epitome of national unity. In the book's introduction, Savarkar writes, 'The nation that has no consciousness of its past has no future. Equally true it is that a nation must develop its capacity not only of claiming a past but also of knowing how to use it for the furtherance of its future. The nation ought to be the master and not the slave of its own history. For it is absolutely unwise to try to do certain things now, irrespective of special considerations, simply because they have been done once in the past. The feeling of hatred against the Mohammedans was just and necessary in the times of Shivaji, but such a feeling would be unjust and foolish if nursed now, simply because it was the dominant feeling of the Hindus then.'[3]

After the British permitted him to leave Ratnagiri, Savarkar gave a speech in Karnavati (Ahmedabad), in which he stated, 'There are two nations: one a Hindu nation (rashtra), and the other a Muslim nation. Those people whose Punya Bhoomi (sacred Land) and Dharma Bhoomi (land of duty) lie outside India are not Hindus. They are not national.'

Dr Hedgewar opposed Savarkar's notion. However, he remained publicly silent on the matter since the Sangh did not hold the idea of a sacred land as central to its ideology. Senior journalist Dilip Deodhar says, 'Hedgewar said nothing publicly, but there are people in the Sangh who believe Savarkar's Hindutva even today. However, Golwalkar and Deoras do not accept anti-Muslim thought in the Sangh. Savarkar developed a conception of Hindutva and converted Hindu nationalism into a sect. Savarkar believed that until Hindus rally against the outside elements of Muslims and Christians, they cannot become a powerful community or society.'[4]

Hedgewar had borrowed the idea of a Hindu rashtra from Savarkar, who would define a Hindu as one who lives in the land between the Sindhu (Indus) River and the ocean. The first requirement for Hindutva is that the individual—either by birth or by ancestry—must be a citizen of Hindustan. However, geographical identity alone is not sufficient to be called a Hindu. Hindus are bound not just by a love of their motherland, but by their shared blood. They are not just one nation; they are also a single caste, in the sense of a common racial or ethnic lineage. This kinship grants them Hindutva. The third requirement is cultural unity. This Hindu culture forms a bond stronger than that of shared ancestry, race or geography. In his opinion, a Muslim who has lived in India for several generations, loves his fatherland and has the same blood flowing in his veins, but still does not become a Hindu because he does not share the cultural foundation of the Hindu civilisation and its shared history and literature. Moreover, language is central to cultural identity. According to Savarkar, one's mother tongue can be Hindi, Gujarati, Tamil, Marathi, Telugu, Malayalam, Bengali, Punjabi, but Sanskrit is the true spiritual and cultural language of the fatherland. Is it possible for Muslims or Christians to fulfil the four conditions and be considered Hindus? Savarkar says, 'No, because their holy land, their sacred land, lies in Arabia or Philistine. Their religions were not born in India, and hence their love and loyalties are divided. They cannot sacrifice everything for their fatherland because they will have to place their holy land above their fatherland; and since their holy place is not in India, they cannot be Hindus, and they cannot get the nationality named Hindutva.' Savarkar mentions a Sanskrit shloka (verse):[5]

> आसिन्धुसिन्धुपर्यंता यस्य भारतभूमिका ।
> पितृभूः पुण्यभूश्चैव स वै हिन्दुरिति स्मृतः ।।
>
> (The land of India, from the Indus to the ocean, is the sacred land of our ancestors. Anyone who considers this land as their own is considered a Hindu.)

In his 1939 book, *We, or Our Nationhood Defined*, Golwalkar said, 'The foreign ethnicities in India should adopt Hindu culture and language. They should have no ideas other than to take pride in the Hindu race and culture, or should live in India completely under the control of the nation, make no claims, not consider themselves worthy of any special rights, forget getting any special treatment: they shouldn't even aspire for citizen's rights.'[6]

Sarsanghchalak Mohan Bhagwat says, 'As a nation, our identity is that of a Hindu. Some consider it a pride to be called Hindus, while others don't feel the same sense of pride, but that doesn't matter. Some people would not say so in public owing to "material considerations" or "political correctness", but would do so in private. Some people have forgotten this, and they are also one among us, Indians like us. Like when the question paper comes to us in an examination, we first answer the easy questions, and then go on to the more difficult ones. Similarly, we first bring together those who consider themselves Hindus. We have no enemies, neither in the country nor in the world. There would be people who hold enmity towards us, but our goal is not to let go of our aspirations while protecting ourselves from them; on the contrary, we aspire to bring them along and bond with them. This is real Hindutva.

'Dr Ambedkar had also said in the Constituent Assembly that the foreigners won because we were fighting among ourselves, and they succeeded in enslaving us. I am telling you his feelings, you can read his words. He said that we are sitting in Parliament in opposite camps and against each other. This is a compulsion of the system and despite that we are all one. If we do not develop brotherhood with each other, we don't know what kind of times we will face. The Sangh works towards this feeling of brotherhood, and the basis for this brotherhood is unity in diversity. The world calls this traditional thought "Hindutva", and that is why we say that ours is a Hindu rashtra (nation). It doesn't mean that we don't need Muslims. The day such a thing is said, Hindutva will cease to exist.'[7]

Sah-sarkaryavah Dr Manmohan Vaidya notes how Guru Golwalkar offered a broader definition that a shared motherland, common ancestry and similar traditions have accorded a unique identity to all people living in India. This is the Hindu identity. In the Indian context, it is not the state but the citizens who make up the nation. Even though different rulers and states ruled over us, we remained a nation. Addressing Savarkar's Hindutva, Nilanjan Mukhopadhyay says, 'Savarkar is a paradox, a contradiction. His book is called *Hindutva*. Hedgewar established the Sangh, taking inspiration from him, but the Sangh did not follow his path. The RSS does not accept Savarkar's definition of Hindutva, but the BJP government gives it a lot of importance. From Atal Bihari Vajpayee to Narendra Modi, everyone is stressing on giving Savarkar the national honour. During the Vajpayee government, it was proposed that Savarkar be awarded the Bharat Ratna, but the then President K.R. Narayanan did not accept the recommendation, and Savarkar could not get the nation's highest civilian honour.'[8]

At the convocation ceremony of the Aligarh Muslim University on 24 January 1948, the Prime Minister Nehru had said, 'You are Muslims and I am a Hindu. We may adhere to different religious faiths or even to none, but that does not take away from that cultural inheritance that is yours as well as mine. The past holds us together; why should the present or the future divide us in spirit?'[9]

Sangh ideologue K.N. Govindacharya, clearing the fogs of his memory, recalls that, before the Kumbh mela was organised in 1966, the Vishva Hindu Parishad was established in 1964. At that time, the VHP focused on two aspects. First, all the people born in India must come together on a common platform and think about the welfare of the entire society. This was Guru Golwalkar's vision, and everyone reached out to Guruji regarding this. He even met Karpatri Maharaj, the founder of the Akhil Bharatiya Ram Rajya Parishad. 'As far as I know,' Govindacharya says, 'Karpatri Maharaj had asked Guruji, what is dharma? In reply, Guruji had said, "What is dharma? You must explain this. You are the one who can elaborate on this topic. Of course, I will try my best to walk the path that you guide us on and to awaken society." Guruji was active in the 1966 Kumbh Mela, exactly the way Lord Krishna had once picked up used food plates from people. He was a guide and a beacon. Guruji had said at the mela, "To strengthen Hindu society, to protect spirituality and life philosophy, to conserve and propagate it, to maintain coordination with Hindus living overseas, to mobilise them for the protection of Hindus and Hindutva, and to help them is our goal."'

हिन्दवःसोदराः सर्वे, न हिन्दूः पतितो भवेत्।
मम दीक्षा हिन्दू रक्षा, मम मंत्रः समानता।।

(All Hindus are brothers; no Hindu should ever be deemed fallen.
My vow is the protection of Hindus; my mantra is equality.)

Golwalkar believed in the philosophy of *Dharmo Rakṣhati Rakṣhita*—dharma protects those who protect it. The British still ruled the country when the RSS was founded in 1925. At that time, the motto of the Sangh was to free the Hindu rashtra, but once the country gained independence, the Sangh focused on ensuring the development of the Hindu rashtra and dharma. In the daily oath taken by the Sangh's swayamsevaks, they pledge themselves to the prosperity of Hinduism, its culture and the nation. In the oath, the swayamsevak vows that:

सर्वशक्तिमान श्री परमेश्वर तथा अपने पूर्वजों का स्मरण कर मैं प्रतिज्ञा करता हूं कि अपने पवित्र हिंदू धर्म, हिंदू संस्कृति, तथा हिंदू समाज का संरक्षण कर हिंदू राष्ट्र की सर्वांगीण उन्नति करने के लिए मैं राष्ट्रीय स्वयंसेवक संघ का घटक बना हूं। संघ का कार्य मैं प्रमाणिकता से, निस्वार्थ बुद्धि से तथा तन, मन, धनपूर्वक करूंगा और इस व्रत का मैं आजन्म पालन करूंगा. भारत माता की जय।

(In the name of Almighty God and our ancestors, I hereby vow that I have become a unit of the Rashtriya Swayamsevak Sangh to protect our sacred Hindu dharma, Hindu culture and Hindu society and to achieve the all-round development of the Hindu nation. I will do the Sangh's work sincerely with a selfless mind and with all my body, heart, and wealth. I will observe this vow all my life. *Bharat Mata ki Jai.*)

The Sangh believes that, based on historical and archaeological evidence, India has been a nation for at least 8,000 years. It is not a 'new nation' or a nation in the making. India is an ancient nation, and people live here based on a common religion, their jati (race/ethnicity) and nationality. It is not a union of nations or a subcontinent, but a single country from north to south.

उत्तरं यत्समुद्रस्य हिमाद्रेश्चैव दक्षिणम् ।
वर्षं तद्भारतम् नाम भारती यत्र सन्ततिः ॥

(The land which lies to the north of the ocean and the south of the Himalayas is called Bhāratavarṣa [India], where the descendants of Bharata live.)[10]

The Sangh believes that India is a Hindu rashtra, and those who have built it and given it its identity are Hindus. Hinduism defines the country's religion, culture, and society. Its philosophy and way of life are also Hindu. Bharat is not merely a land mass, but a revered deity. The perspective with which the Hindu community regards its rivers, mountains, flora and fauna is sacred and divine.

> हिमालयं समारभ्य यावत् इन्दु सरोवरम्।
> तं देवनिर्मितं देशं हिन्दुस्थानं प्रच्यते॥
>
> (From the Himalayas in the north to the Indu [Moon] Sarovara [lake] in the south. That land created by the gods is called Hindustan.)[11]

Every sage has expressed his views on Hindutva and Indianism, and each is of significance. Rabindranath Tagore, in his book *Swadeshi Samaj*, writes, 'The feeling of "unity in diversity", the establishment of unity in diversity—this has been the fundamental concept of dharma or religion in India. The Indian soul does not consider differing points of view to be their opponents, it does not consider people its enemy. That is why it accepts all divergent paths and assesses their greatness from their light.

'Owing to this quality of India, we should not consider any other society or community as our opponents. Hindus, Buddhists, Muslims and Christians will all meet at one point. This point will be non-Hindu but especially Hindu. However foreign its parts may be, its life and soul will remain Indian.'[12]

Mahatma Gandhi said that truth is Hindutva. What Gandhi said about Hindutva, Swami Vivekananda, Subhash Bose, Rabindranath Tagore and Dr Ambedkar have said—not about Hindu society, but regarding Hindutva. The term 'Hindu' did not exist during the time of Lord Ram, but the essence of Hindutva that existed then remains the same today. Krishna, who transcended all boundaries, lived according to the same Hindutva. Shivaji Maharaj upheld the respect of Mirza Raja; he, too, followed Hindutva. That is why Hindutva is one—it cannot be different based on individual perspectives.

Swami Vivekananda said that the secret of dharma lies not in principles but in behaviour. Being good and doing good is the entire essence of dharma. However, our religious traditions and principled behaviour have not been practical expressions for Hindutva, as they failed to protect Indians from invaders and the slavery of the British. The message of Hindutva is that generosity, tolerance, non-violence and all-embracing lose their value when they lead to cowardice and defeat. We can overcome our past humiliations only by letting go of the kind of tolerance and inclusiveness that weaken us. As Hindus, we must organise ourselves and build military strength so that the entire world recognises our might.[13]

Pune, in Maharashtra, was a centre for intellectuals. Dr Hedgewar was once attending a meeting, where a heated discussion was underway about Hindutva. During the meeting, one intellectual loudly exclaimed, 'Which fool claims ours is a Hindu rashtra?' Dr Hedgewar responded even more forcefully. 'I say that until even a single Hindu is alive, this will be a Hindu rashtra.'

Bhagwat positions a 'staunch Hindu' as an extremely generous Hindu—one who believes in truth, non-violence and diversity. The Iranians, Pathans and the Arabs gave the word 'Hindu' to us, literally referring to those living on this side of the Sindhu River. If we accept this nomenclature, the difference between 'us' and 'them' would begin to dissolve. The word that Hindus have historically used for themselves is 'Arya'. By embracing this name, our cultural scope expands remarkably, encompassing Iran, Afghanistan and Pakistan as part of this broader cultural sphere. When we apply inclusive broad nomenclature to any Indian citizen, faith, caste, language, attire, or food habits become secondary. In essence, this rich and vast diversity itself becomes the defining feature of identity.

Bhagwat has said that Hindus do not consider anyone their enemy, but 'for the same Hinduness we have to protect Hindu dharma (religion), Hindu sanskriti (culture) and Hindu society. In the process, we may have to explain, we may have to fight, if necessary.' He adds that the talk of extremist and moderate Hindutva is irrelevant because if Hindus become more fanatic, it means they will be more liberal. He gives the example of Mahatma Gandhi, saying that he was a "kattar (hardcore) Hindu". In addition, he cited Gandhi's writings in *Harijan*, where Gandhi had declared himself a "fanatic Sanatani Hindu".[14]

In discussions on nationalism and secularism, Govindacharya believes these terms were born in Europe and are not fully appropriate in the Indian context. The concept of the nation is a construct of the state, while ideas like nationalism are rooted in materialism. During the independence movement in India, many leaders who had studied in Europe were influenced by these Western concepts. However, the Indian idea of nationalism is fundamentally different. Indian culture talks about oneness and harmony. People here believe that 'You are okay, I am okay.' You may call it spiritual nationalism if you want.

Writer and senior journalist Ashutosh says that the RSS wants to convert the Hindu religion into a 'cult'. The Hindu religion is unfettered, natural, eternal, spontaneous ... they want to tie it to one thought. The Sangh wants Hindus to become a religion that has one book or scripture, one God, one thought process and behaves similarly. Even the food habits should be one and wear identical clothes, which means they become monomorphic, while the beauty of the Hindu religion is its diversity. They are devotees of Shiva and Vishnu; a Hindu is Krishna and Radha.[15]

During an event, someone once asked Dr Manmohan Vaidya, 'What is the difference between Hindutva and Hinduism?' He answered,

'Both are the same; one is an English term, and the other is in Hindi. They are as different as "gulab" and "rose". Dr Radhakrishnan's book, *The Hindu View of Life,* is in English, and that is why he uses the word Hinduism; otherwise, he would have used Hindutva. Had Savarkar written *Hindutva* in English instead of Marathi, he would have perhaps used Hinduism. I believe that the correct translation of Hindutva should be Hinduness instead of Hinduism.'

In a Parliament speech, Vajpayee made a profound point regarding untouchability, saying, 'We are not ready to accept that untouchability is a part of the Hindu religion. Untouchability is a sin and a curse. It is a blot on us. Till this blot is not erased, we will not be able to stand with our heads held high in this world, and I don't believe that Hindu scriptures mandate untouchability as a practice.

'If the scriptures have been interpreted in this manner, that interpretation is wrong and we will not accept it. I would go a step further to say that even if God himself comes and asks me to accept untouchability, I will refuse to accept such a God. God cannot do anything like this, and neither can those who are his devotees.

'Haven't castes divided Hindutva completely and made it impossible to have a separate identity? Dr Ambedkar had said that Hindutva is nothing without castes. A Hindu is a Hindu only when he has to oppose Muslims. Indeed, the RSS has always been in favour of breaking the caste system. There is no caste-based discrimination in the shakhas and programmes of the Sangh; on the contrary, in the Sangh camps, no attempt is made to find out the caste of any person, and everybody is treated equally.'[16]

Govindacharya tells us that in 1984, Professor Yashwant Rao Kelkar identified two challenges facing the Sangh and its organisations: ideological and the style of functioning. Ideologically, every karyakarta must take an oath to protect Hinduism, but there has to be clarity and uniformity at least among the district-level karyakartas; otherwise, confusion will prevail among the organisations within the Sangh Parivar.

Hindu and Hindutva have so many shades, so many spectrums, that there is a danger of a 180-degree turnaround without a clear consensus within the Parivar.

Govindacharya raises critical questions: if the Sangh leadership says that all people living in India are Hindus, then who are the infiltrators? What does it mean when we say the number of Hindus is declining? If everyone in undivided India is considered Hindu, then why is the Hindu religion said to be in danger? He explains that it is important to have clarity on these pressing matters. While society may face threats, the Hindu religion and culture are not in danger. This is an internal ideological turmoil. Apart, there is a discrepancy even at the operational level. The ideology and the Sangh and its framework—the 'grammar'—of its interrelationships with affiliate organisations differ. Relationships are founded on the principles of self-reliance, complementarity and cooperation. All must clearly understand and share these principles. However, no structured training has been provided to ensure this alignment.

Ambedkar's anti-Hindu stance involved not only the issue of hatred of Hindus towards Muslims. He held the opinion that, more than Muslims, the Hindu rashtra was a detrimental concept for Hindus. He considered it against the Dalits and women. And to combat its dangers, he presented the Hindu Code Bill in the constituent assembly on 11 April 1947. Before Independence, the Hindu community did not grant men and women the right to divorce. The men had the freedom to marry more than once, but widows were forbidden to remarry, and the family property inheritance excluded women. The Hindu Code Bill introduced significant reforms and aimed to eliminate discriminatory practices within Hindu society that some staunch traditionalists sought to preserve in the name of custom. It granted equal rights to a man's property for his widow, sons and daughters. It also proposed rules for the division of the assets for those who died without leaving behind a will. Additionally, the daughters received from their father's estate only half of the assets that the sons received. This bill gave legal status to two kinds of marriages, civil and traditional, and prohibited Hindu men from marrying more than one woman. It also introduced the legal right to divorce for women. Because of vehement opposition, the bill was sent to a select committee on 9 April 1948.

When Ambedkar tabled the bill in 1951, voices of protest echoed through the Parliament and the country's streets. From the Sanatani Hindus to the Arya Samajis, almost everyone seemed to be against it. Discussions continued for three days in Parliament, but the first parliamentary elections had not yet occurred at the time, so the members of the Parliament were not direct representatives of the people of India. As a result, many argued that they did not have the moral right to pass such a landmark bill. There was also widespread resentment over why the bill targeted only Hindus and codified their laws when polygamy remained permissible in other religions. Many felt that any new law should apply equally to all communities, instead of calling for a Uniform Civil Code. In Parliament, the pro-Hindu camps of the Jana Sangh and the Congress opposed the bill. Outside, the RSS, Hindu Mahasabha and other Hindu organisations actively resisted it. Many such organisations protested on the streets and organised rallies. Karpatri Maharaj called it an intrusion into the Hindu religion, a legislation that went against Hindu traditions, culture and scriptures. He even challenged Nehru to a public debate on the issue. Although Nehru was in favour of the bill, he postponed it considering that the country's first general elections were fast approaching.

Ambedkar had said that he would be more delighted to witness the Hindu Code Bill passed than even the Indian Constitution.[17] Because the parliament could not pass the bill, Ambedkar resigned as the law minister. Later, Prime Minister Nehru divided the Hindu Code Bill into several parts, and the first Hindu Marriage Act was put in place in 1955. Apart from permitting divorce, this bill labelled polygamy illegal and granted both men and women the right to have inter-caste marriages. In

1956, the Hindu Succession Act, the Hindu Minority and Guardianship Act and the Hindu Adoptions and Maintenance Act came into force. While talking about the Sangh and the Emergency, Ram Bahadur Rai noted that during that period, a suggestion was put forth to open Sangh shakhas for non-Hindus. That using the word 'Indian' instead of 'Hindu' would increase the organisation's acceptability. Balasaheb Deoras was in favour of the idea, but the others objected to it, and the decision was stalled. Now, Mohan Bhagwat has stated that regardless of whether we like it, the Sangh has incorporated this in its agenda. He emphasised that the word 'Hindu' cannot be accepted in a purely generic or universal sense. According to writer Banwari-ji, if a cultural map of India were to be drawn, it could be complete and well-organised based on the country's deities. Shiva is the god of fearlessness, and we find his stories all over the Himalayan region. Apart from the Himalayas, he is the guardian of the border areas. He is established in almost all our principal seats of dharma right, from Kashi in the north to Kanchi in the south. Similarly, Lord Ram is the epitome of righteousness, and his stories connect the vast expanse of our country. Vrindavan is the land of Krishna, and his stories and tales are spread from the east to the west.

We have made all our deities the symbols of the qualities and virtues that are needed to regulate the society's moral compass. Through the rituals, observances and festivals related to Shiva, Ram, Krishna, Buddha and Mahavir, we protect and preserve the values they espouse and attempt to cultivate them in our lives. Moreover, there are many other deities and significant figures who form the foundation of our practices in other cultural spheres. At the heart of all lies truth. For us, happiness is meaningful only when it is grounded in truth. That is why we do not consider our observances and fasts as merely part of karmakanda (ritualistic tradition), but as practices deeply rooted in values and purpose. In 1995, a three-judge bench of the Supreme Court, led by Chief Justice J.S. Verma, overturned the Bombay High Court's verdict that had annulled the election of Maharashtra legislators for using the word 'Hindutva' during their election campaign. The Supreme Court had called Hindutva 'a way of life or state of mind'. However, the court ruled that the statement made by the Shiv Sena leader Manohar Joshi—the first Hindu state in India was formed in Maharashtra—was illegal under the election laws. Human rights activists, legal experts and political parties widely criticised this decision. Nevertheless, since then, the Sangh Parivar has frequently referred to and utilised this ruling whenever it serves their purpose. A year after the 1995 judgement, a three-judge bench of the Supreme Court expressed its objection to J.S. Verma's decision and suggested referring the matter to a five-judge bench. A similar case involved BJP leader Sunderlal Patwa in Madhya Pradesh, where in 2002, a five-judge bench requested the matter to be sent to a seven-judge bench. The hearing came up again under the Chief Justice T.S. Thakur on 25 October 2016. The bench stated that there was no need to reconsider the 1995 judgement of the Supreme Court. But the political debate about Hindutva was ignited all over again.[18]

Although Hindu Dharma advocates harmony and tolerance, a section of society continues to be hot-headed and cannot tolerate criticism about any aspect of their religion. When Prabhash Joshi, chief editor of *Jan Satta*, wrote about the demolition of the Babri Masjid, people viciously attacked him for his detailed coverage. He was called a mulla (a Muslim cleric), Jaichand, and Mir Jafar. Faced with death threats, Prabhash Joshi had said, 'I am a Hindu and believe in the soul's immortality. My religion gives me the power to fight against immorality (adharma), not on the cowardly violence borne out of reaction and vengeance, but with the power of my faith, my ideas, my nonviolence and the indestructible strength of my religion. Being a Hindu means having a direct connection between me and my God. I don't have to go to him through the Pope, an archbishop or a father. I don't need a fatwa (decree) from any mulla (cleric) or a maulvi (Islamic scholar). I am not bound by any Shankaracharya or religious leader. My religion gives me absolute freedom to choose and decide on my deity, my method of worship and my lifestyle based on my faith. I don't need to sport a tuft, wear the sacred thread, wear a dhoti-kurta, perform Sandhyavandan daily, visit the temple, worship every day, go on pilgrimages or bathe in sacred rivers. This religious freedom gives me the innate quality of being secular and democratic.'[19] Nobody could have explained the openness of the Hindu religion better.

In his book, *Hindu Hone Ka Dharma*, Prabhash Joshi writes, 'The philosophy of the Hindu religion gives me the freedom and capacity to face any circumstance openly and to find solutions myself. My religion frees me from the pressures of time and situations because it considers time to be cyclic and eternal. After all, it considers the soul (atma) indestructible, impervious and unaffected, and also considers it eternal, omnipresent, immutable, static and timeless. I don't need to believe in the Vedas. If our religion were not pluralist, there would have been only one Veda instead of four. I don't need to consider the Upanishads as my scriptures. Even the Upanishads are not one, but there are 108. There are eighteen Mahapuranas. It is not mandatory to consider the Gita the final scripture, like the Bible, Quran or the Guru Granth Sahib. The Gita is a part of the Mahabharata, and many of its shlokas are from the Upanishads. There are several Puranas, innumerable scriptures. But these aside, there is a long tradition of Saguna (with form) divine and the Nirguna (formless) divine. The devotees consider having a Guru compulsory, but even Saint Kabir, who considered the Guru to be ultimate, said that "The guru will bear the consequences of his actions, and the disciple of his." This means that in the last moments, even your guru cannot save you. That is why the ultimate truth has to be accepted.'[20]

If we talk about the Constitution and religion, it is clear that Article 25 grants every citizen the freedom and right to profess, practice and propagate any religion. However, reports of forced conversions, especially of people from backward and tribal regions, led the government to realise the need to address this reality. In response, states where there had been instances of Hindus being forcibly converted to Christianity through coercion and pressure passed preventive legislation. Orissa enacted the first such law—the Orissa Freedom of Religion Act—in 1967. Other states enacted similar laws, Madhya Pradesh in 1968 and Arunachal Pradesh in 1978. At that time, the Christian organisations said that propagating their religion was a core tenet of Christianity and approached to court against these laws. Later, the Supreme Court clarified that changing one's religion is not a fundamental right because the freedom of one individual must not infringe upon the freedom of another.

Following Orissa's lead, Chhattisgarh followed in 2000 and Gujarat in 2003. In 2006, a law was enacted requiring individuals to inform the authorities one month in advance of any religious conversion. Chhattisgarh enacted a similar provision. Importantly, this issue was not restricted only to the BJP-led governments. The Congress-led government of Himachal Pradesh and later the Rajasthan government in 2007 also passed laws and prohibited forcible religious conversions.

The chief minister of Uttar Pradesh and the head of the Gorakhnath Math, Yogi Adityanath, who believes that the country has suffered because of the vastly misunderstood concept of secularism, told me, 'I believe that nobody can deny that the word "secularism" is the biggest lie since Independence; Nobody can deny this, especially those who understand religion correctly. Religion is a synonym for duty, moral conduct and ethical values. When the system is not biased towards any sect, religion or community and moves forward with a feeling of equal respect for all religions, that is when it will be an ideal one. If you keep any system neutral from all these, it will become meaningless. Yes, all of us have our rituals and traditions. We cannot force own faith on others.'[21]

Senior journalist, the late Ved Prakash Vaidik, said another identity has latched itself onto Hindutva, and that is of practising vegetarianism. Dietary preferences have become intrinsically connected to religious identities. However, there were many within the BJP and Sangh Parivar who consumed meat but chose not to do so in public. I remember Atal Bihari Vajpayee as someone who would hide nothing about his life, and everybody knew he enjoyed having fish.

Different BJP leaders have made varying statements about the consumption of beef and meat. There are no issues about beef consumption in the Northeast. Prime Minister Narendra Modi also stated that food habits have nothing to do with culture—everyone can eat whatever they choose as long as they can digest it! Sarkaryavah Dattatreya Hosabale has said that the Sangh has no objection if someone consumes meat or beef under compulsion. Most vegetarians are not because they have understood its benefits, but because their families have traditionally been vegetarian. They have adopted vegetarianism as part of their tradition. Similarly, non-vegetarians are also simply continuing their family traditions, often without giving it much thought.

Mohan Bhagwat emphasises that the very meaning of Hindutva is the protection of all. Hindutva is an idea embraced by the Sangh, but it isn't the Sangh's creation; this is a timeless idea in India. Bhagwat explains that the word 'Hindu' entered the scriptures in the ninth century, and it hadn't existed before that. When the word Hindu appeared, Hindustan followed, appearing in the vernacular language. Guru Nanakdev had called this land Hindustan. The registration of Muslims travelling to Mecca was done under the name of Hindavi Mussalman. He adds that there is no objection to the use of the word 'Hindu,' but if one prefers, they may use the term Bharatiya instead. Bhagwat clarifies that the real confusion lies with the word 'dharma'. Outside India, there is no equivalent concept to dharma. What is called 'religion' elsewhere typically corresponds to 'karmakanda'. Hindu dharma is not a shaastra (treatise); rather, human dharma is the shaastra, meant for the entire world. Hindutva doesn't accommodate provinces, states or modes of worship. The form of the foundation of sects (sampradayas) is about embracing one and all. Wherever Indians went, they did not plunder or exploit, while the people of other countries looted and plundered the lands they entered. We have mistakenly taken karmakanda for Hindu dharma, when in fact, Hindutva goes far beyond ritual and encompasses universal values.[22] Terapanth is one of the prominent sects (sampradāya) within the Śvetāmbara branch of Jainism. It was Acharya Mahapragya, a revered national saint respected across all faiths and sects. He would say, 'I am a Terapanthi, and the reason is that I am a Sthanakvasi Jain (a reformist sect within the Śvetāmbara tradition of Jainism). The reason I am a Śvetāmbara is because I am a Jain, and I am a Jain because I am a Hindu. This is the most beautiful aspect of Indian practice. I can be a Terapanthi, Sthanakvasi, Śvetāmbara Jain and a Hindu at the same time. The reason is that Hindu thought doesn't see any dichotomy in this diversity. This is a different expression of the same thing. This has been India's tradition. But when the connection with the deep roots starts to weaken, the explanation also starts to change. Then we start saying that I am a Hindu, but I am a Jain. I am a Jain, but a Svetambara. I am a Śvetāmbara but a Sthanakvasi Jain; and I am a Sthanakvasi but I am a Terapanthi. And when the connection with the roots becomes gradually weak, and a situation comes when I may be a Jain, a Swetambara, a Sthanakvasi, and a Terapanthi, but I am not a Hindu. And then politics on this begins.'[23]

Atal Bihari Vajpayee, a leader extremely capable of understanding the essence of Hinduism, in an essay on the Hindu dharma, wrote, 'The main reason for my attraction towards the Hindu religion is that it is the most superior religion of humans. The Hindu religion is not associated with a single book, nor with a particular founder who becomes irrelevant with time. The structure of the Hindu faith is formed from Hindu society, and this is the reason why this religion has been conserved and is blooming for innumerable eras.'[24]

Vajpayee had once said, 'You know, I used to wear the sacred thread till I decided to dedicate my life to the Sangh. I removed it because I believed that this sacred thread distances me from other Hindus. Earlier, the tuft of hair and the sacred thread were the two identities of Hindus. These days, not many people sport tufts. But it will not be right to say that they have abandoned the Hindu religion just because of that. Of course, when the tuft was forcibly cut, it was our duty to protect them.'[25]

In December 1992, at the Dr Rajendra Prasad lecture series, Vajpayee presented a landmark speech on secularism. Denouncing it as a 'western' concept, he instead accepts Gandhi's principle of religious harmony. When describing dharma, he notes, 'We need to understand the difference between "dharma" and "religion". Religion is related to certain specific devotions or faiths. Until a person believes in them, he or she remains a member of that religion or faith, and the moment he or she leaves those beliefs, he becomes an outcast from that religion. However, dharma is not solely dependent on faiths and beliefs.'[26]

In the same lecture, Vajpayee mentions Gandhi: '*Sarvadharma samabhav* (equality of all faiths) is not against any dharma. It is in favour of respecting all religions. It can be said that the Indian conception of secularism is more positive. It teaches us a way of living.' At the end of his speech, Vajpayee recited a verse from Guru Gobind Singh:

> देहरा मस्जिद सोई, पूजा औ नमाज़ ओई,
> मानस सबहि एक पै, अनेक को प्रभाव है।
> अलख अभेख सोई, पुरान औ क़ुरान कोई,
> एक ही सरूप सभै, एक ही बनाव है।

> (The temple and the mosque are the same, as are the worship [pooja] and the prayer [namaz]; all human beings are one and all are created by the same One.)[27]

Gandhi was a devout Hindu, but he staunchly rejected the concept of Hindutva. He wrote, 'Religion is a personal matter which should have no place in polities. It is in the unnatural condition of foreign domination that we have unnatural divisions according to religion. Foreign domination gone, we shall laugh at our folly in having clung to false ideals and slogans.'[28]

At one of Gandhi's inter-faith prayer meetings held on 21 September 1947, we find a mention of the RSS during a conversation between Guruji Golwalkar and Dr Dinshaw Mehta: 'I told Guruji that I have heard that the palms of this organisation has blood on their hands. Guruji assured me it is a lie and said that his organisation is not an enemy of anybody. Its goal is not to kill Muslims; on the contrary, it wants to protect India to the best of its ability. Its purpose is to maintain peace. Guruji also asked me to make his views public.'[29]

At that time, a section of Hindus was vehemently demanding a law to ban beef. In a prayer meeting in Delhi on 25 July 1947, Gandhi said, 'In India, no law can be made to ban cow-slaughter. I do not doubt that Hindus are forbidden the slaughter of cows … I have been long pledged to serve the cow, but how can my religion also be the religion of the rest of the Indians? It will mean coercion against those Indians who are not Hindus … How can I force anyone not to slaughter cows unless he is himself so disposed? It is not as if there were only Hindus in the Indian Union. There are Muslims, Parsis, Christians and other religious groups here … Besides, some prosperous Hindus themselves encourage cow-slaughter. True, they do not do it with their own hands. But who sends all the cows to Australia and other countries where they are slaughtered, and whence shoes manufactured from cow hide are sent back to India? I know an orthodox Vaishnava Hindu. He used to feed his children beef soup. On my asking him why he did that, he said there was no sin in consuming beef as medicine.'[30]

In his book, *The Myth of the Holy Cow,* historian D.N. Jha has researched that during the Vedic period people not only consumed beef, but they also considered serving meat the peak of hospitality. Jha cites the example of Rishi Yajnavalkya, who mentioned that beef was his favourite. However, Jha adds that in the post-Mauryan era, bans on beef began to be imposed, and it was eventually completely forbidden. During this period, especially in the Brahmanical texts, cow slaughter for food came to be seen as wrong, and the scriptures mandated that those who slaughtered cows should be excommunicated from society. In the *Vyas Smriti*, it was entirely prohibited. In medieval India, cow slaughter became a major source of tense relationships between Hindus and Muslims, leading to communal riots and multiple issues.

Journalist N.K. Singh notes that there has been much discussion about when cow slaughter and beef consumption began. Additionally, a new debate has emerged over whether the feelings of different religions and individuals must be respected. Most researchers agree that for the last 2,500 years, Hindu religious scriptures, traditions, and rules have prohibited cow slaughter and have accorded a revered status to the animal. The question arises: if a faith has developed within a community over 1,500 years, doesn't it hold greater significance when compared to the law of the land? Since the Indian Constitution has not directed the state to implement a uniform civil code out of respect for religious decrees that are over 1,300 years old, and has instead placed them under the section of Directive Principles of State Policy, does the state's duty toward this belief change? Moreover, isn't it appropriate for other religions to respect this belief as well, to maintain mutual harmony and peace?

N.K. Singh points out that another significant issue is the courts' judgments on socio-cultural and emotional issues. In 1959, the Supreme Court ruled that the slaughtering of cows over sixteen years of age was permissible, as they become unproductive and cause a strain on fodder and other resources. However, in 2005, the same court reversed its decision and imposed a fresh ban on cow slaughter. Citing the National Commission for Cattle, the court said, '... It cannot be accepted that bulls and bullocks become useless after the age of sixteen. It has to be said that bulls and bullocks are not useless to society because, till the end of their lives, they yield excreta in the form of urine and dung, which are both extremely useful for the production of bio-gas and manure. Even after their death, they supply hides and other accessories. Therefore, to call them "useless" is totally devoid of reality ... An old bullock gives 5 tonnes of dung and 343 pounds of urine in a year, which can help in the manufacture of 20 carts' load of composted manure.[31]

The Rig Veda considers the cow holy and its killing and consumption as an activity to be abstained from. In many places, it has been prohibited.

In the constitution of independent India, there is not only an emphasis on cow protection, but Article 48 of the Directive Principles of State Policy instructs the states to prevent cow slaughter. Consequently, about twenty states in India have passed laws for cow protection which include Uttar Pradesh, Gujarat, Haryana, Rajasthan, Andhra Pradesh, Telangana, Bihar, Jharkhand, Assam, Madhya Pradesh, Chhattisgarh, Maharashtra, Odisha, Punjab, Tamil Nadu, Karnataka, Himachal Pradesh, Jammu and Kashmir, Chandigarh and Delhi. At different times, many organisations, including the RSS, ran movements for protecting cows and pressured the state governments, leading to the formulation of these laws.

The RSS has passed several resolutions for cow protection and also conducted many programmes. The Akhil Bharatiya Pratinidhi Sabha passed proposals for cow protection in 1952, 1958, 2000, 2001 and 2010. Similarly, the Akhil Bharatiya Karyakari Mandal in 1995 and the Kendriya Karyakari Mandal in 1996 passed similar proposals stressing cow protection in various conferences. Guruji Golwalkar stated that if some communities consume beef in some regions of the country, people should make efforts to help them understand the need to stop. However, if the act is conducted for political gain, it should be denounced and opposed. The Vishva Hindu Parishad has also been actively involved in cow protection since its inception.

In 1986, Rajmata Vijaya Raje Scindia led the establishment of a new department for cow protection. Moreover, in 1996, the Gau Vigyan Anusandhan Kendra (GVAK) was set up to promote panchagavya, a traditional Hindu formulation made from five cow-derived products, considered sacred and beneficial. This includes cow dung, milk, buttermilk, curd and ghee (clarified butter). Several Sangh-related organisations use cows that no longer produce milk to produce gaumutra (urine) and dung for Ayurvedic products, which allows them to save the animals from slaughterhouses and strengthen the rural economy.

In ancient times, visiting temples offered a glimpse of the deity's idol and a chance to introspect, connecting with oneself for the 'internal God'. Traditionally, idols were installed in dark spaces (the garbhagriha or sanctum sanctorum), and the deity could only be seen when illuminated with the light of oil lamps. This symbolises that God lives deep within the individual's mind, and one must seek Him through self-awareness. That is the true essence.

Devotees would decorate the idols beautifully to keep their minds mesmerised by their presence. They made idols of marble and adorned them with attractive attire and ornaments. This was like visiting a market, where people enjoy looking at beautiful clothes, pleasant aromas, fruits and delectable food. Our ancestors understood that the human mind is drawn to such sensory delights, so they placed these things close to capture attention, helping the mind focus on God.

There is a beautiful Shruti (text) in the Vedanta:

अप्सु देवा मनुष्याणां दिवि देवा मनीषिणाम्।
बालानां काष्ठ लोष्ठेषु बुद्धस्यात्मनि देवता ॥[32]

(The God of humans is in the waters; the God of the wise is in the sky; the God of fools is in wood and stones; The God of the yogi is within.)

When someone asks, 'Where is God?', the wise man answers, 'Love is God for human beings. Intellectuals see God in every divine power and quality. The less intelligent see God in wood and stone idols. Intelligent people see God within themselves.' Most Hindus are idol-worshippers, and although they consider God formless, they worship God with form. But this is not the only aspect of the Hindu religion. In the census of 2011, 28,50,000 people marked themselves as 'religion not stated' category.[33] Of those, 5,00,000 lived in small villages and hamlets of Uttar Pradesh (rather than in metro cities such as Delhi and Mumbai) and owned small businesses. These individuals live in communities where the temple's bells ring close to their homes; they can hear devotional hymns (aartis) sung and religious festivals being regularly celebrated. There are all-night jagrans for Sai Baba, yet nobody in the community is disturbed, and social bonds remain intact. This too reflects the beauty of Hinduism. In India, people even honor followers of the materialistic Charvakas (followers of materialistic philosophy) as rishis. Osho may have been driven out of America, but he still has lakhs of followers in India.

Former union minister Arif Mohammad Khan asks, 'Is Hindutva a new concept? If Hindutva is not based on the Rig Veda, if it is not based on the Upanishads, then where is Hindutva from? It has a place to accept every kind of diversity. It is all-inclusive. I believe that if you are trapped in preconceived notions and somebody fills your brain with hatred, then you cannot see reality. The Upanishads say that if you consider anything as not yours, it will create fear in your mind. Indian tradition says that the body is mortal … *Aham brahmasmi … tatvamasi,* which means that we humans are bound by the bond of the soul. The conscious source is connected. If I am lynching someone, who am I killing? I am killing nobody but myself.'[34]

Osho would narrate a story to his followers. Once, a king summoned all the scholars in his court and said, 'I need a short aphorism because I don't possess the time to read heavy texts. Neither do I require them. This aphorism should be one sentence long, and its wisdom must come in handy at all times. It should be useful in moments of sorrow, in happiness, in victory, in defeat, in life, in death.'

The scholars worked relentlessly, but they couldn't agree on such an aphorism. Finally, one said, 'We are in big trouble. This is a major debate, a serious conflict, and we haven't been able to reach a consensus. I have heard that a Sufi saint is staying outside the village; let us go to him.'

The king and the group of scholars approached the saint. Removing a ring from his finger, the saint offered it to the king and said, 'Wear this; there is a small piece of paper under the gem, and an aphorism is written on it. My guru gave it to me, and since I never felt the need for it, I never opened it. However, there is one condition. Only when you have no options left and have reached a dead end, must you open the chit and read the aphorism. You must wait until the very last moment. With my guru's blessings, I never encountered such a situation where I needed the aphorism. But there certainly must be a secret in it.'

The king wore the ring. Time passed, and several times was he tempted to read what was written on the chit. But he remembered the saint's condition and never opened the chit. Several years later, the king lost a war, and his enemy took over his kingdom. The defeated king, having lost his family, friends and subjects, mounted his horse and fled to save his life. As the king rode through a valley, he heard the enemy army following him. The king knew his life was in danger. Soon, he reached the edge of a deep ditch. There was no way forward, and there was no way to turn back.

Suddenly, the king remembered the ring. He removed it from his finger, lifted the stone and took out the chit of paper. He finally read the aphorism: 'This too shall pass.' A smile appeared on the king's face. Everything was over, he realised. He was no king. He had lost his kingdom. There was no peace in his peace. He realised that if the good times could pass, then even the bad times could not be permanent. Perhaps, he thought, the aphorism was true, and there was nothing more to be done. The words had struck a chord deep within him. The moment he realised that the fear and anxiety he had been feeling would pass, it was like an illusion had shattered. He felt a wave of calm wash over him. The sound of hooves faded. Perhaps the enemy had taken another path. The forest was dense, the mountains treacherous, and the soldiers would probably not be able to find the king. Relieved, the king slipped the ring back onto his finger.

After a few days, the king gathered his friends and attacked the enemy. This time, he won the war and regained his throne. Elated at his victory, the king remembered the ring and took a second look at the aphorism. The euphoria of victory vanished in an instant. The king's ministers asked, 'You were so happy a moment ago, but now you are silent. What happened?'

The king replied, 'When everything passes, there is nothing in this world to be sad or pleased about. Remember, whatever is happening will pass. If you understand this aphorism, what else do you need? Your attachments will begin to loosen, and you do slowly distance yourself from all that is destined to fade … Everything that you are proud of, you boast about will pass just like your temporary youth.'

Prabhash Joshi says that the explanation of dharma that Vyasa has given in the Mahabharata is relevant to this day, and in the context of present-day democracy.

> धारणात् धर्म इत्याहुर्धर्मो धारयते प्रजाः ॥
> यत्स्यात् धारणसंयुक्तं स धर्म इत्युदाहृतः ॥

> (Everything will pass … this youth, the conceit, the fleeting life like that of a butterfly … everything will pass. Two days of activity and fun followed by a deep stillness, the deathly silence.)

Dharma is the set of principles that uphold the people and society. Whatever has the power to sustain or support is called dharma. The grandeur, inclusiveness and positive spirit of Indian society and the Hindu tradition are rooted in these principles. We must strengthen them—because in doing so, they grow stronger and, in turn, sustain us.

When Veda Vyasa had completed writing the Mahabharata, he felt despair and failure. He wrote: 'Urdha baahu (I am saying, raising my hands high, but nobody seems to listen to me). By following the path of dharma, one can attain wealth, desire, and liberation, yet nobody follows dharma.'

Prabhas Joshi says, 'I know that the scholars of Hindutva would say that if nobody follows dharma, then why should we follow it? They want to do a Mahabharata, and that is why I want to show them the essence of the Mahabharata, a verse from the *Bharat Savitri*:

> न जातु कामात्न भयात्न लोभाद् धर्म त्येज्जीवितास्यायि हेतोः ।
> नित्यो धर्मः सुखःदुखे त्वनित्ये नित्यो जीवो धातुरस्य त्वनित्यः ॥

It is inappropriate to abandon dharma, even when desire, fear, greed or life are influencing one's actions. Dharma is eternal, while sorrow and happiness are momentary. The body is temporary, but life is timeless. People may abandon dharma in the name of Hindutva, but I feel it is more virtuous to die for my dharma. Somebody else's dharma is not for me. This command from the Gita is the dharma of me being a Hindu.'

10

The Lamp of Faith Is Aglow

On the night of 30 July 2019, Muslim women were celebrating at BJP MP Ravi Shankar Prasad's residence. Such a scene was unprecedented. Ravi Shankar Prasad, the union minister for law and justice in the Modi government, had not yet returned home from the Parliament, but the women had already begun gathering at his house. Both houses of the Parliament had just passed an act criminalising the practice of triple talaq (talaq-e-biddat). The moment marked a hard-won victory for Muslim women, who had overcome several hurdles to achieve this victory. It was also a significant milestone Modi government in terms of image-building. For decades, the BJP had carried an anti-Muslim image—yet here were Muslim women, seemingly standing with the party. From Shah Bano to Shayara Bano, history appeared to have come full circle.

In 1986, the Rajiv Gandhi government, despite projecting a youth-oriented and progressive image, had overturned the Supreme Court judgment in the *Shah Bano* case. Indore's Shah Bano had approached the court, demanding alimony after her husband had divorced her, while her husband argued that as a Muslim, he was obliged to pay maintenance only for three months after the separation (iddat) period. The Supreme Court ruled in favour of Shah Bano when Rajiv Gandhi, a year into his prime ministerial term and enjoying a brute majority in the Lok Sabha, introduced legislation that nullified the impact of the ruling. In contrast, the Modi government had upheld and advanced the Supreme Court's ruling in the *Shayara Bano* triple talaq case. The *Shayara Bano* case was a landmark 2017 Supreme Court ruling in India where a 3–2 majority declared instant triple talaq unconstitutional, affirming that it violated the fundamental rights of Muslim women under Articles 14 and 21 of the Indian Constitution. In both instances, there had been pressure from fundamentalist Islamic groups, but the Modi government held its ground. There are different opinions about the Act, but 31 July 2019, will certainly be remembered as historic when the president signed the Triple Talaq Bill, leading to the enactment of the Muslim Women (Protection of Rights on Marriage) Act in 2019.

For decades, the BJP—especially Prime Minister Modi and the RSS—suffered significant electoral setbacks owing to their anti-Muslim image in Indian politics. Non-BJP governments had long used this image to instil fear in the Muslim community, consolidating their vote bank while sidelining several other political parties. However, their hypocrisy regarding the Muslim community stood exposed in the Parliament. What was surprising was that many Opposition leaders vocally opposed the bill outside the corridors of the Parliament but were not present during the Rajya Sabha vote. This absence worked in favour of the Modi government, as it lacked a majority in the Upper House to pass the bill. In the Rajya Sabha, there were ninety-nine votes for and eighty-four votes against, while thirty members from ten parties were not present. Earlier, on 25 July, 303 members had voted in support and eighty-two against it in the Lok Sabha.

After this law, it will no longer be easy for Muslim men to utter talaq three times and divorce their wives. Muslim women can now file a complaint through their families, receive maintenance for themselves and their children from their husbands, and get their husbands imprisoned for a term of three years, if the husband refuses to pay alimony. However, laws against triple talaq have already come into force in several countries in the world, including Pakistan, Bangladesh and Sri Lanka. But the Muslim community in India remains particularly enraged because the law makes a provision for the husband to be punished. During the debate on the bill, Ravi Shankar Prasad told the Congress that, on the issue of triple talaq, it remained stuck in the same position it had taken during the *Shah Bano* case, despite the passage of forty years. When Rajiv Gandhi's government overturned the Supreme Court's ruling, Arif Mohammad Khan, then a minister, had resigned in protest against the decision. It remains a matter of speculation how pleased the Muslim community truly was with Gandhi's decision, but it certainly angered the Hindu majority. At that time, the Muslim Personal Law Board had assured Rajiv Gandhi that they would run a campaign for improving the personal laws of the Muslims and take decisive measures to do away with triple talaq, but they did nothing for thirty-five long years.

Arif Mohammad Khan eventually faded from the political spotlight after his stint in the V.P. Singh government and the Bahujan Samaj Party. However, when the Modi government appointed him as the governor of Kerala, I happened to meet him a week before the appointment and had a long conversation. The first question I asked him was: 'What was the use of the fight that you undertook more than thirty years ago, when the situation has remained unchanged till now? Mentally, we are still stuck in the same discussion, aren't we?'

Dressed in a crisp white kurta, Khan answered with his intelligent smile, 'I do not agree with this. This country has changed a lot. You can make a law in two days, but it does take time to change habits. Extremists and self-appointed guardians of religion have not changed their minds yet, and this fight against them will be long drawn. However, we are not alone; young Indians are with us.'

Arif Mohammad Khan narrates an incident from his constituency, Bahraich. A gentleman called him, distraught, saying that his daughter and son-in-law were going to visit him from Andhra Pradesh for their vacation, but that very morning, his son-in-law had divorced his daughter. Many people had tried to reason with the young man and his family, but they were not ready to listen. Khan says, 'Then I wrote a letter to the prime minister, and he called me for a meeting on 8 October. I told the prime minister that we had rendered the Supreme Court's decision in the *Shah Bano* case ineffective by making a law in 1986. In the same manner, the Supreme Court's judgment on the matter of triple talaq would also become ineffective if we did not pass a law on the triple talaq issue soon. This has to be declared a punishable offence. I also gave the prime minister a letter that the president of the Islamic Council in Pakistan had written to the then prime minister of Pakistan four years ago. The letter said, "Pakistan declared triple talaq illegal in 1962, but talaq (divorce) has not stopped because it had not been pronounced a punishable offence." Now the president of the same council in Pakistan, Dr Qibla Ayaz, has cited the Supreme Court of India and passed a proposal again.'

On 28 December 2017, Ravi Shankar Prasad tabled the bill in the Lok Sabha amidst considerable chaos. Prasad, an exceptional lawyer known for his cross-examination skills, highlighted a case from Rampur, where someone simply divorced a woman for waking up late in the morning. All India Majlis-e-Ittehadul Muslimeen MP Asaduddin Owaisi, who always opposes the government, protested, 'Triple Talaq Bill is unconstitutional. It is a violation of the Constitution's Articles 14 and 15.'[1]

Prasad cited examples in favour of the bill from all over the world: 'Even Islamic nations like Bangladesh, Egypt, Morocco, Indonesia, Malaysia, and Pakistan have regulated Triple Talaq. According to a law that was promulgated in 1961 in Bangladesh, triple talaq has to be given to the wife in writing. If the husband does not do this, he will be punished. As per the 1961 law, even in Pakistan, in case of triple talaq, a husband has to give his wife a written notice of talaq, and if he does not follow this rule, there is a provision for one year of imprisonment and a fine of five thousand rupees.

Minister of State for Foreign Affairs M.J. Akbar then narrated a story during the Parliament's discussion. 'When the reporter of the English newspaper the *Guardian*, Taya Zinkin, asked Jawaharlal Nehru in an interview in 1960–61 what his biggest achievement was, he answered, "The Hindu Code Bill. Zinkin asked again, "Don't Muslim women have a right to change?" Nehru said, "The time was not right." The question I have had for the past forty years is, when will the right time come?

'People are told that Islam is in danger, but only a few Muslim men's power is in danger. What is Sharia? The real meaning of sharia is not law. It means a medium or a path. The path was philosophy, but the lawmakers were human. Among the Sunnis, there are at least four schools of Sharia. One is Imam Abu Hanifah, the second is Imam Malik ibn Anas, the third is Imam Muhammad ibn Idris al-Shafi'i, and the fourth is Imam Ahmad ibn Hanbal. There are four kinds of laws. Saying that these laws cannot be changed is wrong. They can be changed based on reasoned interpretation (ijtihad).'[2]

On 22 August 2017, a Constitutional bench of the Supreme Court declared triple talaq unconstitutional. Of the five judges on the bench of the Supreme Court, three declared the practice a violation of fundamental rights to equality and therefore unconstitutional. The court questioned why independent India should continue to tolerate such an archaic custom, when even several Islamic nations ban the practice?

In 2016, Shayara Bano from Uttarakhand filed a petition in the Supreme Court seeking a prohibition on triple talaq, polygamy and Nikah-halala. A victim of triple talaq herself, Shayara Bano argued that triple talaq is neither a part of Islam nor a matter of faith. She cited the rules of the Muslim Personal Law Board and how the body considered it a crime. Shayara Bano challenged the Dissolution of Muslim Marriages Act, stating that it had failed to protect Muslim women from being subjected to multiple marriages. In total, seven petitions were filed by Muslim women, claiming that triple talaq was both unconstitutional and un-Islamic. In response, the All-India Muslim Personal Law Board argued that no sensible Muslim would suddenly utter triple talaq impulsively, and they considered the issue overblown.

However, while Muslim women welcomed the law, the men were furious. This outrage may have stemmed from a deep-rooted mistrust and hatred of the Sangh and the BJP. Arif Mohammad Khan says, 'The politicians scared the Muslims with Modi's name, and in 2014, people said that if Modi wins, survival would become difficult for minorities in India, riots would occur, and there would be attempts to make India a Hindu rashtra. But when nothing like this happened in 2019, people said that Modi had become involved in Muslim appeasement; he made laws against triple talaq, or gave scholarships to five crore Muslim children. After he won the 2019 elections, Modi said in the first meeting of the BJP parliamentary committee that alongside *sabka saath sabka vikas* (together with all, development for all), we have to win sabka vishwas (trust of all).'

Does it mean that Modi has changed? Arif Mohmmed Khan says, 'I do not think that Modi has changed. He is aware of his constitutional responsibilities. You tell me, did Modi take any such action in his first term that shows hatred towards any specific community? He has worked towards mitigating the insecurities, distrust and misunderstandings of one particular section of society. After Independence, there has not been a single year when there have been riots in some part or other of India, but there have been no riots in the last five years. Some people mention mob lynching, but the number of mob lynching cases in the last five years has been far less than those that happened in 1950.[3]

'For about sixty years after Independence, Congress governments ruled at the centre and in most states. The party has always claimed to be well-wishers of the Muslims, but the true extent of what they did for the community was revealed by the Sachar Committee, which was itself constituted by the Congress. Notably, when the BJP came to power, it did not discontinue any programmes or policies previously created for Muslims by the Congress. However, it introduced a new slogan: *Sabka Saath, Sabka Vikas.*

Khan says with bitterness, 'Just because some prime minister says that the minorities have the first right over the country's resources, have they got all the resources? Politicians who do politics by building walls of cemeteries build walls between communities so that people can't come close to each other.'

In 2005, the UPA government had constituted the Sachar Committee to assess the socio-economic status of Muslims. This six-member committee, chaired by Justice Rajinder Sachar of the Delhi High Court, presented its 403-page-long report in Parliament on 30 November 2006. The report provided a comprehensive analysis of the social, financial and educational state of the Muslims in the country, along with recommendations to improve their conditions. One of the most striking findings was that the situation of Muslims was even worse than that of the Scheduled Castes and Scheduled Tribes. Although Muslims comprised 14 per cent of India's population, their representation in the bureaucracy was found to be less than 3 per cent. Among the key recommendations was the establishment of an Equal Opportunities Commission. Following this, a Ministry of Minorities Affairs was established with a budget of ₹150 crore, aimed at improving the financial situation of 18–20 crore Muslims in the country. Unsurprisingly, the move faced resistance, with critics labelling it as 'appeasement' and claiming it had nothing to do with a genuine concern for Muslims. This opposition was politically motivated to appeal to a Hindu base. Nonetheless, the Ministry of Minority Affairs, formed during the UPA government with an initial budget of ₹143 crore, now operates with a budget of ₹2060 crore. The central government claims to have implemented seventy-two of the seventy-six recommendations of the Sachar Committee and to have increased the funding for various projects. What does this signify? Khan reflects on an earlier moment in his political career. He recalls that when the V.P. Singh government had decided to form the Minority Finance Commission, he had opposed it. He had warned, 'This measure harms the very people applauding it. You are making a mistake. You are deepening divisions in society.'

Arif Mohammad Khan mentions a speech by Maulana Azad in which he had said, 'Even then I gave expression to my conviction, and I repeat this today, that in the texture of Indian politics nothing is further removed from the truth than to say that Indian Muslims occupy the position of a political minority … This error, on the one hand, brought confusion into the minds of Musalmans about their own true position; and, on the other hand, it involved the world in misunderstandings, so that the picture of India could not be seen in the right perspective.'[4]

It is well known that Vajpayee was just as popular among Muslims as he was among other sections of society. As president of the Jana Sangh, Vajpayee had declared that the party considered all Indians equal and opposed the permanent division of people into majority and minority categories. In a democracy, this distinction should be determined by political factors, not by religion, language or caste. The Jana Sangh, he said, stood for equal treatment of all minorities and believed that any discrimination meted out against them was unjust. If such discrimination occurred, the Jana Sangh would raise its voice against this discrimination.[5]

After nearly eight years of Congress rule, why did the condition of Muslims not improve? And why did Muslims allow themselves to be misled? One reason is that a large section of the Muslim community in India continued to view the Sangh and its affiliated organisations as communal. When Sarsanghchalak Mohan Bhagwat said in his lecture series in September 2018 that Hindutva is incomplete without Muslims, it may have promoted a subtle shift in perspective among Muslims. However, much more remains to be done in this regard, and it is the Sangh that must take the first step, beginning with its swayamsevaks, and the Sangh has to do this first among its swayamsevaks.

Sah-sarkaryavah Dr Manmohan Vaidya says, 'I have had the experience of attending shakhas since childhood. I have never heard or seen any hatred or contempt against Muslims or Christians in the Sangh.'[6] In 1971, Vaidya was assigned the responsibility of a shakha near Ajani station, close to the government medical hospital quarters. One day, a new group of about twelve children joined the shakha, among whom were two boys: Aamil Khan and Firoz Khan. For the first time, Vaidya had encountered Muslim participants in a shakha. Two days later, as part of community outreach, Vaidya visited the children's home. Their father, Basheer Khan, was an ambulance driver. Vaidya introduced himself and informed Basheer that his children had been attending the shakha for the past two days. Basheer invited him in for tea, but at the time, Vaidya did not drink tea. Recounting the experience, Vaidya says, 'I felt that if I refused, he might think I was doing so because they were Muslims. So, I drank half a cup of tea, and that was my first experience of drinking tea. I am surprised when I see false propaganda that the "Sangh scorns Muslims" or "considers them enemies".'[7]

A senior Sangh official later commented on the long-standing impact of such negative narratives. He noted that when Sarsanghchalak Bhagwat spoke about this in Delhi, it was natural for those who had previously kept away from the Sangh to feel that the organisation now shows openness and welcomes new ideas. That's why, he said, someone even likened it to glasnost.

Dr Manmohan Vaidya says, 'When Pakistan was created, its constitution, following Semitic thought, did not give non-Muslims equal rights as Muslims. However, the Indian constitution, according to Hindu tradition, granted equal rights to all religions. This is the Hindutva of India's constitution. The impact of Semitic thought is behind the concept of "minority" in the Constitution.' He further argues that historically, while resisting invasions, Hindus had to fight against Muslim marauders. This over time developed into an anti-Muslim sentiment within segments of the Hindu society. However, he emphasises that all Muslims and Christians in India were originally part of the Hindu fold. It was because of certain internal weaknesses and social shortcomings within Hinduism that some people adopted different modes of worship. Nevertheless, they remain an integral part of India, just as much as the Hindus. He observes, 'Even after taking strict precautions and measures to ensure that Hindu society does not suffer from the anti-Hindu actions of Muslims, we must not forget that one time, they were a part of Hindu society. To think of India's future without including them is a sign of separatist ideologies, which do not align with Indian traditions. Therefore, even if there are instances of Muslim opposition in response, awakening Indian-ness, or Hindutva, among India's Muslims and bringing them along in building India's future is the true identity of Hindutva.'[8]

Our Constituent Assembly believed that the Partition of our country was, in part, a consequence of the system of 'reserved seats' or separate electorates. For this reason, the Assembly aimed to abolish two things at their roots: the caste system and the separatist electoral system. However, the country had become habituated to the existing framework, and so the members of the Constituent Assembly introduced a compromise in the form of constitutional provisions: articles 29 and 30. These articles state that if a linguistic or religious minority establishes its educational institutions, the government shall support it just as it supports other private institutions, with no discrimination. The Constitution does not permit discourse on Hindu–Muslim lines. Yet over time, we have shifted to using the language of 'majority' and 'minority', with 'minority' becoming synonymous with Muslims.

Senior journalist N.K. Singh opines that the age-old conflict between the Hindus and Muslims has taken on a political dimension after the formation of the Indian National Congress. At that time, Syed Ahmad Khan considered himself the most suitable candidate for the Congress party's presidency, but the party chose Badruddin Tyabji instead. Reportedly, this decision annoyed Sir Syed Ahmed, leading him and several Muslim organisations to pursue a separate political identity and ultimately advocate for a separate nation.

In 1917, the British attempted to create an illusion of limited autonomy through the Indian Independence Act. The Viceroy's Council included a few Hindu members. Then, a major incident took place in 1924 when a radical named Abdul Rashid shot dead Swami Shraddhanand, a prominent Arya Samaj leader. V.D. Savarkar later cited two occasions on which Gandhi referred to Rashid as 'Abdul bhai' from public platforms. Around the same time, eighteen-year-old Gopinath Saha attempted to assassinate the police commissioner of Calcutta, Charles Tegart. But because of a case of mistaken identity, Saha killed another officer. Two days later, Gandhi paid tribute to Swami Shraddhanand at the Congress convention in Guwahati but continued to address the assassin as Abdul bhai. He stated he would keep calling him by that name because the real culprit was certainly not Abdul, but the divisive ideas that created rifts between Hindus and Muslims.

However, Gandhi made no mention of Gopinath Saha and even rebuked Deshbandhu Chittaranjan Das for praising Saha. Singh says, 'The Sangh was born under such an environment in 1925. It was not as if the founder of the Sangh, Dr Hedgewar, was not a revolutionary, but at the core of the Sangh was the suppression of the Hindu history and Hindu dignity with the blade of the sword and the devious plot of the British to create divisions between the Hindus and Muslims. Since the condition did not change for the next fifteen years, this deficiency became stronger with time. During the same period, Savarkar, with his irrefutable logic, wrote books on Gandhian ideology and the splendour of Hindutva, which gave the Sangh's developing concept a steely framework.'[9]

Savarkar wrote in his book, *Essentials of Hindutva*, 'As long as the Muslim does not accept and acknowledge not only our country but our culture and history, and doesn't consider our blood as his own, and he is not only loyal to our land, but considers it revered, till then he cannot be a part of the Hindu circle.'[10] This interpretation clearly reinforces the idea that anyone who is not a Hindu has no rightful place in this Hindu rashtra.

In his book, *Thoughts on Pakistan*, Ambedkar has said, 'Islam is a close[d] corporation and the distinction that it makes between Muslims and Non-Muslims is a very real, very positive and very alienating distinction. The brotherhood of Islam is not the universal brotherhood of man. It is a brotherhood of Muslims for Muslims only. There is a fraternity but its benefit is confined to those within that corporation. For those who are outside the corporation there is nothing but contempt and enmity.'[11]

Ramesh Shiledar says, 'Savarkar believed that if one changes his religion, his loyalty changes as well. However, the Sangh believes that if one changes their religion, only their method of worship changes, but their nationality and ancestry do not. But in reality, that did not happen, and Jinnah introduced the two-nation theory, and the Congress accepted it. Thus, the question is: who is communal? The Sangh did not sign the documents of partition; the Congress did. The Sangh has always believed that 90 per cent of India's population is Hindu, so they must organise, unite, and become cultured. Guru Golwalkar would say, "We were divided, and that is why we remained slaves. Therefore, the responsibility lies with us." External forces exploited this opportunity. Islam forcibly converts people, while Christians do service and then convert people. If 90 per cent of the Hindus become more united, the remaining 10 per cent will also join the same stream.'[12]

But isn't it true that both the Hindu Mahasabha and the Muslim League believed in the two-nation theory? In 1939, the two parties came together to form a government in the North-West Frontier Province and Sindh. Interestingly, both partners were against the Quit India movement and supported the British. In March 1943, it was this very coalition government in Sindh that introduced and passed the resolution calling for the creation of Pakistan.

Even after this resolution was passed in April 1943, the Hindu Mahasabha and the Muslim League formed yet another coalition government in the North-West Frontier Province. It has often been alleged that on 30 December 1937, during the nineteenth session of the Hindu Mahasabha, Savarkar formally introduced the two-nation theory, when he said, 'India cannot be assumed today to be a unitarian and homogeneous nation. On the contrary, there are two nations in the main; the Hindu and the Moslem in India.' He clarified his words in a speech on 15 August 1943 at Nagpur, saying, 'I have no quarrel with Mr Jinnah's two-nation theory. We, Hindus, are a nation by ourselves and it is a historical fact that Hindus and Muslims are two nations.'[13] He further clarified, 'And as it has happened in many countries under similar situation in the world, the utmost that we can do under the circumstances is to form an Indian State in which none is allowed any special weightage of representation and none is paid an extra-price to buy his loyalty to the State.'[14]

However, the Hindu Mahasabha and the Muslim League appeared to have no moral qualms about forming coalition governments. In the North-West Frontier Province, Abul Kasem Fazlul Huq was the prime minister, while Dr Syama Prasad Mookerjee was the finance minister.

On 23 April 1965, Pandit Deendayal Upadhyaya said at the Jana Sangh convention: 'It is the duty of Hindu society towards the nation to take into its own hands the great task of re-Indianising those aspects of Indian life that have been made west-oriented by the foreigners. Hindu society should lovingly assimilate them, and this is the only way communalism can end and true nationalism be realised.'

One must note that Savarkar insisted Muslims blend their blood with that of the Hindus and 'Hinduise' themselves to be considered worthy of living in India. There was a world of difference between the ideologies of Savarkar and Upadhyaya. In some ways, Upadhyaya's ideologies shook the foundation of the Sangh. The thoughts of both Savarkar and Guruji had long shaped the Sangh, whereas Upadhyaya, despite his intellectual contributions, largely confined himself to symbolic roles such as lighting ceremonial lamps. For the past few decades, the Sangh has remained in a state of ideological dilemma.

Writing in *Six Glorious Epochs of Indian History*, Savarkar says, 'The old invaders—Shakas, Huns, Kushans, and Greeks—after coming to India, became assimilated into Indian culture, lost their separate identities, and became Indian. However, the Muslims did not adopt Indian culture and traditions. These Muslim invaders not only wanted to crush Hindu political power but also sought to establish complete Muslim rule over India... They aimed to destroy the very blood, bones, and marrow of this nation, which is rooted in the Hindu religion.'[15] Golwalkar asserted that the last 1,200 years of Indian history have been marked by religious battles, during which attempts were made to annihilate the Hindus. The Partition of India was not only a division of land but part of a broader religious conspiracy. Golwalkar believes, 'Ever since that evil day, when Moslems first landed in Hindusthan, right up to the present moment the Hindu Nation has been gallantly fighting on to shake off the despoilers. It is the fortune of war, the tide turns now to this side, now to that, but the war goes on and has not been decided yet. Nor is there any fear of its being decided to our detriment ... In a nut-shell, we may state that in this land of ours we have lived for God knows how long, a great Nation of the grandest culture, that though, for the last thousand years or less, the land has been infested with murderous bands of despoilers in various parts, the nation has not been conquered, far less subjugated, that through all these years it has engaged in a terrible struggle to free the land of this pest and the great struggle is still relentlessly raging with varying success to both sides. In short our history is the story of our flourishing Hindu National life for thousands of years and then of a long unflinching war continuing for the last ten centuries, which has not yet come to a decisive close.'[16] He also added, 'In the coming of the British they found an opportunity to fulfil their desire. They played their cards shrewdly, sometimes creating terror and havoc, and ultimately succeeded in brow-beating our leadership into panicky surrender to their sinful demand of Partition ... There are sure signs that an explosive situation similar to that of 1946-47 is fast brewing and there is no knowing when it will blow up. Right from Delhi to Rampur and Lucknow, the Muslims are busy hatching a dangerous plot, piling up arms and mobilising their men and probably biding their time to strike from within when Pakistan decides upon an armed conflict with our country.'[17]

Once, in a conversation between Vinoba Bhave and Golwalkar, the question arose about the difference in the thought processes between the Hindus and Muslims. Golwalkar told Vinoba that there are good and bad people in every society. However, it is observed that Hindus even if they are rascals in individual life, when they come together in a group, they always think of good things. When two Muslims come together, they propose and approve of things which they themselves in their individual capacity would not even think of. They start thinking in an altogether different way.[18]

K.S. Sudarshan had said in 1993, 'There is a strong influence of Arab culture in Islam because it was born there. However, because Turkey came under the influence of European civilisation, it changed colours. Iran was influenced by the Zoroastrians, while in Indonesia, there is a strong Hindu influence. In Indonesia, Islam did not stop the Muslims from considering the Ramayana and Mahabharata as their sacred texts and never prohibited them from taking Ram and Krishna as their ancestors. What do Indian Muslims have to lose if they consider Ram and Krishna as their ancestors, and Ghazni, Babur and Ghori as foreign invaders?'[19]

In 1977, following the Emergency, the Sangh's Pratinidhi Sabha held a meeting. Sarsanghchalak Balasaheb Deoras proposed the Sangh should open its doors to the Muslim community. However, Yadavrao Joshi, Moropant Pingle, Dattopant Thengadi and several others opposed this suggestion.

Two years later, in 1979, the RSS formally announced its intention to welcome people of other faiths, including Muslims. Despite this declaration, the initiatives did not move forward in any substantial way. Ironically, the members of the RSS and Muslims engaged most meaningfully during the Emergency, when authorities jailed Muslim leaders from organisations including the Jamaat-e-Islami alongside RSS members. Deoras's proposal was undeniably bold, and it attracted criticism for it even within the Sangh. Discussing this period in his book, *Lost Years of RSS*, Sanjeev Kelkar notes: 'The then Maharashtra RSS chief K.B. Limaye expressed his discontent in a letter, writing, "You have been given the position of the chief of the RSS held by Dr Hedgewar. Kindly run that Sangh and try to foster its growth. Do not try to change it. If you think a change is necessary, start a new RSS. Leave the RSS of Doctorji for the Hindu consolidation to us. If you change this RSS … I will not be able to have any relationship with that Sangh. (Chouthaiwale, n.d.)."'[20]

Yet, Deoras did not change his path and continued with his efforts.

Despite the RSS opening its doors to Muslims in the 1970s, why does it still carry an anti-Muslim image? Senior journalist K.G. Suresh believes that this development is part of an agenda driven by the organisation's opponents. He notes, 'Till date, I have neither met a single RSS office-bearer who speaks against Muslims, nor does the RSS conduct any anti-Muslim programmes. In fact, the Muslim Rashtriya Manch is now actively working within the Sangh … Do you consider the law against triple talaq anti-Muslim? If Hindus and Muslims share the same ancestors, then why object to Lord Ram? Do you consider the issue of love jihad anti-Muslim? The Sangh certainly talks about the change in the country's demography or about the issue of Bangladeshi infiltrators, but it has no objection to Muslims who are living in India.'

In 2019, a programme was organised in Delhi, focusing on Dara Shikoh, Aurangzeb's brother. Senior RSS officials were present at the event, whose underlying message was that Indian Muslims should aspire to be like Dara Shukoh, and not Aurangzeb. During the event, Sah-sarkaryavah Krishna Gopal, a prominent spokesperson for Hindutva, asked, 'How many Parsis are in India ... hardly 50,000, Jain 45,00,000 and about 80,00,000 Buddhists are there... Jews are only 5,000. They are not afraid of anyone … Muslims are more than 16 crore, then why are they afraid ...'[21]

Senior journalist Ashutosh comments, 'Why does the RSS believe Indian Muslims draw inspiration from Aurangzeb? The real problem is how people view history. Secular historians consider Indian history to be a chronicle of power struggles among kings, regardless of whether they were Hindu or Muslim. These rulers [have] committed both good and bad deeds in their pursuit of power and governance, including acts of oppression and welfare. However, the Hindutva commentators interpret medieval history as a series of religious conflicts.'

Ashutosh believes that the manner in which Article 370 was amended has generated a sense of insecurity among the Muslims. Similarly, identifying infiltrators through the NRC in Assam has instilled fear. However, RSS leaders don't feel the need to clarify that Buddhism, Jainism, and Sikhism are not considered foreign. Their definition of Hindutva accepts these religions as inherently Indian because they regard India as their holy land (punya bhoomi) and their fatherland (pitru bhoomi). This is why these communities have never been subjected to the kind of treatment that is evident in the writings of Golwalkar and Savarkar towards Muslims. According to the proponents of Hindutva, the followers of Islam and Christianity cannot be entirely loyal to the Indian nation because their holy lands lie outside India. Parsis and Jews, on the other hand, are so few that they barely count in a population of 1.3 billion.

Muslims need not live in fear if the RSS—provided the RSS genuinely changes its stance and begins treating them the same way it treats Hindus.

Sincere implementation of the vision Mohan Bhagwat articulated could improve the communal atmosphere. However, as long as most BJP leaders keep suggesting that Muslims should 'go to Pakistan' at the drop of a hat, the fear will not diminish—it will only deepen. While some people may appear concerned about the plight of Muslims, Mohan Bhagwat clearly states, 'The happiest Muslims in the world live in India, because we are Hindus.'[22]

Aniruddha Deshpande is responsible for communicating the Sangh's ideology to influential individuals from a wide range of backgrounds, beliefs and viewpoints. The Sangh invites these individuals to participate in its programmes and activities—but their participation is entirely voluntary, and no one imposes anything upon them. Commenting on Bhagwat's idea that Hindutva is incomplete without Muslims, Deshpande says: 'It means we should be united in our sense of nationality and identity. Muslims may have developed unity regarding the country, but harmony (samrasata) is still not visible. A small percentage of Muslims are doing good work, but I think it will still take some time. The Muslim Rashtriya Manch is also engaged in promoting this harmony and tries to help people understand that singing 'Vande Mataram' and chanting 'Bharat Mata ki Jai' are not against Islam. As for Christians, it's a different matter—their focus lies more on religious conversion. They now see themselves as closer to the British and don't seem to have a strong connection with India.'

At the Shri Gururamrai Udasin Ashram in Delhi, a senior RSS official discussing Muslims raises a question: 'The RSS is trying to increase engagement between Hindus and Muslims and integrate Muslims into the national mainstream. But who among the Muslims is working to bring a change in their mindset? Muslims are citizens of India, and should they not accept the traditions of this country? Why do they consider Tipu Sultan their hero instead of Shivaji Maharaj? The most important thing is that the mainstream national ideology should be one. Does the entire responsibility lie only with Hindu society?'

Another important question is: can we still consider people who have been part of a country for a thousand years outsiders? The reality is that they are part of the household, and we must learn to live together. Therefore, when Mohan Bhagwat says that Hindutva has space for Muslims in India, even this generosity can come across as patronising or overly hegemonic. This reflects a mindset that still views Muslims as outsiders. Does the Sangh ever say it will accommodate Sikhs, Buddhists or Jains in India? This is their country too—and the Sangh must firmly internalise this understanding about Muslims as well. Another important issue related to Muslims is that of madrasas. Many believe that Muslim children should also attend mainstream schools, as the religious education provided in madrasas often lacks the breadth needed for a well-rounded education. Some even go so far as to accuse madrasas of harbouring or aiding terrorist elements, though there is no credible evidence to support such claims. While the government provides some aid to these madrasas, in general, their conditions are very poor, especially in western Uttar Pradesh and Bihar. The highest concentration of madrasas in India exists in western Uttar Pradesh, and these institutions are primarily funded by local community donations, which are seen as acts of virtue. However, patrons do not send their children there. Instead, they enrol their children in better-quality schools, while it is largely children from impoverished regions of eastern Uttar Pradesh, Bihar, West Bengal and Odisha—areas marked by dense populations and deep poverty—who study in these madrasas. Many times, families are told that if their children study in madrasas, three generations of their families will go to heaven.

Arif Mohammad Khan says, 'I once asked a friend in Bangalore why the Imam at the local mosque was from Eastern Uttar Pradesh or Bihar? Aren't there any children in your area who can become imams? He replied, "Forget about imams—come and see the madrasas here. All the children are from those same regions." We need to introspect in earnest when education is a fundamental right now, why are we still not providing modern education in those backwards areas? When the Vajpayee government made education a fundamental right, only one organisation opposed it—the All-India Muslim Personal Law Board. From a purely religious perspective in Islam, the day prophethood began, education was declared essential. Hazrat Ali said that even worship is not possible without education. The reason the Personal Law Board opposed this move was that they get children for the madrasas of western Uttar Pradesh, eastern UP and Bihar. If the government were to establish a complete modern education system in those regions, the Personal Law Board would stop receiving children from there. The Law Board members go to the poor fathers in these backward areas and say, "We will give your child six pairs of clothes a year, and a hundred rupees per month." Then they lure them with promises of heaven, both in this life and the afterlife. Hearing all this, the poor fathers are convinced. If a parent has [the option of] a good school for their child at their doorstep, why would they send them far away? The people running the madrasas receive donations based on the number of students. This is why the All-India Muslim Personal Law Board opposed the idea of making education a fundamental right.'

In 2010, Arif Mohammad Khan's book, *Text and Context: Quran and Contemporary Challenges*, was released. In it, Khan argues that many of the personal laws commonly referred to as 'Islamic law' are, in fact, human interpretations, many of which directly contradict verses from the Quran. As a result, he contends that the so-called book of Islamic law itself is problematic, and the commentary on it by Deobandi scholars is even more objectionable. And this is what is taught in madrasas. He says, 'My problem isn't with what is taught to 3 or 4 per cent of children [studying] there. The real concern is that these people now control the public platforms, and they deliver speeches and addresses there. This is not a mistake of the children; I believe that society is at fault because children's minds can be filled with anything, especially when in these madrasas, asking questions is not allowed.'

In his speech before the Arabic–Persian Curriculum Committee in Lucknow, Maulana Azad had once said: 'Our ignorance is such that today, in universities, professors deliver lectures, students take notes, ask questions, and receive answers. But this method is labelled as Western and has been prohibited in our madrasas.' Azad pointed out that the first institute established in Abbasid-era Baghdad, Bayt al-Hikmah, followed this very method of dialogue and inquiry, known in Arabic as Imla. Azad added, 'Today, these people don't even know that this method of "Imla" was prevalent in Bayt al-Hikmah. In madrasas today, the teacher merely recites from the book, and students memorise what was said but cannot ask any questions.'

On the afternoon of 2 July 2015, during the holy month of Ramzan, a press conference at the Press Club stirred in Delhi's political circles. An Iftar party was being organised by the Muslim Rashtriya Manch (MRM), a platform created by the RSS to foster harmony between Muslims and Hindus. The MRM was founded in 2002, and for a long time, was mentored and managed entirely by RSS Pracharak Indresh Kumar. In Delhi, hosting Iftar parties during Ramzan is a common tradition, especially among political parties and leaders. Before the Modi government came to power, even the offices of the prime minister and the president would organise such parties. Attending these events was considered prestigious. They often served as a medium for political signalling—who attended and who didn't frequently sparked speculation and gossip in Delhi's corridors of power. Besides politicians, ambassadors from various countries, editors and senior journalists were also typically invited. These events became known not only for their grand Mughlai feasts but also for the vibrant gossip they sparked.

The controversy surrounding the Iftar party announced by the Muslim Rashtriya Manch wasn't because of the organisation's association with the RSS, but because of the alleged presence of a particular guest. Alongside several politicians, the party had invited Pakistani High Commissioner Abdul Basit. Only a few days earlier, Lashkar-e-Taiba terrorists had killed eight paramilitary soldiers in an attack in Pampore, Jammu and Kashmir. When questioned about the attack by journalists during an Iftar party held at the Pakistan High Commission, Basit responded, 'Let's have the Iftaar party and enjoy ourselves'[23]

This insensitive remark sparked public outrage, prompting the Muslim Rashtriya Manch to withdraw Basit's invitation. The anger escalated so much that the Sangh, through its then-all-India publicity head, Dr Manmohan Vaidya, issued a clarification stating that linking the organisation directly to the RSS was factually incorrect. He stressed that it was an independent body working for national awakening in the country. A senior RSS functionary told me that the Sangh no longer refers to all such groups as its affiliates or uses terms like 'Sangh Parivar' in common parlance. The RSS now considers them independent units working in various sectors and capable of making their own decisions.

In January 1992, when BJP President Dr Murli Manohar Joshi embarked on the Ekta Yatra to hoist the national flag at the Lal Chowk in Srinagar, Narendra Modi served as the coordinator of that yatra. Senior BJP leaders J.P. Mathur and K.R. Malkani were overseeing the journey and had already reached Jammu from Delhi. However, at the last moment, the government cited security arrangements as a reason to halt the yatra. Eventually, under pressure, about sixty people were flown to Srinagar. Upon arrival in Srinagar, they discovered no one had arranged for the flag or the flagpole for the hoisting ceremony at Lal Chowk.

When the BJP's general secretary, Govindacharya, heard about the issue in Delhi, he instructed Indresh Kumar to reach Srinagar and look after the arrangements. Indresh managed to fetch a flag and a flagpole, but nobody had done any prior preparation or rehearsal to ensure the proper hoisting of the flag. At the crucial moment, difficulties arose while mounting the flag onto the pole, but Narendra Modi took charge of the situation.

It is said that the paramilitary forces present in Srinagar had planned for the arrival of 5,000 people to attend the ceremony. However, confusion and disorganisation in the communication of information during the event led to heavy criticism from the media. J.P. Mathur and K.R. Malkani did not return to Delhi until three days after the event, leaving the media in the capital with no clear details for quite some time. The task that had remained incomplete during the time of Balasaheb Deoras, or rather, the initiative that had never properly taken off, was restarted in 2002 with the consent of RSS Chief K.S. Sudarshan. On 24 December 2002, the Muslim Rashtriya Manch was officially inaugurated, with Sudarshan present at the launch. Until his passing in 2012, he continued to attend every national convention of the Manch. However, soon after its formation, communal riots broke out in Gujarat, and the organisation faced massive opposition from the Muslim community. Despite that, the initiative was not abandoned.

Since then, the MRM has undergone several name and structural changes. Finally, in 2006, it came to be known as the Muslim Rashtriya Manch. Its focus, however, remained unchanged. In 2009, when a major Muslim organisation, Jamiat Ulema-e-Hind, issued a fatwa declaring 'Vande Mataram' to be un-Islamic and prohibiting Muslims from reciting it, the Manch strongly opposed the fatwa, stating that it was against both the ethos of Islam and India. Earlier, in 2008, the Manch had organised the Paigham-e-Aman rally from Delhi's Red Fort to Kashmir to support the allocation of land for the Amarnath pilgrimage. In September 2012, the Manch also launched a signature campaign in Jammu and Kashmir, demanding the abrogation of Article 370.

One of BJP's senior leaders, Sikander Bakht, often used to say, 'The time will soon come when Muslims will understand that the BJP and the RSS are not against them, and some narrow-minded people in the Sangh will also realise that this country cannot function without taking Muslims along.'[24]

The BJP lost power soon after Najma Heptulla joined the party, and it remained in opposition for ten years. Yet, Heptulla chose not to leave, determined to dispel the notion that Muslim leaders join the BJP only for political gains. Similarly, the long-standing association of the BJP's chief spokesperson, Syed Shahnawaz Hussain, challenges such accusations. Rising through the ranks along with Sadhvi Uma Bharti in the BJP's youth wing, Shahnawaz was a BJP MP and a minister in the Vajpayee government. Although the Modi administration did not give him a significant role, nor did they offer him a Lok Sabha ticket or a Rajya Sabha seat, he remained loyal to the party. Mukhtar Abbas Naqvi's political journey has also seen its share of highs and lows, yet he, too, never left the BJP. Now, under the Modi government, he has taken an active role in serving minorities through the Ministry of Minority Affairs.

It's not that there had been no attempts to connect Muslims with the RSS before. Even during the Guruji Golwalkar's tenure, similar initiatives had been undertaken. But nothing was ever accomplished. During Deoras's leadership in 1979, he opened the doors of the Sangh to Muslims. Later, they were welcomed into the Jana Sangh and the Bharatiya Mazdoor Sangh. A separate minority cell was formed in the former, which eventually became the Minority Morcha. Even now, the Minority Morcha operates within the BJP, but there seems to be no coordination between it and the Muslim Rashtriya Manch, with both outfits working separately.

In Motia Khan, a Muslim-majority area of Delhi, the office of the Muslim Rashtriya Manch is located on the second floor of one of the spacious flats belonging to DDA. Yet, a steady stream of visitors at the entrance reveals that the organisation draws more than just Muslims. Among those seen coming and going are Christian clergy, pastors, senior government officials and police officers. With a saffron tilak on his forehead, a constant smile and a sparkle in his eyes, waits Indresh Kumar, a senior and long-time RSS leader and head of the Muslim Manch.

I asked him if there had been any opposition within the Sangh to the creation of the Muslim Manch? In response, he answers, 'There were questions, doubts and confusions, of course. The Muslim community suspected whether this organisation aimed to create division within them or whether it would try to split the community. Why was this Manch coming close to Muslims and talking about their welfare? Within the Sangh, there was a misconception, and many members thought it wasn't possible. Earlier attempts had failed to achieve anything significant. But now the dialogue has moved forward. Open dialogue has taken place with Muslims on public platforms. This flow of communication is visible, and Hindus and Muslims are beginning to come together.'

The Muslim Rashtriya Manch has now become a massive movement. Administratively, it operates in fifty provinces, has branches in over 350 districts, and lakhs of Muslims are associated with it. It includes 15,000 to 20,000 intellectuals and 4,000 to 5,000 maulvis (clerics). The Manch has spread to nearly twenty countries worldwide. The Rashtriya Pratinidhi Sabha has 700 to 800 members. Now, the national flag is hoisted in madrasas, and 'Vande Mataram' is sung. A decade ago, the number of participants was in the hundreds; today, it has surpassed 10,000. Earlier, during RSS path sanchalans (marches), riots would break out, but that is no longer the case. In many places, the marches are now welcomed. However, the Muslim Rashtriya Manch's name does not appear on the official list of the Sangh's affiliated organisations.

Indresh Kumar says, 'We have conducted awareness campaigns against terrorism. Awareness has grown about the ills of triple talaq and polygamy. Radical elements have lost and are now isolated, which is why the parliament could pass the law against triple talaq. Earlier, they instilled fear among Muslims by portraying the RSS as a threat and claiming that there would be massacres. But nothing like that happened, and now everyone is beginning to understand that there is no threat.'

The Muslim Rashtriya Manch has launched several initiatives to engage the Muslim community. It has established Parivar Sauhardra Kendras (family harmony centres), opened grain distribution centres to provide food to thousands of families and started aid programmes for divorced women, educational aid and girls' weddings. Kumar says, 'There are two kinds of political groups in the country: positive and negative. The negative ones thrive on creating divisions—by caste, language, region, religion, haves and the have-nots, urban-dwellers and rural-dwellers. They provoke and divide society. Even today, politics is being done based on these divisions. They first manufacture a sense of insecurity and then indulge in politics of self-interest and fear-mongering. But such forces have been defeated in national politics. On the other hand, positive politics aims to bridge divides, uplift the poor and eliminate caste-based discrimination. The RSS vehemently opposes negative politics, or any such divisive social, economic, or developmental policies. Those who are afraid of positive politics try to isolate the Sangh Parivar by spreading fear and portraying it as untouchable.'

Because the ideological foundation of the RSS is rooted in Indian philosophical traditions, the organisation encourages open discussion and new avenues of thought. According to Dr Vaidya, a particular example will suffice to understand the RSS's welcoming attitude. A regional pracharak temporarily oversaw the activities of the Hindu Swayamsevak Sangh abroad. The prayer used by the Hindu Swayamsevak Sangh, however, differed from the one used by the RSS. Upon his arrival, the pracharak noticed two elements of the RSS's prayer were missing in the Hindu Swayamsevak Sangh's version. When he notified a local official about this, the official responded: 'We have followed this prayer for years; Bhide-ji created it, and Guruji (Golwalkar) reviewed it.'

However, when the pracharak mentioned the matter to Dattopant Thengadi, he said, 'If that's true, then it should be revised.' A discussion followed, and in 2000, a new verse was added to the Hindu Swayamsevak Sangh's prayer that had been unchanged for fifty years. That they could discuss and revise a subject as serious as the organisation's prayer based on a pracharak's suggestion reflects the strength of the RSS's functioning.

However, understanding and implementing such changes at the grassroots level takes time and effort. It took nearly a decade for the RSS to fully understand and accept the necessity and utility of the seva (service), sampark (outreach), and prachar (publicity) departments across the organisation even after adding them to the RSS structure in 1990.

A question often raised is: what is the real difference between Hindus and Muslims? Are their identities truly different? If we set aside their modes of worship, what meaningful differences remain? Even among Hindus, there are diverse modes of worship; Shaivism and Vaishnavism have their distinct practices. Similarly, there are differences among Hindus, Jains, Buddhists and Sikhs. Moreover, Hindu philosophy acknowledges that various forms of worship are simply different paths leading to the same ultimate truth.

So, is the difference between Hindus and Muslims one of language? Across India, people speak different languages in different regions. In fact, within a single state, people often speak multiple dialects. The government even formed many Indian states based on linguistic reorganisation, be it Punjab, Haryana, or the states of South India. A Muslim may call Urdu his 'milli' (community) language, but a Muslim from Tamil Nadu often has little to do with Urdu. He speaks Tamil just like his Hindu brethren, and does not understand Hindi well. Geography defines language and not religion. Likewise, a Muslim from Bengal is often not fluent in Urdu, just as Hindi may be difficult for many non-Bengali Hindus. In Gujarat, everyone speaks Gujarati; in Maharashtra, people predominantly speak Marathi. Both Hindus and Muslims from the North-West Frontier region speak Pashto. In Uttar Pradesh and Madhya Pradesh, Urdu is deeply woven into common speech. Munshi Premchand, Rahat Indori, Munawwar Rana, Sahir Ludhianvi and Amrita Pritam belong to everyone. You can't divide them by religion. Those who love, no matter what religion they belong to, often express their love through shayari (poetry). Music and art are not slaves to any religion. Muslim artists in the Hindi film industry sing bhajans, Sufi songs, and chant praises of Vaishno Devi. In

Mathura and Vrindavan, most craftsmen who make clothing for Lord Krishna's idols are Muslims.

Can we identify religion based on clothing? Liberalisation has already blurred those lines, and the difference today is not one of religion, but of affordability. Brands that make clothing don't design for religions, but for markets defined by income. In terms of food habits, Muslims eat meat, so do around 83 per cent[25] of Hindus. Moreover, economic status is a critical factor. A poor Muslim can't afford meat every day and has a daily diet consisting mainly of lentils and vegetables. At the same time, dinner tables at affluent Hindu households remain incomplete without chicken or mutton.

Arif Mohammad Khan concludes, 'Sir, understand one thing. Either you can live with everyone, or you can live with no one. The term "minority" does not simply mean a community that is smaller in number. Rather, it refers to a vulnerable section that relies on others for protection and assurance. In that sense, what is the true status of Muslims? It is unfortunate that even after the Partition of the country, we are still not willing to learn the necessary lessons.'

जो कौम भुला देती है तारीख को अपनी
उस कौम का जुगराफिया बाकी नहीं रहता।

(A nation that forgets its own history loses its geography as well.)

11

The Complete Truth of the Emergency

On the evening of 25 June 1975, Jayaprakash Narayan (JP) held a massive rally at the Ramlila Maidan in Delhi. The air was electric with slogans like 'Vacate the throne, the people are coming!', 'The voice of the people is rising!' and 'Indira's seat is shaking!'. The resistance to the government was growing.

At that very moment, Indira Gandhi was rapidly strategising to consolidate absolute power. For that, it was essential to control JP; otherwise, the political tide could dramatically shift against her. The plan she came up with was so closely guarded that even her more trusted confidants were left in the dark. Even Home Minister Kasu Brahmananda Reddy did not know about her decision to impose an internal emergency. At 8.30 p.m. on 25 June, Indira Gandhi and West Bengal's chief minister, Siddhartha Shankar Ray, drove to Rashtrapati Bhavan and had an informal discussion with President Fakhruddin Ali Ahmed. Reddy was summoned and informed of the decision at 11 p.m., and then the file was sent to the president for him to sign. At midnight, the president, acting on the recommendation of Prime Minister Gandhi, proclaimed a national emergency under Article 352 of the Constitution. The official gazette notification was released the following day on 26 June 1975.

To prevent the Ramlila Maidan rally from spreading nationwide, the electricity supply to newspaper offices on Bahadur Shah Zafar Marg in Delhi was deliberately cut off that very night. Parallelly, Sanjay Gandhi and Om Mehta sat in R.K. Dhawan's (Indira Gandhi's special assistant) office to compile a list of individuals to be arrested.

The next morning, during a meeting of Indira Gandhi's cabinet, Swaran Singh raised the issue of dual emergencies. A state of emergency was already in place since 1971, declared during the war with Pakistan under the pretext of external aggression. In contrast, the government had imposed the new emergency on 25 June 1975 on the grounds of internal disturbances. During the 1962 war with China, Prime Minister Nehru had declared an emergency on 6 October 1962, which Indira Gandhi removed on 10 January 1968. Then, following the outbreak of the war with Pakistan on 3 December 1971, the government put another emergency into effect. However, these emergencies didn't have much tangible impact on the lives of Indian citizens. But the emergency of 25 June 1975 was drastically different. Within two days, the government issued two new orders that would prove deeply consequential—and dangerous—for Indian democracy.

On the morning of 26 June 1975, Prime Minister Indira Gandhi entered the cabinet meeting room with Om Mehta, the then minister of state for Home Affairs. With no formal niceties, she announced to her cabinet, 'Gentlemen, [an] Emergency has been declared. JP, Morarji bhai and several other leaders have been arrested.' A stunned silence fell over the meeting room. It was the cabinet committee on Political Affairs that completed the necessary formalities. The committee briefly discussed press censorship, but issued no official ordinance. They appointed Vidya Charan Shukla as the new minister for Information and Broadcasting, replacing Inder Kumar Gujral, possibly shunting him out of the ministry because of his conflicts with Sanjay Gandhi.

On 27 June, the government invoked Article 359 to suspend the fundamental rights of citizens under Articles 14, 21 and 22 of the Constitution. This move effectively denied people the right to seek legal remedy through Indian constitutional courts for violation of their fundamental rights. In addition, Article 358 was used to suspend the freedoms guaranteed under Article 19 of the Constitution. This included seven core liberties, including the freedom of speech, expression and association. In a sweeping move, citizens were rendered powerless against state action.

MRS GANDHI UNSEATED

At the prime minister's residence, the teleprinter suddenly sprang into action with a clatter. A half-line appeared on the machine: 'Mrs Gandhi unseated.' Indira Gandhi's senior private secretary, N.K.I. Seshan, turned pale. He tore the page from the teleprinter and rushed toward Mrs Gandhi's room.[1]

12 June 1975 became a landmark date in Indian political history. By 10 a.m. of that day, courtroom no. 24 of the Allahabad High Court was already full of people. The sound of shuffling feet had turned the room into a cauldron of tension. Justice Jag Mohan Lal Sinha entered, amidst the watchful eyes of the newspaper correspondents present. The

attention of the nation was fixed on Justice Sinha, who was about to deliver his verdict in the *Indira Nehru Gandhi v. Shri Raj Narain* case.

The backdrop to this pivotal moment is fascinating. Ever since Independence, the Congress party had considered Gujarat as an unshakeable stronghold. Their humiliating defeat in the state assembly elections shattered this belief. A coalition of non-Congress parties, united under the banner of the Nav Nirman Morcha led by Morarji Desai, had swept the polls. But the greater political tremor originated from Uttar Pradesh, where the Allahabad High Court was set to deliver a historic verdict.

At the prime minister's residence on 1 Safdarjung Road, Seshan sat tensely, eyes glued to the teleprinter on his desk. The case before the Allahabad High Court revolved around the 1971 Lok Sabha election in Rae Bareli, in which Indira Gandhi had defeated the Samyukta Socialist Party's candidate, Raj Narain, by a wide margin. So confident had Narain's supporters been of his victory that they had begun celebrating even before the results were officially announced. Indira Gandhi's victory had come as a shock. Refusing to concede, Raj Narain had filed a petition in court, alleging that Gandhi had misused government machinery and resources during her campaign and claiming that as a result, her election victory was invalid.

In March 1975, arguments began in Justice Sinha's court from both sides. After hearing both parties, Prime Minister Indira Gandhi was directed to appear in court in person to record her statement. This was the first time in Indian history that a court had summoned a sitting prime minister to appear in a legal case. This raised a question of protocol: what should be the proper etiquette for a prime minister in court, especially since, by tradition, people stand up when the judge enters. To avoid confusion, Justice Sinha clarified people should only stand for the judge, not for the prime minister. In court, Mrs Gandhi was questioned for nearly five hours.

On 12 June 1975, as fifty-five-year-old Justice Sinha entered the court, his usher announced, 'When the judge delivers the verdict, no one will clap.' Justice Sinha, holding the 255-page judgment, said before he began reading, 'I have concluded all matters related to this case. I will now read them.' He paused for a moment while the courtroom watched with bated breath. He declared: 'The petition is accepted.'

People could hardly believe what they had just heard. Within seconds, the entire courtroom erupted in thunderous applause. Journalists and news agency reporters sprang into action, scrambling out of the courtroom to file the breaking story. Biographer Pranay Gupte, in his book *Mother India*, has written: 'Seshan saw Rajiv Gandhi outside the room [of Indira Gandhi], and gave him the UNI message. It was Rajiv who broke the news to his mother, who seemed to take it stoically at first. Over the next thirty minutes, more wire-service copy was handed to her, spelling out Justice Sinha's verdict.'[2]

Justice Sinha found Indira Gandhi guilty of electoral malpractice, specifically of using unfair means during her 1971 election campaign. Of the seven charges raised by Raj Narain in his petition against Indira Gandhi, Justice Sinha dismissed five and granted her relief on those. However, under the Representation of the People Act of 1951, he ruled that Gandhi was disqualified from contesting any parliamentary or assembly election for the next six years. This judgment would invigorate the non-Congress parties that had begun uniting against Gandhi's government, but shake Prime Minister Gandhi and her close circle to the core.

About fifteen minutes after the verdict was delivered, Mrs Gandhi's lawyers swiftly filed a stay petition before Justice Sinha. They argued that, as the leader of the majority party in the Parliament and a sitting prime minister, Gandhi's immediate disqualification would lead to a crisis of governance. They requested a stay of the judgment to ensure the continuity of the government. Justice Sinha agreed to consider the plea for stay only after hearing the opposing counsel. Indira Gandhi's lawyers then informed the judge that the Opposition had no objection to the request, and Justice Sinha granted a twenty-day stay on the implementation of the verdict. However, rather than use the window to elect a new leader, the Congress party focused on rallying support for Indira Gandhi and staging protests against Justice Sinha. Some Congress MPs like Krishan Kant and Chandra Shekhar urged Indira Gandhi to resign.

Indira Gandhi was made aware of these developments, and she instructed Congress President Dev Kant Barooah to gather signed letters of support from party MPs. On 18 June 1975, 451 of the 500 members attended a meeting of the Congress Parliamentary Party. Each speaker expressed support for Indira Gandhi in their speech. At this very meeting, Barooah made his now-famous declaration: 'Indira is India and India is Indira.' Before him, Sardar Swaran Singh had said, 'What happens to Indira-ji will happen to India, and what happens to India will happen to Indira-ji.'

The opposition parties saw through the Congress's strategy. On 16 June, the leaders had submitted a memorandum to the president, demanding the prime minister's removal, arguing that the Allahabad High Court's verdict had created a constitutional crisis. Trapped in an entangled web of political circumstances, Indira Gandhi consulted her trusted aide, Siddhartha Shankar Ray, over a phone call. Two days later, Ray advised her to declare an internal emergency in the country.

On 20 June, a massive pro-Indira rally was organised at the Boat Club in Delhi, drawing crowds from the city and its adjoining areas. The government machinery was mobilised. On the day of the rally, there was no space left at the venue. At this rally, overflowing with people, Indira Gandhi announced she would not resign and would continue to serve the people of India until her last breath.

Indira Gandhi had started preparing for the Emergency long before it was officially declared. But was her intent to retain absolute control over the system? To understand this, one must look back to what had happened two years earlier. In 1973, her government had appointed Justice Ajith Nath Ray as the chief justice of the Supreme Court, bypassing the seniority of three judges: J.M. Shelat, K.S. Hegde and A.N. Grover. Justice Ray was seen as being close to Siddhartha Shankar Ray, Mrs Gandhi's trusted aide. The overlooked judges had been a part of a majority that just two day prior had declared in the *Kesavananda Bharati* case that the parliament could not alter or abridge the 'basic structure' of the constitution. This stand of the judiciary went against Indira Gandhi's plans to bring in major amendments to the constitution. To do this, she needed a judiciary she could rely on.

President V.V. Giri had objected to the government's approach towards the judiciary, but Prime Minister Gandhi disregarded his concerns. On 3 June, nine days before the Allahabad High Court's verdict in the electoral malpractice case, Law Minister H.R. Gokhale met with Mrs Gandhi and then consulted Justice Ray, who had, reportedly, assured Gokhale that if the Allahabad High Court ruled against Mrs Gandhi, the Supreme Court would have no issue in granting a stay of the verdict.

Around the same time, another significant Supreme Court decision came into focus. Kanwar Lal Gupta, a politician from Delhi, had filed a petition against his winning opponent, Amar Nath Chawla, accusing him of corrupt practices alleging that he had exceeded the legal limit on election expenses. Justice P.N. Bhagwati of the Supreme Court had ruled that expenditure made by others on behalf of a candidate would also be considered a part of that candidate's election expense. On this basis, he had nullified Chawla's election. In Mrs Gandhi's case, the Congress party had submitted an affidavit admitting it had spent three and a half lakh rupees on her election campaign. Under Justice Bhagwati's ruling, her election, too, was liable to be invalidated.

To counter this, Mrs Gandhi had pushed through a change by way of a presidential ordinance that amended Section 77 of the Representation of the People Act. The amended provision stated that expenditures a political party or any individual or group incurred on a candidate's behalf would not be counted toward the candidate's election expenses. Crucially, it also declared that the amendment would apply to all cases pending in the courts. The government later introduced the ordinance in Parliament, and on 21 December 1974, it was formally enacted into law.

Some believe that Justice Sinha's verdict was the primary reason Mrs Gandhi declared the Emergency, even though the Supreme Court had already stayed the judgement on 24 June. The Congress party had hired the renowned lawyer Nani Palkhivala to appeal the High Court verdict on behalf of Mrs Gandhi. Since the Supreme Court was on summer vacation at the time, the appeal was heard by the vacation judge, Justice V.R. Krishna Iyer. Justice Iyer granted a partial stay, allowing Indira Gandhi to participate in parliamentary proceedings but barring her from voting. Legally, she could remain a member of the Parliament, but politically and morally, continuing as prime minister had become difficult. After this ruling, the opposition parties stepped up their political attacks.

Jana Sangh leader Lal Krishna Advani and Congress (O) leader Shyam Nandan Prasad Mishra arrived in Bangalore on 25 June to attend a meeting. Atal Bihari Vajpayee was already there. Around 7.30 a.m. on 26 June, information reached Advani from a local RSS official that Jayaprakash Narayan, Morarji Desai and several key leaders had been arrested at midnight. Rumours floated that the police would soon arrive to arrest Advani and Vajpayee; both had condemned the Emergency and the arrests. As expected, by 10 a.m., the police were there. By then, socialist leader Madhu Dandavate had also been arrested. All four leaders were sent to Bangalore Central Jail. Narayan, Vajpayee, Advani, George Fernandes, Chaudhary Charan Singh, Morarji Desai, Nanaji Deshmukh, Madhu Dandavate, Ramkrishna Hegde, Sikander Bakht, H.D. Deve Gowda, Arun Jaitley, Ravi Shankar Prasad, Prakash Javadekar, Ram Vilas Paswan, Subramanian Swamy, Lalu Prasad Yadav and Nitish Kumar were also arrested allegedly for being threats to national security.

In the Bangalore Central Jail, two large rooms were allocated to house the detained leaders. One room housed Vajpayee and Advani, while in the opposite room were Madhu Dandavate and Shyam Nandan Mishra. Duties under jail manual were assigned to the detained leaders. Vajpayee was given the responsibility of overseeing the kitchen, and under his supervision, good food was prepared. Since leaders and workers from different political parties across the political spectrum were jailed together, they began to foster amiable relationships with each other. Whenever someone got released, he carried messages and tasks from those still inside. In this way, even from inside jail, the detained leaders maintained contact with the outside world.

Loknayak Jayaprakash Narayan was admitted to Jaslok Hospital because of ill health. From the hospital, he sent a heartfelt message: 'I am ashamed that all of you are imprisoned while I am free. This situation is a result of my illness, and being ill feels more helpless than being imprisoned, so I don't know what to say to all of you. I simply say this-my belief is becoming stronger that the sacrifices of thousands, or even lakhs of people, will not go in vain. Indian democracy will overcome these current challenges and emerge from this trial by fire purified like gold.'

Indira Gandhi knew well that opposition parties relied heavily on media publicity for support, which she felt could be easily controlled through press censorship. However, crushing the activities of the RSS's activists would not be as easy. In pursuit of that, Balasaheb Deoras was arrested on 30 June at Nagpur Railway Station. On 4 July, a ban was officially imposed on the organisation. Two days prior, on 2 July, the left-wing government in Kerala had already announced a statewide ban on the RSS. Following the ban, RSS offices were raided and sealed. The government machinery widely publicised the recovery of weapons during these raids. Allegations resurfaced, claiming that the RSS had been agents of the British, had been involved in Gandhi's assassination and were anti-Muslim. These allegations were aggressively promoted through the state machinery. Thousands of RSS workers were arrested. The organisation's schools and shishu mandirs were shut down. Offices of affiliated groups like the Vanvasi Kalyan Ashram were also raided and they were forced to cease operations.

Prior to his arrest on 30 June, RSS chief Balasaheb Deoras had said: 'Due to the judgment of the Allahabad High Court, unfortunately, the prime minister has lost her balance. As a result, an emergency has been declared. National leaders have been imprisoned, and restrictions have been imposed on newspapers. These actions have struck at the foundation of the democratic system and violated the fundamental rights of the citizens.'[3] Deoras urged RSS swayamsevaks to remain calm and handed his responsibilities to Sarkaryavah Madhavrao Mule.[4]

By July, the government had imposed bans on nearly two dozen organisations, including the RSS, Jamaat-e-Islami and the Anand Marg. While RSS and Anand Marg members were kept together in jail, Jamaat members were lodged separately with other Muslim inmates. The Jamaat members protested this religious segregation and demanded that they be detained alongside the RSS detainees, objecting to what they saw as discriminatory treatment. Despite the ban on the RSS, the police could not find any significant objectionable or incriminating material at any of its locations. With the old offices of the RSS sealed, new spaces were needed to continue the movement, so alternative arrangements were made. In many cities, swayamsevaks' homes became the new centres of activity. To avoid police detection, the time and location of programmes, meetings and gatherings had to be changed frequently. Not only the swayamsevaks and leaders, but even their families, especially women, played crucial roles in sustaining the movement. Providing meals and essentials to the families of jailed volunteers was a major responsibility, along with caring for the sick, arranging their hospital care and managing finances under constant threat.

By December 1975, Dattopant Thengadi had gone underground in Gujarat and was trying to involve more people in the movement. RSS volunteers in Gujarat distributed five thousand printed copies of an underground publication to the acharyas attending the Acharya Conference in Pavanar on 2 December. While in jail, L.K. Advani wrote a booklet entitled *A Tale of Two Emergencies*. It was decided that the booklet would be printed and distributed across the country. RSS workers in Mumbai took on this responsibility. It was typed in a single night, photocopied the next night and dispatched to different locations for printing and distribution. Around 40,000 copies of this booklet were distributed.

The Indira Gandhi government claimed both domestically and internationally that the imprisoned leaders were being well cared for. However, the reality was starkly different. Not only ordinary workers, but even prominent leaders like Atal Bihari Vajpayee, L.K. Advani, Biju Patnaik, Piloo Mody and Ashok Mehta denied beds to sleep on for seven days. Describing the condition in jail, Kuldip Nayar has written that that initially there were twenty-eight inmates in the barracks where he was housed, which later increased to ninety-six. There were only three toilets, to use which the inmates had to line up every morning. The toilets were cleaned only once a day and it was difficult to breathe due to the horrible stench. There were no bathrooms so everyone had to bathe in the open. Water would come from only one tap and in that too the water would shut off by nine in the morning.'[5]

Rajmata Vijaya Raje Scindia of Gwalior and Rajmata Gayatri Devi of Jaipur were also mistreated. Both were lodged in the women's ward of Tihar Jail among hardened female criminals. Rajmata Scindia was locked in a dark cell, the kind where death-row inmates are held. The toilets there were unusable, and she was forced to defecate in the open. Mrinal Gore of Maharashtra stayed in a rat and cockroach-infested cell in Akola Jail. Jyoti Basu, a founding member of the Communist Party of India (Marxist), was sent to Jaipur Central Jail. He suffered from hypertension. While in jail, when he heard the news that his son had become extremely distressed with grief, Basu's health deteriorated further.[6]

Ironically, being detained together during the Emergency helped break barriers among people of different ideologies, work cultures, perspectives and even caste and religious divisions. Most efforts became collective, with everyone, in their own way, standing up against the Emergency and the atrocities of Indira Gandhi's regime. Perhaps Indira Gandhi herself did not realise that the very Emergency she had imposed to suppress her opponents would ultimately unite them.

The Lok Sangharsh Samiti—created under the leadership of Jayaprakash Narayan with an aim to organise and coordinate different protests and agitations against the government in power—devised a full programme for a satyagraha, which included observing 9 and 15 August as Kranti Diwas (Revolution day) and Satyagraha day respectively and holding discussions on 2 October (Gandhi Jayanti) on how Indira Gandhi's actions blatantly contradicted Gandhian principles. However, on 29 August, Nanaji Deshmukh, the general secretary of the Lok Sangharsh Samiti was also arrested.

In contrast with the non-violent movement of the Lok Sangharsh Samiti, leaders like George Fernandes were in favour of pursuing more radical efforts to oppose the Emergency, one of which later came to be called the Baroda Dynamite case under which Fernandes was accused of procuring large quantities of dynamite with the objective of blowing up road and rail bridges, disrupting communications, and creating conditions of chaos and anarchy. In Kerala, M.M. Thomas of the Catholic Church also launched a public education campaign against the Emergency.

At that time, countless intellectuals wrote letters to Indira Gandhi. Among them were Jayaprakash Narayan, Balasaheb Deoras, Pejawar matha's Vishwesha Tirtha Swami, Krishnabai Nimbkar and Madhu Limaye, but the prime minister remained uninfluenced. Vinoba Bhave termed the period of the Emergency as the 'Anushasan Parva' (the festival of discipline) which was opposed by other Sarvodaya movement leaders who called it the Aatank Parva (the festival of terror) instead. Subramanian Swamy, Makrand Desai, Nayantara Sahgal, Rajni Kothari, and Laila Fernandes played a key role in mobilising international opinion against the Emergency. Prominent lawyers like Shanti Bhushan, K.K. Venugopal, Santosh Hegde and Ram Jethmalani led the legal battles. In the media, journalists like Ramnath Goenka, Kuldip Nayar, K.R. Malkani, Dinanath Mishra, Nikhil Chakravarty, Vishnu Pandya, Bhanupratap Shukla, Yadavrao Deshmukh, Minoo Masani, Narayan Desai, V.V. John, Barun Sengupta, Rajmohan Gandhi, Raj Krishna, Ajit Basu and hundreds of others bravely faced the atrocities of the Indira government and fortified the movement against the Emergency.

Once the top leaders of the Lok Sangharsh Samiti were imprisoned, those still outside were left to shoulder greater responsibilities. During the Emergency, the RSS's numerical strength and sharp strategising came to the forefront. The organisation's volunteers, with no regard for political, religious or caste differences, offered support to the families of those jailed. They did so with such secrecy and efficiency that people in the government remained unaware of their activities. Perhaps this is why Indira Gandhi had to admit that not even ten per cent of RSS workers had been caught; instead they had gone underground. This is why Indira Gandhi remained adamant about not releasing RSS leaders, despite Bhave's request, even after the decision to end the Emergency was taken and the release of political leaders had begun.[7]

During the Emergency, Balasaheb Deoras said, 'Jayaprakash-ji has said and also written that some members of the RSS are personally involved in his movement, but the RSS is not participating as an organisation. I have also said the same. The movement for social welfare will continue, and people's suffering will naturally find a reaction in such movements. The RSS swayamsevaks are also Indian citizens, and they should be seen as such. Since they are a part of society, the swayamsevaks will naturally express the angst felt by people while being with them. Just because they stand with the people does not prove that the RSS organisation is running a movement.

'Since the lifting of the ban on the RSS in July 1949, there has constantly been talk of banning it again, and that discussion continues even to this day. Even if thousands of RSS volunteers are imprisoned, the RSS will not shut down. The organisation does not carry out its work based on whether it will be banned or not. We must continue our work fearlessly, and even if a ban is imposed, we should think of how to turn it to our advantage for our cause.'[8]

Lifting the ban imposed on it was not the RSS's primary goal. Its foremost aim was to end the dictatorship. When the government sent a conditional proposal to lift the ban on the RSS, the senior leaders firmly rejected it, stating that the restoration of democracy was of utmost priority. After the Emergency was lifted and the ban on the RSS was removed, Balasaheb Deoras said, 'Forget and forgive … There is no place for revenge in the work of the RSS.'

Madhavrao Mule was leading the movement against the Emergency on behalf of the RSS. Although he remained underground and his health remained poor, he continued to work secretly. This eventually caused his untimely death. At that time, the RSS had 1,356 full-time pracharaks (full-time swayamsevaks), of whom 189 were jailed. Madhavrao was supported by a team of senior leaders—Bhaurao Deoras and Moropant Pingle assisted Madhavrao in coordinating the overall effort; Rajju bhaiyya and Kidar Nath Sahani handled the civil liberties front; Babasaheb Bhide, Chaman Lal and Kedarnath Sahni dealt with foriegn relations; Rambhau Godbole and Sundar Singh Bhandari managed the political arena; Jagannathrao Joshi handled Commonwealth engagement and Appa Ghatate led the legal front. Along with them hundreds of other officials and pracharaks remained busy working in their respective roles.

During the Emergency, Dr Subramanian Swamy emerged as a prominent figure within the Jana Sangh. Remaining underground for much of the period, he actively campaigned abroad against Indira Gandhi and the Emergency. In a dramatic moment, he stunned everyone by appearing in a parliamentary session one day in 1976 before disappearing again once it adjourned the same day. Though Swamy could rarely maintain cordial relationships with political leaders, many would come to acknowledge his intellectual brilliance. Recalling those days, Swamy says that the police seized everything he owned, and his wife had to manage household expenses alone while caring for their two daughters. During that time, Atal Bihari Vajpayee wrote a letter urging him to surrender. However, Madhavrao Mule advised against it, conveying that JP wanted him to go abroad and inform the world about the Emergency through various international channels. Swamy says, 'During the first six months of the Emergency, I worked [in India] as a driver for Nanaji Deshmukh. Once, Nanaji was sitting in the back seat of the car, and I realised that intelligence officers were tailing us. So, I sped up the car and took different turns at every intersection to shake them off and save Nanaji from being arrested. Nanaji himself, for a moment, was scared by the speed of the car. Soon, I went abroad, and after I left, leaders like Nanaji, Dattopant Thengadi and George Fernandes were arrested.'

As per the rules of the Parliament, if a member remained absent for more than sixty days while the Parliament was in session, his or her membership could be terminated. That meant Swamy needed to return to India to attend Parliament, but it wasn't a simple task. Swamy recounts, 'If I had bought a direct ticket from the U.S. to India, they would've caught me, because the practice was for the airlines to send the complete passenger list to authorities. So, I bought a ticket to Bangkok instead.'

Instead of taking the connecting flight to Bangkok, once he reached Delhi, Swamy exited the airport. He explains, 'The day I decided to attend Parliament, a condolence resolution was being presented in the morning. In those days, cars could be parked right outside the Rajya Sabha entrance. I parked the car at the main entrance, went in, signed the register and suddenly appeared inside the Rajya Sabha chamber. Members were speaking on the condolence motion. I stood up and said, "Mr Chairman, democracy has been murdered in this country. There should also be a condolence motion on that." Before anyone could understand what had happened, I quickly left.'

After leaving Parliament, Swamy went back to the airport and reached America via Kanpur, Gorakhpur and Nepal. Swamy recalls that later, even after the elections were announced, Vajpayee called him and said, 'Stay there, we are going to lose,' but he still decided to return to India.[9]

L.K. Advani remained imprisoned for nineteen months during the Emergency. Thousands of political activists were jailed at the time under the Maintenance of Internal Security Act (MISA). According to the Shah Commission—set up in 1977 to investigate the excesses of the Emergency—34,988 people were detained under MISA and 75,818 under the Defence of India Rules.[10] There were several dire consequences of the

Emergency and the wrongful imprisonment of leaders—Jayaprakash Narayan suffered kidney failure while in custody, while famous Kannada actress Snehalata Reddy fell ill in jail and later died.

UNDERGROUND CAMPAIGN

Seasoned journalist and lifelong associate of the RSS, Dinanath Mishra, wrote a book on the contribution of the underground movement during the Emergency, *Aapatkal Mein Gupt Kranti*. In the foreword, Vajpayee wrote, 'The underground movement during the Emergency can in no way be compared with the guerrilla struggles that took place in African countries, Vietnam, Bolivia or elsewhere. The most significant reason for this is that India's underground movement was non-violent. While these revolutions were philosophically inspired from the ideology of Marx, the philosophical foundation of India's underground movement came from Gandhi and Jayaprakash Narayan. In a sense, it was an extension of Gandhian techniques of satyagraha and non-cooperation. It was an innovation in the dimension of non-violent warfare. It aligned with the cultural consciousness of India, which is sensitive to every single drop of blood. The non-violent nature of this revolution was not only its destiny but also a tested alternative for mankind to shift from barbaric methods to civilised struggle. In this sense, the outcome of India's underground movement became a milestone in the development of global humanity, in upholding human dignity, the success of democracy, the defeat of old and new forms of imperialism, slavery, and exploitation, and the pursuit of an egalitarian world.'[11]

Dinanath Mishra has often discussed the Emergency and the underground movement with me. The imposition of the Emergency devastated his family. The printing press owned by them was shut down and eventually had to be sold off. Life became extremely difficult for them, but he would often say, 'Brother, this isn't just my story. It wasn't only my family that suffered during the Emergency. Millions of families across the country had to endure a lot of hardship.'

It is also true that while a non-violent underground movement was gaining momentum on one front, leaders like George Fernandes took a different stance. Fernandes believed that adopting non-violent satyagraha, distributing underground literature and spreading awareness about their mission, might help in resisting dictatorship, but was not decisive in shaking up the regime. He felt that the satyagraha did not bother the government very much, and what was truly needed was a movement to instil fear in the government and uplift public morale. To execute his vision, Fernandes planned several acts of sabotage like uprooting railway tracks, blowing up railway infrastructure, cutting off electricity and damaging telephone exchanges. Dynamite was the ammunition of choice to undertake these tasks because it was easily available. Since the Janata Morcha government was in power in Gujarat, Fernandes often went to Baroda since it was relatively safer. There, he met a mine owner who agreed to supply dynamite. From there, the explosives were transported to different parts of the country, and select individuals were trained on how to use them. Reports of explosions came in from Karnataka, Maharashtra and Bihar. The operation was going well until the mine owner became a government informant. One by one, George Fernandes and his associates were arrested.[12]

A big aspect of the Emergency was the total censorship of the media and press in India. Indira Gandhi replaced Inder Kumar Gujral with Vidya Charan Shukla as the minister for Information and Broadcasting. In the cabinet meeting held on 26 June 1975, she outlined the government's media policy and took five major decisions—the Press Council would be abolished; PTI, UNI, Hindustan Samachar and Samachar Bharati would be merged into one news agency; the advertising policy would be revised; any journalists who expressed dissent would be evicted from their government-provided housing, and any foreign journalists who did not accept the government's policies would be expelled from the country.

Additionally, a strict censorship policy was enforced, and a handpicked 'advisory' board of favourite editors was formed to assist the Information and Broadcasting ministry in implementing it. A proposal allowing pre-censorship was approved. Orders were issued prohibiting the publication of any news that could be interpreted as criticial of government action. In effect, all space for dissent was eliminated. Coverage of labour strikes and slum demolitions, and the publication of any photographs related to these events were strictly banned. Even reports of parliamentary walkouts or protests could not be printed. On 4 January 1976, a directive was issued stating that any news related to the Parliament would be subject to censorship and could only be published after prior approval. For this purpose, two officers would remain stationed inside the building to grant clearance for any parliamentary news to be printed. The Press Information Bureau's accreditation of over twenty-four journalists was revoked.

On 11 February 1976, lawmakers enacted the Prevention of Publication of Objectionable Matter Act, making it retroactively effective from 18 December 1975. Placing the act in the Ninth Schedule of the Constitution effectively shielded it from judicial review. The government also weaponised its advertising policy to control the press, using state advertisements as a tool to reward compliant newspapers and punish dissenters. On 8 December 1975, an ordinance was issued abolishing the Press Council of India. Doordarshan and All India Radio became little more than propaganda outlets, echoing only the government's narrative. Referring to this, Advani once said, 'The media was asked to bend, but it began to crawl.'

The merger of the four news agencies initially faced resistance from the agencies themselves. To force their hand, the government decided to cut off a big source of revenue of the agencies, which came from the teleprinters installed in different government departments. PIB discontinued their use. The agencies were also pressurised to clear their outstanding dues to the government. Hindustan Samachar and Samachar Bharati became particular targets. Consequently, all the affected agencies held a meeting on 13 January 1976. UNI's management board was the first one to voluntarily agree to the merger. PTI followed on 15 January, and eventually, Samachar Bharati and Hindustan Samachar also consented. This led to the formation of a new unified news agency called Samachar.

Accusations were made against Samachar Bharati and Hindustan Samachar that some communal elements had infiltrated these agencies. The Hindustan Samachar's president was forced to submit a report which said that a group of employees had dealings with banned organisations, namely the RSS. He requested the ministry of Information and Broadcasting to investigate the matter. On the ministry's directives, the police conducted an investigation and, surprisingly, submitted their report within one day. Following this, Baleshwar Agrawal, the managing editor of Hindustan Samachar, was summarily dismissed for having ties to the RSS. Similarly, Dharamveer Gandhi was removed after being labelled a pracharak. Twenty-three bureau chiefs and seventeen other employees were dismissed on similar charges. Additionally, the head of UNI, G.G. Mirchandani, was also removed.

Although many newspapers suffered under the Emergency, the *Indian Express* group bore the brunt of government retaliation. On 26 July 1975, a high-level meeting with the prime minister resulted in a decision to start investigations into both Ramnath Goenka's business house and the *Indian Express*. The Prime Minister and the Information and Broadcasting Minister, V.C. Shukla, made it clear—corner the *Express Group* at all costs.[13] Pre-censorship of the *Indian Express's* Cochin edition on 13 November 1975 marked the first blow. Similar restrictions on the Bombay and Madras editions followed on 4 February 1976. However, when the Bombay High Court ruled that the pre-censorship was unlawful, the restrictions were lifted from Bombay on 27 May. On 16 August, censorship was imposed on the Bombay, Madras, Cochin, Delhi, Vijayawada, Bangalore, Madurai and Ahmedabad editions of the *Indian Express* and the *Sunday Standard*. The electricity to their Delhi office was cut off on the pretext that dues were pending with the electricity department, even though not a paisa was owed. When this was challenged, the court ordered the immediate restoration of power in the premises. On 4 October 1976, the Delhi Municipal Corporation sealed the press office once again, citing false pending dues. The government also ordered a complete stop on all official advertisements for the *Indian Express*, but even this decision was reversed on 23 March 1977 by the Bombay High Court. Still undeterred, the government instructed the management of the newly established news agency Hindustan Samachar to stop providing any services to the *Indian Express*. Consequently, Hindustan Samachar removed its teleprinters from *Indian Express* offices, but the newspaper still didn't shut down.

In another blow to the press, senior journalist Kuldip Nayar was arrested without any valid reason. The police officer who arrested him wasn't even aware that Nayar was a journalist. He was detained under MISA in July 1975 simply because he had organised a meeting of journalists who were against censorship. Nayar's wife filed a petition in the Delhi High Court challenging his arrest. During the proceedings, it was revealed that the official under whose name the arrest order was issued did not even know of Nayar, so the arrest was ruled to be unlawful. Realising that the court was about to rule against it, the government pre-emptively released Nayar a few days before the verdict and requested the court to dismiss the petition. On the day of the verdict, Nayar was present in the courtroom. The court cancelled the detention order and declared his arrest invalid.

A habeas corpus writ petition was being drafted to challenge the widespread detentions and the very legitimacy of the Emergency itself. However, the opposition had internal disagreements over this legal approach. Some leaders were against turning to the courts, recalling that similar efforts to access judicial relief had failed in 1942. In response,

Atal Bihari Vajpayee made a firm statement: 'This is not 1942, it is 1975. We are citizens of a free country. The judiciary is ours. If we don't knock on the doors of the courts today, tomorrow judges may say, "Had you come to us, we would have delivered justice." That's why we must test the judiciary. This is also a trial by fire for the judiciary … I will consult Advani-ji, Shyam Babu, Dandavate-ji and other leaders on this.'[14]

Everyone unanimously agreed, and petitions were filed in the Karnataka High Court. While in the Bangalore jail, all four leaders—Vajpayee, Advani, Madhu Dandavate and Shyam Babu—challenged their detention under MISA. They were assisted by three lawyers: N. Santosh Hegde, M. Rama Jois and N.M. Ghatate. Both Hegde and Jois later went on to become judges.

The hearing was scheduled for 14 July in the Karnataka High Court. The courtroom was jam-packed. Just a day before the hearing, Vajpayee's health deteriorated, and he was admitted to the Victoria Hospital, where they operated to remove his appendix. After the surgery, doctors discovered that his appendix was fine and there was some other health issue. Later, he was transferred to AIIMS in Delhi, where he underwent surgery for a slipped disc. The court was requested to hear the petition expeditiously since the Parliament session was scheduled to begin on 21 July 1975, and the presence of leaders like Vajpayee, Advani, Madhu Limaye and Shyam Babu in the Parliament was essential.

The next hearing was fixed for 17 July. However, early that morning, a jail official woke them up and informed them that they were being released. The leaders grew suspicious, fearing that it was a government trap. Their suspicions turned out to be true—at around 10 a.m., they exited the jail premises in a vehicle and spotted police vans waiting at a distance. They were told they that were being arrested again. The court was informed of this arrest. Under the fresh orders, all three leaders except for Vajpayee were flown to Delhi in a special Air Force plane. They arrived at the Rohtak Jail around 2 a.m.

Before long, thousands of petitions were filed across the country, and one after another, different High Courts ruled that no matter the circumstances, unlawful detention could still be challenged. In a shocking turn of events, the Supreme Court, in a 4–1 judgment, overturned the decisions of nine high courts. Almost no one in the country had expected such a verdict from the Supreme Court. 28 April 1976 will eventually come to be remembered as a dark day for the Indian judiciary.

The government grew increasingly wary as various high courts across states continued to rule against it. Hundreds of habeas corpus petitions related to MISA detainees were being heard throughout the country. In response, the government argued in each case that, subsequent to the declaration of the Emergency under Article 359 of the Constitution, all fundamental rights—including Article 21, which guarantees the right to life and personal liberty—would be deemed suspended. Thus, no detainee would be entitled to approach the court claiming that his or her arrest was unlawful or malicious. Yet, all the high courts rejected the argument, ruling that despite the Emergency, they retained the authority to hear habeas corpus petitions and deliver judgments accordingly.

The government appealed these decisions before the Supreme Court. In October 1975, the Supreme Court issued a directive to all high courts to treat the government's objection as a preliminary issue, to decide on it first and only then proceed with hearing the rest of the matter. High courts complied with this directive and unanimously ruled against the government's objection. They held that even with the suspension of Article 21 during a period of emergency, the 'rule of law' remained intact, and individuals still had the right to file a habeas corpus petition if the provisions of MISA had been violated during their arrest. The government, however, filed appeals all against these rulings in the Supreme Court. A stay order was issued instructing all high courts to suspend hearings on habeas corpus petitions until the appeals were resolved. A five-judge bench of the Supreme Court headed by Chief

Justice A.N. Ray heard these appeals. During the hearing, Attorney General Niren De, representing the Union government, shockingly argued that during a period of emergency under the Constitution, a citizen's right to approach the court on grounds of deprivation of liberty was 'barred at the threshold'.[15]

After two and a half months of arguments in the *ADM Jabalpur* case, the bench delivered its verdict on 28 April 1976, declaring that the right to habeas corpus was invalid during the Emergency. However, this decision was not unanimous. Chief Justice A.N. Ray, along with Justice P.N. Bhagwati, Justice Y.V. Chandrachud and Justice M.H. Beg, supported the ruling, while Justice H.R. Khanna dissented from it. In his dissenting judgment, Justice Khanna wrote that accepting the government's argument would mean 'that if any official, even a head constable of police, capriciously or maliciously, arrests a person and detains him indefinitely without any authority of law, the aggrieved person would not be able to seek any relief from the courts against such detention during the period of emergency.' He also said that 'our founding fathers made no provision in our constitution for suspending the power of the High Courts under article 226 to issue writs in the nature of habeas corpus during the period of emergency.'[16]

Prime Minister Indira Gandhi was displeased with Justice Khanna's verdict. As a consequence, once Chief Justice A.N. Ray retired, she appointed Justice M.H. Beg in his place. As a matter of tradition, being the senior-most judge, Justice Khanna should have been given the position of Chief Justice of India. He resigned in protest. Even high court judges were not spared for their rulings against the government—thirty-five judges were transferred without following proper procedure. Justice Rangarajan, who had ruled in favour of Kuldip Nayar, was transferred from Delhi to Assam. His colleague, Justice R.N. Aggarwal was demoted and reinstated as a district court judge. The chief justices of Gujarat and Andhra Pradesh were also transferred.

Serious questions about the independence of the judiciary started being raised, with many legal scholars suspecting that the judiciary had come under the prime minister's influence. Later, when the Janata Party formed the government, it chose Justice Y.V. Chandrachud—a member of the bench that heard the *ADM Jabalpur* case—as the next chief justice of India. During his tenure, Indira Gandhi's son, Sanjay Gandhi, was even sent to jail. Nearly thirty-five years after the Emergency, on 2 January 2011, the Supreme Court officially acknowledged that the court itself had violated the fundamental rights of citizens during the Emergency. A bench comprising Justices Aftab Alam and Ashok Kumar Ganguly accepted this truth.[17] Former Chief Justice of India, M.N. Venkatachaliah, in his Khanna Memorial lecture of 2005, stated that the Emergency-era verdict of the Supreme Court should be 'confined to the dustbin of history'.[18]

Veteran journalist Ram Bahadur Rai does not seem to agree with the view that Indira Gandhi imposed the Emergency out of fear of the growing popularity of the Jayaprakash Narayan-led movement. He says, 'Mrs Gandhi imposed the Emergency to stay in power as prime minister. On 24 June 1975, Justice Krishna Iyer hearing the appeal against Justice Sinha's verdict in the election malpractice case had granted only a partial stay of the judgement. Had Justice Iyer given a full stay on the ruling, perhaps the Emergency wouldn't have happened. But his ruling gave strength to the opposition. As a result, Indira Gandhi had to step down as the leader of the Congress Party.'

Rai explains that as per the Shah Commission report, on 25 June, Siddhartha Shankar Ray received a call asking him about the ways in which a national emergency could be imposed without a cabinet meeting. He advised that if the president signed the order, an emergency could be imposed. That very night, Indira Gandhi obtained President Fakhruddin

Ali Ahmed's signature. The next morning, two cabinet meetings were held at 6 a.m. and 8.20 a.m. Following these meetings, the prime minister announced the imposition of the Emergency on All India Radio.

He adds, 'Everyone knows the atrocities that took place during the Emergency, but what is important to note is how Indira Gandhi amended the Constitution solely to secure her position and make herself more powerful. It was during this time that she introduced words like "socialism" and "secularism" into the Constitution—unnecessary words, in my opinion. However, none of the subsequent governments dared to remove them or initiate the necessary amendments.'

Speaking about the RSS and the Emergency, Rai mentions that although the organisation did not take part in the freedom movement, it ended up playing a decisive role in resisting the Emergency, supporting JP's struggle to restore democracy.[19]

Although the RSS claims to have fought a protracted battle against the government during the Emergency, people often accuse then Sarsanghchalak Balasaheb Deoras of writing a letter of apology to Prime Minister Indira Gandhi at the time, expressing the organisation's willingness to cooperate with the government's programmes. Regarding this allegation, Ram Bahadur Rai says, 'Two things are clear. First, the letter did not directly include an apology. And second, and more importantly, Balasaheb Deoras himself did not write that letter. It was written by his associates who were not in jail and sent to the prime minister ... The real game was different. The organisational network of the RSS had strategically surrounded Indira Gandhi and gained access to her inner circle and, as part of a calculated move, began advising her to call for elections.'

Author Nilanjan Mukhopadhyay believes the RSS emerged stronger from its bans: after the Emergency and after the demolition of the Babri Masjid. RSS's contribution during the Emergency was widely discussed, and leaders of other parties, including Jayaprakash Narayan, acknowledged the organisation's strength. It was also acknowledged that where, previously, the RSS had taken nearly two decades to recover and rebuild itself after the ban following Gandhi's assassination, it was able to revive itself faster after the Emergency.[20]

To show the world that she still believed in democracy, Indira Gandhi would frequently speak of the dignity and prestige of the Parliament, claiming that neither the judiciary nor any provision of the Constitution granted anyone the power to curtail its authority. However, in practice, she used the same Parliament to undermine and weaken every other institution or individual. She enjoyed a two-thirds majority, but the only work left for most MPs was to agree with whatever she said. Thirty-three prominent ministers of the opposition parties were jailed. The few opposition members who remained in the Parliament continued to challenge the ruling party. Unfortunately, their voices never reached the public because of strict censorship both within and outside of the Parliament.

To secure parliamentary approval for all the changes undertaken since the declaration of the Emergency, Agriculture and Irrigation Minister Jagjivan Ram presented a resolution in the Parliament on 21 July 1975. He used this opportunity to make a scathing attack on the opposition parties. [Ironically, after the Emergency ended, Babu Jagjivan Ram himself aspired to become the prime minister in the Janata Party government.]

During this parliamentary session, all standard proceedings—question hour, adjournment motions and other legislative proposals—were suspended. In response, MPs from opposition parties devised a strategy to directly target the prime minister. According to the stay granted by the Supreme Court in the election malpractice appeal; Mrs Gandhi could take part in parliamentary debates, but she could not vote. Members of opposition parties took advantage of this ruling: every time a motion was tabled, they would demand a vote on it. This forced the prime minister to repeatedly exit the chamber. They would then use this opportunity to mock Mrs Gandhi and make sarcastic remarks about her. Eventually, in a coordinated meeting, the opposition parties decided to resist this government's motions for a couple of days before staging a walkout in protest, which they ultimately did.

The Lok Sabha eventually passed the motion to approve the Emergency with 336 votes in its favour and fifty-nine against. In the Rajya Sabha, only thirty-three votes were cast against it. Significant resistance in both houses greeted the government's introduction of a bill to extend the term of the Lok Sabha by one year. During the debate, N.G. Gore commented, 'On one hand, our home minister claims that normalcy has returned across the country; the prime minister tells foreign delegates that everything is fine, yet in Parliament, the prime minister, the home minister and the law minister argue that the situation is not normal and hence they needed to extend the Lok Sabha's term by one more year.'[21]

On 15 November 1976, Congress MP Kamalapati Tripathi moved a motion to terminate Jana Sangh MP Subramanian Swamy's membership from the Rajya Sabha, but this faced a lot of opposition. Another MP, Krishan Kant (initially a member of Congress party and later a member of Janata Party) sought an amendment to the motion stating that no expulsion proceedings should be initiated against Swamy, and instead, he should be directed to appear on the first day of the next parliamentary session to clarify his position. The allegation against Swamy was that he had given an interview to the *Toronto Star* on 11 February 1976, which was titled: 'Mrs. Gandhi could be killed, Indian MP in exile says.'[22] Eventually, the motion was adopted and Subramanian Swamy was expelled from the Rajya Sabha.

The fact that habeas corpus petitions were still being accepted by various high courts across the country, despite the suspension of fundamental rights, made Indira Gandhi increasingly worried. Her primary concern was about ensuring a favourable outcome in the appeal before the

Supreme Court against the Allahabad High Court's ruling against her. To secure a court victory, on the one hand, the path of constitutional amendments was adopted, and on the other, changes to election laws were made. The offences based on which Indira Gandhi's election was invalidated were decriminalised retroactively by enacting the Election Laws Amendment Act, 1975, which came into effect on 6 August 1975. Simultaneously, the fortieth constitutional amendment bill was introduced in Parliament which prohibited any court from entertaining petitions challenging the elections of the president, vice president, prime minister or the speaker of the Lok Sabha. It also rendered all pending election-related petitions in courts for these positions null and void. It was presented in the Lok Sabha on 7 August at 11 a.m. and was passed by 1.30 p.m. The next day, on 8 August, the Rajya Sabha cleared it within just a few minutes. Since constitutional amendments require ratification by two-thirds of state legislatures, the Congress-majority states passed it quickly on 8 and 9 August, and on 10 August, the president gave his assent. Thus, on 10th August, the fortieth constitutional amendment bill came to be enacted as the thirty-ninth constitutional amendment act. Indira Gandhi's election was declared valid. However, the hurriedly enacted changes could not withstand judicial scrutiny and were ultimately struck down by the Supreme Court. Justice Y.V. Chandrachud, who while striking down the changes, stated: 'But the function of the Parliament is to make laws, not to decide cases. The British Parliament in its unquestioned supremacy could enact a legislation for the settlement of a dispute or it could, with impunity, legislate for the boiling of the Bishop of Rochester's cook. The Indian Parliament will not direct that an accused in a pending case shall stand acquitted or that a suit shall stand decreed. Princely India, in some parts, often did it.'[23]

Indira Gandhi had long sought to amend the Constitution to impose restrictions on fundamental rights. During the Emergency, it was amended so extensively that it came to be referred to as the 'Constitution of Indira' instead of the 'Constitution of India'. This period is an interesting study of the nature of constitutional amendments, their consequences and the efforts made to undo their effects.

Even prior to the imposition of Emergency, there were successful attempts to amend the Constitution. One example is the amendment that was introduced to remove the basis for Supreme Court's judgement in the *Golaknath* case. In this case, Supreme Court had held that the Parliament's power to amend the Constitution arises from Articles 245, 246 and 248 and not from Article 368. The court also held that from the date of the decision, the Parliament has no right to amend any of the provisions of Part III of the Constitution (the part that deals with fundamental rights) so as to take away or abridge fundamental rights.

Strongly opposing this verdict, Indira Gandhi introduced the twenty-fourth constitutional amendment in August 1971, aiming to overturn the *Golaknath* verdict. This amendment to Article 368 restored to the Parliament the power to amend any part of the Constitution, including fundamental rights. Despite protests from the opposition parties, the amendment was passed. Later, this amendment was challenged in the Supreme Court in the landmark *Kesavananda Bharati* case. In this case, the court ruled that while the Parliament had the power to amend fundamental rights, it could not alter the 'basic structure' of the Constitution. This decision drew a clear line for the extent of exercise of parliamentary authority. Although the *Kesavananda Bharati* case allowed the Parliament to modify or remove the right to property, Indira Gandhi never exercised that power. Nevertheless, she criticised the court's judgment in the *Kesavananda Bharati* case as an impediment to progress.

Under government pressure, Chief Justice A.N. Ray announced that, at the request of the attorney general, he had constituted a new bench to review the decision in the *Kesavananda Bharati* case. This was an unprecedented move—the Supreme Court was preparing to review one of its own decisions even though no review petition had been filed. However, senior lawyer Nani Palkhivala strongly opposed the move and challenged its legitimacy. Ultimately, the new bench was disbanded only after two days of hearing.

In the 1971 Lok Sabha elections held in March of that year, the Congress party had secured a two-thirds majority, which was followed by another landslide victory in the state assembly elections the next year. She used this overwhelming political mandate to tighten her grip on the Constitution. Between 1971 and 1974, fifteen constitutional amendments were introduced and passed by the Parliament, whereas only twenty-two amendments were made to the Constitution in the previous twenty-one years. Most of the amendments during Indira Gandhi's prime ministership were aimed at consolidating the prime minister's powers. With the thirty-ninth amendment, Indira Gandhi had attempted to exempt the elections of the president, vice president, prime minister and speaker of the Lok Sabha from judicial scrutiny.

With the forty-fourth constitutional amendment bill, fifty-nine amendments to the Constitution were proposed—a move which would effectively transform a democratic Constitution into an authoritarian one. The bill was passed in the Lok Sabha on 3 November 1976 by 366 votes to 4, and in the Rajya Sabha, by 191 votes in favour. Since members of opposition parties had boycotted the parliament proceedings, not a single vote was cast against the bill in the Rajya Sabha.

On 18 December 1976, this bill officially became law and came to be known as the forty-second constitutional amendment act. This amendment effectively undermined the supremacy of the Constitution. It established that any amendment made by the Parliament to any part of the Constitution could not be challenged in any court. Furthermore, ordinary central laws could no longer be invalidated by a simple majority judgment—only by a two-thirds majority of a Supreme Court bench (with at least seven members) could they be declared unconstitutional. High Courts were stripped of their authority to review central laws. It gave the Parliament the power to make laws to prevent the formation of anti-national associations or prohibit any existing anti-national associations, with a caveat that such laws would not be deemed void for violating fundamental rights. The amendment transferred more power from the state governments to the central government, eroding India's federal structure. Another amendment was made which created a council of ministers headed by the prime minister to aid and advise the President in his/her functions. This council did not include governors of states.

One significant change was the extension of the term of the state legislatures from five to six years. This had a huge impact in the case of Jammu and Kashmir. At that time, the state was governed by a Congress and National Conference coalition, which was led by Sheikh Abdullah. When the central government proposed extending the term of the state legislatures by a year, Sheikh Abdullah told Mrs Gandhi that, 'We want to walk in step with the rest of the country.' Therefore, in 1977, the Jammu and Kashmir state assembly adopted the proposal to extend its term. Later, after the Janata Party government came to power, it reversed many decisions of Indira Gandhi's government including the extension of term for state legislatures, but this change could not be undone in Jammu and Kashmir because by then, Sheikh Abdullah had become quite powerful, having consolidated significant political power in the region. Therefore, the term for the Jammu and Kashmir assembly remained six years until 2019 when Article 370 was abrogated.

One of the most controversial provisions of the 42nd Amendment was the prioritisation of the Directive Principles of State Policy over the fundamental rights. This change meant that no law that gave effect to the Directive Principles could be declared void for being inconsistent with the rights conferred by Articles 14 or 19. Additionally, the judiciary was significantly weakened, while the legislature was granted extensive powers. The central government gained the authority to deploy forces to any state under the pretext of maintaining law and order, and many state powers were transferred to the central government's control. Questions regarding disqualification of members of Parliament or members of state legislatures could no longer be referred to courts--the question was to be referred to the President whose decision would be final. The amendment added the words 'socialist', 'secular' and 'integrity' were added to the Preamble of the Constitution. These additions have remained unchanged and are still part of the Preamble today. However, organisations like the RSS and BJP dislike the inclusion of the word 'secular' in the Constitution.

Jayaprakash Narayan had started the effort to unite political parties against the Congress much before the imposition of the Emergency. After the success of the Nav Nirman movement in Gujarat and the formation of a non-Congress government in the state, preparations began to remove Congress party from power in Bihar. JP began organising rallies and public meetings across Bihar, demanding the removal of Chief Minister Abdul Ghafoor and the dissolution of the state assembly. On 4 November 1974, at a rally in Patna, the police launched a brutal attack on the protesters. JP was injured with a police baton and fell to the ground. Had Jana Sangh leader Nanaji Deshmukh not intervened to protect him, JP might have sustained serious injuries. This incident likely left a deep impact on JP, both emotionally and politically, reshaping his perception of the Jana Sangh. Atal Bihari Vajpayee and L.K. Advani went to Patna to meet an injured JP. The repercussions of this incident were also heard in Parliament, and on 18 November, a historic rally was called at the Gandhi Maidan in Patna, attracting a massive crowd. This rally marked the formal beginning of JP's 'Sampoorna Kranti (Total Revolution)' campaign.

JP believed that neither a student movement nor the efforts of a single political party were sufficient to challenge the Congress. He therefore resolved to unite non-Congress parties. However, this was by no means a simple task. JP knew that the left-wing parties would be unwilling to collaborate with the Jana Sangh, and overcoming ideological and personal differences among non-Congress leaders was a massive hurdle. One day, JP called Vajpayee and Advani and suggested that they should join the movement. Advani convened a party meeting in Hyderabad to consider JP's proposal. The Jana Sangh leaders felt that this was a valuable opportunity for the party's expansion and agreed to join the movement. However, JP's proposal met with strong resistance from the Communist Party of India and the Communist Party of India (Marxist). CPI(M) General Secretary E.M.S. Namboodiripad met JP and asked him, 'How can you include the Jana Sangh in your movement? After Mahatma Gandhi's assassination, you had led an agitation against the RSS.' Even posters began appearing in Calcutta against JP, asking, '*JP Jana Sangh ek aachhe*? (Are JP and Jana Sangh the same?)'[24] However JP remained undeterred.

To mark a year of the Bihar movement, JP scheduled a protest outside the Parliament on 6 March 1975. He urged all political parties to see beyond their individual flags and symbols and unite on a common platform, insisting that only through such unity could the fight against the Congress be truly effective.

By the time a year of the Emergency had passed, people were exhausted with Indira Gandhi's twenty-point programme and Sanjay Gandhi's five-point programme. They resented the forced sterilisation campaigns, where government officials and leaders, to improve their performance reports and earn brownie points, conducted thousands of forced sterilisations. The encroachment removal drive targeting slums and unauthorised colonies further bruised the Congress's image. Nevertheless, sycophantic Congress party members continued to assure Indira and Sanjay that people were happy and that if elections were to take place, Mrs Gandhi would win with an overwhelming majority because the Opposition had virtually ceased to exist over the past two years.

Under the leadership of JP, the efforts of RSS volunteers had also begun to bear fruit. It appeared every RSS worker was involved in the fight against the Emergency in some capacity. Eventually, Mrs Gandhi decided to hold general elections, and shortly before the announcement, political leaders imprisoned during the Emergency began to be released from prison. Madhu Dandavate and Advani were released from the Bangalore jail. Vajpayee was freed in Delhi whereas Morarji Desai was released in Haryana. On 18 January 1977, Indira Gandhi announced that fresh general elections would be held in March of that year.

Senior journalist Kuldip Nayar told me that it was JP and Acharya Kripalani who decided to form the Janata Party. Initially, JP had not been in favour of forming a political party, but after much persuasion from various quarters, he moved forward with the idea. The party adopted 'socialism' and 'secularism' as its policies, which even the Jana Sangh accepted. A key meeting was held in Bombay on 21 and 22 March 1976. Chaudhary Charan Singh, N.G. Gore, H.M. Patel, Shanti Bhushan, Om Prakash Tyagi, Narayan Desai, S.M. Joshi, Umashankar Joshi, Tridib Chaudhuri, Krishan Kant, P.G. Mavalankar, S. Nijalingappa, Babubhai J. Patel, Uttamrao Patil, Era Sezhiyan, Yadunath Thatte, Digvijay Singh and Aleixo Sequeira were some of the attendees.

JP felt it was impossible to defeat the Congress without the unification of all opposition parties. He clarified that this unity should go beyond a mere alliance and called for a complete merger of all parties. To advance this proposal, a four-member committee was formed, comprising Shanti Bhushan from Congress (O), Om Prakash Tyagi from the Jana Sangh, N.G. Gore from the Socialist Party and H.M. Patel from the Swatantra

Party. The vision document for this new party was prepared and sent to leaders of all the constituent parties—many of whom were still in jail—for their consensus. On 22 and 23 May 1976, a meeting of the available leaders was convened for consultation and deliberation.

The Jana Sangh workers found it difficult to reconcile their merger into the Janata Party. To arrive at a collective decision, a convention of the Jana Sangh workers was organised in Delhi where Vajpayee said in his inimitable style, 'For the reconstruction of India and respecting the Indian public sentiment, we are going to absorb our twenty-five-year-old Jana Sangh into the Janata Party tomorrow—a party that has emerged from the churning of the sea that was the Emergency. Today, we are going to sink our old boat; we are going to extinguish the lamp of Jana Sangh with our own hands ... In the twenty-five years of the Jana Sangh, the sacrifices we have made, the blood we have shed and the heights of hard work that we have demonstrated ... we have tears of sorrow in one eye and tears of joy in the other, remembering our struggles during this period of transition. The joy is for the birth of the Janata Party. We have swallowed the poison that emerged from the churning of the ocean like Lord Shiva did, and now, through the Janata Party, we are going to offer the nectar to the nation.' Vajpayee also told the workers that during the nights of the Emergency, the lamp of the Jana Sangh had been their only source of light. But now that the sun had risen, it was time to extinguish the lamp.[25]

At the Jana Sangh's working committee meeting held in Delhi on 23 January, a resolution was passed stating that if all detainees were not released and the Emergency was not lifted, the Jana Sangh would urge the Janata Party to boycott the elections. Chaudhary Charan Singh also warned that if all restrictions were not lifted before the elections, the Janata Party would reconsider its participation. However, after internal deliberations, everyone agreed, and at the Janata Party's national executive meeting on 31 January, it was unanimously decided to contest the elections together.

It was common knowledge that Nanaji Deshmukh preferred a federation of parties and not a confederation. In a meeting, Charan Singh said, 'Nanaji wants an orange, that is, everyone is different from the inside but the same on the outside, however this won't work in politics.' At that time, even though the Jana Sangh was a sizeable party and Vajpayee a popular leader, the party was still considered politically 'untouchable', and most other political leaders were hesitant to be associated with it. When the proposal to form a new party gained traction, JP secured signatures from Om Prakash Tyagi, Uttamrao Patil and Vasant Rao Patil from the Jana Sangh; Chaudhary Charan Singh, Bhanu Pratap Singh and H.M. Patel from the Bharatiya Lok Dal; N.G. Gore, S.M. Joshi and Mohammad Karim Chagla from the Socialist Party. Accepting their support, JP announced the formation of a new national party at a press conference in Mumbai on 2 May 1976. He called upon the youth and independent individuals to join, although the party's name, flag, constitution and executive were still under discussion. A formal announcement regarding the party was to be made at a conference scheduled in Mumbai at the end of June.

Throughout June and July, discussions continued about forming the new party, but Chaudhary Charan Singh kept introducing new conditions at each meeting. While the Jana Sangh and Socialist Party had accepted the proposal, delays persisted because of the lack of agreement from the Bharatiya Lok Dal and Congress (O). In response to this deadlock, a fresh effort began in the Rohtak Jail. Through the efforts of Jana Sangh's Jagannathrao Joshi and Praja Socialist Party's Samar Guha, a new proposal was signed with sixteen other prominent leaders including Bhairon Singh Shekhawat, Devi Lal, Piloo Mody and Biju Patnaik. This proposal was communicated to workers and underground leaders operating outside. Imprisoning many top leaders together had turned out to be a strategic mistake on the part of Indira Gandhi.

While imprisoned, Chaudhary Charan Singh had been one of the strongest supporters of the merger. He took responsibility for conveying the proposal to leaders held in other jails. In February, when rumours started circulating that Charan Singh had struck a deal with the government and was about to be released, he strongly denied them, saying, 'I may break, but I will not bend.' After his release on 4 March 1976, he promised to expedite the merger. However, once he was free, he kept putting up roadblocks by imposing new conditions on the merger. He insisted that the new party should not give positions to people associated with the RSS because those with dual loyalties and communal thinking had no place in it. Many leaders from the Bharatiya Lok Dal, including Biju Patnaik and Devi Lal, opposed Charan Singh's stance, recognising that without the Jana Sangh, the new party would lack strength and be unable to effectively challenge Indira Gandhi. Despite this, on 31 May 1976, Charan Singh passed an anti-merger resolution at the Lok Dal's national executive meeting.

There were frequent setbacks in the efforts to create a national alternative to Indira Gandhi. At one stage, talks progressed to the point where, excluding the Socialist Party and the Jana Sangh, the merger between the Bharatiya Lok Dal and Congress (O) was nearly completed. The proposed name for the new party was to be 'Bharatiya Rashtriya Janata Congress'. However, the matter did not proceed further because Charan Singh wanted to assume the presidency of this new party. Alternatively, he proposed that Morarji Desai serve as the nominal president while he enjoyed real power as the general secretary. This disagreement prevented the formation of the new party. JP had always acknowledged the significant role played by the RSS in the struggle before and during the Emergency, and was in favour of including in the new party even members who were associated with the RSS. At the same time, leaders from the Jana Sangh, frustrated with Charan Singh, openly declared that if the merger did not proceed, they would chart their own course. Finally, on 26 September 1976, Charan Singh agreed to the merger, and on 27 September, it was decided that the new party would be formed with the unification of all four parties.

Atal Bihari Vajpayee's illness had resulted in an early release from jail, and he subsequently played an important role in bringing about the merger. On 10 January 1977, Surendra Mohan, the general secretary of the All India Socialist Party, announced at a press conference that the parties had agreed upon a common programme for the new political party. He stated that the new party would formally come into existence within a week. However, on 18 January at 8.30 p.m., Indira Gandhi announced the general elections on All India Radio. Following the announcement of elections, an urgent meeting of all leaders of opposition parties was held on 19 January. Everyone confirmed the merger, and on 20 January, a new political party was born in Indian politics—a historic moment. For the first time, multiple parties and ideologies had abandoned their separate paths, beliefs and doctrines to come together as one. A twenty-eight-member executive committee of the party was also formed, with Morarji Desai as the chairman and Chaudhary Charan Singh as the vice chairman. Additionally, four general secretaries were also appointed: L.K. Advani, Madhu Limaye, Surendra Mohan and Ram Dhan.

For Indira Gandhi, the announcement about the formation of the Janata Party, immediately after the declaration of elections, came as a major surprise. The political atmosphere across the country had begun to shift, and several disgruntled ministers, upset with Indira Gandhi's government, were preparing to leave the Congress and join the opposition. Mrs Gandhi received a major blow when Babu Jagjivan Ram resigned from the government. A prominent Dalit leader, he had been a minister in every government since Independence. Along with senior Congress leader Hemvati Nandan Bahuguna and Orissa's Nandini Satpathy, he launched a new party called the Congress for Democracy. Indira Gandhi and other Congress leaders used all possible government resources for the elections. Efforts were made to disrupt rallies and campaigns of the opposition leaders. On the evening of 6 February 1977, JP was leading a major rally at the Ramlila Maidan in Delhi.

Initially, the attendance was low. To divert public attention, the Ministry of Information and Broadcasting had decided to air the popular film of the time, *Bobby*, on Doordarshan that evening, replacing *Waqt*, the originally scheduled film. However, this tactic failed and lakhs of people eventually turned up at the rally.

*

The elections scheduled for 16 March had left the opposition leaders with very little time for preparation, limited funds and no common election symbol. But by the time, election results came to be announced on 23 March 1977, it was clear that Indian politics had transformed dramatically. The Janata Party won 298 seats, and together with the Akali Dal, Congress for Democracy and other allied parties, held a massive number of 345 seats—well beyond the two-thirds majority. Except for South India, the Janata Party's flag flew high across the nation. In South India, they won only six seats and none at all in Kerala. The Congress managed to win just fifteen seats in the southern states. In Uttar Pradesh, it failed to win even a single seat, and Raj Narain defeated Indira Gandhi in Rae Bareli by a massive margin of 55,000 votes. The Congress was completely defeated in ten of the states and union territories.

Among the parties that had merged into the Janata Party, the Vajpayee-led faction, the Jana Sangh, secured the highest number of seats (ninety-three), followed by Chaudhary Charan Singh's group with seventy-one, Morarji Desai's Congress (O) with forty-four, and the Socialist and Democracy factions with twenty-eight seats each. Since all the parties had merged into the Janata Party, the group decided not to appoint the prime minister based solely on numerical strength. Moreover, each faction was to receive three ministerial positions. JP was entrusted with the responsibility of selecting the prime minister. On 23 March, he invited leaders of all opposition parties and the newly elected Janata Party MPs to Rajghat in Delhi. There, seated in a wheelchair, he administered an oath of unity and national service to everyone. However, one important face was notably absent from the ceremony: Chaudhary Charan Singh.

Babu Jagjivan Ram held a majority on the Janata Party's executive committee, and had the committee been empowered to choose the prime minister, he might have become the leader. However, JP believed that Jagjivan Ram had played a role in the imposition of the Emergency and thus retracted his support. Exercising his influence, JP backed Morarji Desai as the leader and prime minister, sparking a power struggle with the party. Raj Narain added fuel to the fire by advocating that Chaudhary Charan Singh be made prime minister.

According to Appa Ghatate, a close friend of Vajpayee's, 'From the Jana Sangh's side, the names proposed for ministerial positions were Vajpayee, Advani and Nanaji Deshmukh, but Atal-ji told Rajju bhaiyya that since Nanaji was one of the key people responsible for collecting party funds, if he became a minister, it could lead to compromises being made, because of which the party might earn a bad name. Rajju bhaiyya then went to Nanaji Deshmukh at the Deendayal Research Institute in Delhi and told him that he should not accept a ministerial post. Nanaji replied, "Please convey this to Morarji Desai."' Subramanian Swamy told me, 'Nanaji was quite upset with Vajpayee over this and spent an entire night sharing his pain with me.'[26] Eventually, Vajpayee became the foreign minister in Desai's government, Advani was assigned Information and Broadcasting, while Brij Lal Verma was given the industry portfolio.

Once the Janata Party was firmly in power, discussions began on reversing the constitutional amendments made by Indira Gandhi. There were differences of opinion within the cabinet: Law Minister Shanti Bhushan favoured keeping the beneficial provisions of the amendments while removing those that weakened democracy. Vajpayee supported this balanced approach. In contrast, Advani argued for the full repeal of the amendments or their full retention, saying that if the amendments strengthened the government, they should be retained as a whole. Vajpayee still maintained that anything that was in the national interest and beneficial for the country should be preserved. A majority of the party members sided with him. However, the revocation of the forty-second amendment to the constitution required a two-thirds majority. The Janata Party, with only a limited presence in the Rajya Sabha, faced a challenge in securing the necessary support.

At the time, Shanti Bhushan was residing at 7 Race Course Road, which later became part of the prime minister's official residence. He invited Congress Lok Sabha leader C.M. Stephen and Rajya Sabha leader Padanatha Mohammed Sayeed for dinner, where he explained that although the forty-second amendment favoured the government at the Centre, the Janata Party still did not want to retain it in its current form. He proposed an alternative: keep only the positive provisions of the amendment, allowing the Congress-backed amendment to technically remain, but with necessary changes. Since the Congress was also concerned about its public image, all parties agreed to hold a two-day consultation meeting. As a result, the forty-fourth constitutional amendment act—that reversed some of the provisions of the controversial forty-second amendment act—came to be passed unanimously, although L.K. Advani and Ram Jethmalani were opposed to it.

In the Janata Party government, Bhaurao Deoras was managing political affairs on behalf of the Sangh. It was becoming increasingly clear to him that the Janata Party government might not last long. At that point, the RSS devised a strategy: RSS workers and leaders would try to gain entry, wherever possible, within the government or government organisations; they would establish themselves there and make their presence felt. The aim was to use whatever time was available to strengthen and consolidate their position. Later, the BJP greatly benefited from this strategy. Rebuilding the organisation proved not to be too difficult. In fact, the massive turnout at the first party's convention held in Mumbai in 1980 took everyone by surprise. It was the outcome of that very strategy that, despite the collapse of the Janata Party, the Sangh Parivar emerged even stronger.

It wasn't long before the Janata Party government began to falter, plagued by petty egos and personal ambitions of its leaders. Some members started feeling that those who had come from the Jana Sangh were gaining more power and were likely to benefit more if fresh elections were held. To counter this, they revived the issue of 'dual membership', with Madhu Limaye leading the charge. He demanded that individuals with ties to the RSS sever those connections. One of those who disagreed with Madhu Limaye's stance was the prominent leader, George Fernandes, but nobody heeded his advice. Limaye knew very well that such a thing was unlikely. Some people were under the illusion that this would divide the Jana Sangh, with the more moderate figures like Vajpayee remaining in the Janata Party and the more aggressive members moving out. But Vajpayee made his position clear: his association with the Sangh was twenty-five years old, while his relationship with the Janata Party was just two years old. He argued that the RSS was a cultural organisation and not a political one, and therefore, there was no conflict in maintaining an association with the RSS.

Regarding the dual membership controversy, Vajpayee addressed the issue in an article entitled 'We Are All to Blame', published in the *Indian Express* on 3 August 1979. In it, Vajpayee highlighted the fact that the greatest problem within the Janata Party was Chaudhary Charan Singh's ego, and that he could never accept being second-in-command in the government. That Charan Singh's supporters and some other individuals wanted to destabilise the Janata Party government and were frustrated that members of the Jana Sangh were not assisting them in that. He said that Sangh Parivar had played no role in the communal violence that had occurred in the country and that fears that the Sangh Parivar would concentrate political power in its own hands were baseless.

Along with this, he also offered some advice to the Sangh Parivar in the article, saying that publications affiliated with the Sangh should not take sides in political power struggles. That the RSS should not involve itself in youth organisations that were in talks with political parties and labour unions. Most importantly, the RSS should declare that its idea of a Hindu rashtra simply meant creating an Indian nation.

Following Vajpayee's article, Balasaheb Deoras addressed the annual Vijayadashami gathering in Nagpur in October 1979 and said, 'Some people say that the Sangh is changing and that it needs to change further. Everything alive in the world changes; change is a part of evolution. What does not change is not alive; it is dead. But change does not mean deviating from one's essential character. The Sangh is evolving according to the needs of the time and will continue to do so in the future as well.'[27]

Achyutanand Mishra says, 'Chaudhary Charan Singh wanted to become prime minister. The Jana Sangh members wanted Babu Jagjivan Ram to take the position, and had that happened, a large section of the Dalit community would have broken away from Congress. But Charan Singh opposed this, saying, "Jagjivan Ram was the one who had introduced the Emergency bill. How can he become the prime minister?"' Eventually, the Jana Sangh threw its support behind Morarji Desai, a move that Charan Singh deeply resented and never forgot. On the same day, George Fernandes also shifted his stance—initially supporting the government and then resigning in protest the very next day. Later, with backing from Sanjay Gandhi and Raj Narain, Indira Gandhi sought to win over Charan Singh by offering him the prime minister's post.

L.K. Advani has written: 'One day, Chandra Shekhar came to my office in the Parliament House and said that he wanted to discuss some important matters with Atal-ji and me. He explained that some people who had earlier supported Charan Singh, including Hemvati Nandan Bahuguna, still wished to remain in the Janata Party, on the condition that Jana Sangh members be removed from the Morarji Desai government. The three Jana Sangh ministers, Vajpayee, Advani, and Brijlal Verma, discussed the matter and then went to Morarji Desai and told him they were willing to resign for the sake of the stability and unity of the Janata Party and the government. Morarji Desai outright rejected the idea and said, "Why do you need to resign? If necessary, I will resign."'[28] Eventually, because of an internal split in the Janata Party, Morarji Desai lost the majority and resigned on 15 July.

Meanwhile, on 8 October 1979, Loknayak Jayaprakash Narayan breathed his last. In a moving tribute to him, Atal Bihari Vajpayee said: 'JP was not merely the name of one person; it symbolised humanity. When one thought of Mr Narayan, two pictures came to one's mind. One was reminded of Bhishma Pitamah lying on a bed of arrows. There was only one difference between Bhishma Pitamah and Mr Narayan; while the former fought for the Kauravas, the latter fought for justice. The second picture was one of Christ on the cross, and Mr Narayan's life reminded one of Christ's sacrifices.'[29]

Because of personal ambitions and internal conflicts among leaders, it soon became clear that the Janata Party would not return to power in the 1980 elections. The Janata Party, which had won 298 seats in the 1977 elections, could secure only thirty-one seats in 1980. The Jana Sangh faction, which had ninety-three MPs in the previous election, got only sixteen seats. Meanwhile, the Congress doubled its seat count from 153 seats in 1977 to 351 seats in 1980. Congress received 66.73 per cent of the votes.

Appendix

SARSANGHCHALAKS OF THE SANGH

- Dr Keshav Baliram Hedgewar (Founder): 1925-1930 and 1931-1940
- Laxman Vasudev Paranjape: 1930-1931
- Madhav Sadashiv Golwalkar (Guruji): 1940-1973
- Madhukar Dattatreya Deoras (Balasaheb): 1973-1994
- Prof Rajendra Singh (Rajju Bhaiyya): 1994-2000
- K.S. Sudarshan: 2000-2009
- Dr Mohan Bhagwat: 2009 till date

SANGH TERMINOLOGY

RASHTRIYA SWAYAMSEVAK SANGH:

- **Rashtriya:** One who has single-minded and unwavering loyalty towards his/her country, its traditions, great leaders and saints, its security and prosperity, and who completely attaches his/her emotional values to the country.

- **Swayamsevak:** A swayamsevak is one who voluntarily serves his nation, society, country, religion, and culture, and works selflessly and sincerely for its security and progress. Once a swayamsevak, always a swayamsevak.
- **Sangh:** An organisation composed of people with the same ideas, who are committed to the same goal, and who are mutually amicable. They work together with complete dedication.

THE SANGH OATH

'सर्वशक्तिमान श्री परमेश्वर तथा अपने पूर्वजों का स्मरण कर मैं प्रतिज्ञा करता हूं कि अपने पवित्र हिंदू धर्म, हिंदू संस्कृति, तथा हिंदू समाज का संरक्षण कर हिंदू राष्ट्र की सर्वांगीण उन्नति करने के लिए मैं राष्ट्रीय स्वयंसेवक संघ का घटक बना हूं. संघ का कार्य मैं प्रमाणिकता से, निस्वार्थ बुद्धि से तथा तन, मन, धनपूर्वक करूंगा और इस व्रत का मैं आजन्म पालन करूंगा. भारत माता की जय.'

'In the name of Almighty God and our ancestors, I hereby vow that I have become a unit of the Rashtriya Swayamsevak Sangh in order to protect our sacred Hindu Dharma, Hindu culture and Hindu society and to achieve the all-round development of the Hindu nation. I will do the Sangh's work sincerely with a selfless mind, and with all my body, heart and wealth. I will observe this vow all my life. Bharat Mata ki jai.'

IMPORTANT WORDS RELATED TO THE SANGH:

Sangh Parivar: Sangh and its associated organisations

Sarsanghchalak: Guide, philosopher, friend of the Sangh (nominated)

Sarkaryavah: Sangh general secretary (mahasachiv) (elected every three years)

Sah-sarkaryavah: Joint general secretary

Pracharaks: Lifelong swayamsevaks working to advance the Sangh's mission

Sangh Ganvesh: Sangh's uniform

Sangh Shiksha Varg: Sangh's training or education camp

Sangh Dhwaj: Saffron flag of the Sangh

Sangh Samanvay: Harmony within the Sangh

Shree Guru Dakshina: Once every year, swayamsevaks present themselves reverentially in front of the flag and offer their token of gratitude to the Guru. This is not like an annual fee, a donation, a fund or financial support.

Baithak: A formal gathering of RSS functionaries that takes place at regular intervals according to geographic needs and responsibilities to plan and review, enhance qualitative development and ideological clarity and to take take strategic and qualitative decisions through consensus.

Naipunya Varg: Specialised training sessions organised by the RSS to enhance physical and intellectual abilities on a weekly basis in urban areas and monthly and fortnightly basis in rural areas.

Saanghik: Swayamsevaks of one or more shakhas assemble for various physical and intellectual programmes.

Sammelan: The volunteers come together for a relatively long period to create an atmosphere of enthusiasm and excitement.

Shivir: Programmes conducted at various levels during different seasons for training swayamsevaks and workers on community living, rules, operations over more than one-day sessions.

Bauddhik Varg: Apart from celebrations, every month a speaker holds a comprehensive analysis session on a particular subject in a programme conducted in a shakha or a geographical area.

Charcha: An internal discussion within a small group (toli) and clarification of subjects in depth through question and answer sessions.

Shanka Samadhan: These are sessions where senior leaders of the RSS clarify those doubts and questions that arise in the minds of volunteers from time to time, which can affect productivity.

Sangh Mandali: On particular days and at specific times, volunteers assemble for one-hour long physical training and intellectual programmes in remote areas or in areas with no shakhas. (Prayer and the flag are not mandatory in these programmes).

Saptahik Milan: Weekly assemblies on specific days and times in areas with no shakhas or in areas with sangh mandalis. Prayers are mandatory at these gatherings.

Shakha: Daily assemblies for one hour at a specific time and place attended by volunteers in uniform. In these assemblies, the code of conduct, physical-intellectual training, flag and prayer are mandatory. Members unfamiliar with the local populace, culture and administration are introduced to these aspects.

Prashikshan Varg: Training classes conducted from time to time, to impart knowledge on subjects like lathi exercises, combat, yoga postures, songs, prayers, etc.

Nitya Karyakram: The activities undertaken in the daily shakhas are a part of this category, for example, games, surya namaskar, lathi training, balance exercises, callisthenics, combat and physical training, group songs, moral teachings, golden words or sayings, discussions, intellectual sessions, etc.

Naimittika Karyakram: These programmes are conducted for a specific purpose or for the development of a particular skill and also to strengthen the shakhas. These include forest walks, cycle trips, community meals, visits to sacred places, annual days, Naipunya vargs (skill development sessions), adventure trips, camps, drills, meetings at different levels and classes, bauddhik vargs, discussions, talent exhibitions, celebrations for birth and death anniversaries of great personalities, and different types of physical and intellectual competitions.

ORGANISATION OF THE SHAKHA

Shakha karyavah: The primary leader of a shakha. His duties involve managing and developing the shakha group, contacting the parents and guardians, and building connections between the shakha and the locality and vice versa.

Mukhya shikshak: Responsible for creating and managing the one-hour shakha sessions, developing group and assembly systems and managing group activities at the shakha.

Gana Shikshak: Responsible for leading and training his group of swayamsevaks, managing and running physical programmes with enthusiasm and maintaining cordial relationships with other group leaders.

Gata Nayak: Group leader within a shakha who maintains contact with the swayamsevaks of his group and their family members, meets new members and brings them to the shakha, and takes an interest in their lives and ups and downs.

SANGH STRUCTURE: ACCORDING TO RESPONSIBILITY

Akhil Bharatiya Karyakari Mandal: National level unit comprising the sarsanghchalak, sarkaryavah, sah-sarkaryavah, and pracharaks.

Karya vibhag: Includes the sharirik shikshan pramukh, bauddhik shikshan pramukh, sampark pramukh, vyavastha pramukh, seva pramukh, prachar pramukh and pracharak pramukh.

Karyakari Mandal sadasya: Members of the executive or working committee. The number of members is variable but can go up to twenty-one.

Kshetriya Karyakari Mandal and Prantiya Karyakari Mandal: Include the sanghchalak, karyavah, pracharak, bauddhik shikshan pramukh, sampark pramukh, vyavastha pramukh, sewa pramukh, prachar pramukh, pracharak pramukh and other members.

Shakha Toli: Smallest unit of karyakartas within a shakha. Includes the shakha karyavah, mukhya shikshak, gan shikshak and gat nayak.

Akhil Bharatiya Pratinidhi Sabha: The highest decision-making body of the RSS, comprising representatives from all levels. The number of members depends on the strength of the district level members. At present, it has about 1400 members. The regional officials are called prant karyakari.

SANGH STRUCTURE: CONSTITUTIONAL

- According to the Sangh constitution, the position of the sarsanghchalak is like that of a 'philosopher and guide' and is supreme. From the perspective of execution, the sarkaryavah is the highest authority. Members of the Akhil Bharatiya Pratinidhi Sabha elect the sarkaryavah every three years.
- The prant pratinidhis elect the Akhil Bharatiya pratinidhis. Avowed swayamsevaks over eighteen years of age and active for at least six years elect the prant pratinidhis.
- The prant pratinidhis choose the sanghchalaks at the state/province level. The sanghchalak appoints the divisional, district level and other office bearers. Sanghchalak pramukhs appoint other officials in their own region/area after consultation with the karyakartas.

THE RAM JANMABHOOMI DISPUTE AND ITS HISTORY

1528: Mir Baqi, the army commander of Mughal emperor Babur, gets the Babri Masjid constructed at the disputed site.

1885: Mahant Raghuvir Das files a petition in the Allahabad District Court and seeks permission to erect a shamiana outside the disputed structure. The court dismisses his petition.

1949: Idols of Ram Lalla are stealthily placed in the central dome of the mosque on the night of December 22-23.

1950: Gopal Visharad files a petition in the Faizabad District Court seeking rights to worship Ram Lalla. Ramchandra Das Paramhans too files a petition to continue the worship and to let the idols remain there.

1959: The Nirmohi Akhara files a petition to be given rights over the disputed site.

1981: The Uttar Pradesh Sunni Waqf Board files a petition seeking rights over the disputed site.

1 February 1986: A local court issues an order for the locks at the disputed site to be opened for the Hindu devotees.

14 August 1986: The Allahabad High Court gives orders for the status quo to be maintained at the site.

9 November 1989: VHP and some Hindu saints perform the *shilanyas* (foundation laying) ceremony at the site.

6 December 1992: The Babri Masjid is demolished by a group of demonstrators.

3 April 1993: The Narasimha Rao government at the centre passes a special act for the acquisition of land at the disputed site.

30 September 2010: The Allahabad High Court passes a judgement that equally distributes the disputed land between the Sunni Waqf Board, Nirmohi Akhara and Ram Lalla (one-third each).

9 May 2011: The Supreme Court stays the Allahabad High Court judgement.

21 March 2017: Chief Justice J.S. Khehar suggests an out of court settlement of the dispute.

8 February 2018: The district court hears the civil petitions.

6 April 2018: Senior advocate, Rajeev Dhawan files a petition in the Supreme Court asking for the matter regarding the review of the comments on the 1994 judgement to be sent to a larger bench.

2 September 2018: The Supreme Court refuses to send the matter to a five-member constitutional bench.

8 January 2019: The Supreme Court constitutes a five-member constitutional bench to be presided over by the then Chief Justice Ranjan Gogoi.

10 January 2019: Justice U.U. Lalit recuses himself from hearing the case. The Supreme Court sends the matter for hearing before a new bench.

25 January 2019: The Supreme Court reconstitutes a new constitutional bench for the hearing of the case. The bench comprises Chief Justice Ranjan Gogoi, Justice S.A. Bobde, Justice D.Y. Chandrachud, Justice Ashok Bhushan and Justice S. A. Nazeer.

8 March 2019: The Supreme Court sends the matter for mediation to a committee, appointing former Supreme Court judge, FMI Kalifulla as the president of the committee.

1 August 2019: The mediation committee submits its mediation report in a sealed envelope to the Supreme Court.

2 August 2019: Due to the failure of the mediation, the Supreme Court decides to have daily hearings on the case from 6 August.

16 October 2019: After continuous daily hearings for forty days, the Supreme Court reserves the case for judgement.

9 November 2019: The five-judge bench under the leadership of Chief Justice Ranjan Gogoi pronounces its judgement, directing that a temple be built at the disputed site, while allotting five acres of alternate land for the construction of a mosque.

6 February 2020: The central government forms a trust for the construction of the temple and appoints Mahant Nritya Gopaldas as its president.

5 August 2020: Prime Minister Narendra Modi performs the Bhoomi pujan ceremony at the disputed site.

30 September 2020: Thirty-eight accused in the demolition of Babri Masjid, including Advani, Murli Manohar Joshi and Uma Bharti, are acquitted.

SANGH ACTIVITIES BY DATE

27 September 2025: RSS celebrates 100 years of existence.

17-19 September 2018: The first lecture series of the sarsanghchalak Dr Mohan Bhagwat is organised in Delhi. It is a three-day series.

10 March 2018: Suresh Bhaiyyaji Joshi is appointed sarkaryavah for the fourth time. The number of sahsarkaryahs is increased to two.

2016: The first Shring Shivir (summit camp) is organised in Bengaluru. 2,195 swayamsevaks from different walks of life, from across the country take part. In the Akhil Bharatiya Pratinidhi Sabha, the 90-year-old 'khaki knicker' is replaced with brown trousers.

2015: Suresh Bhaiyyaji is appointed sarkaryavah for the third time.

2013: The Sangh takes part actively in the Swami Vivekananda's 150th anniversary celebrations.

2012: Suresh Bhaiyyaji is appointed sarkaryavah for the second time.

March 2011: The Ma Narmada Maha Kumbh mela is organised in Mandla, Madhya Pradesh. Thirty lakh devotees take part.

2010: The decision to change the leather belt that was part of the Sangh uniform is taken at the Akhil Bharatiya Karyakari Mandal.

21 March 2009: Dr Mohan Bhagwat is announced as the sixth sarsanghchalak. Sudarshan hands over the reins. Suresh Bhaiyyaji is appointed as sarkaryavah.

The 26000-kilometre Vishwa Mangal Gau Gram Yatra is organised with Sangh support; 8.34 lakh signatures are collected for public awareness. 201 MPs and legislators participate.

2007: The first freedom movement, i.e. the 1857 revolt's 150th anniversary, is celebrated. The third Vishva Hindu Sammelan is held.

10 March 2000: K.S. Sudarshan is nominated as the fifth sarsanghchalak. Mohan Bhagwat is chosen as the sarkaryavah.

17 June 1996: Balasaheb Deoras dies.

11 March 1994: Prof Rajendra Singh (Rajju Bhaiyya) is announced as the fourth sarsanghchalak. Hands over reins to Balasaheb Deoras. The Akhil Bharatiya Seva Vibhag of the Sangh starts. Laghu Udyog Bharati is formed.

4 June 1993: A tribunal constituted by the government concludes that the ban on the Sangh was wrong and annuls it. Akhil Bharatiya Poorva Sainik Seva Parishad (All India Ex-Servicemen Welfare Council) is formed.

6 December 1992: Karsevaks demolish the Babri Masjid.

10 December 1992: The Sangh is banned for a third time.

14 May 1992: Bhaurao Deoras dies. Akhil Bharatiya Adhivakta Parishad (All India Advocates' Council) is formed.

30 October 1990: Kar Seva in Ayodhya continues despite restrictions from the Mulayam Singh government.

25 June 1989: A terrorist attack on a Sangh shakha in Moga, Punjab takes place. One swayamsevak and six others die.

1988: Public contact campaign for Dr Hedgewar's centenary celebrations is organised. 1.5 lakh families are contacted and 11 crores collected for the welfare fund.

6 December 1987: Sarsanghchalak Deoras's gives a salutation at the Ambedkar memorial at Chaitya Bhoomi in Mumbai. H.V. Sheshadri is chosen sarkaryavah. Hindu Sangam is organised in Thiruvananthapuram.

1986: Rashtriya Sikh Sangat (National Sikh Association) is founded.

1985: A nationwide awareness campaign is undertaken on the completion of sixty years of the Sangh.

1984: Anti-Sikh riots take place. Swayamsevaks help the victims. Swayamsevaks participate in the renovation of Golden Temple.

1983: Vishva Hindu Parishad organises the Ekaatmata Yagya Yatra in the country.

1980: Massive public outreach campaign is organised by the Sangh. One crore families from 95,000 villages are contacted.

1979: The second Vishva Hindu Sammelan is held. The Dalai Lama and other Hindu religious gurus from all over the world take part.

30 September 1978: Sarkaryavah Madhavrao Mule dies. Prof Rajendra Singh becomes the new sarkaryavah. Bharatiya Kisan Union is established.

1977: Bharatiya Jana Sangh merges with the Janata Party. Janata party defeats the Congress and forms the government.

22 March 1977: The ban on the Sangh is lifted.

3 November 1977: Loknayak Jayaprakash Narayan addresses swayamsevaks in Patna.

5 July 1975: Second ban is imposed on the Sangh. 189 out of 1356 Sangh Pracharaks from across India are put in prison. Karyakartas, including Sarsanghchalak Balasaheb Deoras, are put in jail. The Lok Sangharsh Samiti is formed.

25 June 1975: Prime Minister Indira Gandhi announces the imposition of Emergency in the country. Balasaheb Deoras distributes a pamphlet among the swayamsevaks to accept the challenge of the Emergency.

1974: The three hundredth anniversary of Chhatrapati Shivaji Maharaj's coronation is celebrated.

1973: Guruji Smriti Smarak is built in the Hedgewar Smriti Mandir.

6 June 1973: Balasaheb Deoras is nominated as the third sarsanghchalak. Madhavrao Mule is chosen as the sarkaryavah.

5 June 1973: Guruji Golwalkar dies.

1972: The foundation-laying ceremony of the Deendayal Upadhyaya Shodh Sansthan takes place. President V.V. Giri inaugurates the

Vivekananda Shila Nyas in Kanyakumari. Akhil Bharatiya Grahak Panchayat is set up.

1966: The first Vishva Hindu Sammelan is organised in Allahabad (now Prayag).

1965: Pakistan attacks India. Then Prime Minister Lal Bahadur Shastri invites Guruji Golwalkar to an all-party conference. Golwalkar assures full support at the meeting. Madhukar Dattatreya (Balasaheb) Deoras is chosen sarkaryavah of the Sangh.

1964: Vishva Hindu Parishad is established.

1963: Sangh is invited to the 26 January Republic Day Parade in Delhi. 3000 swayamsevaks in uniform march with their band. Vivekananda birth centenary celebrations take place. Sangh supports the construction of the grand Vivekananda memorial in Kanyakumari. Guruji travels to Nepal, discusses Hindu welfare with the King of Nepal.

1962: China attacks India. Sangh activates swayamsevaks to help the government and especially the soldiers in every way. General Cariappa visits a Sangh shakha. Bhaiyaji Dani is elected as the sarkaryavah yet again.

1956: Eknath Ranade becomes the sarkaryavah. On Guruji's 51st birthday, a person-to-person contact programme is organised to spread the message of the Sangh.

1955: Swayamsevaks take part in Goa Mukti Sangram. Bharatiya Mazdoor Sangh is launched.

2 August 1954: The swayamsevaks liberate Dadra Nagar Haveli from the Portuguese. Second Chintan Baithak begins in Sindi.

3 June 1953: Syama Prasad Mookerjee dies suddenly in a prison in Kashmir.

1952: The Goraksha movement begins. Swayamsevaks submit 1,75,39,813 signatures to the president. Vanvasi Kalyan Ashram is established in Jashpur. The Bharatiya Jana Sangh, under the leadership of Syama Prasad

Mookerjee, is started. Several swayamsevaks join the Jana Sangh. Guruji Golwalkar takes part in the closing ceremony of 'Abhinav Bharat' started by Savarkar for the freedom of India.

March 1950: First Akhil Bharatiya Pratinidhi Sabha meeting is held. Bhaiyaji Dani is chosen as sarkaryavah. 'Vastuhara Sahayta Samiti' is formed for welfare of Hindu refugees coming from Pakistan.

1949: Draft of the Sangh Constitution is prepared.

13 July 1948: Guruji is released from prison.

12 July 1948: The government removes the ban on the Sangh unconditionally.

5 February 1948: Guruji announces the closure of Sangh shakhas.

4 February 1948: A ban is imposed on the Sangh.

1 February 1948: Guruji Golwalkar is arrested.

30 January 1948: Mahatma Gandhi is assassinated.

18 October 1947: Guruji meets the Maharaja of Kashmir, Hari Singh, and requests him to accede to India. The weeklies *Organiser* and *Panchjanya* are launched.

16 September 1947: Mahatma Gandhi addresses 500 swayamsevaks in Delhi.

15 August 1947: India attains freedom.

3 June 1947: Congress accepts the proposal for Partition. The Sangh creates a goal to protect Hindus from Muslim atrocities. Over 300 service camps are started for Hindu refugees.

16 August 1946: The 'Direct Action' movement of the Muslims starts. 5000 Hindus killed and 15000 injured in Calcutta.

1942: 'Quit India' movement of the Congress. Several swayamsevaks play an active part. Swayamsevaks sacrifice their lives at Ashti-Chimur. Balasaheb Deshpande, the Nagar karyavah of Ramtek is sentenced to death by hanging. (The sentence is cancelled under a collective exemption).

3 July 1940: Madhav Sadashiv Golwalkar (Guruji) is declared the sarsanghchalak.

21 June 1940: Dr Hedgewar dies.

20 June 1940: A day before Dr Hedgewar's death, Guruji Golwalkar is nominated sarsanghchalak.

19 June 1940: Subhash Chandra Bose comes to meet Hedgewar but returns after the meeting owing to Hedgewar's ill health.

9 June 1940: Dr Hedgewar addresses the closing of the third-year students' camp in Nagpur. This is his last speech.

1940: Savarkar addresses the Pune Prantik Baithak. Syama Prasad Mookerjee, along with Dr Hedgewar, expresses concern over the plight of Hindus in Bengal.

1939: Swayamsevaks join the satyagraha against the anti-Hindu Nizam of Hyderabad. First chintan baithak is held in Sindi. Sanskrit commands and prayers are decided at this meeting.

1938: Shiksha Vargs are started in Lahore. Until 1934, shiksha vargs were held only in Nagpur.

1935: The first and second-year shiksha vargs begin in Pune.

1934: Mahatma Gandhi visits the Sangh Wardha camp. He is impressed with the feeling of harmony among the swayamsevaks.

1932: The Central Provinces government prohibits government employees from joining the Sangh.

1931: Dr Hedgewar is released from jail. A Sangh shakha begins in Varanasi. At Bhaiyaji Dani's request, Guruji goes to a shakha for the first time.

1930: Dr Hedgewar quits the post of Sarsanghchalak to join the Jungle Satyagraha from 21 July. Dr L.V. Paranjape is appointed the sarsanghchalak. Congress passes the resolution for Poorna Swaraj (complete self rule). Independence Day is celebrated in all shakhas on 26 January. Black caps are included in the uniform in place of khaki caps.

19 November 1929: Sarsanghchalak Dr Hedgewar is accorded the first salute at the Sangh Sthan. Bal Apte, Dadarao Parmarth, Rambhau Jamgade and Gopalrao Yerkuntwar become pracharaks.

9-10 November 1929: Dr Hedgewar is nominated as the Sangh pramukh. Balaji Huddar is made the sarkaryavah and Martand Rao Jog is appointed as the sarsenapati.

1928: First winter shivir organised. Marching is done with the band playing the song 'Jhanda Hindu Rashtra'. On Guru Purnima Day, the saffron flag is worshipped as the 'Guru' and a guru dakshina programme is held. A total of 84 rupees is dedicated. The first pratigya (oath) ceremony is held. Sardar Patel's elder brother Vitthalbhai Patel visits the Mohite-bara shakha of the Sangh.

1927: The first official's education camp is held.

19 December 1926: All Sanghchalaks come together and chose Dr Hedgewar as the Sangh Pramukh.

28 May 1926: Daily shakha formally starts at the Mohite ka bara. The baton is included, and the use of the word 'aaram' is started. Since the numbers increased, gan (groups) like Kush are created. Prayers in Marathi and Hindi are created. The first march drill is done.

17 April 1926: Sangh is named 'Rashtriya Swayamsevak Sangh'.

27 September 1925: On Vijayadashami (Vikram Samvat 1982 as per the Hindu calendar), at a meeting held at Dr Hedgewar's house 'Shukravadi' in Nagpur, the new organisation is started. All members start assembling at the 'Maharashtra Vyayamshala' in Nagpur and at the 'Itwari Darvaza Pathshala' on Sundays. On Thursdays, the Rajkiya varg (later termed as Bauddhik varg) is held.

Endnotes

1. UNITY IS POWER

1 The Ambedkar Circuit, or 'Panchteerth', encompasses—Janma Bhoomi (Ambedkar's birthplace in Madhya Pradesh's Mhow), Shiksha Bhoomi (the place in London where he stayed while studying in the UK), Deeksha Bhoomi (the place in Nagpur where he embraced Buddhism), Mahaparinirvan Bhoomi (the place of his demise in Delhi) and Chaitya Bhoomi (the place of his cremation in Mumbai).

2 Arun Anand, 'Mahatma Gandhi's Assassination: Blaming RSS, a tale of lies and political vendetta,' *Moneycontrol*, 31 January 2025: https://www.moneycontrol.com/news/opinion/mahatma-gandhi-s-assassination-blaming-rss-a-tale-of-lies-and-political-vendetta-12925410.html

3 Arun Anand, 'How "shock troops" of RSS, including Narendra Modi, led the movement against Emergency,' *Moneycontrol*, 25 June 2024: https://www.moneycontrol.com/news/opinion/how-shock-troops-of-rss-including-narendra-modi-led-the-movement-against-emergency-12755613.html

4 'Why RSS was banned three times in the past,' *Deccan Herald*, 29 September 2022: https://www.deccanherald.com/india/why-rss-was-banned-three-times-in-the-past-1149307.html

5 Manmohan Vaidya, 'The nation must stand for the people,' *VKS Telengana*, 22 December 2019: https://archives.vsktelangana.org/the-nation-must-stand-for-the-people

6 Sunil Ambekar, *The RSS: Roadmaps for the 21st Century*, Rupa Publications, 2019.

7 From a conversation between Dilip Deodhar and Vijai Trivedi.

8 B.R. Ambedkar, *Pakistan or the Partition of India*, Thacker and Company Limited, 1945 at p. 338.
9 From a conversation between Sunil Ambekar and Vijai Trivedi.
10 *Ibid.*
11 'Take message of social harmony to people: Bhagwat to RSS members,' *Hindustan Times*, 19 April 2025: https://www.hindustantimes.com/cities/lucknow-news/take-message-of-social-harmony-to-people-bhagwat-to-rss-members-101745083193810.html
12 'Mohan Bhagwat: "If a Hindu says no Muslim should live here, that person not Hindu",' *Indian Express,* 5 July 2021: https://indianexpress.com/article/india/mohan-bhagwat-if-a-hindu-says-no-muslim-should-live-here-that-person-not-hindu-7389103/
13 From a conversation between Dilip Deodhar and Vijai Trivedi.
14 From a conversation between J. Nandkumar and Vijai Trivedi.
15 Sanjeev Kelkar, *Lost Years of the RSS,* Sage Publications, 2011 at p. 113.
16 'Interview: Sangh does not accept varna system in any form,' *Organiser*, 27 May 2017: https://organiser.org/2017/03/27/118700/bharat/interview-sangh-does-not-accept-varna-system-in-any-form/
17 From a conversation between Arun Kumar and Vijai Trivedi.
18 From a conversation between Swami Vigyananand and Vijai Trivedi.
19 Jean A. Curran, 'The RSS: Militant Hinduism,' *Far Eastern Survey* 19, no. 10 (17 May 1950), 93–98: https://www.jstor.org/stable/3023941/
20 Subhas Sarkar, 'Ekatma Manavvad: The way forward for humanism integrated policy making,' *ET Government*, 25 September 2024: https://government.economictimes.indiatimes.com/blog/ekatma-manavvaad-the-way-forward-for-humanism-integrated-policy-making/113659409
21 From a conversation between Appa Ghatate and Vijai Trivedi.
22 From a conversation between Mukunda C.R. and Vijai Trivedi.
23 From a conversation between Anirudh Deshpande and Vijai Trivedi.
24 Gangadhar Indukar, *Rashtriya Swayamsevak Sangh Kal, Aaj Aani Udya*, Sree Vidya Prakashan, 1983.
25 Indukar, *Rashtriya Swayamsevak Sangh Kal, Aaj Aani Udya* at p. 71; Durga Das (ed.), *Sardar Patel's Correspondence Volume 6*, Navajivan, 1973 at p. 323.
26 *Ibid.*
27 Walter Andersen, 'The Rashtriya Swayamsevak Sangh: I: Early Concerns,' *Economic and Political Weekly* 7, no. 11, 11 March 1972 at pp. 589–97: http://www.jstor.org/stable/4361126
28 Shridhar D. Damle and Walter K. Andersen, *The RSS: A View to the Inside*, Viking, 2018.
29 From a conversation between Sunil Ambekar and Vijai Trivedi.
30 From a conversation between Sanjeev Kelkar and Vijai Trivedi.
31 'Here is what Balasaheb Deoras wrote to Indira Gandhi during Emergency,' *Organiser*, 26 June 2018: https://organiser.org/2018/06/26/120884/bharat/shri-balasaheb-deoras-wrote-to-smt-indira-gandhi/

32 From a conversation between Anirudh Deshpande and Vijai Trivedi.
33 Tarun Vijay, 'A Nation's Sin,' *Indian Express*, 4 September 2018: https://indianexpress.com/article/opinion/columns/dalit-atrocities-protests-empowerment-modi-government-5338130/
34 From a conversation between K.G. Suresh and Vijai Trivedi.
35 'CAA not against Muslim community of India: Nitin Gadkari,' *Economic Times*, 22 December 2019: https://economictimes.indiatimes.com/news/politics-and-nation/caa-not-against-muslim-community-of-india-nitin-gadkari/articleshow/72924516.cms
36 L.K. Advani, *My Country My Life*, Rupa Publications, 2008 at p. 85.
37 From a conversation between Nitin Gadkari and Vijai Trivedi.
38 From a conversation between Devendra Swaroop and Vijai Trivedi.
39 From a conversation between A. Surya Prakash and Vijai Trivedi.
40 'Full text of Pranab Mukherjee's speech at RSS event,' *India Today*, 7 June 2018: https://www.indiatoday.in/india/story/read-here-the-full-text-of-pranab-mukherjee-s-speech-at-rss-event-1254156-2018-06-07
41 Sabareesh P.A., 'Mahatma Gandhi's Tryst with Dr Keshav Baliram Hedgewar at Wardha in 1934,' *Organiser*, 2 October 2021: https://organiser.org/2021/10/02/19165/bharat/mahatma-gandhi-s-tryst-with-dr-keshav-baliram-hedgewar-at-wardha-in-1934/; 'Mahatma Gandhi and Rashtriya Swayamsevak Sangh,' *Organiser*, 18 March 2014: https://organiser.org/2014/03/18/116191/bharat/mahatma-gandhi-and-rashtriya-swayamsevak-sangh/
42 *Ibid.*
43 'RSS and General Cariappa: blasting the myth of CIA "secret",' *VSK Telengana*, 6 May 2022: https://archives.vsktelangana.org/rss-and-general-cariappa-blasting-the-myth-of-cia-secret
44 'Homosexuality Shouldn't Be A Criminal Offence, Says Top RSS Leader,' *NDTV*, 18 March 2016: https://www.ndtv.com/india-news/gay-sex-is-not-a-crime-says-rss-joint-general-secretary-1288405
45 '"LGBTQ Community Part Of Society": Mohan Bhagwat Keeps Up With Times,' *NDTV*, 19 September 2018: https://www.ndtv.com/video/lgbtq-community-part-of-society-mohan-bhagwat-keeps-up-with-times-494399
46 'Understanding growth of RSS from 2014 to 2023 through its Annual Reports,' *RSSFACTS*, 5 September 2023: https://rssfacts.org/understanding-growth-of-rss-from-2014-to-2023-through-its-annual-reports/721/
47 'Everyone Living In India Is "Hindu", DNA Of All Indians Same: RSS Chief Mohan Bhagwat,' *ABP Live*, 15 November 2022: https://news.abplive.com/news/india/everyone-living-in-india-is-hindu-dna-of-all-indians-same-rss-chief-mohan-bhagwat-1563577
48 From a conversation between Dilip Deodhar and Vijai Trivedi.
49 Deeptiman Tiwary, 'JNU row: Behind ABVP's confidence, govt and growth,' *Indian Express*, 24 February 2016: https://indianexpress.com/article/india/india-news-india/jnu-protests-jnusu-behind-abvp-confidence-govt-and-growth-rohith-vemula/

50 From a conversation between Dr Manmohan Vaidya and Vijai Trivedi.
51 *Ibid.*

2. DEDICATED TO THE BLESSED LAND: SHAKHA, SERVICE, ASSOCIATE

1 From a conversation between Nitin Gadkari and Vijai Trivedi.
2 Nagpur Vyayamshala, run by Anna Khote, was one of the first places where young men gathered for physical training and ideological discussions. Dr Hedgewar, would often visit this vyayamshala to identify and recruit committed youth for the Sangh. The Maharashtra Vyayamshala and Pratap Akhada emerged later as additional centers for training swayamsevaks. These institutions helped instill discipline and fostered a revolutionary spirit aligned with the Sangh's goals.
3 N.H. Palkar, *Dr. Hedgewar Charit*, Lokhit Prakashan, Lucknow, 2014.
4 Radhika Ramaseshan, 'Atal bridges a six-year divide,' *The Telegraph*, 26 July 2004: https://www.telegraphindia.com/india/atal-bridges-a-six-year-divide/cid/729506
5 'Annual performance report of the RSS for 2024-25: Key Takeaways and Way Forward,' *Facts About RSS*, 28 March 2025: https://rssfacts.org/annual-performance-report-of-the-rss-for-2024-25-key-takeaways-and-way-forward/1210/
6 From a conversation between Jitendra Tiwari and Vijai Trivedi.
7 From a conversation between Sunil Ambekar and Vijai Trivedi.
8 From a conversation between K.N. Govindacharya and Vijai Trivedi.
9 *Ibid.*
10 *Ibid.*
11 *Ibid.*
12 *Ibid.*
13 Nivan, 'How can there be a Hindu Colony in Hindustan? When Dr Hedgewar visited 'Hindu Colony' and explained the philosophy of "Hindu Rashtra",' *OpIndia* 15 August 2020: https://www.opindia.com/2020/08/dr-hedgewar-hindu-rashtra-india-when-he-spoke-at-hindu-colony/
14 From a conversation between Govind Acharya and Vijai Trivedi.
15 From a speech given by Mohan Bhagwat in a vyakhyanmala held at Vigyan Bhawan in Delhi on 18 September 2018, attended by Vijai Trivedi in person.
16 From an interview between a senior official of Rashtra Sevika Samiti and Vijai Trivedi.
17 'RSS suppresses women, has no female members,' *Times of India*, 15 December 2002: http://timesofindia.indiatimes.com/india/rss-suppresses-women-has-no-female-members-rahul-gandhi/articleshow/96240835.cms.
18 'BMS at a Glance,' *Bharatiya Mazdoor Sangh*: https://www.bms.org.in/bms-at-a-glance/

19 Murari Shetye, 'Goa RSS rebel faction dissolved, merged with parent,' *Times of India*, 7 March 2017: http://timesofindia.indiatimes.com/city/goa/goa-rss-rebel-faction-dissolved-merged-with-parent/articleshow/57503590.cms.
20 From a conversation between K.N. Govindacharya and Vijai Trivedi.
21 From a conversation between Pyarelal Khandelwal and Vijai Trivedi.
22 From a conversation between K.N. Govindacharya and Vijai Trivedi.
23 'About Us – Our Impact,' *Rashtriya Sewa Bharati*: https://rashtriyasewabharati.org/en/impact/
24 'RSS and Freedom Struggle: Salt and Forest Satyagraha,' *News Bharati*, 7 August 2022: https://www.newsbharati.com/Encyc/2022/8/7/RSS-and-Freedom-Struggle-Salt-and-Forest-Satyagraha.html?utm_source https://www.newsbharati.com/Encyc/2022/8/7/RSS-and-Freedom-Struggle-Salt-and-Forest-Satyagraha.html
25 From a conversation between K.G. Suresh and Vijai Trivedi.
26 'How Swayamsevaks Saved Delhi in 1947 from Bloody Coup led by Muslim Officers,' *Organiser*, 26 November 2021: https://organiser.org/2021/11/26/16517/bharat/how-swayamsevaks-saved-delhi-in-1947-from-bloody-coup-led-by-muslim-officers/
27 From a conversation between Atal Bihari Vajpayee and Vijai Trivedi.
28 From a conversation between senior Congress leader and General Secretary, Janardan Dwivedi and Vijai Trivedi.
29 From a conversation between Dilip Deodhar and Vijai Trivedi.
30 Manoj Kumar Mishra, 'Right Wing Politics and Construction of Dalit Identity in India,' *Mainstream Weekly*, 21 September 2024: https://www.mainstreamweekly.net/article15083.html

3. HEDGEWAR

1 From a conversation between Dilip Deodhar and Vijai Trivedi.
2 Shamsul Islam, 'RSS modelled after Nazis and Fascists,' *Frontier* 53, no. 22–25, 26 December 2020: https://frontierweekly.com/articles/vol-53/53-22-25/53-22-25-RSS%20modelled%20after%20Nazis%20and%20Fascists.html.
3 Rakesh Sinha, *Builders of Modern India: Dr. Keshav Baliram Hedgewar*, Publications Division, 2017.
4 *Ibid.*
5 From a conversation between Nilanjan Mukhopadhyay and Vijai Trivedi.
6 Sinha, *Builders of Modern India: Dr. Keshav Baliram Hedgewar*
7 H.V. Sheshadri, *Dr. Hedgewar—The Epoch Maker*, Sahitya Sindhu Prakashan, 1981.
8 Sheshadri, *Dr. Hedgewar—The Epoch Maker.*
9 *Ibid.*
10 From a conversation between Anirudh Deshpande and Vijai Trivedi.
11 *Ibid.*

12 Sinha, Builders of *Modern India: Dr. Keshav Baliram Hedgewar*.
13 *Ibid.*
14 *Ibid.*
15 *Ibid.*
16 Sheshadri, *Dr. Hedgewar—The Epoch Maker*.
17 *Ibid.*
18 'Veer Savarkar always stressed on goodwill and unity: PM Modi,' *The Statesman*, 27 May 2018: https://www.thestatesman.com/india/veer-savarkar-always-stressed-goodwill-unity-pm-modi-1502641247.html
19 From a conversation between Atal Bihari Vajpayee and Vijai Trivedi.
20 Sheshadri, *Dr. Hedgewar—The Epoch Maker* at p. 48.
21 From a conversation between Ram Bahadur Rai and Vijai Trivedi.
22 From a conversation between Ramesh Shiledar and Vijai Trivedi.
23 From a conversation between Dilip Deodhar and Vijai Trivedi.
24 *Ibid.*
25 *Ibid.*
26 Mihir Dalal, 'Inventing Hindu Supremacy,' *Aeon*, 27 February 2024: http://aeon.co/essays/how-savarkar-invented-hindu-supremacy-and-its-cult-of-violence.
27 From a conversation between Appa Ghatate and Vijai Trivedi.

4. GURUJI GOLWALKAR

1 From Atal Bihari Vajpayee's speech in *Karmayogi*, a docu-drama directed by Nitish Bharadwaj and based on the life of M.S. Golwalkar, see 'DVDs of Karmayogi and Sewa Disha released,' *Organiser*, 3 December 2006: https://organiser.org/2006/12/03/31156/general/ra88b08a8/https://organiser.org/2006/12/03/31156/general/ra88b08a8/
2 Anirban Ganguly, 'Not me, only thou …,' *Dr. Syama Prasad Mookerjee Research Foundation*, 25 November 2024: https://spmrf.org/not-me-only-thou/?utm
3 From a conversation between Anirudh Deshpande and Vijai Trivedi.
4 Ranga Hari, *Guruji Golwalkar: Jeevancharitra*, Shri Bharati Prakashan, Nagpur, 2023.
5 *Ibid.*
6 From a conversation between Manmohan Vaidya and Vijai Trivedi.
7 From a conversation between Ramesh Shiledar and Vijai Trivedi.
8 Arun Anand, 'Golwalkar's Leadership: Expanding RSS amidst tumultuous times (1940-1973),' *Moneycontrol*, 21 February 2025: https://www.moneycontrol.com/news/opinion/golwalkar-s-leadership-expanding-rss-amidst-tumultuous-times-1940-1973-12946959.html?s=08; 'Debunking Common Myths On RSS: Understanding RSS's Role In Indian Independence And Beyond,' *The Commune*, 17 August 2024: https://thecommunemag.com/debunking-common-myths-rss-goebbels/

9 Shamsul Islam, 'During the Quit India Movement, RSS was in bed with Muslim League,' *National Herald*, 8 August 2017: https://www.nationalheraldindia.com/eye-on-rss/during-the-quit-india-movement-rss-was-in-bed-with-muslim-league
10 From a conversation between Nilanjan Mukhopadhyay and Vijai Trivedi.
11 '1947 - Sardar Patel's Appeal for Internal Peace & Security' *YouTube*: https://www.youtube.com/watch?v=bcIpdFEHvj0
12 Rajmohan Gandhi, 'The meeting with Golwalkar: What Gandhi really said,' *The Indian Express*, 16 April 2019: https://indianexpress.com/article/opinion/columns/what-mahatama-gandhi-really-said-m-s-golwalkar-rss-chief-5677390/
13 From a conversation between Ramesh Shiledar and Vijai Trivedi.
14 From a conversation between Dileep Deodhar and Vijai Trivedi.
15 Nilanjan Mukhopadhyay, 'Sardar Patel wanted RSS to be merged into Congress but Nehru & Golwalkar stood in way,' *ThePrint*, 15 April 2019: https://theprint.in/pageturner/excerpt/sardar-patel-wanted-rss-to-be-merged-into-congress-but-nehru-golwalkar-stood-in-way/221147/; Hartosh Singh Badal, 'How MS Golwalkar and Vallabhbhai Patel ensured the RSS's survival after Gandhi's assassination,' *Caravan*, 30 January 2019: https://caravanmagazine.in/extract/gandhi-assassination-rss-vallabhbhai-golwalkar
16 'Historic correspondence of Sri Guruji of RSS and the GoI in 1948-49 on Ban of RSS – Justice on Trial,' *Arise Bharat*: https://arisebharat.com/2022/12/27/historic-correspondence-of-sri-guruji-of-rss-and-the-goi-in-1948-49-on-ban-of-rss-justice-on-trial/
17 From a conversation between Mahesh Sharma and Vijai Trivedi.
18 'Sardar and the swayamsevaks,' *Financial Express*, 7 December 2013: https://www.financialexpress.com/archive/sardar-and-the-swayamsevaks/1204627/
19 Balraj Madhok, *Portrait of a Martyr: Biography of Dr. Shyama Prasad Mookerji*, Rupa Publications, 2003.
20 From a conversation between Mahesh Sharma and Vijai Trivedi.
21 From a conversation between Achyutanand Mishra and Vijai Trivedi.
22 Ranga Hari, *Guruji Golwalkar: Jeevancharitra* at p. 303.
23 From a conversation between Arun Kumar and Vijai Trivedi.
24 *Ibid.*
25 From a conversation between Dilip Deodhar and Vijai Trivedi.
26 'A Page from History: How shall we Vote?' *Organiser*, 13 February 2017: https://organiser.org/2017/02/13/112384/bharat/a-page-from-history-how-shall-we-vote/
27 Virag Pachpore, 'Diamond Jubilee of Dr. Hedgewar Smriti Mandir,' *News Bharati*, 5 April 2022: https://www.newsbharati.com/Encyc/2022/4/5/Diamond-Jubilee-of-Dr-Hedgewar-Smriti-Mandir.html
28 Ranga Hari, *Guruji Golwalkar: Jeevancharitra* at p. 101.
29 From a conversation between Manmohan Vaidya and Vijai Trivedi.
30 From a conversation between Appa Ghatate and Vijai Trivedi.
31 From a conversation between Dilip Deodhar and Vijai Trivedi.

32 From a conversation between Manmohan Vaidya and Vijai Trivedi.
33 'Sri Guruji was like a Rishi: Mohan Bhagwat,' *VSK Bharat*, 9 December 2014: https://vskbharat.com/sri-guruji-was-like-a-rishi-mohan-bhagwat/
34 '3 letters written by Sri Guruji Golwalkar, 2nd Sarsanghachalak of RSS', *Vishwa Samvada Kendra*, 1 May 2011: https://vskkarnataka.org/3-letters-written-by-sri-guruji-golwalkar-2nd-sarsanghachalak-of-rashtriya-swayamsevak-sangh/
35 *Ibid.*
36 *Ibid.*

5. BALASAHEB DEORAS: THE PIONEER

1 Diksha Tyagi, 'Birth Anniversary of Balasaheb Deoras: The man who played key role in reawakening Hindu consciousness,' *Organiser*, 6 December 2024: http://organiser.org/2024/12/06/268144/bharat/birth-anniversary-of-balasaheb-deoras-the-man-who-played-key-role-in-reawakening-hindu-consciousness/.
2 From a conversation between Rambahadur Rai and Vijai Trivedi.
3 Dattopant Thengadi, ' Speech on हमारे बाला साहब (Balasaheb Deoras),' 16 July 1996: https://arisebharat.com/2018/06/16/%E0%A4%B9%E0%A4%AE%E0%A4%BE%E0%A4%B0%E0%A5%87-%E0%A4%AC%E0%A4%BE%E0%A4%B2%E0%A4%BE-%E0%A4%B8%E0%A4%BE%E0%A4%B9%E0%A4%AC-on-sri-balasaheb-deoras-by-sri-dattopant-thengadi
4 'Centenary Tribute : Evolution in Parallel,' *Organiser*, 9 November 2015: https://organiser.org/2015/11/09/61716/general/https://organiser.org/2015/11/09/61716/general/
5 Balasahebji Deoras, 'Speech on Social Equality And Hindu Consolidation.': https://arisebharat.com/2013/12/10/social-equality-and-hindu-consolidation-by-balasahebji-deoras/
6 *Ibid.*
7 *Ibid.*
8 'Interview: Sangh does not accept Varna-system in any form,' *Organiser*, 27 March 2017: https://organiser.org/2017/03/27/118700/bharat/interview-sangh-does-not-accept-varna-system-in-any-form/
9 Shishir Arya, 'Bhagwat: Vinoba had said he was "in absentia" member of RSS,' *Times of India*, 8 December 2022: https://timesofindia.indiatimes.com/city/nagpur/bhagwat-vinoba-had-said-he-was-in-absentia-member-of-rss/articleshow/96093364.cms
10 From a conversation between Atal Bihari Vajpayee and Vijai Trivedi.
11 From a conversation between K.N. Govindacharya and Vijai Trivedi.
12 From a conversation between Atal Bihari Vajpayee and Vijai Trivedi.
13 Nilanjan Mukhopadhyay, *The RSS: Icons of the Indian Right*, Westland, 2019.
14 From a conversation between Ram Bahadur Rai and Vijai Trivedi.
15 Vinod Kumar, 'How Jayaprakash Narayan's historic blunder paved the way for BJP's rise, *Print*, 6 October 2019: https://theprint.in/opinion/jayaprakash-narayan-historic-blunder-bjp-rss-sangh-indira-gandhi-emergency/301850/

16 Madhu Limaye, *Janata Party Experiment: An Insider's Account of Opposition Politics, 1977-80*, B.R. Publication, New Delhi, 1994. XX
17 From a conversation between Atal Bihari Vajpayee and Vijai Trivedi.
18 From a conversation between Ram Bahadur Rai and Vijai Trivedi.
19 Ratan Sharda, *Secrets of RSS: Demystifying the Sangh*, Vishwa Adhyayan Kendra, 2014.
20 V.R. Karandikar, *Teen Sar Sanghchalak*, Snehal Prakashan, Mumbai, 2001).
21 From a conversation between Appa Ghatate and Vijai Trivedi.
22 *Ibid.*
23 From a a conversation between Devendra Swaroop and Vijai Trivedi.
24 From a conversation between K.N. Govindacharya and Vijai Trivedi.

6. DEENDAYAL UPADHYAYA

1 From a conversation between Mahesh Sharma and Vijai Trivedi.
2 Mahesh Chandra Sharma, *Deendayal Upadhayaya: Kritatva evam Vichar*, Prabhat Prakashan, 2018.
3 'BJP books a dozen charter aircraft and choppers for its star campaigners in UP, *Times of India*, 2 April 2024: https://timesofindia.indiatimes.com/city/lucknow/bjp-books-a-dozen-charter-aircraft-and-choppers-for-its-star-campaigners-in-up/articleshow/108957983.cms
4 L.K. Advani, *My Country My Life,* Rupa & Co, New Delhi, 2008 at p. 141
5 From a conversation between Nilanjan Mukhopadhyay and Vijai Trivedi.
6 Quotes from 'Integral Humanism' by Deendayal Upadhyaya: https://deendayalupadhyaya.org/quotes/
7 Craig Baxter, *The Jana Sangh: A Biography of an Indian Political Party*, University of Pennsylvania Press, 1969.
8 From a conversation between Dr Mahesh Sharma and Vijai Trivedi.
9 *Ibid.*
10 Pandit Deendayal Upadhyaya, 'The Rationale of Jana Sangh,' *Organiser*, 23 January 1960: https://deendayalupadhyaya.org/the-rationale-of-jana-sangh/
11 Deendayal Upadhyaya, 'Candidate, Party and Ideology All Count,' *Organiser*, 11 December 1961: https://deendayalupadhyaya.org/your-vote-2/
12 From a conversation between Achyutanand Mishra and Vijai Trivedi.
13 Mahesh Chandra Sharma, *Deendayal Upadhayaya: Kritatva evam Vichar.*
14 The judgement of the Supreme Court in the case of *S.R. Bommai v. Union of India* (1994) is one of the most significant constitutional judgments in Indian legal history. It clarified the limits of the President's power under Article 356 of the Constitution, which allows the imposition of President's Rule in states. The *S.R. Bommai* case protected democracy and federalism by preventing the misuse of President's Rule.
15 Mahesh Chandra Sharma, *Deendayal Upadhayaya: Kritatva evam Vichar.*

16 Sudhakar Raje ed., 'Pt. Deendayal Upadhyaya; a Profile,' *University of Michigan*, 1972: https://deendayalupadhyaya.org/thoughts/the-state/
17 Mahesh Chandra Sharma, *Deendayal Upadhayaya: Kritatva evam Vichar* at p. 157.
18 Ram Bahadur Rai and Rajeev Gupta, *Hamare Balasahab Devras*, Prabhat Prakashan, 2017 (translation supplied by the translator).

7. MOHAN BHAGWAT

1 'Pranab Mukherjee describes RSS founder Keshav Baliram Hedgewar as "great son of Mother India",' *Indian Express*, 7 June 2018: https://indianexpress.com/article/india/pranab-mukherjee-describes-rss-founder-keshav-baliram-hedgewar-as-great-son-of-mother-india-5208413/
2 Narendra Kaushik, 'RSS shakhas fight for survival,' *Times of India*, 5 June 2010: https://timesofindia.indiatimes.com/india/RSS-shakhas-fight-for-survival/articleshow/6015003.cms; Isha Jain, 'Modi Effect:2,000-odd RSS shakhas sprout in 3 months,' *Times of India*, 13 April 2014: https://timesofindia.indiatimes.com/news/Modi-effect-2000-odd-RSS-shakhas-sprout-in-3-months/articleshow/33671908.cms; Anahita Mukherji, 'RSS is on a roll: Number of shakhas up 61% in 5 years,' *Times of India*, 16 August 2015: https://timesofindia.indiatimes.com/india/RSS-is-on-a-roll-Number-of-shakhas-up-61-in-5-years/articleshow/48498034.cms; Siraj Qureshi, 'RSS has benefited greatly under Modi government,' *India Today*, 12 March 2018: https://www.indiatoday.in/india/story/rss-has-benefited-greatly-under-modi-government-1187765-2018-03-12
3 PTI, 'People are free to join or leave Sangh: Mohan Bhagwat,' *Business Standard*, 2 December 2016: https://www.business-standard.com/article/pti-stories/people-are-free-to-join-or-leave-sangh-bhagwat-116120101545_1.html; Shiv Sahay Singh, 'Come in close contact with RSS to understand organisation, says Mohan Bhagwat,' *The Hindu*, 16 February 2025: http://thehindu.com/news/national/west-bengal/come-in-close-contact-with-rss-to-understand-organisation-says-mohan-bhagwat/article69225899.ece
4 From a speech given by Mohan Bhagwat in a vyakhyanmala held at Vigyan Bhawan in Delhi on 18 September 2018, attended by Vijai Trivedi in person.
5 K. Jamanadas, '"Pollution" of Ambedkar Statue by Sudarshan on Diksha Bhoomi?': ambedkar.org/News/Pollution%20of%20Ambedkar.htm
6 Anuj Srivas, 'When it Comes to CSR Spending, ONGC Reads the Political Signals Well,' *Wire*, 8 February 2019: https://thewire.in/government/when-it-comes-to-csr-spending-ongc-reads-the-political-signals-well
7 'RSS believes in non-violence and truth: Bhagwat,' *The Tribune*, 20 March 2018: https://www.tribuneindia.com/news/archive/nation/rss-believes-in-non-violence-and-truth-bhagwat-560303
8 'Hindutva wahi jo Vivekananda, Gandhi ji, Tagore ve Ambedkar ka tha: Mohan Bhagwat,' *Prabha Sakshi*, 18 March 2018: https://www.prabhasakshi.com/national/mohan-bhagwat-talking-about-hindutva?

9 From a conversation between Shrirang Godbole and Vijai Trivedi.

8. 'THERE IS NO REST FOR ME, UNTIL I DO RAM'S WORK'

1 PTI, 'BJP has brought end to Ram temple issue, says Babri litigant Iqbal Ansari,' *Deccan Herald*, 23 January 2024: https://www.deccanherald.com/india/bjp-has-brought-end-to-ram-temple-issue-says-babri-litigant-iqbal-ansari-2861042

2 'English rendering of PM's address at the Pran-Pratishtha of Shree Ram Lalla at Ayodhya,' *PIB*, 22 January 2024: http://pib.gov.in/PressReleasePage.aspx?PRID=1998560.

3 From a conversation between Alok Kumar and Vijai Trivedi.

4 'Ram Mandir Bhoomi Pujan: Full text of PM Narendra Modi's speech in Ayodhya,' *Indian Express*, 5 August 2020: https://indianexpress.com/article/india/ram-mandir-bhumi-pujan-full-text-of-pm-narendra-modis-speech-in-ayodhya/

5 'Our hearts should also be the abode of Ram – Dr. Mohan Bhagwat,' *VKS Bharat*, 9 August 2020: http://vskbharat.com/our-hearts-should-also-be-the-abode-of-ram-dr-mohan-bhagwat/.

6 Kishore Kunal, *Ayodhya Revisited*, Prabhat Prakashan, New Delhi, 2016.

7 Manmohan Vaidya, 'A few thoughts on Shri Ram Mandir,' *Sunday Guardian*, 21 January 2024: https://sundayguardianlive.com/investigation/a-few-thoughts-on-shri-ram-mandir.

8 Skanda Puran, Vaishnava Kand, Adhyaya 10, 'Ayodhya Mahatmya', Shlok 18-19.

9 Ayushi Arora, 'Congress's Catch 22 dilemma with Ram Janmabhoomi dispute,' *Deccan Herald*, 22 January 2024: http://deccanherald.com/india/explained-congress-catch-22-dilemma-with-ram-janmbhoomi-dispute-2858009.

10 'Unlocking of Babri Masjid was a "balancing act" by then government: Arif Mohammed Khan,' *New Indian Express*, 28 March 2017: https://www.newindianexpress.com/nation/2017/Mar/28/unlocking-of-babri-masjid-was-a-balancing-act-by-then-government-arif-mohammed-khan-1586887.html

11 From a conversation between Ram Bahadur Rai and Vijai Trivedi.

12 From a conversation between K.N. Govindacharya and Vijai Trivedi.

13 Refer to the judgement of the Supreme Court in the case of *Ismail Faruqui v. Union of India* reported as (1994)6 SCC 360.

14 Hemant Sharma, *Yuddha Mein Ayodhya: A Journey Through History, Riots, Conflict and the Ram Janmabhoomi Dispute*, Prabhat Prakashan, New Delhi, 2018.

15 *Ibid.*

16 *Ibid.*

17 *Ibid.*

18 'Ram belongs to everyone; Ram is within everyone: PM Modi in Ayodhya,' 5 August 2020: https://www.narendramodi.in/text-of-prime-minister-narendra-modi-s-speech-at-bhoomi-pujan-ceremony-of-shree-ram-janmabhoomi-mandir-in-ayodhya-uttar-pradesh-550821

9. THE DHARMA OF BEING HINDU

1 Manmohan Vaidya, 'The nation must stand for the people,' *Sunday Guardian*, 21 December 2019: https://sundayguardianlive.com/opinion/nation-must-stand-people-3.

2 Shruti Kakkar, 'Hinduism is a way of life, don't belittle it: Supreme Court,' *New Indian Express*, 28 February 28: http://newindianexpress.com/nation/2023/Feb/28/hinduism-is-a-way-of-life-dont-belittle-it-supreme-court-2551559.html

3 V.D. Savarkar, *The Indian War of Independence 1857*, Asian Educational Services, New Delhi, 2014 at p. xxiii.

4 From a conversation between Dilip Deodhar and Vijai Trivedi.

5 Vinayak Damodar Savarkar, *Essentials of Hindutva*, Hindi Sahitya Sadan, 1923 (the book was later retitled Hindutva: Who is a Hindu?).

6 M.S. Golwalkar, *We Or Our Nationhood Defined* at p. 102.

7 PTI, 'All Indians are Hindus and Hindu represents all Indians: Mohan Bhagwat,' *Times of India*, 1 September 2023: https://timesofindia.indiatimes.com/india/all-indians-are-hindus-and-hindu-represents-all-indians-mohan-bhagwat/articleshow/103277481.cms

8 From a conversation between Nilanjan Mukhopadhyay and Vijai Trivedi.

9 'Freeing the spirit of Man: Nehru on communalism, theocracy and Pakistan,' *Hindu*, 30 December 2019: http://thehindu.com/society/freeing-the-spirit-of-man-nehru-on-communalism-theocracy-and-pakistan/article30433860.ece.

10 Refer to Vishnu Purana 2-3-01.

11 Refer to Barhaspatya Shastra, Brihaspati Agyam, Rigveda.

12 Arun Anand, 'Why Bengal needs to learn from Tagore's words on resolving conflicts through "Hindu viewpoint",' *Print*, 7 May 2021: https://theprint.in/india/why-bengal-needs-to-learn-from-tagores-words-on-resolving-conflicts-though-hindu-viewpoint/653843/

13 From a conversation between Swami Vigyananand and Vijai Trivedi.

14 PTI, 'RSS believes in non-violence and truth: Mohan Bhagwat,' *Economic Times*, 19 March 2018: https://economictimes.indiatimes.com/news/politics-and-nation/rss-believes-in-non-violence-and-truth-mohan-bhagwat/articleshow/63370556.cms

15 From a conversation between senior journalist, Ashutosh and Vijai Trivedi.

16 From Atal Bihari Vajpayee's speech in Parliament in July 1969: https://elibrary.sansad.in/communities/ca1f325a-61ab-4d3c-857d-f48a9b78b1a2

17 Rajan Chaudhary, 'Dalit History Month: "The Hindu Code Bill" and Dr. Babasaheb Ambedkar's Vision for Women's Equality and Rights,' *The Mooknayak*, 26 April 2023: https://en.themooknayak.com/bahujan-nayak/dalit-history-month-the-hindu-code-bill-and-dr-babasaheb-ambedkars-vision-for-womens-equality-and-rights

18 Harish V. Nair, '"Hindutva is not a religion, but a way of life and a state of mind": Supreme Court refuses to overturn its 1995 judgement,' *Daily Mail*, 25 October 2016: https://www.dailymail.co.uk/indiahome/indianews/article-3872368/

Hindutva-not-religion-way-life-state-mind-Supreme-Court-refuses-overturn-1995-judgement.html

19 Prabhash Joshi, *Hindu Hone Ka Dharma*, Rajkamal Prakashan, New Delhi, 2003.
20 *Ibid.*
21 From a conversation between Yogi Adityanath and Vijai Trivedi.
22 'Hindutva is essentially all-inclusive. It will be the basis of a strong and prosperous Bharat: Dr Mohan Bhagwat,' *Organiser*, 18 September 2018: https://organiser.org/2018/09/18/121461/bharat/hindutva-is-essentially-all-inclusive/
23 From a speech given by Mohan Bhagwat in a vyakhyanmala held at Vigyan Bhawan in Delhi on 18 September 2018, attended by Vijai Trivedi in person.
24 Atal Bihari Vajpayee, 'Death Anniversary of Atal Bihari Vajpayee: "The Sangh (RSS) is my soul," wrote Vajpayee ji,' *Organiser*, 16 August 2024:: https://organiser.org/2024/08/16/15344/bharat/the-sangh-rss-is-my-soul-writes-atal-bihari-vajpayee/Read more at: https://organiser.org/2024/08/16/15344/bharat/the-sangh-rss-is-my-soul-writes-atal-bihari-vajpayee/
25 From a conversation between Appa Ghatate and Vijai Trivedi.
26 Prasar Bharati Archives, 'Sh. Atal Bihari Vajpayee - Rajendra Prasad Memorial Lecture (29.11.1992) Part-2,' *YouTube*, 21 August 2018: https://www.youtube.com/watch?v=CBvAiNBbY38.
27 *Ibid.*
28 M.K. Gandhi, Gandhi and Communal Problems, Centre for Study of Society and Secularism, Mumbai: https://www.mkgandhi.org/g_communal/chap11.php.
29 Ramachandra Guha, 'Gandhi and the RSS,' *Telegraph Online*, 27 September 2019: https://ramachandraguha.in/archives/gandhi-and-the-rss-the-historical-record-the-telegraph.html.
30 M.K. Gandhi, *Collected Works of Mahatma Gandhi Vol. 88*, Ministry of Information and Broadcasting, New Delhi, 1983.
31 Refer to Supreme Court judgement in the case of *State Of Gujarat v. Mirzapur Moti Kureshi Kassab Jamat & Ors.* reported as (2005)8 SCC 534.
32 Refer to Dharm aur vivek ka samanvay—Akhand Jyoti, December 1956.
33 'RGI releases Census 2011 data on Population by Religious Communities,' *PIB*, 29 August 2015: http://pib.gov.in/newsite/printrelease.aspx?relid=126326.
34 From a conversation between Arif Mohammad Khan and Vijai Trivedi.

10. THE LAMP OF FAITH IS AGLOW

1 ANI, '"Triple Talaq Bill Is Unconstitutional," Says Asaduddin Owaisi,' *NDTV*, 21 June 2019: http://ndtv.com/india-news/triple-talaq-bill-is-unconstitutional-says-asaduddin-owaisi-2057158.
2 M.J. Akbar, 'From the India Today archives (2011) | Jawaharlal Nehru: The inveterate democrat,' *India Today*, 26 May 2025: https://www.indiatoday.in/amp/india-today-insight/story/from-the-india-today-archives-2011-jawaharlal-nehru-the-inveterate-democrat-2730772-2025-05-26

3 From a conversation between Arif Mohmmed Khan and Vijai Trivedi.
4 Maulana Abul Kalam Azad's Presidential Address to the Indian National Congress at its Ramgarh Session on 2 March 1940.
5 Vajpayee's Presidential address at the National Executive meeting of the Jana Sangh in Jaipur.
6 From a conversation between Manmohan Vaidya and Vijai Trivedi.
7 *Ibid.*
8 'Hindutva is All-inclusive,' *Organiser*, 22 November 2018: https://organiser.org/2018/11/22/122112/bharat/hindutva-is-all-inclusive/
9 From a conversation between N.K. Singh and Vijai Trivedi.
10 V.D. Savarkar, *Essentials of Hindutva*.
11 Ambedkar, *Thoughts on Pakistan*, Thacker and Company Limited, Bombay, 1941 at p. 332.
12 From a conversation between Ramesh Shiledar and Vijai Trivedi.
13 Mangesh Joshi, 'Was Savarkar really an advocate of Two-Nation Theory?' *Indiafacts*, 17 July 2020: https://www.indiafacts.org.in/was-savarkar-really-the-first-advocate-of-two-nation-theory/
14 *Ibid.*
15 V.D. Savarkar, *Six Glorious Epochs of Indian History*, trans. S.T. Godbole, Rajdhani Granthagar, 1971 at pp. 111-112.
16 Golwalkar, *We, Or Our Nationhood Defined* at pp. 52-53.
17 M.S. Golwalkar, *Bunch of Thoughts,* Sahitya Sindhu Prakashan, Bangalore, 1966 at p. 179, 181-182.
18 'On Hindus and Muslims, Rahul quotes Golwalkar in his reply to EC,' *Firstpost*, 13 November 2013: https://www.firstpost.com/politics/on-hindus-and-muslims-rahul-quotes-golwalkar-in-his-reply-to-ec-1227425.html
19 Christophe Jaffrelot, *The Hindu Nationalist Movement and Indian Politics*, Columbia University Press, 1998.
20 Sanjeev Kelkar, *Lost Years of the RSS* at p. 147.
21 Akhilesh Sharma, 'Over 16 Crore Muslims In India, Have Nothing To Fear: RSS Leader,' *NDTV*, 11 September 2019: https://www.ndtv.com/india-news/krishna-gopal-rss-over-16-crore-muslims-in-india-have-nothing-to-fear-2099485.
22 'Muslims in India are the happiest: RSS chief Mohan Bhagwat,' *India Today*, 13 October 2009: https://www.indiatoday.in/india/story/muslims-in-india-are-the-happiest-rss-chief-mohan-bhagwat-1608838-2019-10-13.
23 'Let's enjoy Iftar: Watch Pak High Commissioner's crass remark in reaction to Pampore attack,' *DNA*, 25 June 2016: https://www.dnaindia.com/india/report-watch-pakistan-high-commission-abdul-basit-shrugs-off-pampore-attack-says-let-s-enjoy-iftar-party-2227861.
24 From a conversation between Sikander Bakht and Vijai Trivedi.
25 'Religion in India: Tolerance and Segregation,' *Pew Research Center*, 29 June 2021: https://www.pewresearch.org/religion/2021/06/29/religion-and-food/

11. THE COMPLETE TRUTH OF THE EMERGENCY

1 Pranay Gupte, *Mother India: A Political Biography of Indira Gandhi*, Charles Scribner's Sons, New York, 1992 at p. 435.
2 *Ibid.*
3 From a conversation between Manmohan Vaidya and Vijai Trivedi.
4 Rajiv Tuli & Prashant Barthwal, 'RSS, Emergency, And The Importance Of Civil Society,' *NDTV*, 25 June 2024: https://www.ndtv.com/opinion/rss-emergency-and-the-importance-of-civil-society-5960038
5 Kuldip Nayar, *In Jail*, Vikas Publishing, New Delhi 1978 at pp. 20–25.
6 'Tihar Jail mein "Kaidi number 2265" thi Gwalior ki Rajmata Vijayaraje Scindia ki pehchaan, jane yeh kissa,' *Jansatta*, 30 September 2021: https://www.jansatta.com/national/the-identity-of-the-rajmata-vijaya-raje-scindia-of-gwalior-was-prisoner-number-2265-in-tihar-jail (translation supplied by the translator); From a conversation between Kuldip Nayar and Vijai Trivedi.
7 From a conversation between K.N. Govindacharya and Vijai Trivedi.
8 *Ibid.*
9 From a conversation between Subramanian Swamy and Vijai Trivedi.
10 B.G. Verghese, 'Shah Commission: Requiem for Mrs. Gandhi,' *India Today*, 30 September 1978: http://indiatoday.in/magazine/indiascope/story/19780930-shah-commission-requiem-for-mrs-gandhi-823047-2014-04-29.
11 Dinanath Mishra, *Aapatkal Mein Gupt Kranti*, Penguin Hindi, New Delhi, 2023 at pp. 4-5 (translation supplied by the translator).
12 Shyamlal Yadav, 'What was the Baroda Dynamite Case, in which George Fernandes was sent to Tihar jail?' *Indian Express*, 8 May 2024: https://indianexpress.com/article/explained/explained-history/baroda-dynamite-george-fernandes-tihar-jail-9316323/
13 Coomi Kapoor, 'The Emergency, 50 years on: When the government pushed, and a newsroom pushed back,' *Indian Express*, 25 June 2025: https://indianexpress.com/article/political-pulse/government-pushed-newsroom-pushed-back-emergency-1975-10086728/
14 From a conversation between Shiv Kumar—aide and close associate of Vajpayee—and Vijai Trivedi.
15 'Forty Years Ago: Habeas Corpus,' *Indian Express*, 16 December 2015: https://indianexpress.com/article/opinion/ editorials/forty-years-ago-habeas-corpus/
16 Refer to the judgement in the case *ADM, Jabalpur v. S.S. Shukla* reported as 1976 SCR 172.
17 'SC admits it "violated" fundamental rights during Emergency,' *India Today*, 2 January 2011: https://www.indiatoday.in/india/north/story/sc-admits-it-violated-fundamental-rights-during-emergency-125864-2011-01-01
18 Ashok H. Desai, 'How the Judiciary Defied the Government to Uphold Constitutional Values During the Emergency,' *Wire*, 25 June 2019: https://thewire.in/history/how-the-judiciary-defied-the-government-to-uphold-constitutional-values-during-the-emergency

19 From a conversation between Ram Bahadur Rai and Vijai Trivedi.
20 From a conversation between Nilanjan Mukhopadhyay and Vijai Trivedi.
21 Rajya Sabha Debates, Vol. 119, 28 October 1976, Column 1040-1045
22 'Rajya Sabha, 1976,' *Digital Sansad*: https://cms.rajyasabha.nic.in/UploadedFiles/Procedure/PrivilegeDigest/English/19/priv-19.pdf.
23 Refer to the judgement in the case *Indira Nehru Gandhi v. Raj Narain* reported as 1975 Supp SCC 1 at para 860.
24 From a conversation between Kuldip Nayar and Vijai Trivedi.
25 From a conversation between K.N. Govindacharya and Vijai Trivedi.
26 From a conversation between Appa Ghatate and Vijai Trivedi.
27 From a conversation between Dilip Deodhar and Vijai Trivedi.
28 L.K. Advani, *My Country, My Life*, Rupa Publications, New Delhi, 2008.
29 M.G. Devasahayam, 'Jayaprakash Narayan: An Idealist Betrayed,' *Hindu Centre for Politics and Public Policy*, 11 October 2018: https://www.thehinducentre.com/the-are na/current-issues/article25188707.ece.

Index